D0900629

Varieties of Liberalization and the New Politics of Social Solidarity

This book examines contemporary changes in labor market institutions in the United States, Germany, Denmark, Sweden, and the Netherlands, focusing on developments in three arenas – industrial relations, vocational education and training, and labor market policy. While confirming a broad, shared liberalizing trend, it finds that there are in fact distinct varieties of liberalization associated with very different distributive outcomes. Most scholarship equates liberal capitalism with inequality and coordinated capitalism with higher levels of social solidarity. However, this study explains why the institutions of coordinated capitalism and egalitarian capitalism coincided with and complemented one another in the Golden Era of postwar development in the 1950s and 1960s, and why they no longer do so. Contrary to the conventional wisdom, this study reveals that the successful defense of the institutions traditionally associated with coordinated capitalism has often been a recipe for increased inequality due to declining coverage and dualization. Conversely, it argues that some forms of labor market liberalization are perfectly compatible with continued high levels of social solidarity and indeed may be necessary to sustain it.

Kathleen Thelen is Ford Professor of Political Science at the Massachusetts Institute of Technology and a Permanent External Scientific Member of the Max Planck Institute for the Study of Societies in Cologne, Germany. She is the author of *How Institutions Evolve: The Political Economy of Skills in Germany, Britain, the United States, and Japan* (Cambridge 2004), among other books, which won the Woodrow Wilson Foundation Award and the Mattei Dogan Award of the Society for Comparative Research. She also writes extensively on historical institutionalism and theories of institutional change, including, most recently, *Explaining Institutional Change: Ambiguity, Agency, and Power* (Cambridge 2010, co-edited with James Mahoney) and *Beyond Continuity: Institutional Change in Advanced Political Economies* (2005, co-edited with Wolfgang Streeck). Thelen has held appointments as a research Fellow or visiting professor at the Wissenschaftszentrum Berlin für Sozialforschung, the University of Gothenburg (Sweden), Nuffield College (Oxford), Sciences Po (Paris), and the Copenhagen Business School, among others. She has served as Chair of the Council for European Studies (2002–2006) and as President of the Society for the Advancement of Socio-Economics (2008–2009). She just completed a term as President of the American Political Science Association's organized section for Comparative Politics. In 2009, Thelen was elected to the Berlin-Brandenburg Academy of Sciences and Humanities in Berlin.

Cambridge Studies in Comparative Politics

General Editor

Margaret Levi *University of Washington, Seattle*

Assistant General Editors

Kathleen Thelen *Massachusetts Institute of Technology*
Erik Wibbels *Duke University*

Associate Editors

Robert H. Bates *Harvard University*
Gary Cox *Stanford University*
Stephen Hanson *The College of William and Mary*
Torben Iversen *Harvard University*
Stathis Kalyvas *Yale University*
Peter Lange *Duke University*
Helen Milner *Princeton University*
Frances Rosenbluth *Yale University*
Susan Stokes *Yale University*
Sidney Tarrow *Cornell University*

Other Books in the Series

Ben W. Ansell, *From the Ballot to the Blackboard: The Redistributive Political Economy of Education*
Leonardo R. Arriola, *Multi-Ethnic Coalitions in Africa: Business Financing of Opposition Election Campaigns*
David Austen-Smith, Jeffry A. Frieden, Miriam A. Golden, Karl Ove Moene, and Adam Przeworski, eds., *Selected Works of Michael Wallerstein: The Political Economy of Inequality, Unions, and Social Democracy*
Andy Baker, *The Market and the Masses in Latin America: Policy Reform and Consumption in Liberalizing Economies*
Lisa Baldez, *Why Women Protest: Women's Movements in Chile*
Stefano Bartolini, *The Political Mobilization of the European Left, 1860–1980: The Class Cleavage*
Robert Bates, *When Things Fell Apart: State Failure in Late-Century Africa*
Mark Beissinger, *Nationalist Mobilization and the Collapse of the Soviet State*
Nancy Bermeo, ed., *Unemployment in the New Europe*
Carles Boix, *Democracy and Redistribution*

(*Series list continues after the Index*)

Varieties of Liberalization and the New Politics of Social Solidarity

KATHLEEN THELEN

Massachusetts Institute of Technology

CAMBRIDGE
UNIVERSITY PRESS

CAMBRIDGE
UNIVERSITY PRESS

32 Avenue of the Americas, New York NY 10013-2473, USA

Cambridge University Press is part of the University of Cambridge.

It furthers the University's mission by disseminating knowledge in the pursuit of education, learning and research at the highest international levels of excellence.

www.cambridge.org
Information on this title: www.cambridge.org/9781107679566

© Kathleen Thelen 2014

This publication is in copyright. Subject to statutory exception and to the provisions of relevant collective licensing agreements, no reproduction of any part may take place without the written permission of Cambridge University Press.

First published 2014

A catalogue record for this publication is available from the British Library

Library of Congress Cataloguing in Publication data
Thelen, Kathleen Ann.
Varieties of liberalization and the new politics of social solidarity / Kathleen Thelen.
    pages cm. – (Cambridge studies in comparative politics)
Includes bibliographical references and index.
ISBN 978-1-107-05316-8 (hardback) – ISBN 978-1-107-67956-6 (paperback)
1. Labor market – Social aspects – Europe.   2. Labor market – Social aspects – United States.
3. Labor policy – Europe.   4. Labor policy – United States.   5. Industrial relations – Europe.
6. Industrial relations – United States.   7. Capitalism – Social aspects – Europe.   8. Capitalism – Social aspects – United States.   I. Title.
HD5764.A6T54   2014
331.1–dc23   2013030085

ISBN 978-1-107-67956-6 Hardback
ISBN 978-1-107-05316-8 Paperback

Cambridge University Press has no responsibility for the persistence or accuracy of URLs for external or third-party internet websites referred to in this publication, and does not guarantee that any content on such websites is, or will remain, accurate or appropriate.

For Amelia and Andy

Contents

List of Figures

List of Tables

List of Abbreviations

3F	United Federation of Danish Workers (SiD + KAD)
AEI	Adult Education Initiative, a.k.a. "Knowledge Lift" (Sweden)
AER	Employers' Reimbursement Scheme (*Arbejdsgivernes Elevrefusion*) (Denmark)
AFDC	Aid to Families with Dependent Children (United States)
AFL-CIO	American Federation of Labor/Congress of Industrial Organizations (United States)
AGV Banken	Employers' Association of Private Banks (*Arbeitgeberverband des privaten Bankgewerbes*) (Germany)
Almega	service-sector employers' association (Sweden)
ALMP	active labor market policy
AMUs	Labor Market Vocational Training Centers (Denmark)
AUB	Employers' Reimbursement System (*Arbejdsgivernes Uddannelsesbidrag*) (Denmark)
AVE	collective bargaining extension clause (*Allgemeinverbindlichkeitserklärung*) (Germany)
BDA	German Employers' Association
BDI	Confederation of German Industries
BIBB	Vocational Training Institute (Germany)
BMAS	Federal Ministry of Labor and Social Affairs (*Bundesministerium für Arbeit und Soziales*) (Germany)
CETA	Comprehensive Education and Training Act of 1973 (United States)
CDU	Christian Democratic Union (Germany)
CO-industri	The Central Organisation of Industrial Employees (Denmark)
CVET	continuing vocational education and training

CvR	Board of Government Mediators (*College van Rijksbemiddelaars*) (Netherlands)
DA	Confederation of Danish Employers
DAG	German Salaried Employees' Union (*Deutsche Angestellten Gewerkschaft*)
Dansk Metal	Danish Metalworkers' Union
DF	Danish People's Party (*Dansk Folkeparti*)
DI	Confederation of Danish Industry (*Dansk Industri*)
EFG	Basic Vocational Training (Denmark)
FDP	Free Democratic Party (Germany)
FNV	Dutch Trade Union Federation (Netherlands)
GAIN	Greater Avenues for Independence (United States)
GAO	Government Accountability Office (United States)
Gesamtmetall	Metal Employers' Association (Germany)
Handels	Swedish Commercial Employees' Union
HBV	Union of Retail, Banking and Insurance (*Gewerkschaft Handel, Banken und Versicherungen*) (Germany)
HDE	German Retail Federation (*Handelsverband Deutschland*)
HK	National Union of Commercial and Clerical Employees (Denmark)
HTF	Commercial Salaried Employees' Union (Sweden)
ICT	information and communication technology
IF Metall	Metalworkers' Union (Sweden)
IG Bau	construction union (Germany)
IG Metall	Metalworkers' Union (Germany)
IGBCE	Chemical Workers' Union (Germany)
IVET	initial vocational education and training
JOBS	Job Opportunities in the Business Sector program (United States)
JTPA	Job Training Partnership Act (United States)
KAD	National Union of Women Workers (Denmark)
KIPP	Knowledge Is Power Program (United States)
Kommunal	Swedish Municipal Workers' Union
Ledarna	Association for Managerial and Professional Staff (Sweden)
LO (Denmark)	Danish Trade Union Confederation
LO (Sweden)	Swedish Trade Union Confederation
MDTA	Manpower Development and Training Act of 1962 (United States)
NGG	German Food and Restaurant Workers' Union
NLRB	National Labor Relations Board (United States)
OECD	Organisation for Economic Cooperation and Development
PEP	Public Employment Program of 1971 (United States)
PRWORA	Personal Responsibility and Work Opportunities Reconciliation Act (United States)

PSE	Public Service Employment (United States)
PVV	Dutch Party for Freedom (*Partij voor de Vrijheid*) (Netherlands)
SACO	Swedish Confederation of Professional Associations
SAF	Swedish Employers' Association
SER	Social and Economic Council (Netherlands)
SES	socio-economic status
SiD	General Workers Union (*Specialarbejderforbundet i Danmark*) (Denmark)
SIF	Union of Technical and Clerical Employees in Industry (*Svenska Industritjänstemannaförbundet*) (Sweden)
SN	Confederation of Swedish Employers (*Svenskt Näringsliv*) (Sweden)
STAR	Labor Foundation (Netherlands)
STW	short-time work policy
STWOA	School to Work Opportunities Act (United States)
SWIT	Swedish IT Program (Sweden)
TANF	Temporary Assistance for Needy Families (United States)
TF	Employers Association for Engineering (*Teknikföretagen*) (Sweden)
TFA	Teach for America (United States)
UAW	United Auto Workers (United States)
Unionen	union for white-collar employees in the private sector (SIF + HTF) (Sweden)
ver.di	United Services Sector Union (Germany)
VET	vocational education and training
VEU	Act on Adult and Continuing Training (*Voksen- og Efteruddannelse*) (Denmark)
WIN	Work Incentive Program of 1962 (United States)
WRR	Scientific Council for Government Policy (*Wetenschappelijke Raad voor het Regeringsbeleid*) (Netherlands)

Preface

This book was motivated by an interest, empirical and normative, in the continued viability of what we have traditionally thought of as the more egalitarian or "social" variety of capitalism found in much of Europe. The institutions that define this alternative model are widely seen as under siege as a result of myriad pressures associated with globalization and deindustrialization. I was interested to learn more about the changes these pressures have wrought, and what possibilities existed for preserving social solidarity in a neoliberal era. A vast literature on the welfare state has taught us a great deal about recent developments in social policy and welfare institutions. Rather than go over this well-tilled ground, I decided to focus on other arrangements that have not figured prominently in the welfare state literature but that do occupy a central position in a different but related body of scholarship, on varieties of capitalism (VofC). Specifically, I explore developments in three institutional realms – industrial relations, vocational education and training (VET), and labor market institutions – that the VofC literature sees as distinguishing the so-called coordinated market economies (CMEs) in Europe and Japan from the liberal market economies (LMEs) of the Anglo-Saxon world.

From the beginning, the VofC literature challenged the idea that contemporary market pressures would drive a convergence on a single best or most efficient model of capitalism. The idea at the very heart of the VofC framework was to insist instead that these two models represent different ways to organize capitalism; each has its own distinctive competitive strengths, and both are durable even in the face of new strains. This has been a reassuring argument for those of us who might otherwise worry about the breakdown of institutions characteristic of the CMEs, which are widely seen as supporting the "gentler" form of capitalism, rather than the alternative "cutthroat" Anglo-Saxon model (Bohle and Greskovits 2009; Acemoglu et al. 2012). Despite the reassurances, however, the fact is that we do observe serious strains and significant changes across all three of the institutional arenas under analysis here, not only and certainly not least in the CMEs. So the question to which this book is devoted is whether the trends we are observing are driving a convergence on the more inegalitarian LME model after all.

In addressing this question, I enter into a lively if frustratingly inconclusive debate. In the course of my research, I became convinced that in order to make progress it would be necessary to disentangle – analytically and empirically – the institutions that have traditionally underpinned coordinated capitalism from those that seem to support egalitarian capitalism. This distinction became the basis for the alternative framework that I propose in this book, which identifies three different ideal-typical trajectories of change: through deregulation, through dualization, and through what I am calling socially embedded flexibilization.

The argument developed in this volume validates the claims of those scholars who have drawn attention to the common liberalizing pressures shaping capitalist development everywhere. Yet identifying distinct trajectories of change is meant to draw attention to the fact that these common pressures are being channeled in different ways. Different varieties of liberalization occur under the auspices of different social coalitions, and this has huge implications for the distributive outcomes in which many of us are ultimately interested. The framework I propose allows us to make sense of observations that appear anomalous in the context of existing models of change, which see every liberalizing move as compromising social solidarity and every defense of traditional institutions as preserving it. In sharp contrast to the conventional wisdom, I find that the successful defense of traditional institutions and policies has often been a recipe for institutional erosion and rising inequality through declining coverage and dualization. Conversely, I find that some forms of liberalization are perfectly compatible with continued high levels of equality and indeed may be necessary to achieve and protect it.

The conclusions I reach here are based on a view of institutions that emphasizes the political-coalitional basis on which they rest. In previous work I found that institutions cannot survive long unless they are actively adapted to changes in the social, political, and market context in which they are embedded. A political-coalitional perspective makes clear why the institutions associated with coordinated capitalism and with egalitarian capitalism coincided and complemented one another in the Golden Era of postwar development in the 1950s and 1960s and why they do not do so now. Such a perspective also explains why the institutions that remain most robust and resilient today are those whose form and functions have been reconfigured under the auspices of new social coalitions that are in many ways very different from those of the past.

I have accumulated a rather daunting list of debts over the course of writing this book, and so it is almost a relief to be able now to acknowledge those who have helped me along the way. A number of institutions provided support and refuge while I worked on this project. The Max Planck Institute for the Study of Societies has been my main intellectual home away from home for well over a decade now, and I am deeply indebted to its directors Jens Beckert and Wolfgang Streeck for keeping the door wide open. During the course of my research I also spent precious months as a research Fellow at Nuffield College thanks to Desmond King, at the Wissenschaftszentrum in Berlin thanks to Jutta Allmendinger, at Sciences Po thanks to Bruno Palier, at the University of Gothenburg thanks to Bo Rothstein, and at the Copenhagen Business School thanks to John Campbell and Ove Petersen. I am grateful to the Radcliffe Institute – and especially to Barbara Grosz and Judith Vichniac – for a very productive leave year in 2010–2011.

I thank the *Annual Review of Political Science* for permission to use Figures 1.2 and 1.5, as well as text from my article, "Varieties of Capitalism: Trajectories of Liberalization and the New Politics of Social Solidarity" (*Annual Review of Political Science*, 15 (June 2012), 137–59), in Chapter 1 of this book. Figure 2.3 originally appeared in Anke Hassel, "The Paradox of Liberalization: Understanding Dualism and the Recovery of the German Political Economy," in the *British Journal of Industrial Relations* and is reprinted here with permission of John Wiley & Sons. Figure 3.2 is reprinted with the permission of the author, Daniel Völk. Figure 4.3 is reprinted by permission of the W. E. Upjohn Institute for Employment Research and the author, John Schmitt. Figure 4.5 is reprinted with permission of the author, Werner Eichhorst, with gratitude to Werner also for providing the data to produce this figure. Finally, I thank Christian Lyhne Ibsen for providing me with Table 2.5.

I began this project while I was teaching at Northwestern University, and I still miss many of my colleagues there, including especially Bruce Carruthers, Fay Cook, Dan Galvin, Edward Gibson, Ann Orloff, Ben Page, Will Reno, Andrew Roberts, and Hendrik Spruyt. More than anyone else I miss James Mahoney, who sets the standard as an outstanding scholar and person. The later stages of this book were completed at my new home in the MIT political science department, where I had the good fortune to work under the inspired leadership of Richard Locke. Beyond Rick, my MIT colleagues Suzanne Berger and Dick Samuels stand out as key sources of support, both intellectual and institutional. Above all else, I have benefited from the broader scholarly community in Cambridge. Collaborations with colleagues at Harvard – especially Dan Carpenter, Daniel Ziblatt, and the incomparable Peter Hall – have provided ongoing intellectual nourishment.

I received valuable feedback as this project took shape through workshops and presentations at various institutions. I thank the participants at Yale University, the London School of Economics, the European University Institute, Harvard University, the University of Chicago, Nuffield College, Waseda University, Sciences Po, the Max Planck Institute, Princeton University, Oxford University, the Wissenschaftszentrum Berlin für Sozialforschung, the

University of Washington, the University of Oslo, Princeton University, and Australian National University, among others.

Colleagues in all of the countries featured in this book, and many more, have read and listened to my arguments over the past several years. While all are innocent of whatever omissions and problems remain, I would never have been able to complete this project without their generous intellectual and personal support. I thank Erik Bengtsson, Pablo Beramendi, Marius Busemeyer, Helen Callaghan, John Campbell, Charlotte Cavaille, Pepper Culpepper, Johan Davidsson, Bernhard Ebbinghaus, Werner Eichhorst, Patrick Emmenegger, Lukas Graf, Jacob Hacker, Anke Hassel, Silja Häusermann, Anton Hemerijck, Martin Höpner, Christian Lyhne Ibsen, Gregory Jackson, Peter Katzenstein, Desmond King, Herbert Kitschelt, Anders Kjellberg, Jette Steen Knudsen, Thomas Kochan, Regina Konle-Seidl, Alexander Kuo, Nicola Lacey, Jonah Levy, Johannes Lindvall, Mikkel Mailand, Philip Manow, Andy Martin, Moira Nelson, Renate Neubäumer, Rita Nikolai, Paul Pierson, Michael Piore, Jonas Pontusson, Justin Powell, Britta Rehder, Bo Rothstein, David Rueda, Mari Sako, Adam Saunders, Steen Scheuer, Gerhard Schnyder, Martin Schröder, Tobias Schulze-Cleven, Martin Seeleib-Kaiser, Heike Solga, John Stephens, Silvia Teuber, Christine Trampusch, Jelle Visser, Margaret Weir, Christa van Wijnbergen, and Anne Wren.

I have had the good fortune to work with fabulous graduate assistants. Jeremy Ferwerda and James Conran did far more than just research for me; their substantive input improved this project in all phases. Elissa Berwick and Andreas Wiedemann provided crucial support in the later stages of production. Kate Searle provides expert staff assistance for all that I do. At Cambridge University Press, Margaret Levi inspires me with her energy and enthusiasm; it has been a joy to work with her on this and so many other projects over the years. I am grateful to Lew Bateman for his unwavering support and patience and to Shaun Vigil for shepherding this manuscript through production with such skill.

Most of the arguments presented here were developed in the context of ongoing conversations with a phenomenal group of scholars who are also dear friends. Many core ideas were conceived in the context of a course I co-taught with Bruno Palier several years ago, and I continue to draw on the many insights he has given me over the years. In Cambridge, an extraordinary group of colleagues and friends have repeatedly rallied to read and comment on work in progress. Our little "Bloomsbury" group has shaped my views in such deep and profound ways that I now have a hard time disentangling their positions from my own. Torben Iversen and David Soskice are possessed of superior minds and hearts; both are intellectual powerhouses as well as phenomenal friends. Cathie Jo Martin is absolutely one-of-a-kind, a tremendous scholar and person. Along with the rest of my women's group – Jenny Mansbridge, Michèle Lamont, and Susan Eckstein – she has kept me centered and sane. Wolfgang Streeck continues to amaze and inspire me with a seemingly endless supply of fresh ideas. I could not have asked for a more supportive colleague or dearer friend. Finally, Peter Hall anchors a vibrant community of scholars of all ages and ranks who share an interest in European political economy. He is a treasured colleague; my life in Cambridge has been immeasurably enriched by my association and interactions with him.

My extended family played a bigger role in my life during the course of this project than any previous one. Elder care issues reconnected me to my far flung siblings – Mike and Nikki, Mary and Russell, Erik and Belle, and especially Pat, with whom I shared two intense but rewarding summers – and I feel more whole as a result. I miss my parents-in-law, our beloved Oma and Opa, who passed away during the course of this project, and I am grateful for the continuing support of my own mother. Most of all, my husband and children sustain me in everything I do. I thank my lucky stars for Ben Schneider who, thirty years in, still makes me a better person. During the course of writing this book, our children Andy and Amelia transformed themselves from independently minded teenagers into deeply interesting and engaged young adults. Different as they are from one another and from me, together they have filled my life with infinite happiness and real meaning. In gratitude for this, I dedicate the book to them.

Kathleen Thelen
Governor's Island, New Hampshire

I

Varieties of Liberalization and the New Politics of Social Solidarity

For the past few decades, much of the scholarship on the political economy of the rich democracies has been organized around a broad distinction between an inegalitarian "liberal" model of capitalism that prevails in much of the Anglo-Saxon world and a more egalitarian "social" model found in many European countries (e.g., Pontusson 1997; Acemoglu et al. 2012). While both models seemed equally viable in the Golden Era of postwar development, many contemporary trends seem to spell trouble for the European social model. The litany of pressures on these systems is long and includes heightened competition in international markets, footloose finance, deindustrialization, declining union power, fiscal distress, and ascendant neoliberal ideology, among others. In light of these trends, some observers have suggested that the Golden Era of egalitarian capitalism may be over and that in the end, there is just one model of capitalism after all – the harsher one in which the market prevails over social solidarity (e.g., Howell 2003; Glyn 2006).

While sharing many of the concerns that animate these analyses, I argue here against the idea of a uniform slide toward Anglo-Saxon-style liberalization. I propose a new, more differentiated way of thinking about contemporary changes in the political economies of the rich democracies. The framework offered here breaks with the continuum models on which much of the traditional literature has been based, in which countries are arrayed along a single dimension according to their degree of corporatism or, more recently, of coordination. In doing so, it reveals combinations – declining solidarity in the context of continued coordination, and continued high levels of equality with significant liberalization – that other frameworks rule out by definition. Moreover, and against the dominant view of institutional stability as grounded in vested interests and straightforward feedback effects, I suggest that the institutions of egalitarian capitalism survive best not when they stably reproduce the politics and patterns of the Golden Era, but rather when they are reconfigured – in both form and function – on the basis of significantly new political support coalitions.

A vast, rich literature on the welfare state has taught us a great deal about recent changes in welfare regimes and social policy. This study therefore does not rehearse developments in this area, but instead concentrates on three other institutional arenas that welfare-state scholars tend not to examine, but that figure centrally in a different, though related, literature on varieties of capitalism (VofC). Specifically, I examine recent trajectories of change in three political-economic institutions – collective bargaining institutions, institutions of vocational education and training (VET), and labor market institutions – that have also been linked directly to the distributional outcomes of ultimate concern in this study.[1] The differences that have traditionally distinguished liberal market economies (LMEs) from coordinated market economies (CMEs) in these areas are well known and can be summarized succinctly. Whereas industrial relations systems in LMEs are characterized by decentralized, unco-ordinated collective bargaining and adversarial relations between unions and employers, CMEs feature highly coordinated bargaining and social partner-ship between unions and strong, centralized employer associations. Whereas LMEs are associated with highly stratified systems of education and training organized around the production of general (widely portable) skills, CMEs fea-ture stronger systems of VET organized around firm- or industry-specific skills. Finally, whereas LMEs are characterized by fluid labor market regimes and weak employment protections, CMEs feature stronger employment protection and associated longer job tenures.

From the beginning, VofC theory challenged the idea that contemporary market pressures would drive a convergence on a single best or most efficient model of capitalism. The core argument holds that these two broad mod-els represent different ways to organize capitalism. Each type operates on a wholly different logic and each does different things well, but both are durable even in the face of new strains. In contrast to earlier corporatism theories that explained the origins and reproduction of key coordinating institutions (such as centralized bargaining) with reference to labor strength, VofC scholars explain this resilience with reference to differences in employer organization and inter-ests in LMEs and CMEs (Hall and Soskice 2001). They suggest that in CMEs employers themselves have a stake in the survival of the institutions that dis-tinguish these political economies from the liberal model; having organized their production strategies around these institutions, firms now rely on them for their success in the market. This logic offered a reassuring picture for those who might otherwise worry about breakdown of the institutions characteristic

---

[1] On collective bargaining, see, for example, Michael Wallerstein's (1999) classic analysis of centralization and wage equality. On skills and training, see Streeck (1991) and Acemoglu (e.g., Acemoglu 1998); and on labor market policy and inequality, see the recent OECD reports (e.g., OECD 2008, 2011a).

of CMEs, which are also widely seen as supporting what some observers have called a "gentler" form of capitalism than that which prevails in the alternative "cutthroat-capitalist" LMEs (e.g., Bohle and Greskovits 2009: 355; Acemoglu et al. 2012).

These predictions have not gone unchallenged. Economic turmoil of the last two decades has set in motion a vigorous debate in the political economy literature. On one side of the debate stand representatives of a powerful liberalization thesis (see especially Streeck 2009; also Howell 2003; Glyn 2006). These authors perceive in contemporary developments an erosion of the arrangements that have distinguished coordinated political economies in the past. As evidence, they can point to the massive changes in global finance that have in many cases released banks from the systems of "patient capital" that were once seen as foundational to the CME model (Höpner 2000; Höpner and Krempel 2003). They note that employer pressures for greater flexibility in other arenas, notably collective bargaining, have had a corrosive effect on coordination and social solidarity (Hassel 1999; Baccaro and Howell 2011). They cite ongoing fiscal strain and relentless pressure on governments to cut costs and relax "restrictive" labor market arrangements that have long offered protection to the weaker segments of the workforce (Trampusch 2009; Streeck 2010; Streeck and Mertens 2010).

These scholars emphasize the commonalities rather than the differences across capitalist countries, particularly with respect to the overall direction of change in LMEs and CMEs alike. Behind this diagnosis is a very different, less benign view of employer interests. In this perspective, employers everywhere seek to extend the reach of the market. The only thing that distinguished the CMEs in the past was that – for various historically contingent reasons – society had been able to resist efforts on the part of capitalists to break free from the political constraints imposed on them. For these authors, globalization and the attendant decline in organized labor's power, as well as the resurgence of neoliberal ideology, bode very ill for the future of coordinated, egalitarian capitalism.

By contrast, defenders of the classic VofC perspective see the divergent institutional arrangements characteristic of LMEs and CMEs as relatively robust and resilient. They point out that the institutional differences between the two models of capitalism have deep historical roots (e.g., Iversen and Soskice 2009; Martin and Swank 2012). As such, these systems have survived all manner of crises (economic and political) over the past century, which were every bit as daunting as today's challenges. Scholars in this camp do not see the institutions of coordinated capitalism as a straightforward product of labor strength against capital; they refer instead to historical research that suggests that many of these arrangements were forged out of cross-class coalitions in which employers were key co-architects (Swenson 1989; Mares 2000; Martin 2000). Clearly, scholars in this camp acknowledge current, ongoing changes in these political economies. However, true to the original anti-convergence theme at the heart of the theory, VofC scholars also tend to insist that most of these developments do not undermine the core logic that separates CMEs from LMEs (Hall and Gingerich 2009). VofC scholars are thus more likely to code observed changes as modifications or adjustments that do not undermine coordination and may in fact be necessary to stabilize it under new prevailing conditions.

At some point, the debate typically devolves into a disagreement on whether the glass is half empty or half full, or sometimes simply into a dialogue of the deaf. As useful as the broad categories of LME and CME have been for other purposes, they present some impediments to exploring the dynamics of contemporary institutional changes as they are unfolding, especially – although by no means exclusively – in the CMEs. A core problem is that the debate as it is currently structured is not equipped with analytic categories that can capture relevant changes that, while not necessarily signaling a breakdown of coordination, do indeed involve some rather consequential shifts from more solidaristic to distinctly less egalitarian forms of coordination (Thelen and Kume 2006; Thelen 2009). To the extent that the changes taking place in many advanced industrial countries involve a combination of relatively stable coordination and declining solidarism, we must confront head on the possibility that a high level of employer organization – while quite possibly still a necessary condition for continued social solidarity within CMEs – is by no means sufficient to guarantee its perpetuation. In this case, models of change built up around a one-dimensional continuum that runs from coordinated to liberal are going to miss the most important changes in the current period.

Moreover, for all their differences, defenders of the VofC perspective and their critics tend to agree on one central point: the best way to preserve egalitarian capitalism is through a vigorous defense of the institutions that have traditionally anchored coordinated capitalism. The empirical analysis presented in this book calls this bedrock conventional wisdom into question. An analysis of developments in the three political-economic institutions under examination here reveals that the successful defense of traditional arrangements has often been a recipe for institutional erosion and dualization, associated with dramatic increases in inequality. Conversely, it turns out that in these areas some varieties of liberalization are quite compatible with continued strong social solidarity and high levels of equality. In short, for the institutions under analysis in this volume, not every coordination-preserving move has solidarity-enhancing effects; and perhaps more counterintuitively still in the context of current debates, not every liberalizing move compromises social solidarity.

This book thus attempts to understand the types of political-economic institutions that support broadly egalitarian outcomes in the sense of a relatively equitable distribution of jobs and income and relatively high levels of economic security for the most vulnerable groups. While building on insights from the VofC literature, I demonstrate what can be gained through two innovations that can advance our understanding of current trajectories of change and their likely implications. First, I argue that recent developments call for greater conceptual clarity to disentangle two phenomena that have come to be unhelpfully conflated in contemporary debates, namely coordinated capitalism and egalitarian capitalism. Second, and based on the conceptual discussion, I propose a new framework that can take us beyond the usual dichotomy between coordinated and liberal market economies and allow us to distinguish among divergent trajectories of liberalization driven by very different political dynamics and associated with different distributional outcomes.

Both these analytic moves flow from an understanding of institutional resilience and change that is explicitly linked to an analysis of the political coalitions on which economic institutions rest. Elsewhere I have argued that institutions do not survive long stretches of time by standing still or even through the faithful reproduction of the founding coalition on which they were originally premised (Thelen 2004). As the world around these institutions shifts, their survival depends on their active ongoing adaptation to the social, political, and market context in which they are embedded. Viewing contemporary developments through a political-coalitional lens, my analysis also explains why it is that the institutions of coordination that most faithfully reproduce the politics of the Golden Era of postwar capitalism of the 1950s and 1960s are sometimes the ones most vulnerable to institutional erosion and decay, while those that remain most robust are those whose form and functions have been reconfigured under the auspices of support coalitions that are in some respects quite different from those of the past. The next sections lay out each of these points one by one.

VARIETIES OF CAPITALISM AND ITS CRITICS

Virtually all political economists agree that industrial relations, VET, and labor market policy are centrally important to defining distinct models of capitalism. However, there are huge disagreements over how to interpret the trends we observe in these three areas. In some cases, the dispute is mostly empirical, rooted in an emphasis on different variables or measures (for an extended discussion, see Thelen 2012). From some perspectives and by some measures, the traditional institutions of coordinated capitalism appear quite stable, whereas from other angles and by other measures, they are undergoing dramatic change. Take industrial relations institutions. Centralized bargaining arrangements in most CMEs have exhibited considerable durability in the face of new pressures over the past three decades, defying previous predictions that they would collapse in the face of an employer offensive (Kapstein 1996; Katz and Darbishire 1999; Martin and Ross 1999). Formal bargaining structures, and industry-level bargaining in particular, have instead proved remarkably resilient. However, collective bargaining coverage (i.e., the number of workers whose employment relations are governed by collective contracts negotiated at the industry level) has shrunk in many countries, and the contents of central contracts almost everywhere have become more flexible than before. In such cases, formal-institutional stability in the level at which bargaining occurs may be masking significant change (Thelen 2009, 2010).

Disagreements between VofC proponents and their critics cannot necessarily be settled with more data or better measures, for it turns out that scholars on different sides of this debate are in fact often looking for change on wholly different dimensions (Höpner 2007). As mentioned earlier, the VofC literature usefully directed our attention to the importance of employer coordination as a core underlying feature distinguishing liberal from coordinated market economies. The key difference is whether employers are capable of strategic coordination among themselves and with labor in order to achieve joint gains through cooperation (CMEs) or not (LMEs) (Hall and Soskice 2001: 8). Following this lead, a good deal of the literature on stability and change has been organized around evaluating how well employers' coordinating capacities are holding up. For example, based on a comprehensive statistical analysis of various aspects of coordination across the full range of advanced industrial democracies, Hall and Gingerich (2009) find that despite some changes, there remains a very pronounced gap between LMEs and CMEs.

VofC critics are unlikely to be impressed by this, not necessarily because they dispute the empirics but because they are not interested in employer coordination at all, but rather in distributional outcomes like income inequality and other measures of social solidarity. Liberalization theorists point to what they see as an all-out employer offensive against organized labor, expressed in a relentless, across-the-board drive for more flexibility, while a related critique mounted by dualization theorists locates the source of new inequalities in a hardening of the line between labor market insiders and outsiders – employed versus unemployed, or those in "standard" full-time jobs with benefits and those in various "atypical" employment relationships.

These differences in vantage point are obviously rooted in wholly different intellectual and disciplinary traditions. The VofC framework comes out of an economic perspective that is concerned primarily with the effects of institutions on economic efficiency, hence the focus on what (following Streeck) we can think of as the "Williamsonian" functions of institutions (i.e., institutions as mechanisms through which firms can achieve joint gains through cooperation). Skeptics often come out of a more sociological or political frame of reference, and are thus really assessing something else entirely – namely, the solidarity-enhancing effects of institutions, or their "Durkheimian" or "Polanyian" functions (i.e., institutions as mechanisms that promote social cohesion).[2] Such differences can contribute to "glass half-empty, glass half-full" dis-encounters because it is possible for firms to benefit from continued coordination with each other over some issues and for some employees, even while the number of workers encompassed by these arrangements declines. In such cases, VofC

---

[2] I am indebted to Wolfgang Streeck (2009) for this distinction.

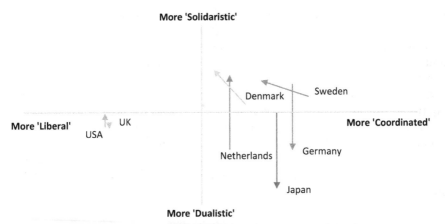

FIGURE 1.1. Trajectories of Change, Selected Countries, 1980s to Mid-/Late 2000s

scholars will see continued relatively robust employer coordination while skeptics will stress the inequalities that result from declining coverage.

Figure 1.1 clarifies this point visually, albeit in a highly stylized fashion.[3] It tracks the relative movement of several key countries in a two-dimensional space based on measures that tap into the concepts around which the literature is organized. The x-axis captures changes on some of the variables that VofC scholars conventionally invoke to distinguish between liberal and coordinated market economies with respect to labor outcomes. It is based on an index composed of three measures: the power of peak employer organizations, labor-management coordination, and wage coordination.[4] The y-axis, by contrast, tracks relative movement with respect to some of the outcomes that VofC critics have identified, focusing especially on variables emphasized by students of inequality. This solidarity/dualism dimension is based on an index composed of three variables: (1) collective bargaining coverage, which captures the reach of the agreements achieved in the context of coordinated bargaining; (2) involuntary part-time employment as a measure of irregular or atypical employment; and (3) youth unemployment as a measure of the extent to which some groups are simply excluded from the labor market altogether.[5] In short, while the x-axis taps the issues of interest to VofC scholars on the extent of

---

[3] I am indebted to Martin Höpner (2007) for this depiction of the issue. In his own work, Höpner draws a different, though related, distinction between "distributive" and "regulatory" liberalization.

[4] All data are courtesy of Duane Swank. Power of peak employer associations is based on the Golden-Wallerstein-Lange index (scores range from 0–4); labor-management coordination is based on an index devised by Kenworthy and Hicks; and wage coordination is based on Kenworthy's five-point index that ranges from plant-level negotiations (1) to binding confederal-level bargaining (5).

[5] All based on OECD data. See the appendix for specifics of the index.

employer coordination, the y-axis captures issues of interest to VofC skeptics with respect to the encompassingness of these arrangements.

This picture – admittedly crude – makes it easier to see why VofC scholars and their detractors have such different views of stability and change. While Germany and Japan remain stable on the VofC dimension, this has not prevented them from moving strongly toward higher levels of dualization. By contrast, Sweden and Denmark managed to maintain high – even slightly increasing – levels of social solidarity (conceived in terms of coverage/encompassingness), despite some formal-institutional liberalization. For reasons to be explored in detail in chapter 5, the Dutch case stands out as moving against the grain and toward higher levels of social solidarity, at least for this period and by these measures.[6]

DISENTANGLING THE RELATIONSHIP BETWEEN COORDINATED AND EGALITARIAN CAPITALISM

The observations in the preceding section call into question conventional understandings of the relationship between coordinated capitalism and egalitarian capitalism. In fairness, the original VofC volume by Hall and Soskice (2001) was not designed to explain equality; instead, it sought to explain different patterns of economic specialization and associated institutional choices or complementarities. However, a good deal of subsequent work has conflated the phenomena of coordination in the VofC sense with egalitarian outcomes, a convention well captured in recent work that distinguishes between "cutthroat" (liberal) and "cuddly" (coordinated) capitalism (Acemoglu et al. 2012). Empirically, these two phenomena – coordinated capitalism and egalitarian capitalism – seemed to coincide in what might in retrospect be thought of as the Golden Era of postwar capitalist development beginning in the 1950s. However, they are analytically distinct, and historically by no means accompanied one another. By most definitions, the German political economy could be seen as strongly coordinated beginning in the late nineteenth century, but as Hilferding (1910) and others clearly understood, this variety of capitalism could be associated with either progressive or deeply reactionary politics.

The debate as it has evolved, however, has mostly overlooked these issues and has therefore been played out in disagreements over how far liberalization has taken CMEs toward LME-type arrangements – thus effectively situating countries on a single continuum and reducing the question of change to movement along that continuum.[7] For example, the landmark volume by Kitschelt et al. (1999b) distinguished three broad political-economic types in which

---

[6] As discussed in Chapter 5, many of the previous gains in the Netherlands have suffered serious erosion since the mid-2000s as a result of the austerity politics of the center-right government.

[7] This continuum-based conceptualization of change is no doubt partly a function of the dichotomous categories around which the VofC framework was organized. However, it is also a function

FIGURE I.2. Varieties of Capitalism and Degrees of Equality in the Golden Era

coordination and equality seemed to be tightly connected. CMEs featuring institutions that provided for national-level coordination (what they called "national CMEs") were associated with high scores on most measures of equality, while liberal countries scored the lowest. Cases of "sector-coordinated CMEs" (coordinated but at an industry level) like Germany came out in between – not as egalitarian as Scandinavia but still more solidaristic than the Anglo-Saxon countries (see also Pontusson 2005a; Martin and Swank 2012).[8] The template that scholars developed to sort and classify country cases in many ways resembled the old corporatism literature, which arrayed countries along a continuum based on their degree of corporatism – with the important difference that now employer coordination replaced labor organization and strength as the master variable (see Figure 1.2).

The dominant models of change in the literature then followed the logic implied by these conventional understandings. So when countries such as Denmark and Sweden experienced strains in peak-level collective bargaining and underwent a shift to industry-level bargaining in the 1980s, many observers coded this as signaling the convergence of the national CMEs on the industry coordination model. A synthetic concluding essay in the Kitschelt et al. (1999a) volume offered three "firm conclusions," one of which was that "national and sectoral coordinated market economies are becoming more alike," with "national CMEs" becoming more like "sectoral CMEs," even if neither was converging on the liberal model (444, 451, 459; see also Pontusson 1997; Thelen 2001). This line of argument is represented in Figure 1.3.

More recently, the Nordic countries have regained their luster and, with that, their status as distinctly successful models of social solidarity and economic efficiency (Pontusson 2009; Martin and Swank 2012); now it is the industry-coordinated systems such as Germany that are often seen as fragile

of the way in which many versions of the liberalization critique of that literature have been formulated (but for a notable exception from which I also draw many core insights, see Höpner 2007).

[8] However, I hasten to add that in much of his other work Pontusson draws a stronger distinction (in kind, not in degree) between Continental and Scandinavian CMEs. He bases this distinction in part on persistent differences in long-term unemployment, a dimension on which Christian Democratic CMEs always performed worse than both the Scandinavian CMEs and liberal economies (Pontusson 2005b).

least egalitarian   most egalitarian

LMEs   sector- or   national-
(e.g., U.S.)   industry-   ◄──────── coordinated
                        coordinated   CMEs
                        CMEs (e.g.,   (e.g., Scandinavia)
                        Germany)

FIGURE 1.3. Hypothesized Direction of Change for National CMEs

and changing in ways that take them toward the less egalitarian Anglo-Saxon model. This line of argument is depicted in Figure 1.4.

However, as closely connected as the notions of coordinated capitalism and egalitarian capitalism came to be in the Golden Era of postwar development (and by extension in the minds of many scholars), nothing in the broader historical record suggests that the two necessarily go together. The origins of many of the institutions that define the CMEs can be traced back to the early industrial period (Crouch 1993; Streeck and Yamamura 2001; Thelen 2004; Iversen and Soskice 2009; Martin and Swank 2012), but clearly these institutions were not designed to promote equality. Their effects on social solidarity had, rather, to do with variation over time in the scope of employer coordination and the purposes to which these coordinating capacities were put.

Neither of these variables is solely a matter of institutions per se, but instead of the political coalitions on which these institutions rest – and this is something that can and does change over time. To give an example, coordinating capacities with respect to worker training in Germany were first established in the artisanal sector. What we could call their solidarity-enhancing side effects grew as the system expanded in scope, first to encompass the machine industry and later to be imposed as a national model to which virtually all youth had access. Conversely, as the reach of the coordinated training system in Germany began to shrink in the 1990s, the result was a rationing of apprenticeships within the still-coordinated system. Previously broad access to training had many solidarity-enhancing effects – above all, providing an avenue through which working-class youth could move into secure and well-paid jobs, especially in manufacturing. In the 2000s, however, increased rationing of access to training fueled new kinds of inequality because those who failed to land

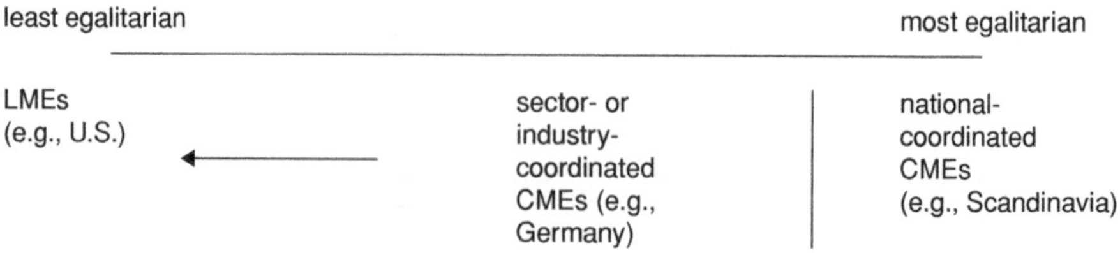

least egalitarian   most egalitarian

LMEs   sector- or   │   national-
(e.g., U.S.)   industry-   │   coordinated
         ◄──────────   coordinated   │   CMEs
                        CMEs (e.g.,   │   (e.g., Scandinavia)
                        Germany)

FIGURE 1.4. Hypothesized Direction of Change for Sectoral (Industry) CMEs

an apprenticeship were doubly disadvantaged in the labor market – shunted into distinctly second-class training and stigmatized as second-rate prospects for later employment (A. Kupfer 2010; Thelen 2011; Busemeyer and Iversen 2012). The general point is that the extent to which the institutions that support employer coordination will have egalitarian side effects is partly a question of the scope or encompassingness of these institutions. This is an issue to which I have tried to draw attention with reference to what I call more segmentalist versus more solidaristic forms of coordination (Thelen 2004).

Beyond this, high capacity for coordination among employers has different consequences with respect to social solidarity depending on the functions to which this capacity is directed. Historically, employers in some of today's most solidaristic countries originally organized not to cooperate with unions but to crush them (Kuo 2009; Paster 2009; Martin and Swank 2012). Too often, scholarship on the political economy of the rich democracies conflates employers' capacity to coordinate among themselves with a willingness to cooperate with labor. However, cooperation does not flow naturally or automatically from the capacity for coordination, even if – as Hilferding (1910) again reminds us – a high level of employer organization can be extremely useful (maybe indispensable) for the political management of capitalism. The more general point is that the institutions for coordinated capitalism do not themselves dictate the uses to which they will be put; the latter is a question of politics and not institutions.

Opening up the analytic space to disentangle the complex (and non-linear) co-evolution of egalitarian capitalism and coordinated capitalism allows us to move beyond the current terms of the debate, which is mostly organized around the questions of whether employers will abandon the institutions of coordination and/or whether labor is sufficiently strong to resist liberalization – or alternatively, whether employer coordination is overall "good" or "bad" for social solidarity. It forces us to think harder about the coalitions and interests – who exactly is coordinating with whom, and to do what – and how differences in the answers to these questions drive variation in the trajectories of change in the rich democracies (see also Iversen and Soskice 2010).

Varieties of Liberalization

Together with Peter Hall, I have elsewhere argued that the term "liberalization" that is typically invoked in the literature may be too encompassing to be useful in assessing the meaning and significance of the myriad developments this term subsumes (Hall and Thelen 2009: 22–24). There is certainly a family resemblance between some aspects of the reforms associated with Danish flexicurity and some of the measures introduced by Prime Minister Margaret Thatcher in the UK in the 1980s, and both can reasonably be treated as cases of liberalization, broadly defined. However, it is not clear that the term then provides us with the kind of precise and discriminating analytic tool we need to grasp the rather different implications of different liberalizing moves.

Especially important for an analysis of political dynamics are the vast differences in the political-coalitional alignments that lie behind what many scholars subsume under the broad liberalization rubric. In some cases (e.g., the UK under Prime Minister Thatcher), liberalization is the result of battles in which interests cleaved largely along class lines (i.e., the familiar story of a neoliberal offensive that pits representatives of organized labor against employers).[9] In other cases, (e.g., Germany) it can be the result of a cross-class coalition that unites rather than separates segments of labor and capital (Thelen and van Wijnbergen 2003; Thelen and Kume 2006). In still other cases, it rests on a coalition that includes both low- and high-skilled workers – including, crucially, white-collar salaried employees – albeit one that presides over the implementation of policies that are distinctly market-promoting (e.g., flexicurity). The broad headline of liberalization conflates these very different political dynamics.

The discussion above suggests a need to distinguish more carefully between different dimensions or aspects of liberalization. In this book, I evaluate developments in industrial relations, VET, and labor market policy in terms of trends in "coordination," using the meaning attached to that term by VofC scholars (i.e., capturing the extent to which employers engage in strategic coordination) (Hall and Soskice 2001). Defined in VofC terms, "high" coordination is associated (in industrial relations) with centralized wage bargaining and associated wage compression, which (in education and training) encourages investments in industry- or firm-specific skills, which in turn supports and underwrites (in labor market policy) long job tenures and associated strong employment protection.

However, if we are interested in the distributive outcomes associated with these institutions, then we must of course also attend to issues of coverage, namely how encompassing are these arrangements? Do they cover a small core workforce, or are unions and/or the state able to impose similar obligations and conditions on firms that would otherwise choose not to participate? The latter are issues to which the critics of VofC have usefully drawn our attention, and the discussion in this book also attends to trends with respect to coverage as a separate dimension of variation.

Employers' coordinating capacities and coverage do not necessarily co-vary. By distinguishing the two, we can identify three distinct ideal-typical trajectories of liberalization.[10] These are depicted in Figure 1.5 and they correspond to (1) deregulatory liberalization, associated especially with LMEs like the United States; (2) dualizing liberalization, associated with conservative Christian Democratic countries such as Germany; and (3) embedded

---

[9] Largely but not entirely because some segments of business did not support Prime Minister Thatcher's early moves against the unions, fearing the shop floor unrest this would generate.

[10] I am grateful to colleagues at the Max Planck Institute in Cologne, and in particular Martin Höpner and Wolfgang Streeck, for emphasizing to me the importance of distinguishing different varieties of liberalization.

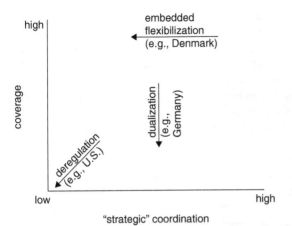

FIGURE 1.5. Revised Hypothesized Trajectories of Change

flexibilization, associated with Scandinavian Social Democratic countries such as Denmark.

By identifying the three different trajectories of change we recognize that liberalization can take many forms and occur under the auspices of different kinds of social coalitions – with important implications for distributive and other outcomes. Moreover, and as I will argue in more detail, these three trajectories of liberalization frequently proceed (again, ideal-typically) through different processes of institutional change: deregulation often through institutional displacement; dualization through institutional drift; and embedded flexibilization through institutional conversion (Streeck and Thelen 2005; Mahoney and Thelen 2009).

Deregulatory liberalization as I am using it here involves the active political dismantling of coordinating capacities (on one or both sides of the class divide) and declining coverage – and with that a marked individualization of risk (Hacker 2006). Deregulation is associated with change through displacement because in these cases institutions and mechanisms for collective labor regulation are explicitly set aside in favor of arrangements that re-impose the discipline of the market. Examples would include the demolition of systems of compulsory arbitration and court-based coordination in Australia and New Zealand (Kitschelt et al. 1999b: 431–432) or, more recently, the rollback in collective bargaining rights of public-sector unions in Wisconsin. This kind of direct frontal assault on institutions supporting the collective regulation of labor relations is perhaps most often on display in LMEs, an association that is not wholly surprising since history suggests that where employers do not themselves possess stable coordinating capacities, they will press vigorously to weaken unions as well.[11]

---

[11] Examples include the open-shop movement in the United States or the campaign against shop steward controls in Britain (see Thelen 2004).

Dualization, by contrast, involves continued strong coordination on the employer side but in the context of a distinct narrowing in the number of firms and workers covered under the resulting arrangements. Unlike deregulatory liberalization, dualization does not involve a direct attack on traditional institutions. Indeed, these institutions often exhibit remarkable resiliency, even as an unorganized and unregulated periphery is allowed to grow outside their ambit, one that is characterized by inferior status and protections for firms and workers outside the core (see also Emmenegger et al. 2011). Dualization takes many forms – for example, maintaining strong employment protections for regular workers while the number of atypical or irregular workers grows, or defending traditional institutions for firm-based training even as the number of opportunities for landing an apprenticeship shrinks, or continued centralization of bargaining but covering fewer sectors and workers (to name a few manifestations).

Whereas deregulation involves a neoliberal offensive in which class cleavages dominate, dualization is often fueled by an intensification of cooperation between labor and management in core firms and industries to the extent that developments in the core leave other firms and workers behind or outside (Thelen and van Wijnbergen 2003; Rueda 2007). For example, such intensification of cooperation in some sectors has contributed to collective bargaining erosion and labor market dualization in Germany and France (Thelen and Kume 2006; Palier and Thelen 2010). The mode of change associated with this trajectory of change is also distinct. Unlike deregulation, which proceeds through outright institutional displacement, dualization often proceeds through a process of institutional "drift."[12] In the current period, this frequently occurs as institutions and practices that were developed for manufacturing fail to take hold outside the industrial core. For example, where membership in unions and employer associations is heavily concentrated in industry, collective bargaining institutions will erode "by themselves" as employment shifts to the service sector.

Embedded flexibilization, finally, involves the introduction of new forms of flexibility within the context of a continued strong and encompassing framework that collectivizes risk. The institutions and policies associated with this trajectory depart from the kind of market-suspending institutions long associated with strategic coordination à la VofC (e.g., the institutions that encourage long-term relations between firms and employees, or underwrite employees' investments in specific skills), and are instead often specifically organized around making workers more – not less – mobile. However, what distinguishes embedded flexibilization from sheer deregulation is that these moves are embedded in policies that promote what Baccaro and Locke (1998) once called

---

[12] Following Hacker and Pierson (2010a), drift connotes transformation "not through the amendment or replacement of existing policies, but through politically mediated inaction in the face of changing social circumstances" (1).

"supply side solidarity," collectivizing risk by focusing resources on enabling society's most vulnerable to get and keep a good job.[13] Implementing such policies frequently involves a functional conversion of existing institutions – whether collective bargaining institutions or labor market institutions – to new goals, and one that is based on a significantly reconfigured social coalition (see also Levy 1999; Bonoli 2005).

Even the most casual reader will not have missed that the broad trajectories of liberalization I just mapped out correspond to Gøsta Esping-Andersen's (1990) famous "three worlds" of welfare. A later section will address the connections behind the political-economic institutions featured in this study and the welfare arrangements so brilliantly analyzed by Esping-Andersen. At this point, however, it is appropriate to ask: What has the literature on VofC had to say about the relationship between these realms? With few exceptions, it sees political-economic and welfare-state arrangements as parallel and complementary. Most VofC scholars see social policy as part of the same set of mutually supportive institutions that define CMEs and that distinguish them from LMEs. To give one example, generous unemployment insurance in CMEs is seen as supporting investment in specific rather than general skills, whereas means-tested social policies in LMEs complement fluid labor markets (low employment protection) and promote investment in general rather than specific skills. In fact, exactly these connections explain why the conventional wisdom so clearly holds that maintaining high levels of equality requires protecting traditional political-economic (and not just welfare-state) institutions and why VofC scholars and their detractors alike view all liberalizing moves as compromising social solidarity.

It is on this point where the framework I am proposing deviates most sharply from the conventional wisdom. Disentangling the question of employers' capacity for coordination lying at the heart of VofC scholarship on one hand from the issues of equality that are so central to the agenda of Esping-Andersen and other welfare-state scholars on the other allows us to see combinations that are difficult to analyze (even hard to conceive) within the context of traditional one-dimensional models of change in which coordination and social solidarity are tightly coupled, either implicitly or explicitly. Dualization, for example, involves declining equality but in the context of continued significant coordination for core firms and sectors in all three of the political-economic realms I examine – industrial relations, VET, and labor market policy. Embedded flexibilization, conversely, involves continued high levels of equality but in the context of developments across all three institutional arenas that can only be characterized as liberal in the sense of market-promoting – sometimes even radically so, since they are precisely *not* premised on protecting workers from

---

[13] I am indebted to Christian Ibsen for bringing the concept of "supply side solidarity" to my attention; Ibsen has himself elaborated these themes in comparisons between Sweden and Denmark (Ibsen 2012).

the market, but instead on actively adapting their skills to changing market conditions.

Generous social policy – and thus a strong welfare state – remains central to the new politics of social solidarity in the context of these changes. But the logic and the functions of social policy are quite different from the traditional model. Rather than serving the complementary (social-insurance) role the literature has traditionally assigned to them, the role of welfare policies increasingly revolves around re-embedding these liberalizing moves in measures that collectivize the resulting risks. I will have more to say about this in the conclusion.

In the meantime, Figure 1.6 provides an overview of cross-national variation (and change over time) on two dimensions that are particularly central to debates on contemporary changes in the political-economic institutions around which my study is organized: long-term unemployment (the most severe form of labor market exclusion) and involuntary part-time employment (as an indicator of the prevalence of "bad jobs"). The countries are clustered into three groups – LMEs, Nordic CMEs and Continental CMEs – plus Japan. The arrows display the average change in the specified indicator from the late 1970s to the late 2000s, and the vertical lines indicate the average value for the cluster in the most recent period.

What we see conforms broadly to the three trajectories of change sketched out above. Long-term unemployment in the Continental CMEs – though declining in the past decades – remains on average a good bit higher than in both the liberal and the Nordic countries. Moreover, the declines in long-term unemployment in Continental CMEs have been accompanied by increases – sometimes dramatic – in the number of "bad jobs" as measured by involuntary part-time employment. Figure 1.6 also adds nuance by revealing some interesting differences even within the usual country clusters. For example, among the Nordic CMEs, long-term unemployment is sharply down in Denmark (from very high levels) since the early 1980s, but it has grown slightly in Sweden to a level that is now above the Nordic average. Meanwhile, among the Christian Democratic CMEs, the Netherlands sharply reduced long-term unemployment, while the level in Germany (already above the Continental average) increased. Finally, involuntary part-time employment in Germany and Italy has increased significantly while remaining more stable (and lower) in the Netherlands. Among the Nordic countries, involuntary part-time employment has declined somewhat in both Denmark and Sweden, though the level in Sweden is higher than in Denmark.

Much of the analysis in this book is devoted to examining trends in three countries that exemplify the broad and diverging patterns of change associated with each of the "families" of countries as identified by Esping-Andersen: the United States as an example of an LME, Germany as a classic Christian Democratic country, and Denmark as a Social Democratic political economy. However, complementary treatments of the Netherlands and Sweden

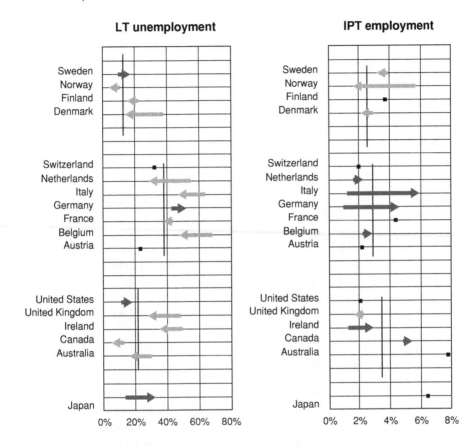

FIGURE 1.6. Trends in Long-Term (LT) Unemployment and Involuntary Part-Time (IPT) Employment, Various Countries, Late 1970s to Late 2000s. *Note:* (a) Sweden 1987; Norway 1989. *Source:* OECD.

provide additional insights into the political dynamics as they unfold in different countries within the same family. My analysis thus highlights core and enduring parallels between most similar cases such as Sweden and Denmark (and Germany and the Netherlands), but it also identifies important differences within each pair in order to provide finer resolution on the interests and political align-ments that are behind the broader cross-national patterns. The analysis sheds light, for example, on why a broad national bargain remains elusive in Swedish industrial relations, while Denmark has settled into a new and apparently quite stable pattern, or why the Netherlands departed in some ways from core fea-tures of the classic Christian Democratic mold while Germany's manufacturing model thrives even as inequality grows. This leads me to a discussion of the politics of change.

EXPLAINING TRAJECTORIES OF CHANGE

How do we account for differences in the trajectories of change in the rich democracies? Elsewhere I have reviewed the literature on the advanced polit-ical economies in some detail (Thelen 2011), but a cursory look at existing scholarship reveals both penetrating insights and glaring gaps. In the following sections, I briefly reprise what I see as the core strengths and weaknesses of the most important perspectives in the literature – power resource theory, dual-ism theories, and theories of employer organization and macro-corporatism – before sketching out my own alternative explanation emphasizing producer group politics and the role of the state.

Power Resource Theory

One of the most prominent and powerful arguments attributes different tra-jectories of change to the strength of the organized labor movement. In the Golden Era of postwar growth, employers may have valued institutions like coordinated wage bargaining as an avenue for securing wage moderation in the context of full employment. However, higher unemployment since the 1970s makes these arrangements superfluous because firms can now rely on the discipline of the market to secure this outcome. As employers press against institutions they now perceive as rigid and confining, power resource theory holds that cross-national differences can be explained by labor's capacity to resist.

In most versions of the argument, there are two facets to labor's power resources – one is the organizational structure of labor unions (typically mea-sured in union density), and the other is the relative power of labor's political allies (typically measured in terms of the electoral strength of the Social Demo-cratic Party and/or Left participation in cabinet government). Power resource theory provides a very compelling first cut explanation of significant and endur-ing cross-national differences, and yet it leaves many intriguing puzzles unan-swered. For example, the Netherlands and Germany have moved on rather different paths since the 1980s, with the Netherlands embracing a variation of flexicurity and achieving significant employment growth, while Germany moved strongly in the direction of dualization in the context of higher unemployment and, increasingly, low-wage employment without social benefits. This is not a difference that is linked in any obvious way to labor's power resources since both countries feature medium (and declining) unionization rates and dominant Christian Democratic parties. Moreover, and as elaborated in Chapter 5, Sweden has struggled more with tendencies toward dualism (e.g., especially Davidsson 2010) than Denmark despite stronger "power resources," whether measured by unionization rates or left-wing dominance.

Secondly, power resource theories frequently involve the claim that globalization is what gives the employer offensive its impetus, by empowering (mobile) capital against (nationally anchored) unions. But closer empirical scrutiny reveals a more complex picture. As mentioned, manufacturing employers – though most clearly impacted by globalization – are not always the ones most urgently calling for institutional reconfiguration. Consistent with VofC logic, these firms are often rather heavily invested in competitive strategies that rely on high-quality production, high skills, and peaceful labor relations, and they continue to be more invested in traditional institutions than, say, employers in lower-wage, lower-skill service sectors. The counter-hypothesis (explored in this book) is therefore that where traditional manufacturing interests dominate the interest associations, the trend is likely toward dualization rather than across-the-board deregulation (see also Palier and Thelen 2010).

Dualism Theories

The idea that employer preferences may be less obvious (and less uniform) than commonly assumed finds a corollary on the labor side in an alternative explanation of the trends documented in the previous section. David Rueda (2007) flips the power resource theory on its head by suggesting that powerful Social Democratic parties allied with strong labor movements may well promote rather than inhibit inequality. Drawing on early labor market segmentation theories, Rueda argues that contemporary market trends have heightened conflicts between labor market "insiders" (i.e., core workers who have jobs and who are intent on preserving their relatively privileged position within the labor market) and labor market "outsiders" (i.e., those who either do not have jobs or are in more precarious forms of employment and thus do not enjoy the same package of wages and benefits as insiders).[14] As egalitarian as their

[14] Rueda's claims in some ways revive arguments made by mainstream economists in the 1980s to explain pervasive involuntary unemployment in some countries with reference to the effects of unions in increasing turnover costs – for instance, costs associated with hiring (searching, advertising, etc.), firing (including severance pay and costs of legally mandated protections), and training – in ways that benefit the currently employed labor market insiders but render the labor market less permeable to outsiders (e.g., especially Lindbeck and Snower 1988). But in other ways, his arguments also bear a family resemblance to the segmentation theories of

policies and preferences may have been in the past, the ongoing fiscal crisis of the state now confronts Social Democratic parties and governments with a more zero-sum choice between vigorously defending the interests of labor market insiders or taking up the cause of labor market outsiders, even where this inevitably now involves an intra-class redistribution at the direct expense of insiders. Rueda's contention is that Social Democratic parties resolve this dilemma by promoting the interests of insiders – against and often at the direct expense of labor market outsiders.[15]

This is an important argument, and one of its great strengths is that it disaggregates the interests of the working class and in so doing highlights the potential for intra-class conflict over policy options. Just as employers are often divided among themselves as a consequence of their different production systems and strategies, so too are workers (including would-be workers, namely the unemployed) divided among themselves on policy preferences based on their situation in the labor market with respect to current and future employment options. What seems less convincing, however, are the causal mechanisms on which the argument rests. Rueda suggests that in order to win elections Social Democratic parties must cater to their core (insider) constituency. However, the differences in preferences between insiders and outsiders that he documents are actually very small.[16] While Rueda is certainly correct to note that Social Democrats now face a more severe dilemma, ultimately cross-national comparisons continue to show that inequality, by almost any measure, is lowest in countries where Social Democracy is the strongest (Pontusson 2009).

Theories of Employer Organization and Macro-Corporatism

Another body of work calls attention to the organization of business and the presence or absence of corporatist channels of interest intermediation. Martin

left-leaning economists in the later 1960s and early 1970s (Edwards et al. 1973; Wilkinson 1981; Gordon et al. 1982).

[15] Rueda cites two conditions that could prompt Social Democrats to promote outsider-friendly policies. One is when insiders are themselves threatened with outsider status (e.g., through unemployment). The other has to do with the existence of corporatist channels of interest intermediation, which could soften union defense of insiders and force them – and, by extension, Social Democrats – to take the interests of outsiders into account. On the latter, however, Rueda's evidence is ambiguous.

[16] Rueda reports an observed difference in preferences on active labor market policies between insider and outsider voters of only about two percentage points – 42% of insiders and 44% of outsiders express willingness to pay more taxes to stimulate employment. The difference between the two groups is smaller still (about one percentage point) when it comes to passive labor market policies, with just over 30% of insiders and just over 31% of outsiders disagreeing that the welfare state costs too much. Among the three measures that Rueda offers, the biggest difference is in employment protection, but here too we are talking about a gap of only 5 percentage points (58% vs. 63% agreeing with the statement that job security is very important) (Rueda 2007: 45–47).

and Swank (2004, 2012) suggest that centralized business associations and national-level tripartite bargaining produce higher levels of social solidarity by facilitating compromise among groups with divergent economic interests, among other things by "transform[ing] employers' preferences" in ways that inspire "greater attention and commitment to collective goals than are found among less organized employers" (2004: 592–593). Emphasizing the political construction of preferences, they note that employers "develop their policy interests in packs" and that national-level employer associations can "facilitate regular meetings with government and labor leaders and expose members to ideas about the benefits of social policies for productivity growth and labor market stability" (2012: 1–2). Through such associations, employers not only come to prefer, but also to act collectively in support of broad social goals.[17]

Corporatism theorists past and present can point to compelling evidence of a strong association between tripartitism and social solidarity, so something is clearly going on here. It is a measure of the staying power of corporatism theory that an entire generation of political economists has committed to memory the names of obscure villages in small European countries where important pacts were concluded. However, there seems to be significant variation over time in how and how well tripartitism works. Denmark and Sweden have both experienced spells of serious economic distress and intense distributional conflict, and the 1980s and 1990s were particularly tumultuous.[18] Both countries experienced very significant neoliberal interludes in which "bourgeois" governments (or in some cases Social Democrat finance ministers with neoliberal leanings) introduced policies that represented a sharp break with the traditional model. Now that the politics have re-stabilized and the economies have rebounded, it is easy to forget that twenty years ago some very astute observers were depicting Scandinavian Social Democracy as being "in disarray," and wringing their hands at the observation that "the major social democratic parties are rapidly ... embracing market liberalism" (Moene and Wallerstein 1993: 385, 388).

Similar observations could be made for other (non-Scandinavian) countries that feature strong tripartitism. Some have been quick to attribute the Dutch

---

[17] There is some ambiguity in Martin and Swank's (2012) account about whether it is business organization or tripartite corporatist bargaining that is more important for the outcomes they seek to explain – and in practice, of course, the two are almost impossible to disentangle because strong business organization is a prerequisite for tripartite bargaining. Thus, while the first part of the book explores the origins of business associations, the second part tends to emphasize corporatist bargaining in explaining contemporary outcomes.

[18] Lundberg and Petersen (2012) note that Denmark in the 1980s and 1990s was characterized by severe conflicts – not just between employers and unions and between the center-right government and the labor movement, but also within the Social Democratic Party itself (5–8). In Sweden, the reforms of the 1990s also generated tremendous conflict between organized labor and employers, as well as "great internal convulsions" in the Social Democratic Party (2012: 9).

employment "miracle" (sharply reduced unemployment and even significant employment growth) to the famous Wassenaar Accord of 1982. However, such accounts tend to downplay the fact that many of the problems that plagued the Netherlands in the 1970s (debilitating inflation through wage indexation) and 1980s (skyrocketing labor costs through promiscuous use of disability pay to ease downsizing) can also be traced to the impact of policies coming out of corporatist bargaining processes.

The strong emphasis on employer organization and bargaining structure in the macro-corporatism literature tends to obscure the political maneuvering and conflicts that animate, complicate, and sometimes derail peak bargaining even in the most corporatist countries. In so doing, these accounts sometimes gloss over the political conflicts that have been played out inside these associations and negotiating structures, and thus miss the massive changes that have transpired in the form and content of corporatist bargaining. In 1990, Swedish employers abruptly withdrew from centralized bargaining and dismantled their peak association's wage bargaining unit in a move that was precisely designed to render continued corporatist bargaining impossible (Kjellberg 1998: 93). Organized employers in Sweden are currently doing everything in their power to marginalize the peak labor confederation Landsorganisationen (LO) and prevent any national-level recentralization. Such observations seem to be at odds with the logic of corporatism theories that emphasize capitalists' willingness and capacity to learn through negotiation and consultation, and to embrace tripartitism and the policies it generates to serve broader societal interests. The fact is that many of the most famous (and famously successful) corporatist bargains were shotgun weddings forged in the shadow of hierarchy (Scharpf 1997; van Wijnbergen 2002; see also Baccaro and Howell 2011: 39).

Producer Group Coalitions and the Role of the State

This point has not been lost on second-generation corporatism theorists, and some authors – including myself in joint work with Cathie Jo Martin – therefore embrace a somewhat different though complementary argument about state capacity in the tradition of Skocpol (1985) (see, e.g., Martin and Thelen 2007). What is foregrounded now is the capacity of the state to cajole and coerce private-sector actors into agreement (or at least compliance) at key junctures. In these versions, the idea that capitalists can be persuaded to act in their enlightened (long-term) self-interest is supplemented or even replaced with the idea that solidarism has to be imposed on resistant employers by powerful state actors.

State capacity and state power clearly matter. What we know from the historical record is that state power was frequently crucial in explaining the origins of many of the institutions of coordinated capitalism, not least in the way that interventions by state actors facilitated employers overcoming their own collective action problems (Crouch 1993; Thelen 2004; Martin and Swank

2012). State capacity also matters today. To continue with the examples in the previous sections, as in some Scandinavian countries (and unlike in Germany), the Dutch state possessed some very strong tools with which to elicit compliance from reluctant employers and for that matter reluctant unions as well. The most important tool in the arsenal was the ability of the government to intervene directly in wage bargaining and impose settlements if the social partners could not come to agreement. This was a power that was repeatedly invoked throughout the 1970s, and it continued to play a decisive role in crucial peak-level bargains well into the 1980s. It is a tool that is utterly lacking in Germany, where collective bargaining autonomy is officially enshrined in the constitution, and this clearly contributed to the failure of tripartite bargaining in that country (Streeck 2005).

Of course, strength is an inherently relational concept so in order to make sense of divergent trajectories of change in the three political-economic arenas of concern here, what we really need to know is: Strong in relation to whom? My short answer to that – and this is really the blunt core of the alternative political-coalitional argument to be laid out in more detail – is "strong relative to manufacturing interests" (see also Palier and Thelen 2010). In a context in which employment in manufacturing is now below 20 percent in all the rich democracies, the strong and resilient cross-class coalition in manufacturing that was so central to the politics of coordination in the Golden Era is no longer able (labor) or willing (employers) to defend traditional institutions – in industrial relations, in VET, and in many aspects of labor market policy – on an economy-wide basis (Martin and Thelen 2007). Where such coalitions continue to dominate the relevant interest associations, they have certainly proved capable of heading off full liberalization and of defending – for themselves – the arrangements long associated with coordinated capitalism. In the process, though, they often indirectly or even directly promote dualism (Palier and Thelen 2010). Alternatively, where manufacturing interests are tightly imbricated in more encompassing organizations, liberalization may in fact proceed further in these three political-economic realms, but under the auspices of a broad alliance of interests organized around socializing the accompanying risks.

My analysis of trends in industrial relations, vocational training, and labor market policy points to the importance of two variables in particular that affect the way manufacturing interests are connected to the interests of firms and workers in other parts of the economy. The first of these variables concerns the level of inclusiveness of interest associations. In the Scandinavian countries, union presence and employer organization are broad and encompassing, so that association membership on both sides of the class divide includes a very diverse set of actors. In many Continental political economies, by contrast, membership in organized interest associations is heavily concentrated in manufacturing. The second of these variables concerns variation in state capacity. As the discussion in the previous section showed, what often distinguishes cases

TABLE 1.1. *Factors Influencing Divergent Trajectories of Change*

		Encompassingness of Producer Group Associations	
		More Encompassing	Less Encompassing
State Capacity	stronger	Denmark	Netherlands
	weaker	Sweden	Germany

of "successful" from "failed" tripartite bargaining is the power of the state to actively broker – with carrots and where necessary sticks – encompassing deals that overcome both internal divisions within the relevant interest associations (unions and employer associations alike) as well as between the two. These two factors – the scope of interest associations and state power – vary independently of one another. For example, despite higher organization among labor and employers in Sweden, the Danish state actually has far more tools at its disposal than the Swedish state does to broker encompassing deals. And while the Netherlands and Germany both share much lower levels of encompassingness, the Dutch state commands more power to force the hand of the social partners than the German state, where employer coordination rests more squarely on voluntarism (Streeck 2005).

Putting the two factors together produces four broad scenarios, captured in Table 1.1. The best case scenario is that in which organized interests are broad and encompassing and the state possesses strong tools to broker and underwrite agreements that reconcile the interests of diverse constituencies within and between these associations (upper left). The worst case scenario – leading to dualism – is that in which manufacturing interests dominate the relevant interest associations and where the state has limited capacity to force more encompassing deals (lower right). One intermediate scenario features broad and encompassing interest associations, but a state with limited capacity to broker deals (lower left). In such instances (e.g., Sweden), manufacturing interests are often still powerful veto players even if they cannot dictate outcomes in other sectors. A second intermediate case is one in which traditional (blue-collar, male) industrial interests continue to dominate interest associations, but the state possesses tools to force the hand of the social partners (upper right). In such instances (e.g., the Netherlands) significant redistributive change is possible, but this outcome rests very heavily on the willingness of the state to sponsor and underwrite the policies needed to re-embed markets after liberalization.

THE NEW POLITICS OF SOCIAL SOLIDARITY

The following sections unpack the logic of the stylized argument as presented in the previous sections. I organize the discussion into two parts, first, addressing changes in interests, and second, in the resulting political and coalitional dynamics.

Beyond Varieties of Capitalism I: The Question of Interests

The question of interests lies at the core of any political explanation. As noted above, the VofC framework posited that coordinated capitalism was held together by a confluence of interests between labor and capital with respect to key institutions and practices. Of particular importance to the outcomes of interest here, organized employers and unions were seen to be jointly invested in (1) centralized and highly coordinated rather than decentralized, uncoordinated collective bargaining; (2) education and training systems promoting specific rather than general skills; and (3) strong employment protections rather than fluid labor markets. It may seem obvious why unions support these arrangements, but recall the key claim that they are stable because employers also support them, albeit for their own, possibly quite different reasons.

The evidence presented in the following chapters provides significant support for these claims – but only for a subset of actors and organized interests centering primarily, though not exclusively on manufacturing. Understanding the new politics of social solidarity requires as a first step acknowledging the profound shift in the political-economic landscape over the past three decades. Manufacturing lay at the heart of the political economies of all the rich democracies in the 1950s and 1960s. This was the engine of growth and jobs in industry accounted for between a third and half of total employment for the period between 1960 and 1973 (OECD 1999).[19] The dominance of industry was shaken in the oil shocks of the 1970s, and while manufacturing rebounded subsequently in many (though not all) of these countries, employment in the sector never bounced back. It is not that manufacturing did not remain important for many of these economies; it clearly did, although the extent to which this is true varies. But what matters for the politics is that everywhere employment in industry has dropped steadily over time to currently between 10 and 20 percent.[20]

The shift in employment to services – including, of course, services to industry itself – has upset previous political dynamics because both firms and workers in these emerging sectors have interests that are very different from their counterparts in traditional manufacturing. On the employer side, I find that service sector firms do not support traditional arrangements and have in fact pushed

[19] The exceptions are countries that continued to employ very large numbers (greater than 30%) in agriculture – namely Greece, Ireland, and Turkey (with Spain and Portugal not far behind). Japan and the United States were on the low end for industrial employment, at 33.4% and 34.7% respectively. Germany, Luxembourg, Belgium, and Austria were at the high end, all with over 40% employed in industry (Germany at 47.8%).

[20] In the UK, the decline in manufacturing employment set in earlier, in 1961 (see the figures in Broadberry 1993: 790).

relentlessly in most countries for more wage differentiation and more flexible labor markets. Clearly a part of this is simply an effort to reduce costs, but beyond this, labor mobility and wage differentiation play a more prominent and sometimes positive role in emerging service sectors. Whereas traditional manufacturing thrives on high employment stability (allowing firms and workers to amortize their co-investment in firm- or industry-specific skills), in high-end services labor mobility promotes skill acquisition by providing incentive and opportunity for workers to enhance their human capital (Becker 1993: 34). This observation is consistent with the original VofC logic (Hall and Soskice 2001), and it explains why many CMEs in the past have experienced skill shortages at the high end (e.g., Smith 2000; Thelen 2004: chapter 1; Daley and Kulish 2012).

Related to this, service-sector firms thrive on general rather than specific skills. This is particularly true at the high end for occupations like software engineering that involve very portable skills. But in low-skill sectors like the retail and hospitality industries as well, a high-quality public school system providing foundational general education and training may in some ways be better equipped than traditional apprenticeship to generate the kind of social and communication skills that employers seek (see especially Iversen and Stephens 2008a). In light of such differences, it is no surprise that the most urgent calls for a reconfiguration of traditional political-economic institutions – industrial relations institutions, educational institutions, and labor market institutions – have emanated from organized employers in the service sectors.

On the labor side, the shift to services has also brought new interests to the fore, including constituencies that we know were never well served by arrangements suited to male blue-collar workers in the era of manufacturing dominance (Klausen 1999: 261). The growing number of working women, for example, may benefit from some forms of liberalization, since existing evidence suggests that they do not do well under many of the arrangements traditionally associated with coordinated capitalism. Iversen and Rosenbluth (2012), among others, have noted the great paradox that "labor market protections and solidaristic wage policies, [although] designed to safeguard society's weak, can have the effect of disadvantaging women" (307). Recent work by Nelson and Stephens (2012) demonstrates that strong employment protections and generous long-term unemployment replacement rates suppress women's employment (161). Such arrangements – traditionally so central to supporting investment in specific skills in manufacturing – put women at a disadvantage because employers anticipate having to bear the costs associated with interruptions for maternity leaves (Estevez-Abe 2006). As long as social protections are strong, more fluid labor markets may in some respects be more congenial for women, whose employment records are more likely to be interrupted for family reasons.

With respect to skill regimes as well, research has shown that women are distinctly disadvantaged in countries featuring traditional firm-based apprenticeship and do better in school-based training emphasizing general skills

(J. Martin 1998: 16; Estevez-Abe et al. 2001; Estevez-Abe 2006). Here again, the possibility of career interruption due to motherhood makes employers reluctant to invest in training women in firm- or industry-specific skills (Iversen and Rosenbluth 2012: 308). Moreover, beyond the question of access to training, more general skills afford women greater flexibility and penalize career interruptions less (Estevez-Abe et al. 2001: 150–151, 159; Estevez-Abe 2006). Women thus stand to benefit disproportionately from institutional reforms that support school-based education and training in more general (portable) skills (Estevez-Abe 2006), and in fact they often outperform men in such settings (Baethge et al. 2007).

Many of these arguments apply equally well to the growing number of salaried employees, professionals, and semi-professionals who see themselves as benefitting from at least some aspects of liberalization. For example, nurses in Scandinavia eagerly embraced liberalization in collective bargaining because centralization and wage compression had been holding their increases back. Moreover, salaried employees will often welcome forms of liberalization that enhance consumer choice.[21] Esping-Andersen (1985) pointed out nearly thirty years ago that as the composition of employment in the economy as a whole shifts in response to economic trends, white-collar groups may prove crucial to the survival of egalitarian capitalism. My analysis affirms Esping-Andersen's original insight about the importance of white-collar constituencies, while also showing that these groups are often not particularly invested in some of the institutions traditionally associated with coordinated capitalism. It is not that they face no risks in the labor market; it is just that existing arrangements fail to cover the very different risks these groups face, which may include issues such as insufficient social security coverage as a result of less continuous career paths, or the need to reconcile work and family (Bonoli 2005). As Silja Häusermann's work in particular has emphasized, well-educated socio-cultural elites (professionals, semi-professionals, and high-skill employees in services) are in many cases core constituencies of Social Democracy and defend a universal welfare state even if they embrace a different variety of universalism in the labor market – one that emphasizes individual development, internationalization, meritocracy, and gender equality (e.g., Häusermann and Kriesi forthcoming: esp. 28–29).

Finally, less-skilled workers generally also face a host of new risks that are not necessarily well addressed by traditional institutions. Such workers clearly benefited in the past from arrangements such as centralized collective bargaining and associated wage compression. However, skill-biased technological change and the transition to services create new trade-offs that pit wage equalization against full employment (Iversen and Wren 1998). Less-skilled workers are the ones most likely to bear the brunt of such trade-offs – either through

---

[21] Unless, of course, reforms introduced under the consumer choice banner aim to inject forms of market competition that threaten a profession's organizational monopoly or integrity, in which case professionals will oppose it (Sako 2012).

unemployment or through low-wage work in dead-end jobs. Given that these groups are the ones most exposed to rapid shifts in labor market conditions, they may not be well served by traditional arrangements organized around the assumption of stable career trajectories, such as training systems that involve heavy upfront investments in particular (industry or occupational) skills. For them, training regimes that are organized around more general (especially basic cognitive) skills, and especially those that provide multiple entry points to allow individuals to acquire new skills flexibly and over the life course may be more suited to helping them manage the uncertainties they face in the labor market.

In short, the transition to a post-industrial employment structure brings to the fore new constituencies that face different risks. How these new risks are articulated and addressed – also in relation to those of other groups – is crucial to the new politics of solidarity. Clearly the old sources of insecurity (unemployment, loss of benefits) remain important, but alongside these there are a host of new issues as well, including single parenthood, skill obsolescence in a period of rapid technological change, less continuous career paths, and the need to reconcile work and family in a context in which women no longer stay at home (see especially Bonoli 2005; Morel et al. 2011). Institutions that protected well against the risks of the 1950s do not unproblematically continue to cover risks that have shifted considerably since that time (Hacker 2006).

The crux of the debate between VofC and its critics discussed in the preceding sections really boils down to the issue of interests. VofC scholars operate on the (often unexplored) assumption that the interests of traditional manufacturing are shared by all employers, and they are therefore forced to ignore a great deal of evidence that in fact employers in CMEs (especially but not exclusively outside manufacturing) have notably not defended traditional institutions, but indeed vigorously promoted changes in them. For their part, however, VofC critics sometimes overlook evidence of continued support for these arrangements within the (still important) manufacturing core, and operate on the equally shaky assumption that traditional institutions meet the interests of (and cover the relevant risks faced by) all workers. In the end, both perspectives are deeply infused with a map of interests that reflects a distinctly industrial logic. And this is why, even though they disagree on so many other things, scholars in these two camps often converge on the idea that the interests of social solidarity are best served through a spirited defense of traditional institutions.

This is the received wisdom that the present analysis challenges. It shows on the one hand that the faithful reproduction of traditional arrangements can in fact promote institutional erosion and increased inequality through dualization, and it demonstrates on the other hand that some forms of liberalization can actually shore up social solidarity by addressing the interests of emerging constituencies that were under-represented in the era of manufacturing dominance. This leads me to a discussion of the political dynamics.

Beyond Varieties of Capitalism II: Political Dynamics and Coalitions

Many of the political choices in the 1950s and 1960s that were so important in shaping welfare regimes (Esping-Andersen 1990) have also had
downstream implications for the politics surrounding current changes in the
political-economic institutions at the center of the present study. Above all,
developments at that time powerfully influenced the political and organizational resources that all of the relevant actors – organized labor, business, and
the state itself – can bring to bear in the current period. For example, and as
is widely known, in Social Democratic countries, the modal response to labor
market shortages in the 1960s was to mobilize women, whose entry into the
labor market in turn fueled demand for an expansion of public services to
support female employment. The shift away from household-based (unpaid)
caregiving created demand for a wide range of services, thus drawing even
more women into the labor market and in particular into the rapidly growing
public sector (Huber and Stephens 2000: 327; see also Pontusson 2009). As
a result of these developments, a large and well-organized public sector came
to form a very important second pillar within the union movement, producing a significant counterweight to manufacturing.[22] Women now constitute a
majority of the organized labor movement in most of these countries.[23]

In Christian Democratic countries, by contrast, the response to labor market
shortages in the 1960s was very different. These countries frequently turned
to state-sponsored guest worker programs to cover labor market shortages.[24]
Women, meanwhile, stayed home in large numbers and continued to support a
traditional male breadwinner model through their role as crucial providers of
unpaid caregiving services (Orloff 1993). That meant that the public and service sectors remained smaller, which in turn allowed manufacturing interests
to continue to dominate producer group politics. In these countries, the structure of union membership often continues to reflect the employment patterns
of the 1950s and 1960s – heavily concentrated among male blue-collar workers in manufacturing and weak in services (Hassel 2011). When women did
enter the labor force in larger numbers, typically in the 1980s and 1990s, the
context had shifted completely to one of high unemployment rather than labor

---

[22] In previous work with Cathie Jo Martin (Martin and Thelen 2007), we observed a strong
correlation between the size of the public sector and solidaristic outcomes (a finding that is
elaborated in more detail in Martin and Swank 2010).
[23] On the electoral impact of the different patterns sketched out here, see especially Huber and
Stephens (2000).
[24] Despite the presumption that these would be limited sojourns, foreign workers often stayed
on. In many cases, manufacturing unions went to great lengths to incorporate them into the
organized labor movement in an effort to forestall downward pressure on wages once markets
tightened up. Where this succeeded, first- and even second-generation immigrants often came
to be rather well integrated into industry (as reflected, for example, in unionization rates) even
if they usually remained poorly integrated in society (Halepli, n.d.; Lacey 2008; Aktürk 2011:
138).

shortages. Women in Christian Democratic countries were therefore more likely to enter as secondary earners looking to supplement family income in a period of heightened economic insecurity.[25]

Drawing together the ways in which previous political settlements interact with changing interests today, we can make out three broad political-coalitional patterns that correspond to the three trajectories of liberalization laid out above.

In the case of liberal economies like the United States, no stable accommodation had been reached within manufacturing between employers and organized labor even in the Golden Era of postwar growth. Here the decline of manufacturing set in motion a pattern of deregulation. Organized labor's strength – initially formidable in the industrial core – rested on tight labor markets and sometimes state support. But absent complementary institutional arrangements to sustain the kind of high-skill, high-value-added manufacturing that could survive in the more turbulent markets of the 1970s, economic downturn sparked ferocious conflict within manufacturing. This is consistent with the original VofC logic (Hall and Soskice 2001; Thelen 2001). The transition to services then took place under the auspices of a coalition between employers in declining and emerging sectors based on a broad neoliberal project, and was accompanied by a marked turn toward the individualization of risk. In these cases, deregulation in the three institutional arenas examined here contributed to striking increases in levels of inequality.

A second pattern – dualization – has prevailed in those CMEs where organized interests and producer group politics continue to be dominated by a strong and often still-competitive manufacturing sector. The paradigmatic cases here are Japan and Germany, where public policy continues to be organized around manufacturing interests. For all the reasons laid out in the VofC literature, industrial firms and their workers will jointly defend – for themselves – traditional institutions and practices. However – and this is where the argument departs from some of the VofC literature – the strong and resilient cross-class coalition in manufacturing that was so central to the politics of coordination in the Golden Era is no longer in a position to exercise leadership of the political economy as a whole (Martin and Thelen 2007). Manufacturing employers will not be at the forefront of demands for across-the-board liberalization, but nor can they be expected to oppose liberalization outside the organized industrial core. Quite the contrary, in fact, since export-oriented firms benefit doubly from the growth of a less regulated periphery – both through lower service prices and through lower taxes.[26] Unions in such cases may well oppose these developments, but without strong anchoring in the affected sectors they will be poorly placed to counter these trends.

---

[25] Iversen and Rosenbluth (2010) show that where traditional family structures persisted longer, women are politically conservative and oppose policies that are likely to raise taxes on male insiders (142; see also Barrows 2011).

[26] Thanks to Martin Höpner for emphasizing this to me.

Finally, a third pattern – embedded flexibilization – is best approximated in the Scandinavian countries. In these cases, manufacturing interests are less dominant within the organized interest associations. Partly for this very reason, traditional arrangements have actually undergone more significant changes – and as we will see, often away from coordination in the VofC sense. However, where emerging new interests (service-sector workers generally, including above all women and low-skilled workers) are well organized and incorporated into institutionalized decision making venues, this has also paved the way for more encompassing and sometimes unlikely reform coalitions (Levy 1999; Bonoli 2005: 442ff; Martin and Thelen 2007; Martin and Swank 2012). In such cases, public policy reflects a "social investment" logic that embraces some elements of liberalization while also rejecting the idea that "any job is a good job" and insisting instead that social policy be used to create "quality jobs" (Morel et al. 2011: 9–10; see also Hemerijck 2013). Thus, while encompassing and inclusive interest associations seem to be important prerequisites for embedded flexibilization, the state plays a hugely important role in brokering and sustaining the coalition supporting this path. In fact, the variety of liberalization associated with this trajectory of change requires more rather than less state involvement, although the goals guiding public policy shift in important ways, above all toward measures (particularly investments in education and training) that underwrite employment (rather than job) security (Peterson 2011: 209; Wren et al. 2012: 142).[27]

Embedded flexibilization departs from many of the traditional arrangements underpinning coordinated capitalism even if liberalizing reforms are embedded in institutions and policies that protect the most vulnerable groups.[28] The new redistributive logic substitutes active engagement for passive support – "prepare, not repair" in the language of its advocates (Morel et al. 2011: 354). While a high degree of employer organization is helpful for the reasons that Hilferding identified, it is by no means sufficient. Instead, as power resource theory suggests, what is crucial is unity and coordination on the labor side, along with the active support of the state to underwrite policies that collectivize risk (Huber and Stephens 2005; Rehm et al. 2012; Hacker et al. 2013). Moreover, and as Chapter 5 on the Netherlands and Sweden demonstrates in particular, because the arrangements associated with embedded flexibilization often rest on "ambiguous agreements" among actors with different and sometimes contradictory interests (Palier 2005: 127, 138), embarking on this

---

[27] The paradox that this form of liberalization requires significant state support has caused the liberal news magazine *The Economist* some consternation. While heaping praise on the Nordic countries as the new "supermodel," the editors marvel at how these countries seem capable of combining successful capitalism (for *The Economist*, that means liberal capitalism) with such a large state (*The Economist*, February 2, 2013).

[28] Embedded flexibilization calls to mind John Ruggie's (1982) concept of "embedded liberalism" (i.e., the observation that after World War II, democracies implemented welfare policies to protect domestic losers in conjunction with their embrace of free trade and finance). I thank an anonymous reviewer for pointing this out.

path requires a rather significant reconfiguration of institutions and policies to "upset inherited coalitional patterns and stimulate the emergence of new vested interests and political alliances" (Patashnik 2008: 3–4). Where they are durable, the resulting arrangements institutionalize what Ahlquist and Levi (2013) call a "community of fate" that reconciles the interests of Social Democracy's traditional blue-collar core with the interests of new constituencies including, notably, women and service employees (Huber and Stephens 2000; Pontusson 2009; Iversen and Rosenbluth 2010; Martin and Swank 2012).

OUTLINE OF THE CHAPTERS TO FOLLOW

The next three chapters explore the propositions laid out above through an analysis of the politics of institutional stability and change in three of the central institutional arenas to which the VofC literature has drawn our attention, namely industrial relations (Chapter 2), vocational education and training (Chapter 3), and labor market policy (Chapter 4). In each area, I compare developments in a classic LME (the United States) and two important CMEs that have traversed rather different paths since the 1980s (Germany and Denmark). These chapters examine the political dynamics and political outcomes that distinguish the three trajectories of change identified in this chapter. Chapter 5 extends and elaborates the argument through an examination of two further cases, the Netherlands and Sweden. The Dutch case gives us an illuminating contrast to Germany, as the Netherlands is a Christian Democratic country that deviated somewhat from the usual Continental pattern to embrace a version of flexicurity sharing some broad similarities with Scandinavia. Sweden provides a useful foil for Denmark, because it gives us an instance of macro-corporatism (including powerful and encompassing unions and well-organized employers) that has been plagued with dualist tendencies that bear some resemblance to the dominant pattern in the Continental cases. Chapter 6 concludes and draws out the implications of my analysis for the study of advanced capitalism and for the politics of social solidarity in the contemporary period more generally.

2

Industrial Relations Institutions

We can begin the analysis of divergent trajectories of change with an examination of developments over the past two decades in industrial relations. This is an area in which scholars who are focusing on different measures often reach wildly different conclusions concerning the relative stability of traditional arrangements (see Thelen 2012). VofC scholars expect stability, at least in CMEs. They argue that even though employers in liberal market economies may well seek deregulation, those in CMEs will continue to support traditional arrangements because their competitive strategies rely on a high degree of labor cooperation, wage moderation, and peaceful plant relations – all elements that the institutions and practices associated with coordinated bargaining safeguard and protect.

VofC critics, by contrast, maintain that employers in CMEs are no more supportive of these arrangements – or for that matter of unions – than their counterparts in the Anglo-Saxon world, and in fact seek at all turns to escape from the regulatory constraints imposed on them by organized labor and the state. VofC critics maintain that globalization has tilted the balance of power against labor, emboldening and empowering firms to increase flexibility and lower costs (Kapstein 1996; Katz and Darbishire 1999; Martin and Ross 1999). The direction of change is the same cross-nationally – neoliberalism – and any observed variation in the pace of institutional change is for them a matter of successful labor defense, not divergent employer preferences.

We can begin to assess these arguments in light of several key indicators of stability and change in industrial relations. Tables 2.1 and 2.2 record change within countries in the period from 1970 to 2010 with reference to two common indicators, the level of collective bargaining and the degree of bargaining coordination.[1] What we see by either measure is evidence of significant formal

---

[1] All four of the tables below are based on data assembled by Jelle Visser. I exclude Ireland and New Zealand, for which Visser does not have data on all four of the measures considered

TABLE 2.1. *Degree of Wage Coordination*

Country	1970	2010	Change
Denmark	5	4	−1
Finland	5	3	−2
Norway	5	4	−1
Sweden	5	4	−1
Austria	5	4	−1
Belgium	4	5	+1
France	2	2	no chg
Germany	3	4	+1
Italy	2	3	+1
Netherlands	3	4	+1
Switzerland	4	3	−1
Australia	3	2	−1
Canada	1	1	no chg
U.S.	1	1	no chg
UK	3	1	−2
Japan	5	4	−1

Note: based on Kenworthy's five-point classification scale
5 = economy-wide bargaining
4 = mixed industry and economy-wide bargaining with pattern setting
3 = industry bargaining with no pattern or irregular pattern setting
2 = mixed industry- and firm-level bargaining, with weak enforceability of industry agreements
1 = none of the above, fragmented, mostly company-level bargaining
Source: Jelle Visser (http://www.uva-aias.net/208)

TABLE 2.2. *Bargaining Level*

Country	1970	2010	Change
Denmark	5	3	−2
Finland	5	3	−2
Norway	4	3	−1
Sweden	5	3	−2
Austria	3	3	no chg
Belgium	4	4	no chg
France	3	2	−1
Germany	3	3	no chg
Italy	3	3	no chg
Netherlands	3	3	no chg
Switzerland	3	3	no chg
Australia	4	2	−2
Canada	1	1	no chg
U.S.	1	1	no chg
UK	3	1	−2
Japan	1	1	no chg

Note:
5 = national or central level
4 = national or central level, with additional sectoral/local or company level
3 = sectoral or industry level
2 = sectoral or industry level, with additional local or company level
1 = local or company level
Source: Jelle Visser (http://www.uva-aias.net/208)

decentralization in all of the Scandinavian countries, as well as in other "most corporatist" countries such as Austria. By contrast, Continental Christian Democratic countries exhibited a more mixed picture, including some movement in both directions, but also a higher degree of stability overall in formal bargaining structures over this same period, again by either measure.[2] Liberal

here (Ireland missing bargaining coverage data for all years; New Zealand missing bargaining coverage data after 2000).

[2] See also Karlson (2010). Based on an index composed of several measures (centralization of wage setting, confederal involvement in wage setting, and government involvement in wage setting), he finds that several of the previously most corporatist countries – specifically, Sweden, Denmark, and the Netherlands – have experienced the greatest decentralization, alongside the liberal UK. By these same measures, Karlson finds that the continental model has seen much less change.

TABLE 2.3. *Collective Bargaining Coverage*

Country	1970	2010	% Change
Denmark	80	85*	+6%
Finland	73	90***	+23%
Norway	65	74**	+14%
Sweden	84	91	+8%
Austria	95	99	+4%
Belgium	85	96	+13%
France	70	92**	+31%
Germany	85	61	−28%
Italy	85	85	no chg
Netherlands	76	84	+11%
Switzerland	50	49	−2%
Australia	90	45*	−50%
Canada	34	32***	−7%
U.S.	30	13	−56%
UK	73	31	−58%
Japan	32	16**	−50%

Note: Bargaining (or union) coverage measures the proportion of employees covered by wage bargaining agreements as a proportion of all wage and salary earners in employment with the right to bargaining, adjusted for the possibility that some sectors or occupations are excluded from the right to bargain – removing such groups from the employment count before dividing the number of covered employees by the total number of dependent workers in employment.
* indicates data from 2007 (latest available)
** indicates data from 2008
*** indicates data from 2009
Source: Jelle Visser (http://www.uva-aias.net/208)

TABLE 2.4. *Union Density*

Country	1970	2010	Change
Denmark	60.3	68.5	+14%
Finland	51.3	70.0	+36%
Norway	56.8	54.8	−4%
Sweden	67.7	68.9	+2%
Austria	62.8	28.4	−55%
Belgium	42.1	50.6	+20%
France	21.7	7.9	−64%
Germany	32.0	18.6	−42%
Italy	37.0	35.5	−4%
Netherlands	36.5	19.3	−49%
Switzerland	28.9	17.2	−40%
Australia	44.2	18.0	−59%
Canada	31.0	30.0	−3%
U.S.	27.4	11.4	−58%
UK	44.8	27.1	−40%
Japan	35.1	18.4	−48%

Note: union density = net union membership as a proportion of wage and salary earners in employment
Source: Jelle Visser (http://www.uva-aias.net/208)

political economies, finally, were already very decentralized to begin with, but those that previously had exhibited some degree of centralization or coordination if anything became more decentralized over this period.

A somewhat different picture emerges if we turn to trends in bargaining coverage and union density (Tables 2.3 and 2.4). By these measures, all of the Scandinavian countries record net increases in bargaining coverage since the 1970s (Table 2.3), while all of the liberal countries register declines (sometimes dramatic declines) in bargaining coverage over this period. Continental Christian Democratic countries again show more mixed results – Austria, Belgium, France, and the Netherlands experienced increases, while Germany, Italy, and Switzerland recorded losses. Trends in union density produce a similar picture (Table 2.4). Here we see a nearly uniform increase in union density in Scandinavia, and an almost uniform decline (again often dramatic) in union density in Continental Christian Democratic and liberal market economies.

Putting the pieces together we see three distinct patterns: (1) formal-institutional decentralization, but in the context of continued broad coverage and strong unionization (much of Scandinavia); (2) formal-institutional stability, but in the context of declining union membership – very often, though not always, accompanied by declining bargaining coverage – especially in the Continental Christian Democratic countries; and (3) formal decentralization coupled with declining coverage and unionization in the liberal economies.

This is a picture that does not comport entirely with either VofC or liberalization theories. Against VofC theories we see significant formal decentralization, not just in the LMEs but also in what were previously the most highly coordinated market economies of Scandinavia. But against liberalization theories, we see not just continued high formal-institutional stability in many Continental CMEs but also continued high coverage and unionization in Scandinavia despite bargaining decentralization. Given this mixed picture of stability and change, adjudicating the theoretical debates requires us to inquire into the express interests of employers and to analyze the political dynamics that are driving these somewhat contradictory outcomes.

Such an examination reveals three different trajectories of liberalization in industrial relations that reflect the patterns introduced in Chapter 1. U.S. industrial relations provide us with a textbook case of deregulatory liberalization, featuring the collapse of unions and with that the further dismantling of what was already a rather patchy system of collective bargaining. Institutions for negotiated settlements between representatives of business and labor, never really stable to begin with, were effectively demolished in the 1980s as a result of an employer offensive powerfully abetted by the state. What remains is not so much a strong collective framework but mostly a set of legal options to which individual workers can turn if employers violate various employment laws. In short, the trend has been toward an individualization of risk and a system in which recourse often runs through the courts as a matter of individual, not collective, labor rights.

The pattern in Germany is different. Here traditional bargaining institutions and practices have remained remarkably robust in manufacturing, where – consistent with VofC logic – employers exhibit continued support for coordination. Rather than conflict, we observe an intensification of cooperation between labor and capital in the interest of what remains a very competitive export sector. However, this system has largely failed to take root outside the industrial core, and the gradual shift in employment to services – where unions have a weaker presence – has eroded collective bargaining coverage (dualization through drift). In line with the logic of drift as defined by Hacker and Pierson (2010a), proponents of change have not mounted a direct frontal assault on traditional institutions, but instead fostered change by resisting reforms that would shore up these arrangements in the face of clear erosion.

Finally, Denmark has not been exempt from liberalization pressures, but these pressures have played out differently. High levels of conflict in Danish industrial relations in the 1970s and early 1980s resulted in the breakdown of peak-level solidaristic wage bargaining and formal-institutional decentralization from the national level to the industry level. These developments were followed by further decentralization, so that bargaining over pay now takes place mainly at the workplace level. However, these liberalizing moves have been embedded in an encompassing set of bargaining structures that collectivizes rather than individualizes risk. Encompassing union organization and a broad presence across the economy have contributed to this outcome, but the state has also played a key role in setting bounds on wage flexibility at the low end of the spectrum and in facilitating a reorientation in peak bargaining to address emerging risks faced by new constituencies.

The next sections flesh out the politics through detailed analyses of developments in these three countries over the past four decades.

INDUSTRIAL RELATIONS IN THE UNITED STATES: DEREGULATION PURE AND SIMPLE

The United States provides us with a case of deregulation pure and simple. The past three decades have seen the collapse of unions, and with that a precipitous decline in the collective regulation of employment relations. The overall trend has been toward the individualization of pay bargaining in the context of ongoing erosion in the statutory minimum wage and a privatization of risk in which bounds are set primarily by laws regulating individual employment contracts (e.g., anti-discrimination laws) with recourse through the courts. The effects of the collapse of organized labor and of collective bargaining are especially dramatic in the United States because so much of the American welfare regime has traditionally been delivered via industrial relations (see especially Hacker 2002, 2006). Thus, the decline in collective bargaining involves not just an individualization of wage setting, but also the loss of other benefits that in other countries are provided to all citizens by the state.

Deregulation in American industrial relations advanced relatively rapidly on two related fronts, one rooted in union-avoidance strategies pursued by individual firms, flanked later by collective efforts to roll back union bargaining rights. Confronted in the 1970s with intensified competition in international markets, American employers seized on opportunities embedded in U.S. labor law to avoid unions and defeat organizing drives. They were powerfully abetted by the state, which especially under President Ronald Reagan fostered a political and legal climate that was hostile to organized labor and that helped to hasten a large scale deregulation in American industrial relations.

In a way, this is an outcome long in the making. In nineteenth century America, ongoing struggles between firms and craft unions over managerial prerogatives undermined the kind of stable accommodation between labor and capital that elsewhere underwrote industrial strategies organized around highly skilled labor and high wages.[3] In most CMEs, unions in the early industrial period explicitly ceded management control on the shop floor in exchange for union recognition, while in LMEs like Britain and the United States, craft unions continued to battle employers over skills. The power of organized labor in the United States varied greatly across regions such that firms in bastions of union strength often found themselves at a competitive disadvantage in national product markets, thus exacerbating competition by introducing what employers perceived as "disruptive distortions" (for a discussion see Thelen 2004: 191–194). Unable to sustain coordination around an agenda to preserve skills and training and to contain wage competition, employers periodically rallied around an agenda aimed at leveling the playing field – by defeating craft controls.

If anything, U.S. firms went further than their counterparts in other LMEs in the wake of these battles over managerial prerogatives, seeking to reduce their dependence on skill altogether (Thelen 2004: chapter 4). Aided by a more expansive domestic market, American manufacturing in the 1920s had already settled on strategies of mass production based on semi-skilled and unskilled labor. In this context, productivity gains were achieved through mechanization, increasing division of labor ("Taylorization"), and a foreman-led "drive" system aimed at relentless rationalization of production and cost cutting. The process was far advanced by the time the Wagner Act was passed in 1935 so that "by the time American unions were stabilized and collective bargaining rights were secured, organized labor in the United States was maneuvering in a more thoroughly rationalized shop floor environment. Union strategies revolved around a narrower form of job control in highly bureaucratized internal labor markets" (Thelen 2004: 177–178).

In retrospect it is easy to see why this arrangement would not be stable. The Wagner Act provided a crucial lift to unions, allowing them to achieve a foothold in firms and to establish and enforce rules (e.g., seniority-based promotion within internal labor markets) to protect workers against the harsh and capricious foremen who presided over the notorious drive system. However, the New Deal industrial relations system was not premised on any confluence of interests, or on any enduring realignment of class relations or power at the national level. The only real expectation was that management would "adapt to union organizing efforts in a pragmatic fashion" (Kochan et al. 1994: 25). Importantly, the Wagner Act did not presume nor did it particularly promote unionization. It simply provided employees with the opportunity to choose to be unionized; as Goldfield (1987) points out, "its explicit purpose was to ascertain whether employees wanted a union and to protect their rights in such expression" (106; see also Kochan et al. 1994: 25).

By defining labor rights as individual rather than collective rights, the law fit with a political-economic landscape in which business interests were

[3] For a fuller analysis, see Thelen (2004).

uncoordinated and distrustful of the state (D. Vogel 1978; Iversen and Soskice 2009), and where unions, too, were centered on narrow economistic goals and voluntarism (Godard 2009: 90–91).[4] Unlike in many CMEs, where union coverage rates often exceed unionization rates, the way that labor rights are institutionalized in the United States means that trends in union membership and collective bargaining coverage track each other almost perfectly (Schmitt and Mitukiewicz 2011: 5, 7). This constellation virtually assured that the organized labor movement that had emerged with such apparent energy in the 1930s and 1940s would ultimately prove a "fragile juggernaut" resting on "an ephemeral deal, not a permanent realignment of class power" (Cowie 2010: 298). As in the early nineteenth century, collective regulation of labor conditions even after labor's full incorporation under the Wagner Act would be vulnerable to unraveling through competitive pressures and concerted business push back.

It did not take long. From 1935 to 1947, the Wagner Act and associated institutions (notably the NLRB) supported union organization. However, already in 1947 the passage of the Taft-Hartley Act marked a first rollback. Passed against intense union opposition, the law banned wildcat strikes, outlawed the closed shop, and held unions liable for damages through industrial action. The Taft-Hartley Act also rendered union certification more difficult by eliminating card checks and other mechanisms through which unions could demonstrate majority support. After 1947, the only route to certification by the NLRB was through elections, and after the Taft-Hartley Act these were elections in which employers enjoyed an explicit right to counter-mobilize (Goldfield 1987: 185). Although observers typically date the onset of the U.S. labor movement's decline to the Reagan era, in fact union power has been on the slide since 1954 – which is to say, the decline set in at the height of the Golden Era of postwar capitalism itself. In that year, union density peaked at 25.4 percent, and it has trended steadily downward since then to just over 10 percent in 2012, according to the Bureau of Labor Statistics.

Deregulation in American Industrial Relations in the 1970s and 1980s

The key point (consistent with classic VofC arguments) is that in the United States, unlike in CMEs like Germany and Sweden, there was really no stable accommodation reached between organized unions and employers – not in the manufacturing core, and not even at the height of postwar capitalist growth. The 1970s and 1980s did not so much upset a previously stable set of institutions as they revealed the flimsy foundations on which existing arrangements rested. As in the past, uneven union presence exacerbated rather than mitigated

---

4 As famously articulated in 1883 by one of the early leaders of the American Federation of Labor, Adolph Strasser, "We have no ultimate ends. We are going from day to day. We are fighting only for immediate objects. . . . We are all practical men" (quoted in Moody 2007: 163).

competition among firms. The union wage premium rose from 19 percent in the late 1960s to 30 percent by the late 1970s (Kochan et al. 1994: 41). And whereas in the booming 1950s this gap could be offset by higher productivity in unionized plants, by the mid- to late 1970s "few managers could find productivity improvements to offset the 20 to 30 percent wage and fringe benefit differences many of them faced" (70). It was only a matter of time before companies in which unions had established a presence responded by moving to an openly antiunion stance.

Even more than in the antiunion "open shop" movement of the early 1900s, international pressures played a role in provoking an employer assault on organized labor in the 1970s. The United States steadily lost ground in low-technology industries like textiles and in medium-technology industries such as machinery, electrical equipment, and cars. Unionized firms responded by embarking on a vigorous campaign to level the playing field by eliminating rigid and expensive job controls. Inspired by the successes of the Japanese, companies experimented with shop floor innovations premised on a small number of broad job classifications, fewer rules governing specific jobs assignments, and more freedom for supervisors (and less weight for seniority) in promotion and transfer decisions (Kochan et al. 1994: 96).[5] Such innovations inevitably provoked conflict with unions, since implementing them necessarily involved renegotiating the work rules to which union rights were themselves attached. The contrast to countries in which industrial unions had prevailed is stark, because there none of these flexibility-enhancing moves involved any kind of assault on union bargaining rights. In fact, in many CMEs employers found themselves running through open doors as work reorganization accommodated organized labor's longstanding humanization of work goals (Locke and Thelen 1995).

American employers, by contrast, saw rigid work rules as the key competitive problem and launched a broad assault on union bargaining rights. Possibilities for individual union-avoidance strategies through employer counter-mobilization in union registration drives were virtually built into the Taft-Hartley Act. Such strategies were perfected in the 1970s. As Bruce Western (1997) points out, "the rising incidence of unfair labor practices, lengthening delays before certification elections, and growing popularity of professional union-busting management consultants all indicate an intensified effort by employers to resist unionization" (48). These trends were reflected in a dramatic rise in decertification elections beginning in the late 1960s. Beyond the already widely used strategy of moving operations to the less unionized South, by the 1970s American firms could just stay put and take advantage of what one observer has called "a sophisticated union avoidance industry" without parallel elsewhere (Godard 2009: 99).

[5] Such issues dominated bargaining in the late 1970s and early 1980s, and unions typically conceded ground. According to a survey conducted by the Conference Board in 1983, 63 percent of firms had secured work rule concessions in recent bargaining (Kochan et al. 1994: 118).

Antiunion management consulting firms were already active in the 1950s, but it was in the 1970s that the use of such services exploded. Whereas in 1962 almost half (46.1 percent) of all NLRB elections were "consent" elections (i.e., not actively opposed by management), by 1977 this was down to 8.6 percent (Goldfield 1987: 193, 200). Based on data from the NLRB, Schmitt and Zipperer (2009) document a sharp jump in the late 1970s and early 1980s in illegal firings in the context of union election campaigns (11). Whereas in the 1960s and early 1970s illegal firings were documented in about 8 percent of such campaigns, this figure rose to 31 percent in the early Reagan years and has mostly stayed above 20 percent since then. In a comprehensive comparison of trends in unionization across the rich democracies, Western (1997) argues that from a comparative perspective what really sets the United States apart is the institutional framework that provides "unique opportunities for employer resistance" (48–49). He singles out decentralized secret ballot elections and employer counter-campaigns as especially uncongenial for union organization.[6] Richard Freeman (2007) concludes on the basis of survey evidence that "if workers were provided the union representation they desired in 2005, then the overall unionization rate would have been about 58%" (2).

The effectiveness of these individual strategies in turn drove decentralization in those few sectors where some degree of coordination had been established in the 1950s and 1960s. Pattern bargaining broke down in the 1980s in industries like coal, steel, rubber, and transportation. In the automobile industry as well, coordination declined as supplier firms opted out of industry-wide deals in large numbers and as Japanese transplants resisted unionization. Where unions did manage to maintain a presence, firms sought separate contracts with the United Automobile Workers. Across the full range of industries, multi-employer bargaining declined step by step as companies withdrew from master agreements either to negotiate company-level deals or to eliminate the union altogether (see, e.g., Goldfield 1987: 46).

Individual union-avoidance strategies and decentralization were accompanied by a concerted collective effort to thwart labor law reform aimed at shoring up unions. With Democrats in power in 1977, the American

---

[6] These patterns have continued into the current period. Examining developments between 1999 and 2003, Brofenbrenner (2009: 10) finds that employers mounted antiunion campaigns in fully 96 percent of NLRB elections and hired management consultants to assist them in their campaigns in three-quarters of such elections. Specifically, he found that the "employer threatened to close the plant in 57% of elections, discharged workers in 34%, and threatened to cut wages and benefits in 47% of elections. Workers were forced to attend antiunion one-on-one sessions with a supervisor at least weekly in two-thirds of elections. In 63% of elections employers used supervisor one-on-one meetings to interrogate workers about who they or other workers supported, and in 54% used such sessions to threaten workers." He also found that even where unions do win an election, in 52% of cases they are "still without a contract a year later, and in 37% are still without a contract two years after an election" (Bronfenbrenner 2009: 2, 8).

Federation of Labor and Congress of Industrial Organizations (AFL-CIO) proposed legislation whose general thrust involved measures to address rampant
union-avoidance strategies on the part of business. Specifically, the idea was
"to speed up representation elections, increase penalties for the skyrocketing
number of unfair labor practices committed by employers, afford unions access
to employer premises to combat 'captive audience' employer union-busting tac-
tics, and grant the National Labor Relations Board (NLRB) additional power
in 'refusal to bargain' cases, while increasing the size of the NLRB and stream-
lining the review process for regional Administrative Law Judge findings" (Ferguson and Rogers 1979: 18). Employers rallied collectively to deluge congress
with petitions to vote against the legislation, which narrowly died in a filibuster.

In Chapter 1, I argued that the effects on social solidarity of employer coordination are not unambiguously positive, but depend crucially on the purposes
to which these coordinating capacities are put. VofC literature usefully draws
attention to the lack of coordination among employers in LMEs, by which
they mean low coordinating capacities in Williamsonian terms specifically. But
these observations should not detract attention from the considerable coordinating capacities that American business has periodically mounted in the
political realm. Just as employers rallied in the 1900s to defeat craft unions, so
too in the period since the 1970s can we observe a remarkable expansion of
business organization and power that was brought to bear in the United States
in the service of a broad neoliberal offensive (see especially Hacker and Pierson
2010c). The two phenomena are not unrelated because where employers lack
the capacity to stably coordinate among themselves in the market, they have
especially strong incentives to prevent unions from doing so as well.

Thus, American employers in the 1980s rallied – just as they had in the open
shop movement a century before – around the more limited agenda of defending
firm autonomy and reasserting "managerial prerogative" (Thelen 2004: 146).
The defeat of President Jimmy Carter's labor law reform was the masterwork
of the Business Roundtable, an organization founded in 1972 and devoted to
the program of enlarging the non-union sector through assistance to companies
in decertification elections and strike breaking, and through the founding and
promotion of pro-business political action committees. David Vogel (1983)
has called the Business Roundtable "the clearest symbol of the heightening of
class consciousness among the American *haute bourgeoisie*" (34). More than a
lobbying association, the Roundtable worked vigorously to promote collective
consciousness among top managers irrespective of narrow sectoral interests
and proved "remarkably successful in imposing a modicum of discipline or
'class solidarity' on what has traditionally been a rather anarchic business
establishment" (35). These developments confirm one of Martin and Swank's
(2012) core insights, namely that "employers are social animals and ... develop
their policy interests in packs," even as it also underscores that the results can
actually either support or undermine social solidarity.

The year 1977 – specifically the defeat of labor law reform – was in this sense
the key turning point in American industrial relations (D. Vogel 1983: 38).

Ronald Reagan's ascent to the presidency four years later only further embold-
ened employers in their union-avoidance strategies. Committed to a firmly
deregulatory and antiunion agenda, President Reagan responded to a strike by
air traffic controllers by declaring the action to be in violation of the law and
by ordering workers back to their jobs against the threat of dismissal. In car-
rying out that threat, President Reagan made clear that organized labor could
not count on any support from the government. Quite the contrary: considerable governmental power was brought to bear against organized labor. These
actions were then also backed up by NLRB appointments that made sure that
union recognition battles would drag on and that antiunion strategies would
not be vigorously prosecuted.

The Impact of Deregulation

A long line of scholarship has established an inverse relationship between
the degree of bargaining coverage and centralization on one hand and wage
inequality on the other (see especially Wallerstein 1999). While wage inequality
was already higher in the United States than in most CMEs – and, for that
matter, other LMEs – declining unionization has played a significant role in
further fueling inequality since the 1980s (Katz 1994: 253; also Card 2001;
Western and Rosenfeld 2011).[7] Wage inequality in the United States – measured
as the ratio of the 90th to the 10th percentile (90/10) – increased between
1973 and 2010 by 51 percent for men and 50 percent for women (OECD
figures). Pay differentials by skill category increased more than in any other
rich democracy as a result, among other causes, of a doubling of the college
wage premium in this period (Katz 1994: 243). Despite a tightening of the job
market in the 1980s, the real earnings of low-wage workers continued to slide.
As Katz (1994) notes, "in the early 1990s, real hourly pay of recent male high
school graduates and young drop outs was more than 20% below that of their
counterparts twenty years earlier" (257).

Exacerbating the effects of declining union coverage was a steady deterioration in the real value of the federal minimum wage starting in 1981. This
development is of course also related to union decline because, as Hacker and
Pierson (2010b) point out, organized labor is a crucial counterweight to the
power of business and the "only major [organized interest group] focused on
the broad economic concerns of those with modest incomes" (57).[8] This matters especially in the United States where, precisely in the absence of broad

---

[7] In what follows, I focus mostly on wage inequality but the picture would be starker still if we
looked at overall compensation (i.e., including benefits). Pierce (2001) finds that inequality in
overall compensation rose even more than wage inequality between 1981 and 1997, especially as
health insurance coverage rates dropped. He speculates that "low wage workers, facing declining
real wages, choose to take a disproportionately large fraction of the compensation decrease in
the form of lower fringe benefits" (Pierce 2001: 1520–1521).

[8] And of course the implications of labor's declining political power reverberate much more
broadly than just the minimum wage, with knock-on effects for a wide range of policies (e.g.,

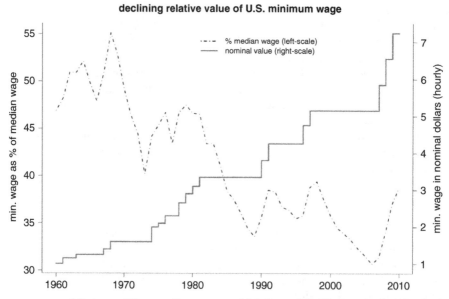

FIGURE 2.1. Minimum Wage as Percentage of Median, and Changes in the Nominal Value of the Federal Minimum Wage, 1960–2010. *Source*: stats.oecd.org and US Dept of Labor (http://www.dol.gov/whd/minwage/chart.htm).

and encompassing collective bargaining, a statutory minimum wage provides essential protection for the lowest-paid workers in the country.

The statutory minimum wage was first introduced in the United States in the Fair Labor Standards Act of 1938, and nominal increases occur through amendments to that law. The real value of the minimum wage thus depends crucially on the government acting to adjust its level to compensate for inflation, or as Shierholz (2009) puts it, "workers earning the minimum wage must literally wait for an act of Congress to get a raise" (1). Writing in 2009, he points out that the real value of the minimum wage was approximately 20 percent below its peak value in the 1960s. The last increase was passed by Congress in 2007, and implemented in three stages. In 2009, a full-time worker earning the minimum wage in the United States brought home an annual income of about $15,000, well below the poverty level for a family of three (1).

The general consensus in the economics literature is that the decline in the minimum wage contributed significantly to growing inequality in the 1980s at the low end of the distribution (the 50/10 ratio, i.e., the ratio of earnings of those at the 50th percentile and those at the 10th percentile). Figure 2.1 above charts trends in the federal minimum wage in the United States – its nominal value (solid line, right scale) and as a percentage of the median wage

tax policy and social services) that also profoundly affect the level of inequality (Hacker and Pierson 2010c, 2010b).

(broken line, left scale). As indicated, the 1980s saw a dramatic decline in the value of the minimum wage from about 45 percent of the median wage to less than 35 percent, without any move to increase its nominal value. Two stepwise increases in the minimum wage provided some relief in the early 1990s, but after the 1996 adjustment following President Bill Clinton's reelection, the value of the minimum wage was again allowed to sink. Overall, the pattern since 1978 is erosion in the real value of the minimum wage, periodically corrected through acts of Congress. These adjustments result in slight upticks in the value of the minimum wage relative to the median wage, but the clear long-run trajectory is rather sharply down.

Moreover, in the absence of union representation, low-wage workers in the United States are especially vulnerable to "wage theft." A 2008 survey of low-wage workers in the country's largest cities (Chicago, Los Angeles, and New York City) revealed that 26 percent of such workers were paid less than the legal minimum wage in the previous week and 76 percent of those who were legally entitled to overtime pay did not receive it (Bernhardt et al. 2009: 2–4).[9] Enforcement of labor standards is, even by the government's own admission, patchy to say the least. In March 2009, the Government Accountability Office (GAO) released a report bearing the sobering title: "Wage and Hour Divisions' Complaint Intake and Investigative Processes Leave Low Wage Workers Vulnerable to Wage Theft."[10] Enforcement of minimum standards in the United States depends heavily on individuals taking the initiative (whistle-blowing). However, low-wage workers usually lack the resources to mount legal challenges and are also understandably hesitant to confront their employers.[11] In this way, too, the absence of collective representation through unions results in an individualization of risk.

Alongside the growing gap between the low and median wage earners, a larger gap has also opened up at the upper end of the distribution (the 90/50 ratio, i.e., the gap between those at the 90th percentile and those at the 50th). After the precipitous collapse of wages at the very low end in the 1980s, the gap between the median earners and workers in the lowest (tenth) percentile flattened out in the 1990s, reflecting the minimum wage adjustments noted above. The 90/50 gap, by contrast, continued to grow. Even leaving aside the spectacular increases among the very rich (e.g., especially, Piketty and Saez 2003), the 1990s and 2000s saw the entire upper end of the distribution

---

9 The authors also found evidence of illegal antiunion activities. For example, over 40 percent of employees who made a complaint or attempted to form a union experienced illegal retaliation, and half of workers who informed employers about a serious workplace injury were subject to illegal retaliation.

10 http://www.gao.gov/new.items/d09458t.pdf. See also the coverage in The New York Times http://www.nytimes.com/209/03/25/washington/25wage.html.

11 The NLRB of course can act on its own. However, until very recently, the five-member board lacked a quorum because Republicans had blocked the confirmation of Obama appointees (Hicks 2013).

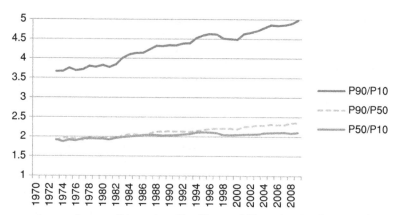

FIGURE 2.2. Income Dispersion (Pre-Tax and Transfer) in the United States, 1970–2008. *Source*: OECD Stat database.

pull away from the median. Figure 2.2 tracks changes in the 90/50 ratio, the 50/10 ratio and the 90/10 ratio. What it makes clear is that wage inequality – already higher than in any of the other advanced industrial countries before the crisis of the 1970s – has grown steadily since then. The result is a level of overall wage inequality that stands out in international comparisons and in which workers in the top decile earn fully five times more than those at the bottom. For comparison, the 2008 figure for Sweden was 2.2, for Germany 3.3, and for the UK 3.6.

In explaining these trends, economists tend to focus on broad technological changes that have "shifted labor demand away from middle management, clerical, and high-wage production jobs (the middle-class jobs of the mid-20th century)" (Blagg 2012: 26). An important analysis by Autor et al. (2008) points more specifically to skill-biased technological change in which information and communication technologies (ICT) complement educated workers performing abstract work while substituting for moderately educated workers performing more routine tasks (301 and passim). A more complete analysis of education and training policy appears in Chapter 3. At this point it is sufficient to note that bargaining decentralization and the collapse of unions contributed to the growth in the wage gap at the upper end as well. Whereas in the 1950s manufacturing workers had entered the ranks of the solidly middle class, with all that this implied in terms of home ownership and enhanced (often credit-based) consumption, the collapse of manufacturing and the assault on union rights cut deeply into the wages and benefits that had once naturally accompanied well-paid and secure employment for blue-collar workers (Hacker 2006; Weir 2010). The weakening of private-sector unions has undermined the bargaining power of many middle-class workers even as families saw their health care and higher education costs rise (Blagg 2012: 26).

Returning briefly to the theoretical debates outlined in Chapter 1, developments in American industrial relations could be invoked by either VofC scholars or their liberalization detractors. The U.S. case is wholly consistent with the VofC framework – after all, American employers lacked strong strategic coordinating capacities to begin with, and wage inequality and job mobility certainly drive the kind of education wage premiums we observe here. But the case is also consistent with liberalization theories, since the assault on union rights has indisputably been a function of a neoliberal campaign by employers. Moreover, viewed against the backdrop of the other theories discussed in Chapter 1, the U.S. case seems overdetermined: weak power resources, lack of a dedicated "left" political party, and the absence of corporatist interest intermediation all point in the same direction. In the current study, then, the United States is an important limiting case, providing a point of reference that will allow us to distinguish between deregulation and dualization on one hand and deregulation and embedded flexibilization on the other. To illuminate these differences, however, and to evaluate the causal claims advanced by VofC scholars and their critics, we need to assess developments in countries that appear more anomalous in light of VofC arguments, or liberalization arguments, or ideally both. The German and Danish cases provide such an opportunity.

GERMAN INDUSTRIAL RELATIONS: DUALIZATION THROUGH DRIFT

On the surface, German industrial relations seem to offer striking support for VofC theory. This is a classic CME, and one in which firms entered the crisis years of the 1970s heavily invested in competitive strategies that rely on high-skill, high-quality production. Consistent with the logic of VofC, heightened competition in international markets since that time has if anything intensified cooperation between labor and capital in the manufacturing sector and shored up traditional institutions and practices, including coordinated wage bargaining and labor–management cooperation at the firm level. For good reasons, many observers attribute the country's current strong economic performance partly to continued strong social partnership in the export sector.

Paradoxically, however, intensified cooperation between labor and capital within manufacturing has in many ways deepened the erosion outside the industrial core where unions and traditional bargaining institutions have never really taken root. By the mid-1990s at the latest, industrial relations in Germany had become increasingly bifurcated between a stable core (where traditional institutions and social partnership still held sway), and a growing periphery concentrated especially in emerging service sectors (where weaker unions struggle against employers whose interests with respect to labor relations are very different from those of industry). These two parallel systems are almost mirror images of each other – continued stability and enhanced cross-class cooperation in manufacturing alongside more conflictual relations and low bargaining coverage in other areas, particularly services. In the next sections I look at each, briefly, in turn.

Stability in the Manufacturing Core

Much of the liberalization literature revolves around the claim that global-ization drives deregulation by providing employers with motive and opportu-nity to escape traditional "rigid" centralized bargaining arrangements. They have strong motives to seek change, since intense competition in international markets forces them to seek, through all available means, ways to reduce labor and other production costs. At the same time, globalization is associated with increased capital mobility, which provides opportunities to act on these needs by tipping the balance of power in their favor, as nationally anchored unions will be pressed into concessions against the threat of firm exit or firm failure.

This picture does not resonate in the industries most affected by globaliza-tion in Germany. Manufacturing famously lives off exports, but in Germany it is in the export industries where traditional institutions are most robust. For many years now, manufacturing employers have been outspoken defenders of industry-wide bargaining, which they value as providing a way to keep wage negotiations and associated conflict off the shop floor. They have consistently emphasized that Germany needs strong industrial unions that are capable of enforcing their policies ("Der beste Mann" 2003: 24; also "Falscher Ort, falsche Zeit" 2003: 2). They support industry-wide bargaining for the order and pre-dictability that it helps to impose on the labor market (e.g., "Wir müssen mehr leisten" 2003: 18; "Flächentarif als Modell" 2006: 21).

German manufacturing firms appreciate the advantages of dealing with strong and unified bargaining partners. This explains their tepid response to a 2010 Labor Court ruling that gave upstart rival unions the right to operate alongside the dominant industrial unions. The decision represented a striking departure from previous court decisions that had mostly upheld the princi-ple of one company, one union. The main union in the metalworking indus-try, IG Metall, has long tussled with the smaller, more conservative Chris-tian Democratic Metalworkers' Union. Hence, the ruling might have been seen as an invitation for employers to exploit this competition to secure con-cessions from the larger and less pliant IG Metall. Far from welcoming the change, however, Ulrich Brocker, who was then the managing director of the Metal Employers' Association (Gesamtmetall), criticized the outcome. He argued that "when competing unions pose an ongoing challenge to peaceful plant relations, one of the crucial advantages of the branch agreement is lost" ("Bundesarbeitsgericht," 2010). The head of the national association of Ger-man Employers, Dieter Hundt, worried openly about union fragmentation and competition, invoking the British example as a warning about the harm this can cause to industry ("Wirtschaft warnt" 2010). The peak union confedera-tion and the central employers' association in Germany thus spoke with one voice in denouncing the court's decision, arguing that collective bargaining autonomy and branch agreements had always been central supports for the country's industrial competitiveness (see also "Tarifeinheit" 2010: 68; Lesch 2010).

In manufacturing, cooperative relations are if anything stronger still at the plant level, where – in large firms especially – works councils are powerful co-managers without whose active cooperation production would quickly grind to a halt.[12] Union representatives at that level share with employers a strong interest in the firm's success, and both sides are keen to avoid conflicts that would undermine the company's position in international markets. These shared interests are reflected in the growth since the 1990s of company-level "Pacts for Employment and Competitiveness" (*betriebliche Bündnisse zur Beschäftigungs- und Wettbewerbssicherung*) (Rehder 2003). Such deals involve trade-offs in which managers commit to job security for employees in exchange for flexibility, especially regarding working times (Hassel and Rehder 2001).[13] The collapse of export markets during the financial crisis of 2008 did not destroy these agreements; mostly, in fact, labor and capital took the opportunity to renew their vows. For example, in the midst of the downturn, Daimler guaranteed the jobs of all workers at its largest German plant until 2019 (ABC News Associated Press 2009). Siemens likewise promised to preserve the jobs of all 128,000 of its Germany-based employees until at least 2013 (Schneibel 2010).

We know from previous research that strong local cooperation sometimes complicates industry-wide coordination.[14] However, works councils' formidable legal rights also shore up industry-wide wage bargaining because German employers are keen to keep distributional issues off the shop floor. Because labor's plant-level powers give them highly effective "hold up" power, firms prefer industry deals. Whereas in Sweden and Denmark employers have pressed relentlessly – and, as we will see, successfully – for a decentralization of wage formation, German manufacturing employers have not abandoned industry-wide bargaining, including wage scales that impose serious constraints

---

[12] In addition to plant-level codetermination through works councils, labor also enjoys representation on the company-level supervisory boards of larger companies. Codetermination at the company level is often seen as more controversial because of statements made by leaders of some employers' associations calling for a rollback of labor's rights at this level. However, careful research shows that German managers do not, in fact, hold the same dim view of company-level codetermination and do not share a desire to change it (Höpner and Waclawczyk 2012).

[13] An important industry-wide agreement in 2004, the Pforzheimer Agreement specifically allows for opening clauses – local deviations from industry contracts based on agreement between union and firm – and offers room for local negotiators to make these kinds of trade-offs.

[14] See, for example, Thelen and van Wijnbergen (2003). Complications arise when local actors fail to perform the functions asked of them by industry leaders. Thus, for example, an industry lockout in 1995 collapsed in the face of resistance on the part of Gesamtmetall's members firms, who were reluctant to risk alienating their works councils in the context of a fragile economic recovery. In 2003, it was labor leaders who defected, when a strike by IG Metall on behalf of Eastern workers collapsed in the face of resistance by powerful works councils in the West who worried about the impact on firm competitiveness of continued disruption in production.

on how employers distribute pay increases among individual workers.[15] In fact, wage bargaining in metalworking in some ways became even more coordinated after 2002, when the employers' association conceded a longstanding union demand for unified wage scales for white- and blue-collar workers (Schulten 2002; Stettes 2005). This development moves in the opposite direction from that in Scandinavia, where since the 1990s local actors exercise more discretion in how to distribute wage increases on a local and even individual level.

Strong social partnership in the industrial sector in Germany was vividly on display during the recent financial crisis. At the first sign of trouble, IG Metall and Gesamtmetall jointly lobbied the government for legislation to extend existing subsidies for so-called short time work (*Kurzarbeit* – subsidized temporary working time reductions) to avoid layoffs.[16] This resulted in an extension of the period during which such workers would be supported from six months to eighteen months. Wage negotiations in 2009 then complemented these developments, with bargaining centering on how much firms would top up the state subsidies. The most generous such agreement was negotiated in the chemical industry – which increased compensation to cover 93 percent of workers' regular net wages – but a similar arrangement was worked out in metalworking as well.

The following year, with industry still feeling the effects of the crisis, IG Metall earned headlines as a union "willing to compromise" by declining to set forth any wage demands at all (Reich 2010; see also S. Vogel 2009c). The union instead focused entirely on employment security and training, paving the way for an unusually consensual bargaining round (Krämer 2010). The unexpectedly rapid economic rebound gave employers the opportunity to return the favor by unilaterally pulling forward previously deferred wage increases in order to acknowledge the sacrifices that workers had made in the company's interest. Daimler's director of labor relations, Wilfried Porth, framed the move as a way of acknowledging the workers' contributions to over-coming the crisis: "the commitment of our German employees is an important reason why Daimler could recover so quickly" (Daimler AG 2010; see also S. Vogel 2011).

All in all, one is struck more by the continued commitment on the part of Germany's core export firms to traditional institutions and social partnership. Instead of mounting an attack on traditional industrial relations arrangements, manufacturing employers have sought flexibility within the context of existing bargaining structures, maintained strong and cooperative relations with pow-erful works councils, and even acceded to the industrial union's longstanding demand for unified wage scales for white- and blue-collar workers. Germany's

---

[15] Local-level bargaining is discretionary, and subsequent industry-level wage increases are applied to the contractual wage scales negotiated at the industry level (i.e., not including local wage drift).

[16] Short-time work policies are discussed at length in Chapter 4.

social partners earned lavish praise for their cooperation in the recent crisis. Christian Democratic Labor Minister Ursula von der Leyen raved: "the well-practiced cooperation between the social partners saved many jobs in the crisis" (Groll and Marcus 2012).

However, ongoing compromise with strong unions at both the industry and plant levels has in many ways been underwritten by more flexible relations outside the core (Palier and Thelen 2010; also Chapter 4). Local-level agreements stabilizing employment at the plant or company level are often accompanied by measures in which services previously performed within the company – from cafeterias to cleaning – have been outsourced to lower-cost producers. Similarly, job security for core skilled workers has involved increased use of temporary agencies to cover unskilled tasks. While in many other countries temporary agency workers are concentrated in services, in Germany they are far more prevalent in manufacturing – 34.8 percent of temps work in manufacturing, against just 15.5 percent in services (Mitlacher 2007: 582). Of the workforce at the Mercedes-Benz factory in Wörth, for example, almost 10 percent consists of temps; at another auto plant, the proportion is nearly one-third (29 percent) (Deckstein et al. 2006; Mitlacher 2007: 591–592). Since 2003, German labor law allows agency workers to be assigned to receiving companies for unlimited duration, and nearly half of all temps who work in large firms are engaged for very extended periods on renewal (Vanselow 2009: 6; Eichhorst and Marx 2012a: 23). Extensive use of agency workers provides a buffer against fluctuations in production and saves on labor costs as well, since agency workers' wages are on average 25 to 30 percent lower than those of permanent employees (Eichhorst and Marx 2012a: 23).[17] In this sense, stability for workers within the industrial core and flexibility for those outside the core are two sides of the same coin.

Drift on the Periphery

Bargaining coverage remains much more robust in Germany than in LMEs like the United States. Nearly 70 percent of workers are still covered by union contracts.[18] This is a far cry from coverage rates in the United States, which are closer to 10 percent. Still, there are indisputable signs of erosion in Germany, and a very different pattern of industrial relations prevails outside the manufacturing core. In services, unionization rates are in the 10 to 20 percent range (compared to 50 percent or more in manufacturing), and while employment in these sectors has been growing, unionization has either not kept up or,

---

[17] According to Eichhorst and Marx (2012a), 4 percent of all metalworking employees are temps, but among low skill-workers specifically the percentage is much higher at 30 to 50 percent in medium to large firms.

[18] Over 50 percent are covered by an industry-level contract, and another 20 percent by company contracts that often copy the industry deal (Vogel 2010).

often, has declined. It was largely in response to such declines that Germany's main service sector unions merged in 2000 to form a single overarching union, the United Services Sector Union (ver.di). All five of the participating unions had experienced a slippage in membership in the 1990s, ranging from a drop of 18 percent in the Deutsche Angestellten Gewerkschaft (DAG) – the union of salaried employees – to a drop of 36 percent in the Gewerkschaft Handel, Banken und Versicherungen (HBV) – the union for retail, banking, and insurance. The merger was thus partly designed to consolidate resources and avoid costly jurisdictional conflicts (Schulten 1999a; Scheele 2001).

In a context like the German one, in which employer organization is more important to bargaining coverage than union membership, higher levels of employer organization might compensate for weak union presence.[19] Banking provides an example of this. Despite low organization rates on the union side (approximately 14 percent among private banks), the banking industry is concentrated among a handful of dominant players that together account for 90 to 95 percent of all employment, and they continue to prefer to coordinate with each other and with unions in order to keep the state at bay. The result is 85 percent coverage in western Germany (59 percent in eastern Germany) despite the low organization rates (S. Vogel 2010). Sounding very much like representatives in manufacturing, the head of collective bargaining for the employer association for private banks, Arbeitgeberverband des privaten Bankgewerbes (AGV Banken), emphasized the virtues of encompassing branch-wide collective bargaining as useful in holding competition in bounds. "All of the big players definitely want it" (AGV Banken, interview 2010).

However, banking is more the exception than the rule in services, because firms in other sectors are either less well organized, or – more often – simply want different things. At the very high end of the skill spectrum, such as in the ICT industry, there is no unified collective bargaining system. Some ICT workers are covered by sectoral contracts, others by company-level contracts, but many are outside the system altogether (Dribbusch 2009: 6). At the low-skill end (e.g., retail and hospitality industries), the sectoral boundaries are clearer and industry-wide structures are in place. In these cases, the decline of collective bargaining coverage is more the result of firms dropping out of the employer associations or never joining them to begin with (Eurofound 2011: 10).

Traditional mechanisms for extending collective representation of labor interests in poorly organized sectors now fail to do so. One longstanding feature of German labor law offers the possibility for the government to extend collective bargaining coverage to unorganized firms under specific circumstances – through the *Allgemeinverbindlichkeitserklärung* (AVE). In industries in which at least 50 percent of all employees work in firms that are covered by an

---

[19] In Germany, all workers employed within a firm that is a party to the contract negotiated by the employers' association are covered, whether they belong to the union or not.

industry contract, either of the parties to the contract can petition the government to declare its terms universally binding (i.e., also binding for non-member firms).[20] Whereas in the past invoking such provisions was unproblematic, employers in key industries outside of manufacturing now oppose the use of extension clauses.[21] Collective bargains in retail trade, for example, used to be routinely declared generally applicable but since 2000 the national employers' association, Handelsverband Deutschland (HDE), has blocked extension clauses with the argument that it does not wish to endorse the imposition of what it considers to be outdated wage scales and working time arrangements (HDE, interview 2010). In the hospitality industries – another low-wage sector – a few bargaining regions have AVEs for framework contracts but not for wages, which in this sector are among the lowest in Germany (DeHoGa 2010: 3).

These trends in part reflect the interests of service sector firms themselves, but collective bargaining shrinkage outside the core has been abetted also by manufacturing employers who benefit from lower service prices. Requests for AVEs must be approved by a parity committee composed of three representatives each from unions and employer associations outside the petitioning industry. Unions are typically in favor of the use of extension clauses since the alternative is non-coverage. However, the employer representatives who sit on the board – including, without exception, representatives of industry – now seek to limit the use of extension clauses, which they see as compromising a firm's free choice as to whether to belong to the contract or not (BDA 2007a).[22] Tellingly, the one area in which employers are keen to negotiate collective contracts is for agency workers. Under German labor law, workers in a firm who are performing the same tasks are entitled to the same pay unless they are covered by a separate contract. Since manufacturing specifically relies

---

[20] For a full listing of regions and industries covered by extension clauses, see BMAS Verzeichnis der für allgemeinverbindlich erklärten Tarifverträge, Stand 1. Januar 2011.

[21] The number of AVE has fallen more or less continuously, from about 5.4 percent of contracts in 1991 to about 1.5 percent today, and most of these do not cover wages but are instead framework agreements ("Niedriglöhne" 2010: 5).

[22] There exist possibilities for the government to act without the express approval of the parity board. The posted workers law (*Entsendegesetz*) passed in 1996 was designed to protect certain industries from wage dumping by foreign firms active in the German market. Under this law, minimum wages that are laid down in an existing industrial contract – covering again a minimum of 50 percent of the sectoral workforce – can be declared binding for the entire sector (not just all German firms but foreign firms active in Germany as well). This law has long covered the construction industry, and it has also been invoked by a number of construction-related sectors like electrical and related handicrafts, painting, and building cleaning services. For a short time, it covered the postal services sector, before that application of the law was declared unconstitutional in 2010 (Vogel 2009a). The most recent additions are the care industry and the temp industry (Meiritz and Wittrock 2008; "Unternehmen fordern Mindestlohn," 2010), but the number of sectors that can be covered in this way is highly restricted by the wording of the law, and not likely to grow.

so heavily on temps, employers have been eager to strike separate deals with unions. This explains the 100 percent coverage rate for this particular group of atypical workers despite extremely low union organization rates, estimated at between 5 and 16 percent (Vanselow 2009: 7).

The Impact of Dualization through Drift

The pattern of industrial relations in Germany can be characterized as a case of dualization, featuring strong coverage and collective representation in the (still-significant) core economy, alongside an emerging "patchwork" (*Flicken-teppich*) of regional- and sector-specific arrangements alongside "large unreg-ulated zones of wage-setting without binding minimum standards" (Weinkopf and Bosch 2010: 2; also Bosch et al. 2009: 45; Bispinck 2010a). Consistent with VofC logic, we observe significant intensification of coordination among firms and cooperation between unions and employers in manufacturing. However, where VofC sees all feedback as positive and operating to stabilize the exist-ing system, precisely this cooperation has had deeply destabilizing collateral effects – exacerbating differences between workers who are covered and pro-tected by these arrangements and those who are not.

The erosion of collective bargaining coverage has played a significant role in the emergence in Germany of a growing low-wage sector in recent years. Between 1995 and 2008 the number of low-wage workers – defined by the OECD as those earning less than two-thirds of median income – rose nearly 50 percent, from 4.4 million to over 6.5 million (Bispinck 2010a: 1). The share of low-wage full-time workers as a percentage of all full-time employees rose in Germany from 13.8 percent in 1993 to 17.3 percent in 2003 (Bosch 2008: 18). According to statistics of the Federal Employment Agency, by 2010 the low-wage sector accounted for over 20 percent of all full-time employees ("Hunger-lohn" 2010). For comparison, this puts Germany at the level of LMEs like the UK (21.7 percent) and the United States (25 percent), and well above Scan-dinavian countries (e.g., Denmark at 8.5 percent) and some other Christian Democratic countries like the Netherlands (17.6 percent) (Bosch et al. 2009: 7–8).

In Germany, dualization has proceeded largely through drift, emerging grad-ually and as a "natural" consequence of the shift in employment out of man-ufacturing (where unions are strong) and into services (where they are not). As noted at the outset, union membership still largely reflects the employment structure of the 1960s, with strongholds in manufacturing and low represen-tation in services (Hassel 1999: 501).[23] The trends are similar though less

---

[23] In 1981, 58 percent of union members were blue-collar workers, and in 2002 the percentage was still over half (51.1 percent). The share of white-collar members has been rising (from 24.2 percent in 1981 to 32.5 percent by 2002), but this lags behind employment growth in those sectors (Addison et al. 2007: 9).

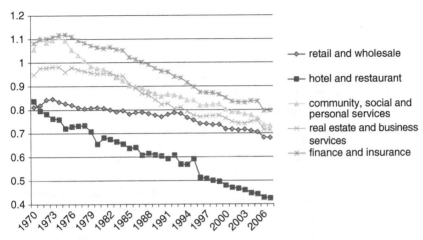

FIGURE 2.3. Hourly Wage in Services as Share of Manufacturing Wages. *Source*: Hassel (2012: 15).

pronounced on the employer side where organizational levels are low outside of manufacturing (495). Labor compensation in services has declined steadily against wages in the manufacturing core, particularly since the 1980s, as Figure 2.3 shows.

Dualization in German industrial relations exhibits a pattern of change through drift; unlike in the United States, there has been no direct assault on unionization and traditional bargaining institutions. Instead, change has transpired more gradually and quietly; collective bargaining coverage shrinks "naturally" as the share of employment increases in those sectors in which unions have a weaker presence. However, as a political phenomenon drift typically also involves elements of not-so-benign neglect, as political actors also actively resist reforms that could adapt institutions in response to observed changes in the political and economic context (Hacker and Pierson 2010a). Recent debates in Germany on the introduction of a statutory minimum wage (which Germany lacked) are revealing in this respect.[24] The German Food and Restaurant Workers' Union (NGG) – representing poorly organized workers with low skills – has, for more than a decade now, supported the introduction of a statutory minimum wage (Schulten 1999b). By 2004, Germany's new (and more encompassing) service sector union ver.di was also in favor. The peak employer confederations – the German Employers' Association (BDA) and the Confederation of German Industries (BDI) – have both vigorously opposed

---

[24] As this book goes to press, the Christian Democratic Party and the Social Democratic Party had just entered into negotiations over the formation of a "Grand Coalition." The Social Democrats identified the introduction of a nationwide, legally binding minimum wage of 8.5 euros as one of their core demands.

these initiatives (Dribbusch 2004; BDA 2007b). But until relatively recently they were not alone. The powerful IG Metall initially also opposed legislation in this area, worried that a statutory minimum wage could put downward pressure on wages in their sectors (Dribbusch 2004; Güßgen 2006; Bosch et al. 2009: 40–41). By 2006, IG Metall had come to strongly endorse a resolution presented at the national trade union congress, but other manufacturing unions – notably the Chemical Workers' Union (IGBCE) – remained resolutely skeptical (Dribbusch 2009: 4).

In opposing minimum wage legislation, German employers have framed their position not as an attack on union rights or traditional industrial relations practices but as a spirited defense of existing arrangements, in particular Germany's hallowed and constitutionally anchored principle of collective bargaining autonomy, *Tarifautonomie*: "The state must stay out of wage formation.... Any government intervention ... compromises collective bargaining autonomy and puts the traditional system of wage formation at risk" (BDA 2007b, 2010). This argument resonates with the liberal Free Democratic Party (FDP), which has been vehemently against any such legislation. But it also carried weight with some unions who preferred a negotiated minimum wage bargained between the social partners and worried that a statutory minimum wage would compromise their power and privileges and result in lower settlements.

Ongoing controversy – over whether a statutory minimum wage was needed and if so who, exactly, would be involved in setting it – explains why a previous proposal for a statutory minimum wage brought by Christian Democratic Chancellor Angela Merkel fell flat, despite surveys that showed that a huge majority of Germans (86 percent) supported the general idea (Dettmer et al. 2011). The head of the Bundesvereinigung der Deutschen Arbeitgeberverbände (BDA), Dieter Hundt, categorically rejected the Merkel proposal: "we don't need any further regulations" (87). But representatives of organized labor also responded gingerly (Spiegel 2009). The heads of ver.di (Frank Bsirske) and of the peak Confederation of German Trade Unions (Michael Sommer) greeted the general idea with some enthusiasm, but the heads of other unions worried about the specifics (Spiegel 2011b). The head of IGBCE denounced the CDU's initiative as a "farce," and the head of the construction union IG Bau criticized the proposal as "inconsistent with the constitution" (Spiegel 2009, 2011a).[25]

[25] The issue was also contested within the Christian Democratic Union (CDU) itself (Spiegel 2009). In 2009, the government passed legislation that outlaws "immorally low wages." The original Act on the Setting of Minimum Working Conditions (*Gesetz über die Festsetzung von Mindestarbeitsbedingungen, MiArbG*) goes back to 1952 but was never in fact invoked. Poverty-level wages in poorly organized sectors put the issue back on the agenda, however (Kraemer 2011). The revised (April 2009) law allows the state to set a wage floor for such sectors based on recommendations from a committee of experts (Bispinck 2010a: 3). The process, though, is cumbersome, to say the least. Unions, employers' associations, or state governments can request the application of the law, and such requests are referred first to a

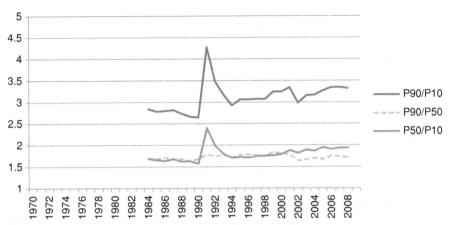

FIGURE 2.4. Income Dispersion (Pre-Tax and Transfer) in Germany, 1984–2008.
Source: OECD Stat Database.

The unions did, however, line up in 2013 behind the Social Democratic Party's proposal for a uniform statutory minimum of 8.5 euros per hour.

Many of the jobs that will be affected by minimum wage legislation are part-time jobs that also lack standard benefits. These so-called mini-jobs (discussed at length in Chapter 4) comprise a large share of the emerging low-wage sector in Germany. However, creeping dualization in German industrial relations also manifests itself in trends in earnings among full-time workers, as Figure 2.4 shows. Ignoring the blip at the time of unification, we see that the 90/50 ratio (high earners to median earners) has been stable since 1992, while the 50/10 ratio (median to low earners) has risen since the late 1990s from about 1.7 to almost 2.0. Although overall levels of income inequality are less dramatic than what we saw for the United States, Germany has also been ineffective in preventing the wages of low-skill workers from falling behind. The decline in the fortunes of the lowest decile (also in relation to the median) seems clearly related to the trends documented in this section, where many low-wage, low-skill workers no longer enjoy collective bargaining coverage. The wage gap in the upper half of the distribution has by contrast remained more stable, partly perhaps because of the linkages noted between blue- and white-collar wage scales in leading sectors, but also no doubt as a function of low organization among white-collar employees relative to skilled blue-collar workers.

committee of seven "neutral" experts who determine whether such an action is warranted. If they decide positively, then the Ministry of Labor and Social Affairs composes a second committee, made up of representatives of the relevant union and employer association to decide the level of the wage. The areas in which such a law would likely be invoked would include call centers and the hospitality industry (Bosch et al. 2009: 47), but it has yet to be invoked.

The politics that promote the ongoing erosion of collective bargaining in Germany are thus a good bit more complicated than typically suggested by arguments about a straightforward neoliberal offensive. Manufacturing unions have been successful in defending, for themselves, many of the core arrangements characteristic of the traditional model, not least because – as VofC theory emphasizes – manufacturing employers continue to support such arrangements as crucial to their continued success in world export markets. The problem is that the strong and resilient cross-class coalition that presides over German manufacturing – so central to the politics of national coordination in the Golden Era – is no longer willing (employers) or able (unions) to exercise leadership for the economy as a whole (Martin and Thelen 2007).

The politics of change have not taken the form of the anticipated neoliberal attack on traditional institutions along the lines we saw for the United States. In Germany, proponents of change do not seek to dismantle existing institutions; instead – consistent with the logic of drift – they focus on preventing reforms that would address the ongoing erosion in union coverage. Above all, they defend the principle of *Tarifautonomie,* which keeps the state at arm's length. As a result, institutional change proceeds mostly through drift, as employment has shifted away from organized labor's industrial strongholds and into areas – above all services – in which the traditional system had never really taken root.

DANISH INDUSTRIAL RELATIONS: EMBEDDED FLEXIBILIZATION

Trends in Danish industrial relations are in some ways the mirror image of those in Germany, for this case combines significant formal-institutional decentralization with continued high levels of collective bargaining coverage. Denmark featured prominently in the corporatism literature of the 1970s for its highly centralized bargaining arrangements and solidaristic wage policies that narrowed wage differentials within and across sectors. But in the late 1970s and 1980s, peak-level bargaining gave way to coordinated industry bargaining, and subsequent organizational changes brought further decentralization of wage bargaining. In Denmark today fully 85 percent of private-sector employees have their pay set at the company level, with industry contracts containing only minimum wage floors and in many cases no pay clauses at all (Dansk Arbejdsgiverforening 2013). Wage setting in Denmark is thus far more decentralized than in the organized sector in Germany, where industry bargains lay out (often detailed) wage scales that determine how pay raises will be allocated, and where local bargaining is informal.

The trends in Danish industrial relations over the past two decades can only be characterized as liberalizing, and earnings inequality rose significantly in Denmark between 1990 and 2008, although from a low initial level (Pontusson 2013: 12, 34). The changes in collective bargaining institutions were actively sought by employers, who were initially abetted in their efforts to reconfigure Danish industrial relations by skilled unions in the export sector and – in the 1980s – also by a bourgeois government committed to a broad neoliberal agenda (see, e.g., Ibsen et al. 2011). Yet these changes have transpired in a way that distinguishes them both from Anglo-Saxon deregulation and from German-style dualization. Whereas in the United States wage individualization went hand in hand with the collapse of unions and a decline in collective bargaining, in Denmark coverage rates remain high and unions themselves preside over the negotiation of the terms and extent of wage flexibilization within procedural frameworks that are still highly coordinated. Coordinated bargaining limits wage differences resulting from corporate profitability (thus maintaining pressure on firms to increase productivity) while allowing for more differentials due to education and investment in human capital. Corporatist arrangements and actors have not been dismantled with the decentralization of wage formation, but instead turned to new purposes, taking up issues such as training and parental leave that address new risks and cater to new constituencies, including, increasingly, those also outside the manufacturing core.

Despite characterizations that emphasize consensus and cooperation in Europe's most corporatist countries, the changes in Danish industrial relations over the past decades have involved considerable tumult and conflict. Whereas Germany has drifted to higher levels of inequality through dualization, the changes in Denmark – although ultimately supportive of higher levels of social solidarity – have been more overtly conflictual. The breakdown of solidaristic wage bargaining in the 1980s revealed a considerable rift between public-sector and private-sector unions, and reopened a longstanding one between skilled and unskilled unions. Changes in bargaining arrangements in that period heightened industrial conflict and fueled "violent conflicts" between organized labor and the government (Due et al. 1994: 194; see also Campbell and Hall 2006: 15).

In Germany, change proceeded gradually and without major conflict partly because the losers – unskilled, unorganized workers outside the industrial core – are poorly organized and represented. In Denmark, by contrast, the reconfiguration of bargaining was tumultuous and difficult precisely because the losers were well organized and fought back. Although unable to prevent the breakdown of solidaristic wage bargaining, representatives of unskilled workers did resist initiatives that would have incorporated their separate organizations into industrial unions dominated by skilled workers. The continued influence of unskilled workers' unions within the peak trade union confederation Landsorganisationen (LO), alongside the growing influence of salaried white-collar workers in the same organization, set the scene for the functional conversion of traditional arrangements to new goals and purposes. This shift was based on a political exchange in which decentralization in wage formation was traded against progress on a range of non-wage issues (Ibsen 2012). The result is a reorientation of collective bargaining away from the previous focus on equalizing pay across occupations toward supply-side solidarity and an emphasis on securing equal access to good jobs for all workers (Baccaro and Locke 1998; Ibsen 2012).

Crisis and Change in Danish Industrial Relations

Collective bargaining in Denmark in the 1950s and 1960s was highly central-ized and, as in Sweden, organized around "solidaristic wage policies" that drove significant wage equalization within and across sectors (Dølvik 2007: 22). In Denmark, unskilled workers were organized into their own separate unions,[26] and in fact from the 1950s through the 1980s, the Danish General Workers' Union (SiD) was the largest union in Denmark (for membership shares, see Ebbinghaus 2000: 188). Alongside the National Union of Women Workers (KAD), which also represented low-skill employees, the SiD used its influence within the LO to push vigorously for agreements that granted extra wage hikes to low-pay groups (Due et al. 1994: 189–90). As a result, wage dispersion among Danish workers decreased significantly – by 54 percent among man-ual workers between 1963 and 1977, and by 26 percent among white-collar workers between 1972 and 1980 (Schulze-Cleven 2009: 187).

It is widely accepted that wage solidarism contributed to Denmark's sub-stantial economic problems in the 1970s. Tight labor markets in the 1960s intensified competition for skilled manufacturing workers and generated sig-nificant wage drift, as Danish "employers could not – and hardly wished to – prevent workers in the higher pay-brackets from gaining further frequent pay rises during the agreement period" (Due et al. 1994: 189). However, central bargains then granted compensatory increases for low-skill workers, fueling an upward wage spiral that continued even as unemployment grew after the oil shock of 1973. These developments contributed both to Denmark's skyrocket-ing inflation and to a fiscal deficit that ballooned to 9 percent of GDP over the course of the 1970s (Schwartz 1994: 544).

These dynamics sparked "intense distributional conflicts" (Iversen 1996: 414) on a number of fronts – within the union movement between workers employed in exposed and sheltered industries, between skilled and unskilled unions, between the organized labor movement and employers, and between unions and both left- and right-wing governments. Public-sector budget cuts in the late 1970s set off demonstrations and wildcat strikes by public-sector work-ers who suffered "a rapid deterioration of relative wage increases" (J. Andersen 1984: 252). Private-sector unions in manufacturing, though, applauded these moves as necessary to restoring Danish competitiveness. The 1970s thus "wit-nessed a radicalization of non-manual public employees alongside a move to the right among [manual] workers" (J. Andersen 1992: 101).

---

[26] This was a legacy of the triumph in Denmark of craft unions which meant that unskilled works had to found their own organizations.

Contrary to the image of corporatist negotiation as facilitating compromise and consensus, industrial relations in Denmark in the 1970s were conflictual in the extreme. Four out of five bargaining rounds ended in stalemates that had to be broken by direct parliamentary imposition of wage settlements (Scheuer 1992: 186; also Ebbinghaus 2000: 161). The LO and the government repeatedly "collided despite extensive consultations, and the government increasingly resorted to statutory incomes policies and restrictive high interest policies to contain inflation and speculation against the currency" (Iversen 1996: 419). The Social Democratic Party itself became increasingly split between a left wing more closely aligned with unskilled and public-sector workers (and defending the LO's policy of wage solidarism and cost-of-living indexation), and a right wing more closely associated with skilled workers, especially in manufacturing, who advocated taking a firmer line against wage increases in the public sector (Schwartz 1994: 551).[27]

Ongoing economic turmoil and a seemingly intractable political stalemate helped unseat the Social Democrats in 1982 and bring to power a center-right coalition government headed by confirmed neoliberal reformer Poul Schlüter. Schlüter implemented a number of dramatic changes to macroeconomic and labor market policies that were intended to stabilize the economy but that were also "clearly aimed at diminishing union influence and membership" (Scheuer 1992: 188). Coordination through the social partners ground to a halt as the government adopted a strict austerity program to combat deficits and inflation aggressively – all against fierce union opposition (Vartiainen 2011: 8). The most important changes included pegging the Danish krone to the German mark, liberalizing capital markets, and suspending the cost-of-living indexation of pay and of most public transfers as a centerpiece of a broader set of public spending cuts (Ebbinghaus 2000: 161).

The early years of the Schlüter government were very turbulent times in industrial relations, as unions of unskilled workers fought tenaciously against a coalition of employers and skilled unions who together engineered the decentralization of bargaining from the peak to the industry level (Due et al. 1994: 150; Iversen 1996: 422–423). The new regime was consolidated in 1987 in a joint confederative Common Declaration that is often coded as a triumph of Danish corporatism and consensus-building (Dølvik 2007: 22). The 1987 settlement did mark an end to the conflictual and chaotic period that had preceded it, but this should not obscure that there were real winners and losers. As Due et al. (1994) noted, the main unskilled workers union (SiD) "vehemently opposed" the breakup of peak-level bargaining (191–192). The move to industry-wide bargaining diluted the influence of both of the unskilled workers

---

[27] Anthonson et al. (2010) argue that, by causing a fissure in the previously close relationship between the Social Democratic Party and the LO, these developments paradoxically contributed later to more encompassing deals by closing the distance between the Social Democrats and other centrist parties.

unions (SiD and KAD) by effectively splitting them up into different negotiating areas. While these unions were able to resist full absorption into the industrial unions, the demise of national coordination in wage bargaining inevitably meant that SiD, like the LO itself, "was relegated to a less important role" (EIRR 1998a: 5; see also Scheuer 1992: 184; Petersen 1997c).[28]

Organizational changes on the employer side consolidated these developments, in large part to prevent a return to the status quo ante. In 1991, the metal employers' association merged with employer associations in other exposed industries to form a new employers' association called Dansk Industri (DI), which encompassed the entire industrial sector (Ebbinghaus 2000: 160).[29] Trade unions were more or less forced to adopt corresponding changes "to avoid a further decline in their influence" (Due et al. 1994: 229). Thus by 1992, the exposed sectors formed CO-industri, a bargaining cartel for both blue- and white-collar unions in industry. These developments – the breakdown of wage solidarism and the reconfiguration of bargaining – brought a definitive end to the era in which the LO and the DA could orchestrate wage setting centrally.

One of the explicit aims of the newly ascendant DI was to rationalize bargaining by moving to a system of "one enterprise, one contract" and to prevent the return of wage solidarism by decentralizing negotiations over pay to the company level. Two different wage systems have traditionally coexisted in Denmark, so-called normal pay and minimum pay systems. With normal pay contracts, wages are set at the industry level and simply applied with no flexibility at lower levels (i.e., no local bargaining). Minimum wage contracts, by contrast, only set a pay floor below which no individual can fall, but they leave room for local bargaining above this floor. As a practical matter, most workers are paid well above the minimum rate, so that the wage floor only applies to a tiny minority of entry-level unskilled employees. For most workers, then, the minimum wage is irrelevant and their wage increases are determined entirely via company-level bargaining (Ibsen 2012: 7).

Minimum wage contracts had long existed in the metalworking industries, but under DI leadership the model diffused widely. As Table 2.5 shows, after 1989 the number of workers covered by the normal pay wage system declined as those under a minimum pay wage system grew (Scheuer 2007: 243). In 1989, 34 percent of employees in the LO/DA area were covered by the normal

---

[28] SiD and the other union of unskilled workers, KAD, would later join forces, merging in 2003 to form 3F.

[29] Subsequently, the DI continued to grow by essentially absorbing more employer associations, and now also includes a large number of service sector firms, overcoming the traditional divide between services and manufacturing despite the decline of the DA. In fact, DI now dominates the executive committee of the DA, and by extension can dominate the use of DA's continued formal powers (e.g., veto power over agreements and power to call lock outs) (Ibsen 2012: 15).

TABLE 2.5. *Share of Employees (DA/LO area) Covered by Various Wage Systems*

	1989	1991	1993	1995	1997	2000	2004	2007	2010
normal wage/*normalløn*	34	19	16	16	16	15	16	17	15
minimum wage/*minimalløn*	32	37	13	12	21	23	27	57*	54
minimum pay agreements/ *mindstebetaling*	30	40	67	61	46	42	35		
figureless agreements/*uden lønsats*	4	4	4	11	17	20	22	26	31

*Note: After 2004, the data for minimum wage and minimum pay agreements were collapsed into a single category.
Source: Dansk Arbejdsgiverforening, Arbejdsmarkedsrapport 2005; 2013.[30]

wage system, but by 2010 this has dwindled to just 15 percent.[31] Moreover, in a growing number of cases, central contracts no longer even establish a minimum wage. Under so-called figureless agreements, industry contracts do not contain pay clauses at all but instead just lay out principles to which local bargainers are meant to adhere. As Table 2.5 shows, this type of contract has risen from just 4 percent of all employees in the LO/DA area in 1989 to nearly one-third by 2010 (see also Due and Madsen 2008: 517; Arbejdsgiverforening n.d.: 5).

In contrast to the "noisy realignments and political conflicts" in the move from peak-level to industry-level contracts of the 1980s, the subsequent decentralization to the firm or individual level unfolded more quietly "without much pomp and ado" (Vartiainen 2011: 12; see also Due and Madsen 2008: 519–520).

The Role of the State and the Revival of the LO

Even as wage negotiations were increasingly moved "out to enterprises" (Due and Madsen 2008: 519–20), coordinated industry-wide bargaining took on important new functions in Denmark. A crucial political realignment occurred in 1998 in the context of a major crisis in Danish industrial relations. Unions and employers in manufacturing had taken the lead in bargaining and reached a settlement that was meant to set the pace for the economy as a whole. But unions of unskilled workers unexpectedly mobilized at the local level against the agreement, which was defeated in a ratification vote in which a clear majority

[30] Minimum wage bargaining "often takes the form of 'pay-sum bargaining'... [where] the shop steward will bargain with management over the aggregate size of the pay rise for the group of workers he or she represents," but where it is "then up to management (or supervisor) to allocate the award to employees; pay increases for individual workers may vary widely" based on individual performance or qualifications (Scheuer 1998: 165).

[31] The industries that still have normal pay systems include transport, food processing, textiles, cleaning, hotels/restaurants, and hair dressers (thanks to Christian Ibsen for clarifying).

(56 percent) rejected the proposed settlement (Petersen 1998a). The rejection of a major settlement based on agreement between the social partners in the leading industrial sector – and the ensuing general strike[32] – suddenly put the newly stabilized system at risk.

The problem had its roots partly in discord on the employer side as a result of the move from coordination through the DA to coordination through the industrial sector, DI.[33] There was some grumbling on the part of some large companies and among DA affiliates (e.g., transport, construction, and services), whose own bargaining was held up by protracted negotiations in the industrial sector (Petersen 1998c, 1998d). Their leaders resented being relegated to the role of "spectators" in collective bargaining (Petersen 1998e). Commerce was especially irritated at being dragged into a conflict with its unions that it had not sought (Petersen 1998d).

On the labor side, as well, some LO affiliates outside manufacturing chafed at having the content and terms of their contracts set by industry, whose membership base in many cases was quite different from their own (Petersen 1998e). They noted with irony that the employers' associations in the DA had sought to decentralize bargaining only to then abdicate to DI. As LO President Hans Jensen put it, "The Danish model is a good model which has shown its efficiency. However, support for the model presupposes that the social partners negotiate their own results in their respective sectors. If there is no ... democracy in the decision-making process the system will collapse. And this should be noted by DA" (quoted in Petersen 1998e). Additional problems on the labor side had their roots in the transition from normal to minimum wages (i.e., the increased room for company-level wage formation). The rule of thumb for industry-level negotiations under the new minimum wage system is that the central bargaining partners settle at a figure that amounts to about a quarter of the anticipated wage increase, leaving the rest to local bargaining (Ibsen 2012: 14–17). But in 1998 when the proposed industry-level figure in the lead agreement was revealed, it was disappointing to members of many LO affiliates. The increase appeared especially meager to unskilled workers outside manufacturing who, with the end of wage solidarism, could no longer count on contractual top-ups to match wage drift in industry.[34]

In general, the new context of decentralized (but patterned) bargaining behind DI and CO-industri sidelined the LO and the DA and confronted unions

[32] The strike lasted eleven days and directly involved almost one-fifth of all Danish workers. Many more were indirectly affected (Madsen 1998).

[33] One source of strain was that the DI and its union counterpart CO-industri had signed a three-year agreement in 1995, while other DA and LO affiliates had signed two-year agreements. DI was keen to resynchronize, which was partly a matter of timing but which also involved issues of substance, since industry did not negotiate in 1997 and thus lagged behind other sectors on pension contributions (Petersen 1998b, 1998c).

[34] The members of unskilled unions also opposed proposed changes to the rules governing early retirement (see Chapter 4).

with a profound challenge (Petersen 1997a). The question was "how to provide visible benefits for their members in industry-level agreements when wage bargaining and working time was being decentralized" (Ibsen 2012: 2). The dilemma was resolved as the LO sought a new role for itself by turning to non-wage issues. At its next (1999) congress, the LO explicitly embraced training as a centerpiece of its new strategy. The shift from distributional to supply side issues involved a deal between the metalworkers' union (Dansk Metal) and the SiD (now 3F, after a merger with KAD) (16). As in the 1980s, skilled metalworkers still had an interest in localized bargaining since such arrangements allow them to benefit from higher skill premiums without the inflationary drag of wage compensation for low-skill workers. Meanwhile, unskilled unions "saw solidaristic skills provision as a bulwark against globalization and relocation of low-skilled work" (2). In other words, decentralization in wage formation and working times were explicitly exchanged for an "expansion in the scope of collective bargaining" as "other forms of security" beyond wages were incorporated into central contracts (Andersen and Mailand 2005: 3).

This was a transition that was brokered by the state, beginning with a legislated end to the 1998 conflict. Unlike in Germany, where the state is prohibited from intervening in collective bargaining, the Danish state has considerable powers to force a settlement through its power to link agreements across industries and force a single up or down vote, and, failing that, to impose a settlement directly through legislation (see especially Ibsen 2013). In 1998, the government directly imposed a settlement, and one whose content broke with the traditional practice of adopting (broadly) the terms of the agreement as negotiated by the social partners. Instead, the government-imposed settlement included additional concessions to the LO that reflected the interests of constituents, especially women, outside of manufacturing (J. Madsen 1998; Petersen 1998d). In (failed) negotiations to try to salvage a negotiated deal and stave off government intervention, the LO had demanded extra holidays and extra leave days for parents. The government settlement added one day of leave for all workers, plus – in an issue of special salience for the heavily feminized public sector – two additional days of leave for parents of young children (rising to three days over the course of the contract), with the cost partly offset by tax relief for companies that would cost the state DKK 400 million per year (Petersen 1998d).

Subsequent state actions operated more through the introduction of statutory entitlements that invited and often subsidized further initiatives in collective bargaining. These moves allowed the LO and the DA to find a new role in an era in which DI dominance in wage matters is uncontested. Although these new contracts are still normally worked out first with manufacturing in the lead, continued institutionalized LO influence is important in maintaining strong representation for the unskilled constituencies it represents and for ensuring that whatever gains are made in the DI-sphere on non-wage issues are diffused to the rest of the economy as well. One example of the kind of non-wage issues taken up in these venues is collective bargains that place employees with diminished work capacity in so-called light jobs. Older workers and other groups had been covered by statutory provisions in the past but "only in the last ten years [have] various 'light jobs' arrangements [been] included in collective agreements" (Andersen and Mailand 2005: 18). Along these lines, a 2012 agreement for older workers converted some pension payments into a system of reduced working hours (i.e., senior days off).

Another issue that has been taken up in collective bargaining (in this case in connection with labor market reforms discussed in Chapter 4) is training. Existing provisions already entitled any employee with nine months' service to take two weeks of unpaid leave for training. A 2007 agreement, however, establishes a co-administered skill development fund (*kompetenceudviklingsfonden*) to provide paid leave. Workers can apply for training, including for periods longer than two weeks. If the proposed training is part of the company's skill development plan, the worker receives 100 percent of his/her wage; if it is not part of that plan, then 85 percent (Ibsen and Mailand 2009: 106). A subsequent 2012 agreement makes it possible for workers to "bank" these weeks over three years in order to accumulate a right to six weeks of training. Another arrangement allows redundant workers an additional two weeks of notice to be taken in training, paid for out of these funds (Ibsen 2012: 8).

The agreements on training are a part of several leave schemes negotiated by the social partners in key sectors since the 1990s. These arrangements are based on statutory entitlements but augmented by collectively bargained provisions that top-up capped allowances to cover a larger share of a worker's normal wage during the leave period (Ibsen and Mailand 2009: 106). Since most of these initiatives involve financing new benefits through required contributions into funds that are jointly administered by the signatories to the agreements, these developments lock firms into industry settlements. The training agreement, for example, requires firms to pay a specific sum (initially 35 euros) per employee into the fund annually to finance additional training for any employee with more than nine months' seniority (Mailand 2009: 6). With these agreements unions have assumed a new role in social policy and at the same time institutionalized new forms of long-term cooperation with employers in administering the funds.[35]

In this way as well, collective bargaining in Denmark also accompanies and supplements state social policy. Supplementary pensions, for example, hold special attraction for professionals with relatively high incomes but less than continuous employment records. In fact, Christine Trampusch (2007) codes Denmark as an instance in which collectively negotiated benefits compensate for welfare-state retrenchment in ways that shore up social solidarity even in a period of austerity (198). Of course, the solidarity-enhancing effects of such moves depend heavily on how encompassing collective bargains are. In

[35] I am grateful to Christian Ibsen for pointing this out to me.

Germany, where coverage has shrunk to cover only the (privileged) core, the replacement of statutory entitlements with collectively bargained benefits is more likely to exacerbate rather than alleviate inequality. Accordingly, Trampusch (2007) finds that the most solidarity-enhancing effects of collectively bargained benefits are found in countries like Denmark, France, and the Netherlands where coverage rates are high – and notably not in Germany, where they are lower (210).

Other aspects of recent collective bargains in Denmark go beyond compensatory measures to cover a retreating state. In fact, what is striking about the kinds of non-wage issues that figure most prominently since the 2000s is that they frequently address non-traditional constituencies like women and salaried professionals, and cover new sorts of risks such as maintaining skills in a period of rapid technological change and balancing family and work. The 2004 bargaining round, for example, was dominated by the issue of parental leave. A broad cross-party coalition of female politicians urged the social partners to take this matter up in collective bargaining and indeed strongly hinted that failure to do so would result in legislation on this issue (Mailand 2006: 383–384). The (male-dominated) metalworkers – who already had such an arrangement – denounced the move as political interference in free collective bargaining, while the (heavily feminized) clerical workers' union (HK) welcomed it. The result was a collectively bargained settlement to "increase the period of fully paid childbirth-related maternity/paternity leave from 14 to 20 weeks [available to both men and women]... as well as introducing further 'pregnancy leave' of four weeks for women" (C. Jørgensen 2004: 1). The agreement also allows parents to take up to a week of fully paid leave in the event of the hospitalization of a child under 15 years of age. Initially the funds to cover parental leave were set up on a sectoral basis – one for industry and one for the rest of the DA area (Andersen and Mailand 2005: 22). But in the meantime the funds have been combined to even out the costs of maternity leave between sectors that employ a large number of women and those that do not. This amounts to a redistribution of resources from manufacturing to services and from traditionally male blue-collar workers to women and service employees.

Embedded Flexibilization

The developments in wage formation described in the previous sections clearly move Danish industrial relations in the direction of liberalization. But the variety of liberalization we observe in this case is distinct from both U.S.-style deregulation and German-style dualization. Unlike in the United States, union influence is still very strong; it is just organized around different goals than before.[36] Unlike in Germany, constituencies outside the industrial core are well

---

[36] Although there are also signs of trouble ahead. The overall organization rate in Denmark is 67.2 percent, close to the 1985 level (69.8 percent) but down from a high in 1995 of 73.1 percent. However, especially since the center-right government's reform of the unemployment

organized and in fact continue to exert significant influence at the national level through the LO. In Germany, union density is strongly skewed toward male blue-collar workers and membership declined as employment in manufacturing fell. In Denmark, unions have a strong presence outside manufacturing, in services and particularly among women. In 1966, the organization rate for women in Denmark was 53 percent – already an enviable figure from the perspective of most Continental countries. By the late 1990s, the organization rate among women had grown to equal that of men (88 percent). The women's share of the organized labor movement rose from 20 percent to nearly half of the members of the LO between 1950 and 1999 (Ebbinghaus 2000: 168–169). By 2008, Danish women made up a majority of the organized labor movement, compared to Germany where female unionists are still outnumbered two to one (Carley 2009). Relatedly, the share of white-collar employees in Danish unions has increased steadily since 1970 and by the early 1990s, the HK (National Union of Commercial and Clerical Employees) had overtaken the SiD to become the largest union in the LO (Scheuer 1992: 182; Due et al. 1994: 150). Higher-skilled salaried employees are also well organized and, unlike in Sweden, (see Chapter 5) most of the growth in unionization among this group has not come at the expense of the LO but within the peak confederation itself.[37]

The interests of the various constituencies within the LO are far from uniform, and as we have seen, internal conflicts have sometimes erupted into very public displays of disaffection. State power has played a key role not just in brokering deals between labor and capital, but also in sustaining linkages across employees who are differently affected by liberalization. In contrast to Germany, with its constitutionally anchored ban on state intervention in "free" collective bargaining, the Danish state has more tools at its disposal. The Danish Mediation Institute enjoys strong powers to link agreements across industries, and the threat of government intervention is often sufficient to sustain a relatively high level of coordination across distinct bargaining units.[38]

Such linkages have forestalled fragmentation and helped to shore up the influence of national actors, in particular the LO. These effects and strong union representation (including in low-skill sectors) manifest themselves in continued relative equality in wages despite widespread wage decentralization.

---

insurance system in 2002, so-called alternative (essentially yellow) unions have been on the rise in Denmark, and the overall organization rate drops to 59.1 percent if we exclude members of these unions (Due et al. 2012).

[37] In Sweden, the organizational divide between salaried and blue collar unions is sharper. In Denmark, a white-collar confederation was founded in the 1950s but subsequently stagnated at around the 16 percent of the union movement that it commands today (Ebbinghaus 2000: 163–164). Overall, the Danish LO has been far more successful than its Swedish counterpart in reaching beyond its traditional blue collar base to incorporate new groups, including beyond low-level clerical to other salaried groups (Scheuer 1992: 182).

[38] See, especially Christian Lyhne Ibsen (2013) on the importance of state mediation in Denmark.

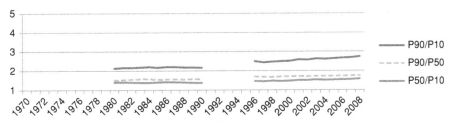

FIGURE 2.5. Income Dispersion (Pre-Tax and Transfer) in Denmark, 1980–2008.
Source: OECD Stat Database.

Figure 2.5 examines trends in wage dispersion in Denmark over the past three decades. Overlooking the gap in the trend line (years for which no data are available), we see that between the time that bargaining decentralization began in 1981 and the late 1990s, wages had become more dispersed and the 50/10 and 90/50 ratios continued to grow in the 2000s, albeit at a very moderate rate compared to Germany and, especially, the United States. The comparison to Germany is especially instructive at the low end. The 50/10 ratio rose in Germany by 23 percent between 1990 and 2008, from 1.57 to 1.93, while in Denmark it rose less in that period (about 14 percent) and by 2008 had just reached the 1990 level for Germany at 1.57.

The comparatively small increases in wage dispersion between the median and the 10th decile in Denmark is a function of higher levels of union organization overall and continued encompassing organization on the labor side, both of which mediate against the dualization strategies described for Germany (Kjellberg 2011a: 69). Moreover, and beyond the issue of pay, the state has played a crucial role in promoting the shift in bargaining to include new non-wage issues that appeal to the interests and address the risks faced by growing union constituencies at both ends of the income spectrum. The collective agreements noted in the previous sections – on pensions, on education and training, and on parental leave – were all initiated by the state, based on statutory entitlements on which collective bargaining agreements then build. Agreements on these issues have not only encouraged continued cooperation between labor and capital through funds that are jointly administered, they have also created shared interests among constituencies that are otherwise differently affected by liberalization (Ahlquist and Levi 2013). Parental leave, for example, redounds to the benefit of dual income families and women workers, whether they are salaried professionals or hotel cleaning staff. Training leave likewise helps workers invest in their own human capital no matter what their starting point.

In short, continued high levels of unionization and organizational links across sectors and between low- and high-skill groups provides an organizational counterweight to the centrifugal forces that liberalization inevitably unleashes, while the state-brokered reorientation in the content of corporatist bargaining – away from the wage issues that divided public- and private-sector workers (and low- and high-skill workers) in the 1970s and 1980s – has played an important role in shoring up the position of the national union confederation.

TRAJECTORIES OF LIBERALIZATION IN INDUSTRIAL RELATIONS

Trajectories of change in industrial relations institutions in the United States, Germany, and Denmark exhibit three distinct varieties of liberalization. In the United States, collective bargaining had always rested less on a stable cross-class alliance and more on a fragile balance of power that was undermined in the 1970s and 1980s by economic turbulence and a powerful alliance of business interests intent on wholesale, across-the-board deregulation. The result has been a collapse in unionization and a steady decline in collective bargaining coverage.

In Germany, by contrast, traditional bargaining arrangements have proven more resilient. A high degree of formal bargaining centralization continues to enjoy the support of powerful employers' associations and unions in the manufacturing core. In this case liberalization has proceeded gradually – not through a direct frontal assault on traditional bargaining arrangements, but more through a process of institutional drift. Existing arrangements lose their grip as an increasing number of firms operate outside otherwise stable bargaining structures and as more and more workers find themselves outside the reach of collective agreements.

Denmark, finally, exhibits a third pattern – embedded flexibilization. In this case, formal structures have undergone rather profound changes and wage bargaining is if anything more decentralized than in Germany. These reconfigurations involved significant conflict and tumult – between labor and employers, among unions representing different constituencies, and between organized labor and governments of all stripes. In the end, representatives of unskilled workers were unable to defend traditional arrangements organized around wage equalization, but state interventions have shored up national associations of labor and business and kept industry tightly imbricated in more overarching arrangements. Traditional bargaining structures were not dismantled, but were instead converted to new purposes, from wage setters to coordinators of local bargaining that now covers a wider range of issues than before.

3

Vocational Education and Training

Skill formation forms a second arena of importance within the VofC literature – VET being one of several complementary institutions that distinguish LMEs from CMEs. LMEs feature systems that encourage the acquisition of general skills, while the systems of education and training in CMEs provide strong vocational training in industry- or firm-specific skills. These differences are important not just in economic terms; they also have relevance to the political and distributional outcomes of central interest in this book. In LMEs, educational stratification often reflects and reinforces economic inequalities. In CMEs, by contrast, well-developed vocational tracks traditionally have offered opportunities for working-class youth to move into stable and relatively well-paid work, especially in manufacturing.

The transition to the new "knowledge-based" economy poses important new challenges to both models (Morel et al. 2011: 1). The outsourcing of lower-skilled manufacturing jobs and the automation of production and services have transformed the kinds of competencies and skills required in these political economies. The relevant changes involve "not only a shift away from more narrow job-specific skills toward broader, more analytic general skills... [but also] a much more rapid turnover in the content... of training than in the past" (Mayer and Solga 2008: 2). This chapter considers the ways in which different national systems of education and training have been reconfigured to address these new challenges.

I begin again by situating the three cases at the center of the present study within a cross-national framework. While there is no shortage of typologies of VET, the one proposed by Busemeyer and Trampusch (2012) provides a particularly useful point of departure. They distinguish two dimensions along which training regimes vary. One is the degree of public commitment to vocational training, which taps the extent to which the state supports VET "as a viable alternative to academic higher education" and a means to promote the

TABLE 3.1. *Types of Vocational Education and Training Systems*

		Involvement of Firms in IVET	
		low	high
Public Commitment to VET	high	*collectivist, state-based* Finland, Norway, Sweden, France	*collectivist, firm-sponsored* Germany, Austria, Switzerland, Netherlands, Denmark
	low	*liberal* United States, UK	*segmentalist* Japan

Source: Adapted, with minor modifications, from Busemeyer and Trampusch (2011: 12).

integration of young people with weak academic qualifications into education and employment (12). The other is the extent to which private-sector companies are directly involved in initial vocational education and training (IVET). This second dimension captures an older distinction classically drawn in this literature between school-based and firm-based training systems (see also Lynch 1994). Sorting a number of country cases along these two dimensions produces the typology depicted in Table 3.1.

Here again, we see a mostly familiar pattern. The Anglo-Saxon countries are clustered in the lower left (liberal training regime) quadrant; in such countries there is low public commitment to VET and also little firm involvement. Public schools provide general education; youth acquire vocational skills subsequently (if at all) and largely on the job. Japan, by contrast, exemplifies what I have elsewhere called a "segmentalist" system. As in the liberal systems, the state is not deeply involved in VET, but firms play a stronger role in skill formation in the context of company-based careers and long-term employment relations (Thelen 2004). Most of the Scandinavian countries cluster in the upper left quadrant, characterized by high public support for VET but relatively low firm involvement. These cases are typically characterized by "comprehensive' schools that do not sort children into vocational tracks during high school but that support vocational training through publicly funded vocational schools. Most of the Continental countries, finally, cluster in the upper right quadrant – high public commitment to training coupled with strong firm involvement. These countries do more tracking at the high school level, channeling youth into either vocational or academic pathways. In all cases, firms play a central role in the provision of vocational training, often accompanied by a school-based component.

Turning to the three cases under consideration here, the United States has traditionally fit squarely in the liberal model when it comes to education and training. Although higher education in the United States is the envy of the world, there is very little infrastructure for vocational training and the quality of public education at the primary and secondary levels is highly uneven. Denmark and Germany, by contrast, both fall squarely within the kind of collectivist skill regime long associated with CMEs. In this respect Denmark differs from most of the other Scandinavian countries where school-based vocational training dominates. Instead, as in Germany, IVET involves a combination of school-based training and firm-based experience. And in both Germany and Denmark the social partners (employer associations and unions) play a key role in the planning and administration of VET at the national level.

Busemeyer and Trampusch (2012) focus their attention on initial vocational training, as opposed to adult education or continuing vocational education and training (CVET) and, within that focus, on the collectivist systems. They identify what they call four "neuralgic" points of contention within such training regimes (17–19). These concern (1) who controls the content and quality of training (the issue of monitoring), (2) who provides skill formation (the balance between school and firm-based components), (3) who pays for skill formation (the balance between firms and state), and (4) the relationship between VET and general education (the issue of permeability between the two spheres).

For present purposes, and looking across a broader range of countries, two further questions seem crucially important. One concerns the relationship between IVET (for youth) and CVET (for adults). In the past, the most successful systems of VET involved heavy upfront investments in firm- or industry-specific skills (i.e., high-quality apprenticeships). The costs of such investments were typically shared by firms and workers and the fruits of these investments were then also jointly amortized over the course of a worker's (long) career within the firm or industry. However, in a context characterized by rapid technological change and a shift in employment to services, adult education and continuing vocational training play a more important role – allowing workers to avoid skill obsolescence and easing the transition, especially for the most vulnerable groups, in the event of job loss.

A second, more general and even more important question is who controls access to high-quality training.[1] Does the private sector monopolize access to vocational training or can the state directly influence the number of apprenticeships on offer (see especially Busemeyer and Iversen 2012)? Is VET widely available or it is rationed based on financial resources or other factors? To the extent that career opportunities in the new knowledge-based economy depend heavily on human capital endowments, access to training at all levels has enormous implications for economic equality and social solidarity.

The trajectories of change we observe in education and training policy are strikingly similar to those in industrial relations. In the United States, the trend in education policy has if anything exacerbated inequality. A number of initiatives in the 1960s and again in the 1990s sought to establish an infrastructure through which working-class youth could acquire vocational skills. The failure of these programs, however, only reinforced the idea that skill formation

---

[1] I am grateful to Marius Busemeyer for emphasizing the importance of this to me.

was best left to the market. The state has since retreated from almost all government-sponsored training and embraced a more hands-off "college for all" approach that is focused on increasing enrolments in various forms of postsecondary education. Enrollment is up, but completion rates, especially among lower socioeconomic groups, are very low. And although opportunities for CVET and adult education exist in community colleges of varying levels of quality, they are often only loosely linked to later job prospects.

Germany, by contrast, features a popular and well-functioning apprenticeship system. In this country, all the relevant actors have rallied to adapt the traditional system to the new challenges noted. Ongoing reforms in the content of training have rendered what was already a high-quality system for IVET even better. However, successful adaptation to new technological and market challenges has increased the costs to firms of providing apprenticeship training. Because the German economy relies almost exclusively on the private sector to sponsor apprenticeship, these developments have resulted in a rationing of such training and with that, new inequalities based on institutionalized dualization in training opportunities and later career trajectories (Busemeyer and Iversen 2012; Thelen and Busemeyer 2012). Moreover, recent reforms have notably not addressed a persistent and longstanding weakness in Germany in the provision of CVET for adults. Access to CVET in Germany is largely limited to workers who already have jobs and in whom firms, for their own reasons, are prepared to invest further. By contrast, few opportunities exist for workers to take the initiative to update their own skills, and the infrastructure for low-skill unemployed workers to receive training that will enhance their chances of reintegrating into the labor market is weak to say the least.

In Denmark, finally, the response to the economic and technological changes noted here has been a significant liberalization of training along a number of related fronts. Reforms over the past two decades have, as in Germany, broadened the content of skills. But Denmark also implemented a number of reforms that Germany has specifically rejected, introducing new flexibilities in the process through which skills are acquired. Policies have expanded access to training through modularization in the credentialing process and through an aggressive dismantling of traditional boundaries – between IVET and CVET, between blue- and white-collar training, between training opportunities for skilled and unskilled workers, and between training offerings for the employed and the unemployed. The Danish system has some problems of its own, but in this case the state is actively involved in promoting and financing a very broad training effort. Unlike in Germany, where training is almost exclusively a matter of firm voluntarism and heavily focused on apprenticeship for youth, in Denmark a well-institutionalized and generously funded system for CVET and adult education provides opportunities for skill development over the life course and opens up avenues back to employment for labor market outsiders.

EDUCATION AND TRAINING IN THE UNITED STATES

The United States is famous for its superior system of higher education but also infamous for its distinctly inferior system of VET. For reasons that I have explored elsewhere (Thelen 2004: 148–214), apprenticeship in the United States had mostly withered by the 1920s, surviving in only a few trades, mostly construction. What remained of firm-sponsored skill formation consisted (and consists) of short-term on-the-job training. Unlike in some CMEs, there is no separate system of vocational schooling at the secondary level. Instead, American high schools are in principle organized around a college preparatory curriculum. However, whereas the United States used to lead virtually all other countries in college enrollment, almost all the rich democracies have made up the gap and some have even surpassed U.S. levels. Where the United States does continue to stand out, though, is in a high level of stratification in post-secondary education, with world-class elite private universities at the top of the hierarchy and public community colleges of various levels of quality at the bottom. Since we know that income tracks educational achievement closely in the United States – even if it does not seem to close the gender gap – educational stratification parallels and reinforces economic stratification in this country.

In the past, a number of public programs sought to redress these problems, providing targeted support for training for working-class youth. Such programs have been almost completely abandoned. In the 1960s, job training was a central component in President Lyndon B. Johnson's War on Poverty and in the 1990s, as well, the Clinton administration attempted to create an infrastructure for vocational education. Such efforts failed and I will show why. Since the 1990s, the focus of education policy has been on enhancing the performance of public schools, liberalizing education through the introduction of voucher programs ("school choice"), closing the achievement gap to increase the number of lower-class youth who complete high school and, especially, facilitating college access for all. As we will see, enrollments have risen significantly in the last two decades. However, drop-out rates are extremely high and particularly so among youth from disadvantaged socioeconomic status (SES) backgrounds. In light of this, some of the most astute observers of education policy in the United States view contemporary programs and policies organized virtually exclusively around expanding enrollment in four-year colleges as a "cruel charade" that masks the very real difficulties that await many of the most disadvantaged students when they arrive for classes and that contribute massively to their discouragement and, in a majority of cases, their failure to achieve any degree at all (Rosenbaum 2011: 113).

In previous research, I analyzed the historical process through which VET withered in the United States even as it was taking off in other countries (Thelen 2004). In the early twentieth century, at around the same time that high-quality firm-based apprenticeship training became institutionalized in Germany, vocational education institutions in the United States were being written off as "lyceums for losers" (Hansen 1999: 21). Instead of VET for the working classes, American education was configured around the interests and aspirations of middle-class children. Public funding for vocational training dried up and ambitious youth faced strong incentives to avoid vocational training like the plague and to pursue a more academically oriented education that opened many more opportunities for advancement in a labor market that rewarded general, not specific, skills.

The contrast to Germany is especially stark. There, a high-quality system of VET has not only survived but thrived. Policy makers have upgraded the system on an ongoing basis to keep pace with technological and other changes, so that the vocational tracks remain extremely attractive, including among more academically inclined youth. In the United States, by contrast, all efforts in the postwar period to strengthen VET have failed. I track the evolution of policy in this area through three phases – beginning with initiatives in the 1960s and 1970s to forge links between vocational training and labor market policies, followed in the 1990s by attempts to institutionalize a stronger vocational track to address manufacturing decline, and finally superseded by a commitment to a "college for all" strategy that focuses on college enrollments (although not necessarily on college completion) without much connection to subsequent job opportunities.

Training Policy between Manpower Development and the War on Poverty

In the United States, the first sustained debate on VET reform in the postwar period emerged in the 1950s. Across most of the rich democracies this was a period of extraordinary growth, but core American industries were already experiencing competitive pressures. Thus, at the very same time that European policy makers were devising strategies to address acute labor market shortages, American policy makers were dealing with unemployment, concentrated especially in the industrial heartland. Policy makers understood the problem mostly as emanating from technological change, and Democratic congressmen from hard-hit regions began to lobby for legislative action to assist jobless factory operatives in preparing themselves for new job opportunities. Paul Douglas of Illinois and Joseph Clark of Philadelphia were among those who led the call for area redevelopment projects (Weir 1992: 66–67). Their case was bolstered by an important report by the National Manpower Council in 1955 that argued for increased state involvement in training (Kremen 1974).

This would not be the government's first postwar foray into this field. In fact, the United States subsidized practical job training on a very significant scale under the GI Bill of 1944. This program is best known for encouraging veterans to attend and complete college, but in fact more GIs took part in subsidized vocational training: "whereas 2,155,988 GI's took advantage of the college subsidies between 1944–1951, more than four and a half million

GI's used the job training or the on-the-job training programs during the same period" (Wilson 2004: 16). This program was hugely popular, appealing as it did to the middle classes and channeling patriotic sentiments. President John F. Kennedy followed the same broad script, attaching the problem of structural unemployment to the new "imperatives of the Cold War" (read: the Sputnik challenge) in making the case for stronger government involvement in education and training (Kremen 1974: 1). One result was the Manpower Development and Training Act (MDTA) of 1962, the first major federal job training program in the United States.

Training under the MDTA never took off in large numbers, however.[2] One reason is that public support waned once Kennedy's successor, Lyndon B. Johnson, began to direct more of the funding toward the urban poor (Weir 1992: 65–66). One of the centerpiece components in Johnson's War on Poverty was the Job Corps, formed in 1964 to offer support to disadvantaged youth. Patterned after Franklin D. Roosevelt's Civilian Conservation Corps, the express mission of the program was to help young people (aged sixteen to twenty-four) "improve the quality of their lives through vocational and academic training" (Job Corps mission statement). Other programs targeted long-term unemployment among adult populations. The Work Incentive (WIN) Program founded in 1967, for example, allowed welfare recipients (covered by Aid to Families with Dependent Children) to receive occupational or pre-occupational training – either through federal manpower programs or through institutionalized training of various sorts (Gold 1971: 491).[3]

The labor market policies of the Johnson era are discussed at length in Chapter 4. In the present context the important point is that the links between government-sponsored and/or subsidized training and the War on Poverty proved fatefully toxic (Weir 1992). Unlike earlier efforts on behalf of GIs and industrial workers, the middle classes were not invested in programs that were aimed at disadvantaged groups and they came to resent the tax dollars that were being devoted to them. In fact, perversely, the close association of federally funded training with welfare policies stigmatized those who were meant to benefit. By the 1970s, publicly sponsored and subsidized training evoked such negative connotations that program participants "were actually less likely to be hired than similarly qualified candidates who were not part of a federal program" (93–94; also Rosenbaum 2001: 263). Most of the training programs associated with the War on Poverty met the same fate as many of President Johnson's other well-intentioned initiatives, either abandoned later or limping along in much reduced form.

---

[2] 600,000 unemployed persons were supported by MDTA between 1962 and 1968 (Wilson 2004: 16).

[3] While the Job Corps program enjoyed some success, many of the other training programs associated with the War on Poverty produced mixed results at best (Schochet et al. 2008: 1864).

Subsequent initiatives with respect to training rejected targeting and embraced a broader approach (Lafer 2002: 117). The most important such initiative was the Comprehensive Education and Training Act (CETA) (for a listing of major programs, see Katz 1994: 275–281). Passed in 1973 under President Richard Nixon in response to growing joblessness among middle-class Americans, CETA had both a training and a public works component. Rejecting former president Johnson's centralized approach (direct federal support for specific populations), President Nixon organized the CETA program into block grants to states. This arrangement had the desired effect of reducing the role of the national government, but decentralized administration also left the program open to misuse as patronage by local politicians (Weir 1992). In a period of rising unemployment, the program tilted away from the training part of its mission and was mostly used to prop up employment through funding to various public service programs. CETA was then caught up in a series of corruption scandals in the late 1970s and funding was reduced under President Carter before it was disbanded entirely under his successor Ronald Reagan (Weir 1992).[4]

Reform Efforts of the 1990s

In the Reagan era, the rhetoric of small government held sway, and so the issue of training reform was mostly off the agenda through the 1980s. This neglect persisted despite the publication in 1983 of an unflattering characterization of the state of U.S. skills by the National Commission on Excellence in Education. The committee's report – bearing the ominous title *A Nation at Risk* – emphasized the impact of inadequate education and training on the American economy. The German and Japanese economies had rebounded from the oil crisis based on strong manufacturing exports, and the report drew invidious comparisons to the United States, where chronic skill shortages were seen as contributing to the inability of American firms to keep pace. A subsequent study in 1990 by the Commission on the Skills of the American Workforce – *America's Choice: High Skills or Low Wages* – was even more explicit in pointing to the deficiencies in the system of American education, particularly in the area of vocational skills.

These reports revealed a large and growing gap in skill formation and education between the United States and Europe. Comparisons to Germany were

---

[4] The successor program, the Job Training Partnership Act (JTPA) of 1982, was a poorly funded initiative that mostly reflected President Reagan's lack of interest in all such programs. Republican Senator – later vice president – Dan Quayle authored the bill and conceived of it mostly as a social policy rather than an economic measure, as Lafer (2002) puts it: " . . . a kind of Republican affirmative action" (159). While the program enjoyed some success at the level of adult training, the emphasis on youth training in disadvantaged communities continued to fuel stigmatization. Randomized trials revealed that young JTPA participants earned less than young men with arrest records: "Subsidized on-the-job training lowered the earnings of those without an arrest record by $578 for women and $3012 for men" (Bishop 1995: 11).

especially sobering. Christoph Büchtemann et al. (1993) found that only about 50 percent of U.S. school leavers received any kind of postsecondary skill credential. For most, the only training they would get would be fleeting and on the job. In a comparison to Germany, the authors underscored significant differences in the educational trajectory of youth in the two countries. Within the first year after graduating or dropping out of high school, a majority of American youth were either working (52 percent) or looking for a job (10 percent). In Germany, almost 80 percent of youth at that stage were instead receiving some form of training. The differences five years after leaving secondary education were even more striking. Almost 80 percent of American youth were in jobs by this time and only one in ten was in some form of education or training. By contrast, in Germany four out of ten German youth were still in some kind of training five years out (99). The patterns of employment converged after about twelve years, but of course by then German youth had a stock of skills that their American counterparts lacked.

Reaganomics had no place for government interventions to solve such problems, placing its faith instead in the market. The case for intervention on grounds of structural unemployment seemed in any case moot in a period in which unemployment was falling – even if poverty was increasing, not least as a result of the failures noted in Chapter 2 to update the minimum wage through both of President Reagan's terms in office.

Continued economic growth and an overwhelming Democratic victory in 1992 provided an auspicious context for reform. In his first term, President Bill Clinton proposed the establishment of a nation-wide apprenticeship system modeled on the German example (Büchtemann et al. 1993: 97). Clinton's secretary of labor, Robert Reich, was a longtime fan of the German system and understood it well. The 1994 School to Work Opportunities Act (STWOA) marked an important departure from previous efforts. Whereas earlier programs had targeted disadvantaged groups, STWOA was tirelessly emphasized by its proponents as "the most universal, non-means-tested effort to date ... intended to help all students who have not yet completed high school, regardless of their economic status" (Halperin 1994: 4–5). Focusing on high school and the transition to postsecondary education, the legislation "addresses the needs of all students [while also] 'remember[ing]' the needs of 'The Forgotten Half' who are not going to four-year colleges immediately after high school graduation" (5).

The legislation was pitched by Secretary Reich (1996) as both an education and a labor market reform, and it was specifically designed to bridge the historic gap between labor market policy and training policy in the United States. This was a policy that would simultaneously benefit non-college-bound youth and lift American manufacturing back to greatness. The rhetoric was soaring and as one astute observer has noted, much of it paralleled the discourse surrounding the Smith-Hughes Act of 1917, the last major effort to bolster American manufacturing through apprenticeship training (Stephens 1995; also Thelen 2004: 195, 210). In both cases, the proponents of change emphasized the inadequacy of existing educational institutions to prepare youth for the workplace. In both cases, reformers stressed the urgency of reform in the face of technological change and intensified international competition. Both laws sought to strengthen the link between school curricula and the needs of firms (Stephens 1995: 30).

Both initiatives, one might add now with the benefit of hindsight, failed – but not for lack of trying. The passage of the STWOA was accompanied by complementary legislation, the National Skill Standards Act, which called for the establishment of a National Skill Standards Board (also modeled on the German system) charged with identifying broad occupational clusters in which standardized skill sets could be adopted that would render training more transparent and skills more portable, including across state boundaries (Kreysing 2001: 32–33; Bosch and Charest 2008: 438). But as in 1917, the STWOA foundered on the familiar shoals of collective action problems among firms and lukewarm support from organized labor (Thelen 2004). Skill standards set by the National Board were voluntary, and set out only recommendations with which institutions of higher education, employers, trade associations, and unions could at best be implored to comply. As in the early twentieth century, employers were too disorganized to implement standardization, and organized labor feared that federally funded initiatives would compete with union-run apprenticeship programs (Kreysing 2001: 33) or become a management tool in a context of significant antiunion sentiment (Imel 1999).

Moreover, the STWOA could never impose a national framework for skill standardization and certification. Given state authority in the area of education, the best the federal government could do was to charge states with developing their own programs to facilitate school-to-work transitions fitted to local circumstances. So when the federal funding for STWOA ran out in 2001, the continuation of the programs that had been initiated under its auspices depended on state governments (Brown 2002). While some states remained committed, most others let the program expire. As in the past, a large part of the problem was that teachers and parents were not focused on vocationally bound youth; the communities that were most mobilized were instead more interested in devoting resources to improving high schools generally and investing in the academically bound (Kreysing 2001: 34). With that, the ambitious vocationally oriented initiatives of the Clinton years faded quietly away and have shown no signs of revival since.

Education Reform since the 1990s: The Promise and Pitfalls of College for All

The politicization of programs targeted to the lower classes in the 1960s and the failure of the Clinton apprenticeship initiatives of the 1990s led to the abandonment of these projects. But other elements of education policy survived, although the focus in this area shifted in emphasis from job training to

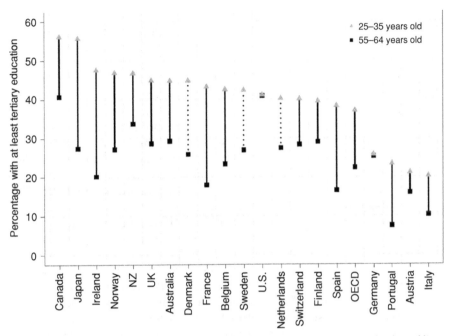

FIGURE 3.1. Tertiary Education Attainment by Generation, 2009. *Note*: The dotted lines identify the countries that figure most centrally in the present analysis. *Source*: OECD (2011c: 30).

expanding opportunities for higher education. This pivot fit with the Clinton administration's embrace of a centrist New Democratic agenda. In the U.S. context "education had the universal characteristics that job training, with its remedial orientation, lacked ... [and] the middle class already cared deeply about higher education" (Weir 1998: 288). Education thus became a central element in President Clinton's Middle Class Bill of Rights, part of an "unabashed ploy" after 1994 to win middle-class support for the New Democratic agenda (288).

Unlike VET, higher education was an area in which the United States was traditionally a leader. Forty years ago, more Americans had attained a college degree than in any other rich democracy. This is no longer the case. Figure 3.1 records the share of the population that had attained a tertiary degree for two generational cohorts, ages fifty-five to sixty-four and ages twenty-five to thirty-four. It shows that the former U.S. lead in this area has evaporated. Other countries have not only reached the same level, but many have surpassed the United States by this measure.

What is also notable in the present context is the clustering of LMEs and Scandinavian CMEs near the front of the pack, as many of the continental

CMEs continue to lag behind in this area (Japan, France, and Belgium being notable exceptions). Some of the biggest advances among CMEs are recorded by Norway, Denmark, and Sweden, while Italy, Germany, and Austria have not moved very much in forty years.

Given the growing importance of higher-level skills in the new knowledge-based economy, much recent education policy in the United States has been aimed at preparing children for college. The U.S. education system is marked by great unevenness (and in very many cases, demonstrably failing institutions) at the primary and secondary levels, so some reforms have focused on lifting the performance of weaker primary and high schools. Many of President Clinton's initiatives in this area provided support for state-based programs to develop and apply standards to the content and performance of public schools – including extensive use of testing to establish metrics for quality. Clinton's successor George W. Bush built on some of the scaffolding thus created with the controversial No Child Left Behind Act that established achievement targets for schools and imposed sanctions on those that failed to meet them. These initiatives to improve the quality of public primary and secondary schools (including also President Barack Obama's Race to the Top program) are linked to a broad "college for all" agenda organized around closing the achievement gap and encouraging students to think beyond high school to a higher degree.

Such programs have actually been very successful on one level. More youth than ever before are going on to some form of postsecondary education: a large majority (75 percent) of youth who complete high school do in fact enroll in college within two years of graduation (Rosenbaum 2011: 572). Clearly this varies by SES, but even in this respect the numbers are at first glance encouraging. Over the last three decades, the proportion of minority and low-income students in college has doubled (Stephan et al. 2009: 572–73). Whereas in 1980, the percentage of students from low SES backgrounds going on to postsecondary education was under a third (32 percent), by 2007 it was over half (56 percent) (Osterman 2011: 129). Some of these enrollments are in four-year institutions, but community colleges have played the much bigger role in this development. Enrollments in two-year colleges have risen over the past four decades, from 20 to 38 percent of all enrollments (Stephan et al. 2009: 573). Between 1963 and 2006, enrollments in four-year public institutions and private universities/colleges nearly doubled, but community college enrollments rose more than seven-fold during this period (Osterman 2011: 129).

In the absence of any significant firm-based training and with the failure of most public training programs, community colleges in fact are the core institution providing vocational training in the country today.[5] Increased demand

---

[5] In 1993 fewer than 2% of high school leavers were in apprenticeships, amounting to 0.2% of the workforce in the United States (Büchtemann et al. 1993: 98), and not much has changed since then. Today there are only 450,000 registered apprenticeship programs (i.e., those certified by the Department of Labor or a state agency), of which 56% are in construction and 11% in the military (Osterman 2011: 149).

has driven proliferation and diversification in the community college landscape (Stephan et al. 2009). Different types of institutions – including new private community colleges – cater to different regional businesses and local populations. Community colleges also provide a key training ground for a number of middle-skill occupations in growing industries such as health care and information and communication technology (Osterman 2011: 136–137).

At many such institutions, open admissions policies that essentially guarantee admission to all applicants have clearly boosted enrollment. However, dropout rates are extremely high and concentrated on precisely the low SES groups who would benefit most from training. Stephan et al. (2009: 574) show that only about half of students entering college attain any degree at all within eight years, and the completion rates at public two-year colleges are particularly low. Among full-time students in two-year institutions, only 22 percent who enrolled in 2005 had achieved their degrees three years later. The completion rate for part-time students after three years, understandably, was even lower (15.5 percent) though this figure rises to between 23 and 42 percent if one takes a somewhat longer time frame (Osterman 2011: 139–40).[6]

In short, programs organized around the "college access for all" motto turn out to succeed better at the level of ambition than in reality. An overwhelming number of American youth plan to attend college. In 2004, less than 1 percent of high school graduates had no plan to attend college; all others expressed this as a goal. While some envisioned getting a community college degree, the vast majority (89 percent) were planning to get a BA. In the end, more wind up in two-year programs. While open admissions policies have the laudatory effect of increasing enrollment, Rosenbaum points out that they often also inadvertently foster the impression that high school performance does not matter. His research shows that 40 percent of college-bound students do not think that their performance in high school is relevant to their future (Rosenbaum 2011: 114). These students are then surprised when they are placed in remedial classes when they get to college, as indeed almost 60 percent of them are (Osterman 2011: 141). But in such courses, students are not earning credit toward a degree. This is the point at which many become discouraged and drop out. In fact, the drop-out rate among low-achieving seniors who enroll in college of any sort is an astounding 80 percent (Rosenbaum 2011: 113).

Moreover, the connection between education and labor market prospects at the low end of the skill market remains tenuous at best in the United States. Unlike in countries with better institutionalized vocational tracks, incentives and networks are missing for children from lower SES backgrounds. Youth who believe that there is little connection between hard work in school and job prospects later are often right. One of the most striking findings in Rosenbaum's (2001) research is that employers who hire high school graduates are uninterested in their performance in school. Despite ongoing complaints about

---

[6] Osterman provides figures for completion rates after six years from several states, which range from 23% in Connecticut (total award or transfer) to 42% in Texas (Osterman 2011: 139–140).

the inferior training of high school graduates in basic literacy skills, American firms demonstrate a surprising indifference to any indicators that might help them distinguish students who worked hard in high school from those who did not. They overwhelmingly do not request transcripts and they consider teacher evaluations irrelevant or unreliable, relying instead on the impressions they glean from their own (usually brief) interviews with job candidates. Asked what were the most important factors in their hiring decisions, 76 percent indicated that they consider interviews "very important' against only 18 percent who consider grades "very important" (136 and chapter 6 passim).[7] High school students who plan to join the workforce after graduation rationally respond to these signals with their own indifference to high school performance.

The skills problem in the United States thus runs a good bit deeper than just the lack of a strong system to support VET. Rosenbaum (2001) sums up the situation in American education as well as anyone I know, noting the "tragic irony" of the American school system, in which egalitarian ideals mean that American policy makers are "uncomfortable with creating a substantial vocational education system and instead offer a college preparatory curriculum to nearly all students" – a trajectory that does not necessarily serve students of low SES backgrounds well because it does not come to grips with the problems that such students have in actually succeeding in such a system (116).

The Retreat of the State and the Individualization of Risk in U.S. Education and Training Policy

The trajectory of change in U.S. training policy has mostly involved a retreat on the part of the state from direct sponsorship of training and a move away from programs targeted to address the needs of the most vulnerable in society. Instead of the government assuming responsibility, the United States mostly has turned to market solutions, even in the area of education policy. At the level of community colleges, private institutions charging significant fees now compete vigorously with public institutions based on promises of a smoother transition into employment after graduation. At the high school level, public schools increasingly compete not just with private alternatives, but also with a growing number of charter schools that operate with public funding but outside of the usual public regulatory framework (e.g., almost always without unions). Enrollment in charter schools quadrupled to 1.6 million between 2000 and 2010 (NCES 2012).

In some ways the dramatic entry of non-profits like Teach for America (TFA) or the Knowledge is Power Program (KIPP) into American education policy only underscores the extent to which private actors feel compelled to

---

[7] Of course there is a chicken and egg issue here, in which the type of jobs on offer at the low end of the American labor market may not, in fact, require much in the way of cognitive skills (on the problem of a low-skill equilibrium, see also Finegold and Soskice 1988).

pursue alternatives outside the dominant public-policy channels. Some of these developments have undoubtedly enhanced opportunities for low SES youth to gain access to higher education and with that, the opportunity to compete for higher-quality jobs. At the same time and as many observers have noted, education-oriented non-profits like TFA are not able – and were not designed – to address the deeper structural problems that underpin much of the achievement gap (Ravitch 2012).

In sum, in the case of VET, the emphasis in the United States has often been on securing short term improvements on superficial measures (e.g., getting students into college) and without much attention to whether they then stay in school or if they have any idea what they are training for. The current public-policy emphasis on high school completion and enrollment in a college – but without regard for prior preparation let alone successful completion – involves the same pattern of individualization of risk we observed in industrial relations, and will see again in the area of labor market policy (Chapter 4). In a system like the one in the United States, where in principle all high schoolers have access to college, the onus is on the individual when he or she fails. Educational stratification therefore continues to reflect and reinforce pre-existing inequalities in SES. And since income closely tracks educational attainment, the transition to the new knowledge-based economy has been a boon for those who have been able to acquire high-end knowledge and credentials. Those whose formal education ends with a high school degree (or less), by contrast, mostly look onto a landscape that features precarious, dead-end employment with low pay, few or no benefits, and virtually no possibility for further training.

GERMAN VOCATIONAL EDUCATION AND TRAINING

In contrast to the United States, Germany's vocational training system has long been considered the crown jewel of the country's political economy. Most observers see Germany's high-quality apprenticeship model as a crucial contributor to the continuing competitive strength of its manufacturing sector in international markets. But here, too, the economic and technological changes noted at the beginning of this chapter pose an important challenge. The apprenticeship system grew out of the handicraft sector, and industry remains the traditional core of the German training model. However, new service-sector occupations – and indeed many of the industrial jobs that remain in Germany – depend increasingly on more general and abstract kinds of knowledge, rather than the firm- and industry-specific skills that traditionally defined the model (Mayer and Solga 2008: 1–2).[8] The increasing importance of general

---

[8] The automobile industry – the heart of German manufacturing – is indicative of these trends. Fully one-quarter of all employees at the largest Mercedes-Benz assembly plant (in Sindelfingen, Germany) work in the research and development department (Lamparter 2012: 22).

skills raises new issues for CMEs like Germany with training systems organized around firm-sponsored training.

The German system remains wildly popular among all the major stakeholders. In fact, it is hard to think of another political-economic institution to which all the relevant parties – business and labor, Social Democrats and Christian Democrats – are as committed as the VET system. Ongoing reforms over the past twenty years have responded to new technologies and market challenges, and there are in Germany many signs of successful adaptation. Despite its obvious and continuing strengths, however, the model is now bedeviled with a set of challenges that have led many longtime observers to worry about its future (Stratmann 1994; Baethge 1999; Troltsch 2005; Ulrich 2005). The most important recent problems do not concern the quality of apprentice training in Germany (which is high and ever-rising), but have instead revolved around the quantity of in-plant training opportunities.

The dominant mode of change, similar to that in industrial relations, has been toward dualization. As in industrial relations, in training policy too we observe an intensification of cooperation within the industrial core and strong cooperation to adapt the traditional model to new challenges. A part of that adaptation has involved innovations to broaden the content of training and, with that, often to lengthen training as well. Such ongoing upgrading of training has done a great deal to shore up the traditional model and to maintain its attractiveness to German youth.

However, these same measures have driven an increase in the costs to firms of training, and with that, also a decline in firm participation. This is true in manufacturing, where small firms have dropped out of the system, and in the service sector where traditional apprenticeship has not taken root to the same extent as in industry. Shortages in training slots in recent years have produced a rationing of apprenticeship as some youth land training slots that segue (as before) into stable long-term employment, while others find themselves trapped in various transitional programs that lead neither to a proper apprenticeship nor to stable employment (Busemeyer and Iversen 2012; Thelen and Busemeyer 2012). Moreover, the long-standing underdevelopment in Germany of continuing (as opposed to initial) vocational education and training means that youth who fail to land an in-firm training slot cannot count on a second chance for later training. On the contrary: early disadvantages in the German training market are compounded over time, as those who fail to secure a high-quality apprenticeship at the start of their careers are also more likely to land in jobs that offer fewer chances for later skill development.

Shoring Up the Model

The basic features of the German vocational training system are relatively easy to summarize. Skill formation in Germany takes place through practical firm-based training, accompanied by a more theoretical school component.

The system is strongly collectivist in that employers train not narrowly and for their own needs but broadly and to standards that are set nationally by committees composed of representatives of business, unions, and the state. These features distinguish the German system both from the liberal model – where training is mostly on the job and company-specific – and from more school-based systems like that in much of Scandinavia. Unlike in more segmentalist systems such as Japan where training is mostly accomplished in large firms, small firms have traditionally played a very strong role in German apprenticeship training.

The German system is entirely voluntary in that firms do not have to take apprentices and there is no training levy for those who do not (as there is in Denmark, discussed later in this chapter). Firms that do take apprentices, however, are required to train to nationally defined standards with respect to both the quality and content of training. The resulting standardization of training around well-defined occupational profiles has generated a relatively plentiful stock of skilled workers that has so famously facilitated the kind of high-skill, high-value-added production regime for which Germany is now well known (Streeck 1989). Organized labor has traditionally played an important role not just in administering and overseeing this system, but also in pushing for ever broader skill profiles. For example, in the 1970s and 1980s, unions succeeded in reducing the number of shorter two-year apprenticeships, insisting on more elaborate three-year training periods for most occupations (Busemeyer 2009; Thelen and Busemeyer 2012).

The German training system is wholeheartedly embraced by manufacturing and, as already mentioned, it also enjoys wide popularity in society as a whole. As a result, there has typically been strong cooperation across party lines and also across the class divide to implement reforms over the years that are designed to update skill profiles and create whole new training programs for emerging occupations. It is not hard to find many signs of successful adaptation of the traditional model to technological and market developments that call for new types of skills. Ongoing updating and the need for broader and more theoretical skill profiles resulted in an increase in the average length of training from under thirty-four months in the mid-1980s to close to thirty-seven months since 1990 (BIBB 2005: Figure 7.1).

Massive changes in the quality and content of training in Germany over the last few decades have been achieved in reform waves marked more by consensus than conflict between the social partners. In 1984, even as the union and employers' association for the metalworking sector were locked in a major conflict over working time reduction, they still managed to negotiate a complete reorganization of the occupational structure in the metal and electrical industries. The reforms consolidated forty-five previously separate occupations into sixteen new ones with broader and more theoretical training, and also introduced several new forty-two-month apprenticeships. Further reforms in 2005 merged several of the sixteen separate occupations together to form five basic occupations, each with broader training (Bosch and Charest 2008: 434). This later change reflected the increased abstract competencies that are now required even of manual workers, and it accompanied the collective bargaining round described in Chapter 2 that combined the wage scales of blue- and white-collar workers.

Other major reforms have taken place since the late 1990s in which the tri-partite National Vocational Training Institute has updated training ordinances on a wide scale (see, e.g., BMBF 2000: 8ff; 2001: 145ff). This has involved the modernization of hundreds of other occupations and the creation of dozens of wholly new occupational profiles such as in ICT. Between 2000 and 2005, seventy-six revamped and twenty-six new occupations were recognized, with over thirty in 2004 alone and dozens more the following year, making this the "biggest modernization push since 1969 when the Vocational Training Law was passed" (BMBF 2005: 2). Of the 344 training courses currently offered in the German apprenticeship system, 43 are wholly new occupations intro-duced in the last decade and 171 have been modernized to adapt the training to changes in technology and the job market (Wiesmann 2012).

The rise of the service sector and the blurring of the line between blue- and white-collar work – and indeed between specific and general skills – poses special challenges in Germany since the secondary education system is premised on early tracking of students and a relatively sharp (although not impermeable) divide between vocational and academic tracks.[9] Traditionally, manufacturing drew on youth from the more vocationally oriented tracks. These included pupils coming out of the lower secondary schools (*Hauptschule* pupils, who leave school at around age fifteen), who often made their way to employment in larger firms after completing an apprenticeship in a small handicraft shop, as well as pupils from the alternative intermediate secondary schools (*Realschule* pupils, who leave school at age sixteen). Such students have virtually no chance of landing an apprenticeship in service sectors like banking, insurance, media services, or even many health care professions, which recruit almost exclusively out of the upper secondary track (Gymnasium).

But even within manufacturing, firms now demand heightened competencies and draw increasingly on students with university-entry certification. Accord-ing to the leading expert on the German automobile industry, Ulrich Jürgens

---

[9] While in principle there are pathways from the lower primary and secondary tracks that lead to higher education, in practice the gulf is wide and not easily overcome. Powell and Solga (2011) show that only about 1% of students in higher education do not have the *Abitur*, largely because it is difficult to get credit for education and learning outside the usual track (56, 59). In general, school segregation continues to be seen as broadly legitimate in Germany (55). Partly as a result of continued early tracking, but also no doubt of the continued attraction of the VET system, Germany lags behind most of Europe in enrollments in higher education (see Figure 3.1). In 2008, only 28% of Germans between ages thirty and thirty-four held tertiary certificates (which includes professional schools, technical colleges, and universities). This is one of the lowest rates in Europe and far below the European Commission's (EC) target of 40%.

(pers. comm.), about half of all Volkswagen employees in Germany completed the *Abitur* (the academic-track high school credential). Competing both with universities and with service sector alternatives, industrial firms have also sought ways to enhance the attractiveness of apprenticeship for otherwise more academically inclined youth. One such initiative involves new forms of collaboration among firms and between employers and unions with institutions of higher education to create hybrid educational institutions at the intersection of higher education and traditional firm-based vocational training. These institutions travel under different names in different states (e.g., vocational colleges or dual study programs).

These dual study programs were originally piloted in Baden-Württemberg in the late 1960s when leading companies were concerned that newly created pathways to university would reduce interest among youth for more traditional firm-sponsored training.[10] Daimler-Benz, Bosch, and Standard Elektrik Lorenz co-sponsored the first vocational academy as an alternative to the classic university model, in a sense adapting and absorbing elements of that model into the apprenticeship system itself by sponsoring their own theoretical training. More recently, existing universities of applied sciences (*Fachhochschulen*) in some regions have begun offering dual study programs in collaboration with local firms and based on a curriculum that firms help to shape.[11] Participating firms can thus influence the training of their higher technical personnel, exercising extensive input into the course curriculum as well as full control over the practical component.

Applicants cannot enter dual study programs directly, but instead must be hired as apprentices by cooperating firms. The training itself involves rotating shifts of about three months each in theoretically oriented classes and practical experience in their training firm. This model is popular among academically inclined youth (and their parents) because it allows them to earn, simultaneously, both a recognized higher education degree – typically a bachelor of engineering or science – and a vocational certificate (Kupfer and Startz 2011). Unlike their peers in university, dual study trainees are paid apprentice wages, and they are also often hired by the firm after graduation. For their part, firms like the system because it keeps vocational training attractive for high-achieving youth and allows the employer to get to know the apprentice before possibly hiring him or her on a permanent contract. Through such programs, firms counteract academic drift in the sense of losing high achieving youth to the university, and also are able to complement the student's theoretical training with practical firm-based experience so that those who complete their degrees are immediately in a position to contribute to the company. The absolute

[10] This was in a context in which changes to the education system resulting from the student movement were aimed at democratizing education in Germany by softening the strict system of secondary school tracking.
[11] See also www.ausbildungplus.de, which provides a nationwide overview of dual study courses.

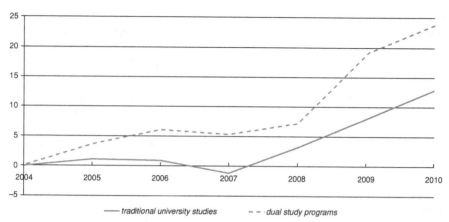

FIGURE 3.2. Relative Increase in Dual Study Students versus Traditional University Study, 2004–2010. *Note*: solid line: traditional university studies; dotted line: dual study students *Source*: Völk (2011) based on data from BIBB AusbildungPlus 2004–2010 Statistisches Bundesamt.

number of dual apprenticeships remains modest, with just over 50,000 students registered in such programs in 2010. However, this type of program has become extremely attractive, and even more so after the 2008 financial crisis. In fact, in the 2000s, dual study courses have been growing at a significantly faster rate than traditional university studies, as Figure 3.2 shows.

In 1982, Baden-Württemberg was the first state to embrace vocational colleges as fully recognized institutions in the state's tertiary education system. Since that time, the basic model has spread to other states in response to growing firm interest in offering such courses of study (see especially Baethge et al. 2007).[12] The fields most prominently represented by such institutions include the so-called MINT subjects – mathematics, computer science, natural sciences, and engineering (BIBB 2011b).[13] Engineering alone accounts for a quarter of all such courses of study (Graf 2011). If anything, the Bologna process (the creation of a bachelor's degree) has promoted these forms since in the German context a bachelor's degree is not taken to mean a liberal arts education but a degree that often involves greater practical orientation.

Drift on the Periphery

These developments and innovations all speak to the will – shared by all the relevant parties – to collaborate to adapt the traditional system to keep pace with new technologies and market trends. Taken together, these efforts go

[12] In the meantime as well, *Fachhochschulen* in more regions have begun offering dual study programs in collaboration with local firms.

[13] The acronym comes from the German: Mathematik, Informatik, Naturwissenschaften, Technik.

far toward refuting the image of the German system as rigid or inflexible (cf. Herrigel 1996). On the contrary, the consensus is that the quality of German training is high and only getting better (Bosch and Charest 2008: especially 443–444). The result has been that the demand for firm-sponsored training among German youth remains extremely robust, even among higher achieving youth. In 2008, about 33 percent of school leavers with a university entrance qualification were headed to VET and not higher education (Powell and Solga 2011: 59). In 2011, more German youth signed apprenticeship contracts than enrolled in university (570,000 apprenticeships vs. 520,000 university enroll-ments) (Wiesmann 2012). About 20 percent of the university graduate cohort in Germany held not one but two degrees, having first gotten a vocational certification before going on to university. The dual study programs described in the previous section are especially attractive; a study in Baden-Württemberg found that the students who were opting for such programs had higher *Abitur* scores than those who were going on to university (Wiarda 2011).

The problem in Germany is not the quality or the continued attractiveness of firm-based training. It is rather the quantity of training slots on offer. The number of apprenticeship slots offered by firms has trended downward since the early 1990s and typically drops most in times of recession. This has peri-odically produced a serious imbalance between continued strong demand on the part of youth for firm-based training on the one hand, and the number of training places offered by firms on the other. The extent of the problem is itself hotly contested in the literature.[14] Official statistics tend to suggest a closer fit between the demand for and the supply of apprenticeship slots, but experts point out that these figures understate the problem by removing apprenticeship-seekers who wind up in some "alternative arrangement" whether by choice or by default. Based on survey data, estimates by Joachim Ulrich (2008) of the Federal Institute for Vocational Education and Training (BIBB) suggest a sig-nificant and growing imbalance, so that by the 2006, there were only about 75 training slots for each 100 youth seeking such a slot (9). In any event and no matter what the measures, no one disputes that there were significant shortfalls in training opportunities beginning in the mid-1990s and continuing well into the 2000s.

The causes of this decline have been explored elsewhere (Culpepper and Thelen 2007; Thelen and Busemeyer 2012), but two factors figure prominently. The first is the secular decline of manufacturing, which has been the traditional core of the German training system. The service sector (the only real source of employment growth in Germany) has yet to embrace the traditional dual system of training on the same scale as in manufacturing.[15] The apprentice ratio

[14] As many observers have pointed out, the official statistics tend to understate the problem. For the official statistics, see BIBB (2011a). For a discussion of what the official statistics capture and miss, see Thelen (2007a: 251).

[15] The system is quite well established in a few sectors (notably banking) but much less so in many other service sectors (see, for example, Quack et al. 1995; Quack and Hildebrandt 1996).

(i.e., the number of trainees to total employees) in the metal and electronics industry stayed relatively high over the late 1990s and early 2000s despite an overall decline in jobs in the sector, at eleven or twelve apprentices for every 100 employees. But in primary and secondary services, the figure is much lower, between three and five apprentices for every 100 employees (Werner 2004: 59).

As Anderson and Hassel (2012) point out, there is no inherent reason why apprenticeship cannot be adapted to the service sector and indeed some areas – notably banking – corroborate this point. However, they also note that "there are some indications that school-based training systems might fit more easily with the skill requirements of service sector firms and therefore enhance service sector employment" (188). They cite recent research that establishes a strong link between rising educational attainment and employment in services. They cite Iversen on service-sector firms' particular reliance on "social skills" and they echo Estevez-Abe's findings about the disadvantages faced by women in training regimes that rely on firm-sponsored training (188). In the end, they conclude that "school-based systems have a distinct advantage over firm-based systems in the provision of general skills that are so central to the service economy" (191).

A second factor is the cost of training itself. The same pressures that have driven the laudatory and successful upgrading of apprenticeship training described in the previous section have also, of course, made it more expensive for firms to provide such training. Small firms, including in the handicraft sector (the historic core of the German apprenticeship system) have an especially hard time meeting the higher standards and broader skill profiles and have dropped out of the system in very significant numbers (Steedman and Wagner 2005: 21–22; Thelen and Busemeyer 2012).[16] But even large firms in the manufacturing core felt the pinch, and this has led to a stratification in training in which some apprentices are placed in full three- or four-year apprenticeships while others are offered less elaborate two-year slots more tailored to the firms' own needs (Neubäumer et al. 2011; Thelen and Busemeyer 2012). Unions oppose moves such as this because they have an interest in broader training and continued high skill portability (Solga 2009: 18). Nonetheless, the number of two-year apprenticeships has grown, and far more rapidly than traditional three- to four-year training slots (Thelen and Busemeyer 2012: 83).

The biggest problem in the German training system today is access to high-quality training, especially for lower SES groups. Apprentices in industry, commerce, public services and the free professions are increasingly recruited from

---

[16] The cost of training rose across the board but as Steedman and Wagner (2005) point out, other firms did not experience a similarly large net increase because they were able to realize higher returns to training by incorporating trainees more into production. In the handicraft sector, similar productivity increases were not possible, since training was already largely accomplished within the work environment (21).

upper secondary schools, and some occupations (e.g., banking and ICT) now de facto require a general higher education entry certificate as a prerequisite for being offered a training contract (Powell and Solga 2011: 56). The most coveted types of firm-sponsored apprenticeships (e.g., the dual study courses described in the previous section) are very expensive to maintain, and when firms do offer these options it is just to a select few. Between 2004 and 2010, the number of different dual study courses on offer rose by 50 percent, but the number of students accepted to these programs rose just 23 percent. As Kupfer and Startz (2011) note, "This suggests a growing differentiation and specialization in the subject-related content of dual study courses, coupled with only very modest expansion of the number of places offered" (30).

Increased competition for firm-sponsored training severely disadvantages youth at the lower end of the educational spectrum. As noted previously, apprenticeship traditionally operated as a path to secure and relatively well-paid jobs even for youth from the lower secondary tracks. Pupils with an intermediate secondary certificate (*Realschulabschluss*) now have far fewer choices than before, and in most states the situation is dire for those with a lower secondary certificate (*Hauptschulabschluss*). Such pupils used to land training spots in handicraft firms, but declining participation in training among such firms now means that fully 50 percent of youth who leave school with this lowest educational level fail to land any in-firm training slot at all. The *Hauptschule* educational track is becoming such a dead end that Chancellor Merkel recently mooted the idea of abolishing it altogether by merging it with the *Realschule* to form a single *Oberschule*. But small manufacturing firms in Bavaria and Baden-Württemberg continue to draw on this track for apprentices and they rushed to the defense of the *Hauptschule*. The proposal also ran into stiff opposition within Chancellor Merkel's own Christian Democratic Union (CDU); party whip Peter Hauk vowed to "fight for the preservation of the system" (Führin and Pfister 2011: 41).

In fact, almost any initiative that is designed to equalize opportunities within the context of Germany's highly stratified secondary school system has become a kind of third rail issue politically. Even actors on the Left are loath to touch this, since parents of children in the higher education tracks furiously defend against de-tracking. Ironically, and as Edelstein (n.d.) points out, "the education expansion of the 1960s and 70s result[ed] in a broadened support base for the Gymnasium." The middle classes are now inside the system, and this has been "especially consequential for the school politics of the Social Democrats (SPD), the traditional proponent of the integrated model, parts of whose clientele had now become deeply invested in the [existing three-track] system" (14). A recent initiative in Hamburg – jointly sponsored by the Greens and the conservative CDU – underscores the difficulty of reform. The idea was to extend the time that all children are together from the fourth to the sixth grade – a modest proposal that still left ample room for tracking. However, middle-class parents were wary of any change that might compromise the quality of education for their Gymnasium-bound children, and mobilized to defeat the proposal in a referendum (Darren and Levitz 2010).[17]

In the meantime, students coming out of the lower educational tracks in most states in recent years have faced great difficulty in landing high-quality firm-based apprenticeships. Acknowledging the problem, the German government created a state-financed "transitional" system (*Übergangssystem*) for youth who are waiting for a normal in-firm training slot to open up. Rather than a single unified institution or policy, the transition system consists of a wide variety of different measures and programs, "a patchwork of different kinds of opportunities, with different target groups, different sponsors, and different responsibilities and goals" (Baethge 1999: 50). What unites these programs is that they specifically do not lead to any vocational certification and operate instead as a holding pattern as these participants wait for "real" in-firm apprenticeships to open up. Initially conceived as a temporary measure, Germany's transition system grew steadily – and faster than any other segment of the training market – so that in the mid-2000s nearly as many youth were in the transition system as in a normal dual apprenticeship (BIBB 2011a: 31–32; Thelen and Busemeyer 2012).

The development of the transition system has thus been associated with an increase and a deepening of disparities in the German training market.[18] A study commissioned by the government of Baden-Württemberg identified the specific groups most likely to wind up in the transition system, and the results are not surprising. Over 80 percent of youth who fail to achieve *Hauptschulabschluss*, the lowest school leaving certificate, and half of those with only this certificate wind up in these programs (Baethge et al. 2007: 39). Youth with "migration backgrounds" who used to find training positions and later work in the handicraft sector or industry are also over-represented in the transition system (35, 39, 42–43). The youth who land there are thus doubly disadvantaged, shunted into second-class training and stigmatized later in the job market as well.[19]

One obvious solution to shortfalls in the number of private-sector training slots would be to introduce full-time school-based VET as an alternative to firm-based training, with Denmark (discussed later in this chapter) serving as a possible model.[20] However, this option has never enjoyed much support in Germany. In the 1970s, other countries with strong in-company apprenticeship (i.e., Austria) moved to upgrade and expand school-based alternatives, and in

---

[17] I thank Benjamin Edelstein for drawing this example to my attention.

[18] Baethge et al. (2007) note that only about 40% of those in the transition system ever make it into a "real" apprenticeship or skill appropriate job (51).

[19] Young women, by contrast, typically stay in school longer and also do better in school than their male counterparts. Accordingly, fewer girls fall into the transition system and are then also far less likely to become unemployed than young men.

[20] Some occupations, like nursing, have always involved school-based training. The numbers of trainees in such occupations/training has increased since the 1990s as a result of the shift to services, but it is still much smaller than the dual system (Ulrich 2008: 5).

Germany as well the 1970s saw a movement for reform (see especially Buse-meyer 2009: 79ff; also Thelen 2004: 240–269). Proponents of reform argued in favor of democratizing VET, and sought the full integration of vocational training into the public school system, or alternatively and more modestly, an increase in the school component in relation to the dominant firm-based com-ponent. These proposals were vigorously opposed by the CDU and employers' associations, who rejected them as unwelcome revisions to a training system that was widely perceived to be working well. Reprising battles that had been played out decades earlier, organized employers rallied against excessive state intervention (*Verstaatlichung*) as well as an overly "bookish" approach to training (*Verschulung*).[21] They backed up these demands with a very credible threat to boycott training altogether, something that struck fear in the hearts of German policy makers, who by this time were almost wholly dependent on private-sector training (Busemeyer 2009: 86).

Another proposal at the time sought to modify the financing of vocational training by introducing a training levy through which non-training firms would help offset the costs incurred by those firms that did train. In the 1970s, the SPD managed to pass a law establishing the possibility of such a training levy under certain specified conditions.[22] However, even firms that train do not welcome state interference in these matters. Employers thus remained opposed and took the case to the Constitutional Court, where it languished before being struck down in 1980.[23] Employers, meanwhile, mobilized on their own initiative to keep the levy at bay by orchestrating a voluntary increase in the number of training slots on offer. The 1981 law that replaced the previous (overturned) legislation no longer contained the controversial financial provision. Since that time, employers have repeatedly cut short all discussion of levies – and, for that matter, school-based alternatives – by meeting complaints of shortages in training opportunities with promises (sometimes kept) to increase the number of training slots.

In the meantime, smaller birth cohorts have begun to shrink the gap between the number of training slots on offer and the number of "qualified" youth to fill them. German industry now complains of a shortage of trainees, and low-pay sectors have a hard time recruiting youth. Some firms and local chambers of commerce have responded by recruiting apprentices from Eastern Europe (e.g., Bulgaria, Poland, Hungary) (Buhse 2012).[24] But the imbalance is partly a

---

[21] For earlier conflicts along these same lines in the late nineteenth and early twentieth centuries, see Thelen (2004: chapter 2).

[22] Namely, if the supply of apprentice slots did not exceed the number of applicants by at least 12.5%.

[23] Not on the substance but on a procedural issue (a full account of the episode appears in Thelen 2004: 265–266).

[24] Immigration has also become a strategy for coping with shortages in higher-end skills. German firms now seek to capitalize on high unemployment in struggling neighboring countries like Spain, offering young trained engineers salaries that are twice what they could get at home (Daley and Kulish 2012).

function of weak educational attainment in Germany, as firms pass over youth they deem to be "unsuited" for training. This would explain the paradox of employer claims of apprenticeship shortages even though a very large number of German youth – more than 30 percent – are still entering the transition system (BIBB 2011a: 32). Even if demographic changes (i.e., declining youth cohorts) have eased the situation somewhat since 2005, overall the past two decades have amply exposed the weaknesses of a system such as the German one that relies so heavily on the private sector to provide access to training.

The incentives to reform the system fundamentally have if anything weakened over time. Firms currently have their pick of apprentices and do not want to compete with a school-based alternative. They continue to threaten that creating alternatives to the current apprenticeship system would prompt the private sector to stop training altogether (Solga 2009, 2010). Moreover, unions have also now come around to defend the traditional system. As Busemeyer (2009) shows, despite their support for reform proposals floated by the SPD in the 1970s, unions by the 1980s had moved to a position more closely aligned with employers in defending the traditional system (see also Ebner and Nikolai 2010; Anderson and Hassel 2012: 190). They defend firm-sponsored apprenticeship on grounds that this is the only form of training that clearly leads to stable employment, and of course, given the weakness of the alternatives, they have a point. Anderson and Hassel (2012) summarize the dim prospects for serious reform: " ... the coincidence of employers' and unions' preferences regarding the maintenance of the system is likely to continue even in the face of increasing strains in meeting the training needs of low-qualified school leavers.... In addition, the continuing weakness of the service sector is likely to help maintain the dominance of manufacturing firms in political decision-making" (190).

Other actors join in the defense of the traditional system for their own, sometimes very different, reasons. For example, those handicraft firms that continue to engage in training do not relish competing against school-based alternatives because they rely on apprentices as a cheap extra hand in production; and by the third year, apprentices are almost fully qualified but are still paid low apprentice wages. The artisanal chambers and chambers of industry and commerce, while more open to more differentiated apprenticeship models, oppose moves that would compromise their role as crucial intermediaries in the area of skill certification. Moreover, policy makers continue to code school-based vocational training as inferior, and even those forms of training that specifically involve more classroom-based learning and that blur the line between higher education and vocational training (e.g., the new dual study programs) operate within the voluntarist, private-sector-led logic of the old system (Solga 2009: 8; 2010).

The dominance of the private sector in the German training model has meant that training efforts are closely linked to developments in the labor market. Ulrich (2008: 6) documents the tight connection in Germany between the number of training slots offered by the private sector and the number of hires into full-time standard jobs with full benefits. In other words, in good times firms are hiring and also taking more apprentices. But the reverse is also true, that in economic downturns firms tend to become more conservative both in hiring and in taking trainees. In some ways, the logic is the opposite of state-sponsored active labor market politics, which are strongly countercyclical in that they respond to downturns and corresponding higher unemployment with more, not less, training.

The Underdevelopment of Continuing Vocational Education in Germany

Perhaps even more importantly, in Germany the disadvantages for those who fail to secure a high-quality in-firm apprenticeship early in their careers persist over time, since the training system is organized around a very significant front-end investment but very little adult continuing training. Crouch et al. (1999) have argued that the very strength of German apprenticeship may have contributed to the country's longstanding deficit in CVET: "It might be considered that the strength of the apprenticeship system makes this kind of skill provision less necessary since in some countries... further training is 'remedial,' compensating for the deficiencies of initial training" (145). The "perverse effect," as they note, is that Germany's high-quality system for IVET may have contributed to the underdevelopment of CVET (146).

This gap in the German system is now widely recognized, but given the relatively weak presence of the state in the training market, it is difficult to bridge. Local labor representatives can press for additional training and retraining for current employees, and firms themselves may choose to sponsor such measures when it is in their interest to do so. However, both of these mechanisms deepen dualization because by definition training goes to those workers who are already employed and highly valued. A study by Berger and Moraal (2012) notes that "firms concentrate CVET on relatively few employees, the length of training is short and the direct outlays for each are small" (382). In other countries – the Netherlands and Denmark, for example – collectively bargained branch funds support CVET on a broad scale. But such funds play a very marginal role in Germany.[25] Firms are not interested, and unions are generally not willing to make concessions on other fronts in order to push for them (382, 385–386, 389).

The absence of a strong collective framework for CVET to match that of Germany's enviable system of IVET means that continuing education and training "tends to be concentrated on those who already have a high level of skill and education" (Crouch et al. 1999: 146), with not much left for those who – for whatever reason – miss out on the opportunity for firm-based apprenticeship in the first place, nor for those workers who lose their jobs and

---

[25] While there exist collectively bargained funds for training in the temporary agency sector, Berger and Moraal (2012) note that the "fund model" is generally rejected by German employers and not seen as an option for major unions such as the metalworkers (389).

have to transition into wholly new jobs in different sectors. Paraphrasing Berger and Moraal's (2012) summary of the situation, in contrast to Denmark and the Netherlands – where the social partners and the state share responsibility for CVET – in Germany firms are responsible for IVET, the state for training the unemployed, and individuals themselves for CVET (383).

Dualization through Drift

Again in the area of VET, we see a pattern in Germany of an intensification of cooperation – centered especially but not exclusively within the manufacturing core – that shores up the traditional training model in important ways, while inadvertently promoting a decline in its coverage and scope. Successful adaption has thus meant dualization – a shrinking number of ever higher-quality training slots for some, coupled with a growing number of youth with poor training options. The traditional German apprenticeship system has succeeded brilliantly in absorbing and channeling the transition to more theoretical skills, in the process also blurring the line between VET and higher education. But access to the most attractive training slots is mostly out of reach for youth from lower educational tracks. The public transition system stabilizes the traditional system by soaking up demand for training slots in ways that create the illusion that the training market has cleared, but without addressing the core problems created by the country's deep dependence on private-sector voluntarism to deliver a key collective good (Solga 2009: 12).

The German system has thus "flipped" in its distributive effects over the past two decades. Previously heralded as a system in which firms were deeply involved in performing critical public functions, now the private sector has become a key bottleneck. Once celebrated as a system that provided opportunities for working-class youth to move into stable and well-paid work, the system now increasingly sorts winners and losers at a very early stage and in ways that persist throughout a person's career. Manufacturing firms and some high-end services (i.e., banking) are still invested in the system, and high-achieving students coming out of the upper secondary track have more options than ever before. Low-achieving students, by contrast, can no longer count on an apprenticeship as an entry point into secure and relatively well-paid employment. And the underdevelopment of CVET means that early advantages (or disadvantages) tend to be reinforced over time, entrenching dualism.

EDUCATION AND TRAINING IN DENMARK

Among the Nordic political economies, Denmark is most similar to Germany with respect to the structure of IVET (Crouch et al. 1999: 139). Other Scandinavian countries rejected firm-sponsored training in the 1940s and 1950s as inherently biased toward employers, but Denmark maintained a strong tradition of apprenticeship. In 2009, 35 percent of the labor force over sixteen years old had completed some form of apprenticeship education.[26] As in Germany, youth who opt into a vocational track enter a training system that combines school-based learning with considerable in-company training.[27] Moreover, as in Germany, Danish unions and employer associations are heavily involved and equally represented in national-level governance boards that monitor the training and testing through which youth earn nationally recognized credentials.[28]

Despite the many similarities, however, the German and Danish training systems have evolved along different tracks in recent years. The dominant trend in Germany, as we saw, is toward increasing dualization, as some youth continue to benefit from ever higher-quality firm-sponsored training opportunities, while a growing minority is shunted into a distinctly second-class public system on the other. The Danish system also exhibits some insider-outsider dynamics (Martin and Knudsen 2010), but in this case the state is heavily involved and since the 1980s has pushed aggressively to expand access to training at all levels, dismantling traditional boundaries: between IVET and CVET, between blue- and white-collar training, between training opportunities for skilled and unskilled workers, and between training offerings for the employed and the unemployed. Many of these reforms are distinctly liberalizing, promoting exactly the more flexible, modular approach to training and credentialing that the guardians of the German training system have often sought to resist. In contrast to the German pattern of updating the traditional occupational model (*Berufskonzept*) – in which training is still heavily front-loaded and based on following a single (albeit now broader) vocational path for a whole career – the Danish training system supports much more "fluid career pathways and professional identities" (Schulze-Cleven 2009: 225). Through heavy state sponsorship and what some observers call a "radical individualization" of training paths, training policies in Denmark "promote opportunities [for workers] to broaden [their] skill set over the course of a lifetime" (Grollmann et al. 2003: 11; Lassen et al. 2006: 9; Nelson 2012: 181).

Shared Histories and Sources of Divergence

In Denmark as in Germany, the survival of firm-sponsored apprenticeship training into the modern period has much to do with the survival of the guilds

---

[26] http://www.da.dk/bilag/AMR09%2CArbejdsmarkedsrapport%202009.pdf (page 10), with thanks to Mikkel Mailand for the reference.

[27] In Denmark, generally two-thirds of an apprentice's time is spent in the company (Cort 2002: 21).

[28] In Germany, the national Bundesinstitut für Berufsbildung (BIBB) sits at the top of the governance structure and has equal representation of unions and employers. In Denmark the equivalent entity is the in Rådet for de grundlæggende Erhvervsrettede Uddannelser (NEA 2008: 4). In Denmark, separate national trade committees provide advice on specific VET qualifications relevant to their sector (there are about 120 of these), then local training centers assist vocational colleges with local planning of programs. Providers include both enterprises and vocational colleges (NEA 2008: 4).

through the nineteenth century and the strong parapublic role assigned to arti-sanal associations in organizing and administering in-firm training in the early industrial period (Thelen 2007b; Martin 2012). However, important differ-ences emerged over time, especially as a result of differences in the organiza-tion of labor interests in the two countries. Already in the 1920s and 1930s, the organizational separation of skilled and unskilled workers into different unions in Denmark created "dynamic tensions" and "constructive competi-tion" in training institutions (Sørensen and Jensen 1988: 123; Schulze-Cleven 2009: 222–232; see also Kristensen 2006: 314). These differences have contin-ued to shape more recent reform trajectories in IVET and, especially in CVET. I address each of these in turn.

Initial Vocational Education and Training
Both Germany and Denmark entered the postwar period with strong traditions of firm-sponsored apprentice training. In the 1950s, Danish Social Democrats shared with their counterparts elsewhere in Scandinavia the goal of advancing social integration and promoting equal opportunity for youth regardless of class background through the introduction of "comprehensive" schools that com-bined vocational and academic tracks. But as in Germany, firm-based training was well entrenched and enjoyed the support not just of organized business but also of Denmark's skilled unions. When the Social Democrats failed in a bid to extend comprehensive schools, they "shifted course to expand the general skill component of VET" and to assign the state a larger role in vocational schooling (Nelson 2012: 182, 193–195). Thus, instead of aligning vocational and aca-demic tracks more closely as, for example, in Sweden, the Danish government presided over a vast expansion of VET.

The resulting "massification of VET" (Nelson 2012: 192) occurred in a context in which industrial firms were starved for labor, and had turned to recruiting farmers and women, the majority of whom "had only a little pre-vious schooling" (Cort 2002). State initiatives in the 1950s and 1960s sup-ported the upgrading of skills among these groups through changes affecting IVET, and through the introduction of new avenues to acquire credentials through CVET (addressed in the next section). Whereas initial training had been dominated entirely by master apprenticeship, the government in 1956 enhanced the school-based component by mandating day-time instruction at public vocational schools (as opposed to previous after-work courses) as an integral part of apprenticeship (Sørensen and Jensen 1988: 54; Nelson 2012: 192). In addition, new, more specialized apprenticeships were introduced "in connection with the ever-increasing inclusion of unskilled labour in the indus-trial workforce at the end of the 1950s, as part of the major change-over from the society dominated by agriculture and handicrafts to an industry-dominated society" (Sørensen and Jensen 1988: 54; also Nelson 2012: 192). In other words, in exactly the same period that Germany's industrial unions were successfully insisting on longer training for all workers (and presiding over a decline in two-year apprenticeships), Denmark was moving in the opposite direction – inaugurating two-year programs alongside regular four-year apprenticeships to cover demand for semi-skilled labor in industry. Such programs addressed the interests of unskilled workers in Denmark, for whom shorter training programs created new opportunities to move into better-paid work.

Entering the more turbulent economic context of the 1970s and 1980s, there were thus already some important differences between the otherwise similar-looking Danish and German VET systems. These differences grew subsequently, and in ways that have led to two very distinct trajectories of development. Both countries relied heavily on the private sector to sponsor training, and both confronted problems of shortages in training opportunities in the recessionary context of the 1970s. In both countries, Social Democratic governments tried to reform VET to enhance the ability of the state to ensure broad access to high-quality training – but with different degrees of success. First, the Danish Social Democrats succeeded in introducing changes in the financing of firm training, including (in 1978) the imposition of a mandatory levy very similar to the one that failed in Germany. Thereafter, all Danish employers have been required to pay into the Employers' Reimbursement Scheme – *Arbejdsgivernes Elevrefusion* (AER) – based on the number of full-time workers they employ.[29] Training firms are then reimbursed on the basis of the number of apprentices they take in (Cort 2002: 24).

Second, proposals to expand the role of school-based training that were resisted by organized employers in Germany at that time succeeded in Denmark. Thus, in 1972, the Danes introduced an alternative to traditional master apprenticeship in the so-called Basic Vocational Training (EFG) that would allow students to stay in school for an additional year before moving into a shortened period of practical firm-based training of two years rather than the usual three or four (Nelson 2012: 194–196). Similar to the previous two-year apprenticeship, this idea was strongly supported by unskilled unions – especially the SiD and the KAD – but jointly opposed by organized employers and skilled unions. Firms were against the measure because it denied them a year of apprentice labor (important given the dominance in Denmark of small firms); skilled unions opposed it out of fear that it would dilute their skills monopoly. Opponents were unable to derail the legislation, but they did manage to prevent the new model from displacing master apprenticeship altogether, which was the original idea. Instead, EFG was institutionalized as a separate track, and by 1986 enrollment in VET was roughly equally divided between traditional

---

[29] Beginning in January 2013, the employer levy system for vocational education and training is called Arbejdsgivernes Uddannelsesbidrag (AUB). Employers and apprentices conclude education agreements that release wage subsidies that vary according to the apprentice's age and seniority. Thanks to Christian Ibsen for providing the information on this most recent development.

apprenticeship and the EFG system (Sørensen and Jensen 1988: 64–65, 189; Nelson 2012: 195).

Important structural reforms to IVET began to take shape after a center-right government assumed power in 1982. Incoming Prime Minister Poul Schlüter implemented policies promoting decentralization and marketization. As part of its austerity program, the government reduced spending on training and redirected AER funds to cover the firm-based component previously paid by tax financed grants (Nelson 2012: 196). Meanwhile, the minister of education (a member of the Liberal Party) sought to transform the structure and content of training. Embracing a new public management approach, he introduced more market-based incentives into the content and delivery of training (Lassen et al. 2006: 8).

Some of the most significant structural reforms to the Danish system for IVET came in 1989 with the Apprentice Act of that year, which was implemented in 1991 (Nelson 2012). This law abandoned the previous national curriculum and moved these issues to the local level in an effort to make the system more responsive to market signals. Instead of fixed national rules, local training centers would henceforth have more autonomy, and indeed were required to draw up education plans adapted to the needs of local industry and to regional labor market conditions. Government financing was also reconfigured so that vocational schools would receive funding on the basis of enrollment (the so-called taximeter system), thus spurring competition for trainees (NEA 2008: 42; also Nelson 2012: 195).[30]

When the Social Democratic Party returned to power in 1993, they did not reverse the policies of the previous center-right government but instead built on them. They launched an ambitious "education for all" program designed to increase participation in education and to enhance the attractiveness of upper secondary school attendance (Grollmann et al. 2003: 6). Some reforms softened the line between academic and vocational tracks. Up until the year 2000, students who reached the end of the lower secondary system (age sixteen) and who wanted to enter higher education had to pass final exams in a number of subjects. This requirement has now been abolished, so that all students who complete compulsory schooling (primary and lower secondary, to age sixteen) may largely choose for themselves which upper secondary path they wish to pursue (Cort 2002: 16). These steps mark the culmination of many previous attempts at enhancing accessibility to university. Since 2000, state subsidies have increased, "making Denmark one of the most affordable tertiary education systems in Europe" (Nelson 2010: 479–480).

In terms of VET, many of the changes under the Social Democrats expanded the general (as opposed to firm- or occupation-specific) content of skills while

---

[30] Meanwhile, at the level of higher education, in 1989 the government established both a voucher program for tertiary education and an "open education" system to expand opportunities for entry into it.

also increasing individualization in their acquisition. A 1999 law (implemented in 2001) that parallels the reforms in Germany described earlier in this chapter involved a reduction in the number of separate specializations from which apprentices select – from eighty-three groups down to seven broader occupations, although later this was expanded again to twelve (NEA 2008: 42). Unlike in Germany, however, at the same time that the content of training paths was broadened, the acquisition of skills was rendered more individualized. Apprentices now work with "contact teachers" to develop an individual plan for what skills they will acquire and how. The role of these contact teachers is "comparable to a tutor who accompanies the individual trainees throughout the course of training and advises them with respect to their individual education plan" (Grollmann et al. 2003: 12). Apprentices maintain a personal education "logbook" to document competencies as they acquire them "in a kind of portfolio approach" (Grollmann et al. 2003: 12). This unbundling of a singular occupation into component parts – including recognition for the acquisition of partial qualifications (Cort 2002: 22) – remains a very contested issue in Germany.

Another set of reforms undertaken by the Social Democrats addressed shortages in firm-sponsored training by upgrading the status of school-based IVET. In Germany, as we saw, the state-sponsored transition system is basically a holding pattern for youth who fail to land a firm-sponsored training slot, and does not offer formal certification. By contrast, since 1993 the Danish system offers young people who fail to secure an in-firm apprenticeship the chance to complete their training in school-based trade courses (Nielsen 1995: 55). Students who enter into a training agreement with the vocational college instead of a firm are "obliged to continue applying for relevant training placements at enterprises," but if they are unsuccessful they can stay in the classroom and receive full certification on completion anyway (CEDEFOP 2012: 26).

Firm-based apprenticeship is still seen as superior to school-based vocational training, and it continues to dominate – in 2010, there were 73,014 firm-based apprenticeship contracts, as against just 3,677 school apprenticeships.[31] Similar to Germany, firms cherry-pick the youth they deem "most qualified," so children with migration backgrounds are over-represented in the school-based system in Denmark as they are in the German transition system, and the drop-out rate is higher than with firm-based training. However, unlike in Germany, the duration and content of the school path and the company path are the same, and both lead to vocational certification in Denmark (Cort 2002: 22; NEA 2008: 37–38).[32] Moreover, and again unlike Germany, the Danish

---

[31] http://www.uvm.dk/Service/Statistik/Statistik-om-erhvervsuddannelserne/~/media/UVM/Filer/Udd/Erhverv/PDF11/110510_aarsstatistik_for_praktikpladsomraadet_2010.ashx (table, page 6).

[32] The growing importance of the school-based track ultimately required a recalibration in funding. As noted, the AER funds traditionally provided the compensation to apprentices for the

government provides significant financial incentives to firms to encourage them to take apprentices in economic downturns. For example, after the recent financial crisis the state was paying about 10,000 euros per apprentice position (Nelson 2012: 184). A representative of the peak employers' association DA confirms that these subsidies play a key role in encouraging firms to train (interview, 2009).

In Germany, as we saw, the vocational track remains very popular, including among academically inclined youth. This is partly the consequence of the upgrading of training documented in the last section. In Denmark, by contrast, the vocational track as a whole is still more solidly focused on lower and working classes. While the quality of training remains high, middle- and upper-middle-class youth tend to gravitate in larger numbers toward more academic tracks. One sees these signs of stronger academic drift in Denmark as compared to Germany in Figure 3.1. While the number of Danish youth in academic tracks and vocational tracks is currently about equal, the former is trending up and the latter trending down.

The Danish training system has its own problems, and as Martin and Knudsen (2010) have noted, also promotes some insider-outsider dynamics by "forg[ing] barriers to the easy incorporation of marginal low-skill workers into training" (347). The problem they identify is similar to that described for Germany, namely that the very strengths of the training system produce a "mismatch between the educational needs of the low-skilled workers and the available training programs" (354, 357). Lengthy apprentice programs "create a programmatic hurdle for those who need or want fewer skills than are offered by these expansive programs" (357). Firms that want fewer skills are not willing to sponsor costly training, and the existing programs often overshoot what low-skill workers themselves think they need and want. In this way, Denmark's high quality initial training may "enlarge the gulf between core and periphery workers" (347). This gap is felt most strongly among ethnic minorities, and as in Germany becomes more acute in economic downturns. For example, after the financial crisis, ethnic minorities had a much more difficult time landing a firm-sponsored training slot.[33]

Reforms in the late 2000s have sought to address these issues in several ways – by offering the possibility of partial qualifications specifically for weaker students, by implementing reforms that give credit for prior learning through work experience, and by inaugurating so-called new apprenticeships as an alternative path for those with lower aptitude and interest in theory (allowing

---

time they spent away from the firm (in classes) and the increase in non-firm-based training under the new law put pressure on this system. So in 2004 the state took over this cost in exchange for increased employer funding for continuing education and training (Lassen et al. 2006: 33).

[33] See http://www.ae.dk/analyse/indvandrere-efterkommere-har-langt-svaerere-ved-finde-praktik plads. In the previous (low-unemployment) years of 2000–2008, the numbers were more favorable, with success rates well over 50% (Mikkel Mailand, pers. comm.).

them to forego lengthy classroom instruction and proceed directly to practical experience, see CEDEFOP 2012: 22, 31). Such initiatives have encountered much more resistance in Germany, where unions still vigorously defend a more holistic and unified approach and have been skeptical of modularization as "watering down" apprenticeships. Their argument is that rather than reduce the content and length of training to fit what low-skill firms think they want and need, training programs should lift low-skill workers beyond what their jobs require (Streeck 1989).

Adult Education and Continuing Vocational Education and Training

Most importantly, Denmark has emerged as a leader in exactly the area where Germany is a laggard, namely CVET for adults. In sharp contrast to Germany, CVET in Denmark is strongly institutionalized, flexible, easily accessed, and generously supported by the state.

Contemporary differences in this regard again have their roots in differences in the politics of skills and training that go back to the Golden Era. While Denmark's skilled unions were already deeply involved in overseeing apprenticeship by the 1930s, the country's unskilled workers – organized separately – were blocked out of the training system altogether. Tensions between unions representing skilled and unskilled workers predate World War II, when unskilled male workers "realized that to compete with craft workers for jobs they had to upgrade their skills" (Kristensen 2006: 300). Attempts in the 1940s by the Danish Social Democrats to shorten training periods in order to open the traditional apprenticeship system to the unskilled foundered on "fierce resistance" from unions of journeymen and master craftsmen alike. But unskilled unions were able nonetheless to press successfully for a second-best solution through the introduction of evening courses at local Work Technical Schools, through which their members could "prepare themselves to take over the jobs normally held by the skilled" (315).

In the context of labor market shortages in the 1950s and 1960s, the government expanded opportunities for adult unskilled workers to acquire skills in what would become the seeds of an extensive system for CVET. Building out from the evening classes model instituted in 1940 for non-apprenticed workers, the Social Democrats worked with unskilled unions to found full-fledged vocational schools for specialized unskilled and semi-skilled workers. Beginning in 1960, state-run Labor Market Vocational Training Centers (AMUs) offered continuing training for working adults, with a very large share of the costs of training (85 percent) borne directly by the state (Sørensen and Jensen 1988: 57). These institutions were put under the jurisdiction of the Ministry of Labor rather than the Ministry of Education, and they soon "became an important tool in overall labor market policy" (Cort 2002: 25).

AMU courses – publically funded and available to all – introduced training possibilities that were very different from the traditional apprenticeship system and aimed at a completely different clientele. This training "consisted of modular courses of a number of weeks' duration" (typically one to six weeks) (Sørensen and Jensen 1988: 55). Courses were specifically designed in a way that allowed workers – including married women – to acquire skills flexibly. Unskilled workers were allowed to acquire certification gradually by combining "a number of courses that, aggregated with their work experience, would lead to a formal recognition as skilled workers and thus make them eligible for the training offered to the latter" (Kristensen 2006: 300).

These developments accommodated industrial employers' voracious appetite for labor in the Golden Era of postwar growth. They were actively supported by the unskilled workers' unions, who had an interest in expanding their members' access to training and with that to higher-skilled, higher-paid positions in the labor market. These were also – one must emphasize – achieved against intense opposition by skilled workers whose monopoly on skills they compromised. In fact, the institutional separation of the two systems – IVET co-administered by skilled unions and CVET for unskilled unions – set up a competition that would spur continuing education and training in Denmark forward and in ways that help to explain "the fortuitously precocious institutionalization of lifelong learning within the Danish VET system" (Nelson 2012: 181).

The government adopted the same governance structure for these new training institutions as for the traditional apprenticeship model, namely self-management by the social partners with state coordination and financing. The "decisive difference," though, was that in these cases employers negotiated not with skilled unions but with unskilled unions – the SiD and the KAD (Sørensen and Jensen 1988: 56; see also Mailand 2009: 6; Nelson 2012). In fact, the 1960 law that created the AMUs "was regarded by [these unions] . . . as a triumph for a principle of equality, i.e., the winning of a right to basic vocational training for those who had generally been discriminated against with training by society" (Sørensen and Jensen 1988: 89). Unskilled unions in fact referred to the specialized schools as "our schools" (58).[34]

Since the 1990s, important changes have also occurred in the area of CVET. Similar to the changes in IVET discussed in the previous section, these involve a flexibilization of training on three fronts – further modularization of training offerings in order to facilitate the flexible accumulation of skills and credentials, easing of traditional boundaries between IVET and CVET and between training for youth and for adults, and a dismantling of boundaries between training for the employed and unemployed.

---

[34] The institutionalization of opportunities for unskilled workers to upgrade or acquire new skills fuelled demands by skilled unions for parallel arrangements for their members. Thus, in 1965 legislation was passed that opened opportunities for continuing training and skill upgrading for skilled workers too. The new arrangements basically replicated for skilled workers the kinds of possibilities for skill upgrading that had been created for unskilled workers (including arrangements to compensate participants for loss of earnings during training), thus opening opportunities for continuing training to keep pace with technological change (Sørensen and Jensen 1988; Nelson 2012).

Much of the structure through which CVET now flows predates the inauguration of Denmark's famous "flexicurity" turn in the 1990s (see Chapter 4). But state subsidies for training increased dramatically as more stringent work requirements for the unemployed were applied. Between 1993 and 1998, spending on adult education grew faster than any other area of education, increasing by 38 percent (Schulze-Cleven n.d.: 21) and participation in all categories of adult education and training increased by about 36 percent (OECD 2002: 15). In the 1990s, fully two-thirds of spending on further training was allocated to the unemployed in conjunction with activation requirements (Mailand 1999: 3). Although this has declined in the meantime, in international comparisons, the Danes still spend more on training for the unemployed than in virtually any other EU country. As Schulze-Cleven (2009) notes, Denmark had the highest participation rate of all the OECD countries, at 35 percent participation for unemployed and 47 percent for employed (221).

Moreover, one of the hallmarks of the Danish system of training – very different from Germany – is that adult education and CVET for employed workers occurs within the same framework as education and training for the unemployed. This is crucial to reducing the stigmatization that has long plagued the U.S. system and that, as we saw, is a new feature in the German system as well. In Denmark, by contrast, "training measures for the unemployed are – to a large extent – organizationally tied in with the continuing training (or LLL [lifelong learning]) activities of the currently employed" (Schulze-Cleven 2009: 221).

The crucial reforms came in 2000. The Act on Adult and Continuing Training – *Voksen- og Efteruddannelse* (VEU) – was based on a prior agreement worked out in 1999 between the Social Democratic government and the opposition that "merged CVET and further education programs into a single more coherent system" (Lassen et al. 2006: 4). The training reforms were forged in the shadow of the conflicts in industrial relations in 1998 discussed in Chapter 2. Indeed, as we saw, increased state support for training (and for the LO's role in this area) was part of the solution to that crisis. As noted, AMU courses are free of charge and broadly available to the employed and unemployed alike. Most of the courses are very short – up to about six weeks maximum – and they can be done on a full-time or part-time basis, in day-time or evening courses. Most training programs lead to formal qualifications (Cort 2002: 19, 26).

The Danish state also offers support to firms that take in adult apprentices (see, e.g., Ministeriet 2008: 3). Companies that provide training to unskilled or unemployed workers over twenty-five years of age can qualify for state subsidies and tap into funds from the Employers' Reimbursement System (AUB) mentioned earlier. To enjoy the subsidies, the apprentice must have been unskilled or unemployed in the previous period, although under certain circumstances workers who are employed can also qualify for the subsidy (in the case of regional shortages in particular skills). Should firms choose to organize formal training courses at the workplaces themselves, they are sometimes able to collect teacher subsidies as well (Simonsen and Skipper 2006: 2; see also Lassen et al. 2006: 13–14).[35]

CVET is thus very well supported in Denmark and, in fact, nowhere else does the state spend more on further training. As Bredgaard and Larsen (2010) point out, extensive state financing "externalizes the costs of training and education for the firms, and indirectly serves as a government subsidy to the competitiveness of Danish industry.... Since the continuing training is predominantly financed by the public budget CVET activities are more likely to provide general rather than firm-specific skills and more likely to bee [sic] transferable on the external labor market" (5).

As a result of these initiatives and programs, Denmark emerged as the EU leader in lifelong learning. In 2003, participation rates in training and lifelong learning during the previous twelve months were already twice the EU average. Annually, about 60 percent of workers with higher education participated in further training, along with 40 percent of craft workers and 30 percent of formally unskilled workers (Schulze-Cleven 2009: 221). The participation rates in adult education at all levels continue to outstrip the EU averages. In 2010, the percentage of adults participating in education and training in Denmark was 32.8 percent, far above all other countries (Sweden was next, at 24.5 percent; for comparison, Germany was at 7.7 percent) (Ministry of Children and Education 2012: 18).

If there has been a criticism of CVET, it is that most continuing training is taken by the already skilled. It is certainly true that the uptake in CVET increases with level of educational attainment, but in cross-national comparisons the extent of training at all levels stands out. According to the most recent figures, 23.4 percent of Danes with the lowest educational achievement (levels 0–2 of the International Standard Classification of Education, ISCED) participate in such courses, compared to the EU average of 3.8 percent; 30.7 percent of Danes at the next level (ISCED 3–4) participate, compared to the EU average of 8.0 percent; and 41.1 percent of Danes with the highest educational achievement (ISCED 5–6) participate, compared to the EU average of 16.7 percent (CEDEFOP 2012).

The flexibility of the Danish system – providing opportunities to acquire skills flexibly and over the entire life course – operates to the advantage of groups that tend to be disadvantaged in more rigid systems. Women, for example, benefit especially, and they are more inclined than men to participate in continuing adult education for longer periods and at different stages in their careers. For Danish men, training mostly takes place when they are young (twenties to early thirties) and declines after that over their working lives. Women, by contrast, tend to engage in postsecondary training later in life, and

---

[35] As this book goes to press, further reforms of CVET (negotiated by the LO, DA, and government) are making their way to the parliament, but the precise content is not yet clear.

in fact "only women seem to participate more or less equally in vocational training over their working lives" (Simonsen and Skipper 2006: 16; Jørgensen 2009a: 2). Women's participation in training declines with the presence of small children (two years old or younger), but only for those types of training that occur outside of working hours. And take-up rates for women for all types of training increase as children get older.

As noted in the previous chapter, CVET is further supported by collective bargaining agreements that establish workers' rights to take up training (Jørgensen 2009a: 1). Thus, for example, the 2007 agreement for the industrial sector described in Chapter 2 entitles workers to two weeks of training with 85 percent of their wage even if the training is not directly relevant to the company (100 percent if it is) (Schulze-Cleven 2009: 213–15). The same agreement established a competence development fund to cover the costs of this training (Schulze-Cleven n.d.: 24; see also Fleming and Søborg n.d.). Because of the presence and the role of the overarching LO in this area, the arrangements from the leading sectors have been applied broadly so that in the meantime most collective agreements in Denmark grant employees the right to further training (Mailand 2009: 6).

Reconciling Liberalization and Solidarity in the Danish Training Regime

Many aspects of the reforms discussed in the previous sections are decidedly liberal. The skill sets that workers are acquiring are more general than before and the process through which they acquire them more individualized. While German training remains heavily front-loaded on youth and organized around nationally defined occupational profiles, recent reforms to Danish education and training involve liberalization on three fronts: (1) a modularization of training offerings in order to facilitate the flexible accumulation of skills and credentials, (2) an individualization of training paths to accommodate individual preferences and capabilities with respect to the content and pace of skill acquisition, and (3) an aggressive dismantling of traditional boundaries – not just between vocational and academic paths, but also between initial and continuing education and training, between training for youth and adults, and between training for the employed and unemployed – all of which are supported by the National Qualifications Foundation (Ministeriet 2008: 3; NEA 2008: 24; Nelson 2010: 479).

Recent reforms involve a shift from a focus on specific qualifications to more general competencies, from standardization to individualization, from narrow to broad access, and from standardized and uniform to modular training (Cort 2002: 37). The system thus involves liberalization in the content of skills – from more specific to more general, in VofC terms – as occupational and industrial lines are constantly breached. It involves also liberalization in the process of skill acquisition, as individuals accumulate credentials flexibly, in modules and over the course of their employment careers. Importantly – and very different from both Germany and the United States – training for the unemployed is integrated into a comprehensive system of skill development that also serves currently employed workers who are interested in enhancing their own credentials. Since training at all levels enjoys comparatively generous state subsidies and funding, the overall result is a form of liberalization that collectivizes rather than individualizes risks in the market for education and training.

TRAJECTORIES OF LIBERALIZATION IN VOCATIONAL EDUCATION AND TRAINING

An important article by Iversen and Stephens (2008b) echoed Esping-Andersen by identifying three models ("worlds") of human capital formation premised on distinct political-coalitional foundations. A first, liberal model, based on center-right coalitions in majoritarian contexts, caters (ideal-typically) to middle- and upper-middle class voters. Such a system focuses on college preparation and college education and spends relatively less on public primary and preschool education. A second, Christian Democratic model is based on a cross-class alliance rooted especially in manufacturing. This regime-type devotes significant resources to skilled workers (supporting high-quality IVET) and largely ignores low- and semi-skilled workers by investing comparatively less in basic education and preschool programs. A third, Social Democratic variant is based on a center-left coalition. This regime-type invests heavily in primary and secondary education, active labor market policies, and day care and preschools, thus catering to their lower-skill and more feminized constituencies.

The evidence presented in this chapter suggests that such differences – and their distributional consequences – are more pronounced than ever before. Rapid technological change and the steady decline in manufacturing employment have put pressure on all three types of systems. Their responses have important implications for patterns of educational opportunity and inequality. In the United States, recent trends point to increased stratification through the continued underdevelopment of a viable vocational track and through the continued relative neglect of (glaring weaknesses in) primary and secondary education in favor of an overly optimistic "college for all" strategy.

The German pattern, by contrast, continues to cultivate and protect a high-quality vocational track, which fails periodically to generate training opportunities for all. Moreover, the lack of any accompanying system of CVET is becoming a crucial liability in a context in which the pace of technological change puts a premium on ongoing skill acquisition (Nelson 2010: 464). Politically, the system continues to serve the interests of the manufacturing core very well, and as such plays an important role in sustaining the German export model. However, precisely the successful defense of the traditional training model – against the "encroachment" of the state (associated in German with the epithet *Verstaatlichung*) and against "inferior" school-based models

(*Verschulung*) has also left the German political economy very dependent on the private sector to provide this crucial collective good (Busemeyer 2009). The quality of training is very high but uneven access to training and periodic rationing have also fueled dualization in the German training market.

By contrast, recent reforms in Denmark have pushed for flexibility on precisely these fronts and the resulting system – far from ideal and of course with problems of its own – nonetheless appears to offer an overall more inclusive training model. This applies not just to IVET but also *a fortiori* to CVET and lifelong learning. In Germany, CVET has still not quite shed the connection with remedial training, and the state programs that exist are mostly residual, while in Denmark a relatively well-developed system of CVET offers more flexible and open access to training at all levels and at all points in life (see, especially, Schulze-Cleven 2009, 2011).

In this case as well, state policy has been crucial in expanding educational opportunities and in subsidizing the participation of both firms and employees. While the take-up rates for education and training are higher among more skilled workers, the state specifically provides funding and a framework for low-skill, hard to employ groups (i.e., precisely the constituencies that the private sector is most likely to neglect), so that even after many years of center-right governance, Denmark continues to lead the EU (by a significant margin) in the number of adults participating in CVET. As importantly, the existence of a shared general framework for training covering youth and adults, skilled and unskilled, and employed and unemployed dampens fragmentation across these groups and encourages instead the development of a "community of fate" (Ahlquist and Levi 2013) among these diverse interests, and a shared commitment to the system as a whole.

4

Labor Market Policy

Labor market policy is a third arena in which divergent trajectories of liberalization are evident and have a profound impact on equality and social solidarity. Governments influence the operation of labor markets in a wide variety of ways. The political economy literature puts heavy emphasis on employment protection legislation and unemployment benefits, and for good reason. Employment protection legislation affects the ease with which employers can lay off workers, and the level and duration of unemployment benefits influence the incentives that workers face in the market. These factors play a role in my analysis as well, but in this chapter I focus attention more on two other types of policies through which governments influence the operation of labor markets: active labor market policies (ALMPs) and short-time work (STW) policies.

Of the two, ALMPs have captured the lion's share of attention. Following Katz (1994), the term refers to "measures targeted at the unemployed and disadvantaged (low-wage) workers with the intent of improving the functioning of the labor market" in one of three ways: by investing in education and training to upgrade these workers' skills, by stimulating employment either through direct job creation in the public sector or through subsidies to the private sector, and by facilitating reintegration into the labor market by assisting the unemployed in job searches and by matching them to openings (259). Although in fact their distributive effects vary significantly depending on which of these facets is emphasized, most observers see ALMPs as outsider-oriented in that the spending is targeted at those at the low end of the skill spectrum and the unemployed (Rueda 2007; Martin and Swank 2012).[1]

---

[1] There is some evidence that ALMPs are effective at fighting unemployment (see, e.g. OECD 2006: 211). But firm conclusions have been hampered by inconsistencies in what exactly is captured under the broad heading of ALMP in different countries. The most thoughtful analyses – by John Martin (1998) of the OECD, Giuliano Bonoli (2012), and Werner Eichhorst and Paul Marx

STW policies, by contrast, have not received much attention, partly because they are much smaller in budgetary terms. Although traveling under different labels in different countries, where they exist, STW policies are much more similar in form and function, differing mostly in the generosity and duration of benefits to recipients. These policies provide subsidies to firms experiencing cyclical downturns to allow them to avoid layoffs and instead cut working times while compensating workers for the reduction in their hours. Such policies provide relief to employees while allowing firms to weather downturns "without incurring dismissal costs, preserving the human capital specific to the firm and reducing the costs of turnover" (Arpaia et al. 2010: 3; also Sacchi et al. 2011: 5).

Broadly speaking, ALMPs address structural unemployment, while STW policies operate to alleviate cyclical unemployment. Whereas ALMPs are outsider-oriented and organized around facilitating the (re-) entry of hard-to-employ groups, STW policies are distinctly insider-oriented and benefit workers that employers are interested in retaining anyway.[2] As such, government policies toward STW give us a different picture than what we get looking just at ALMP. In combination, government policy toward ALMP and STW can tell us a great deal about what different countries seek to do in terms of labor market policy.

ACTIVE LABOR MARKET POLICY

I begin, as in previous chapters, by situating the three country-cases in a broader cross-national context before engaging in a more detailed analysis of the political dynamics that have shaped labor market policy over time in each of them. Figure 4.1 provides data on ALMP expenditures across a number of countries between 1985 and 2010 (broken out into five-year intervals). Taken together, the dark gray and black bars record expenditures on ALMPs (the dark gray bar gives average spending specifically on training for each five-year segment), and are best interpreted in relation to unemployment levels (the dots indicate averages for the corresponding period). This figure confirms what is already widely known among students of the political economy of advanced capitalism, namely that the Nordic countries generally combine lower levels of

---

(2012b) are clear in pointing out that ALMPs are a moving target, comprising an ever-evolving basket of programs that vary both across countries and over time. In general, however, spending on ALMPs in both their more punitive and positive aspects is directed at the workers with the most tenuous position in the labor market.

[2] This is confirmed by an OECD evaluation of STW schemes during the 2008–2009 recession, which found that "by helping to preserve the jobs of workers with permanent or open-ended contracts, without providing additional job stability to temporary workers, STW schemes have a tendency to enhance the position of insiders relative to outsiders and thereby further increase the degree of labour market segmentation" (Hijzen and Venn 2011: 27).

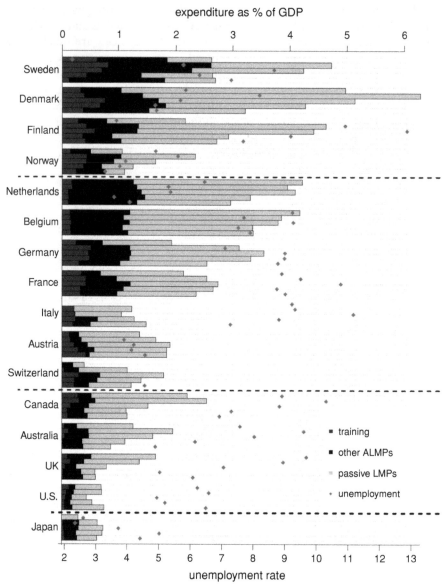

FIGURE 4.1. Spending on Labor Market Policies, and Unemployment Rates. *Note:* For each country, bars refer in descending order to 1985–89, 1990–94, 1995–99, 2000–2004, and 2005–10. Data unavailable for Italian and Japanese LMPs before 1990 and Italian non-training ALMP before 2000. Harmonized unemployment rates unavailable for Austria and Germany before 1990 and Switzerland before 2010. *Source:* stats.oecd.org.

unemployment with more generous spending on ALMPs,[3] and that LMEs are laggards in spending on ALMP no matter what the level of unemployment. Continental political economies occupy an intermediate position, especially when spending levels are considered in relation to unemployment, though there are some stand-out cases, such as the Netherlands since the 1980s, where unemployment has been relatively low and ALMPs have become a very central part of the economic model. But aside from this case (discussed at length in Chapter 5) none of the Christian Democratic countries reaches Social Democratic levels when viewed against unemployment.

Figure 4.2 provides a more disaggregated picture of labor market policies in the five countries examined in some detail in this study. This figure breaks out labor market policy expenditures into passive and active components (light gray indicates spending on passive, dark gray on training-oriented measures, and black on all other active measures.[4] The dashed line indicates the unemployment rate (scale on right).

A full discussion of each country follows, but a few things are worth noting. For Denmark, the 1990s saw a dramatic decrease in passive support relative to active measures. Also striking is the way that spending on labor market policies in Denmark tracks changes in the unemployment rate rather closely – when unemployment goes up, passive and, increasingly, active spending also rise. On the other end of the spectrum, the United States spends very little on passive supports and close to nothing on ALMP. Germany is an intermediate case, spending less on both active and passive measures than Denmark despite overall much higher levels of unemployment through the 1990s and 2000s. Chapter 5 discusses the Netherlands and Sweden in detail, but what stands out in these figures is a general decline in labor market spending of all sorts in Sweden since 1990 despite high unemployment. By contrast, spending on labor market policy in the Netherlands is higher, though it remains skewed toward passive measures and with very little devoted to training.[5]

SHORT-TIME WORK POLICIES

STW policies have a very different meaning and valence. As indicated, these policies are designed to allow firms to avoid laying off workers in economic downturns by providing government subsidies to pay workers "a wage replacement allowance in order to compensate a temporary reduction in working time" (Sacchi et al. 2011: 5). Despite the subsidies, such policies are not costless to the firms and workers who benefit from them. Firms are often responsible for

---

[3] Finland being the notable exception on unemployment.
[4] I take this illuminating format for presenting the data from Bonoli (2012: 95) and have simply updated to include more years.
[5] However, as elaborated in Chapter 5, CVET in the Netherlands is funded mostly through collectively bargained funds. Direct state financing plays a small role, but the government supports such training by extending the terms of collective agreements on training to cover virtually all firms in the sector in which they are negotiated.

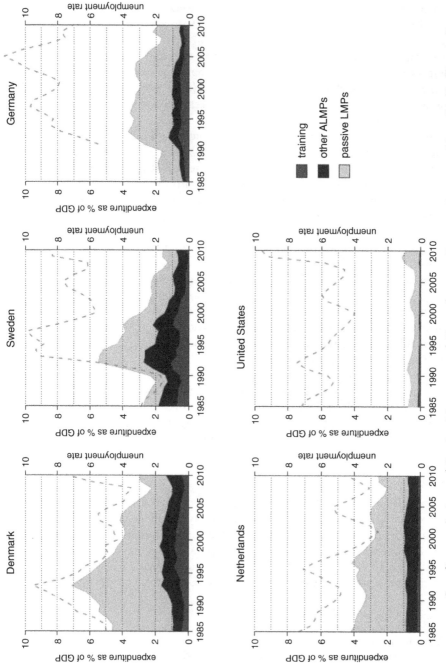

FIGURE 4.2. Spending on Active and Passive Measures, and Unemployment Rates, 1985–2010. *Note:* Broken line indicates unemployment rate. Passive labor market policies (LMPs) consist of income support for unemployed, underemployed, and early retirement. *Source:* stats.oecd.org.

continuing to pay social contributions for workers despite reduced hours, and workers experience a decline in pay. While workers typically prefer this to the alternative of layoffs, they cannot access STW subsidies directly and as a matter of individual right. Employers have to apply for this type of support, and they only invoke such policies in cases where they are keen to retain these workers (3). In sum, while employees experience STW as a source of employment security, from the employer's point of view, these policies provide a way "to hoard labour – in particular, skilled workers – during temporary downturns" (5).

In most countries that have STW programs, subsidies are, in principle, available to firms and workers in all sectors. In practice, however, it is invariably manufacturing firms that dominate the actual use of these programs (Arpaia et al. 2010: 14, 17, 21, and passim).[6] The reason is consistent with VofC logic: where employers and employees have both invested in industry-specific skills, they will share an interest in employment continuity (Estevez-Abe et al. 2001; Hall and Soskice 2001: 16).[7]

Unlike ALMP, it does not make sense to look at trends over time in STW because this is a cyclical policy that is invoked only in downturns. However, during such downturns, STW (where it exists) is a key labor market instrument. To get a sense of cross-national variation, Figure 4.3 provides data on the use of STW policies in the immediate aftermath of the recent recession, a major shock shared by virtually all the rich democracies.[8]

The pattern that emerges is instructive. Notably absent are the UK and Sweden, both of which lack this policy tool.[9] The countries clustered at the bottom include other Anglo-Saxon countries right alongside other Nordic countries in their low commitment to STW policies. Only marginally more employees were covered by STW policies in Denmark and Norway than in Canada during the crisis. By contrast, the Christian Democratic countries dominate the top of

[6] In some countries (e.g., Belgium) STW subsidies are specifically reserved for blue-collar workers. In Italy, too, STW subsidies are exclusively available to industry, construction, agriculture, and certain crafts (Sacchi et al. 2011: 8).

[7] In some countries, notably Germany and Japan, STW coverage was extended during the recent crisis to cover agency workers, since they now make up a significant share of manufacturing employment. However, as Hijzen and Venn (2011) note "even if workers in non-regular jobs are eligible for STW in principle, the incentive for firms to place them on STW is likely to be considerably weaker than for their core workforce. Participation in these schemes tends to be costly for employers, while hiring and firing costs tend to be low for workers in non-regular jobs" (9).

[8] Clearly, some of this variation is due to the depth of the shock, related – among other things – to relative reliance on exports. But these figures should also be considered in the context of variation in the generosity of STW policies (level of support, duration), which is more purely a matter of public policy. In general, though, the countries that use these programs most extensively also offer the most generous support (see the summary of program features in OECD 2010).

[9] In Sweden, the engineering industry concluded a collective agreement on STW in 2010, but the government declined to offer subsidies (interviews, Teknikföretagen and Facken inom Industrin, 2010).

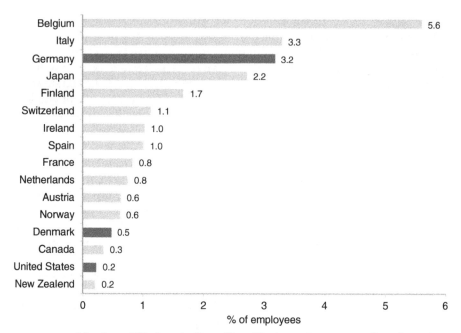

FIGURE 4.3. Number of Workers in Short-Time Work as a Percentage of Total Employment, 2009. *Note*: Neither Sweden nor the UK has a legislated STW policy. *Source*: Schmitt (2011: 16), based on OECD figures from 2010.

the chart. Belgium made massive use of such policies, followed by Italy and Germany (also Japan). In fact, all the countries with the strongest and most generous STW schemes are conservative welfare regimes in which manufacturing interests dominate. Austria appears to be an outlier in this regard, with relatively low STW spending in the crisis. But in Austria, another program provides a functional alternative to STW, and one that employers much prefer. Temporary suspension contracts (*Aussetzverträge*) resemble STW in their logic; they "consist in a voluntary agreement between employees and their employer to terminate the employment relationship in time of crisis" and re-establish it in the upturn (Sacchi et al. 2011: 12–13). This option turns out to be cheaper for employers because the worker goes on unemployment benefits so that, unlike with STW, the firm is not obligated to pay social contributions for the period of contract suspension.

CROSS-NATIONAL VARIATION IN LABOR MARKET POLICY

Putting these two dimensions – ALMP and STW – together, we can get a picture of the relative strength of support for "outsiders" (ALMP) and "insiders" (STW). Table 4.1 sorts countries by their level of commitment to ALMP, which

TABLE 4.1. *Relative Spending on Active Labor Market Policies and Short-Time Work Policies*

	relative spending on ALMPs		
	higher >1%	higher (>12) Belgium Switzerland	lower (<12) Germany Italy Japan Finland Ireland
	lower <1%	Denmark Norway Sweden Netherlands	UK United States Canada Australia New Zealand France Austria*

(left margin, rotated: Relative Reliance on STW Policies)

Note: STW spending is based on OECD figures as reported in Figure 4.3 above.

Relative spending on ALMP is average ALMP spending per unemployed (following Vis (2010: 52), share of total labor market spending devoted to ALMP measures divided by number of unemployed), 1985–2007, based on figures from Armingeon database[10]).

* However, as noted in the text, *Aussetzverträge* are a functional substitute for STW

can be (somewhat crudely) high or low, and their level of commitment to STW policies, again crudely high or low.[11] As we see, most of the Nordic countries (with the exception of Finland) score high on ALMP but low on STW. Continental European political economies are spread across two quadrants – those that devote low resources to ALMP and significant resources to STW (Italy and Germany; also Japan), and those that devote significant resources both to ALMP and to STW (Belgium and Switzerland). LMEs invest neither in ALMP nor in STW policies.

The country-cases at the center of this study conform to type when it comes to these two important labor market policies. Typically for an LME, the United States features fluid labor markets (low employment protection but also underdeveloped STW policies) and it is a laggard with respect to active labor market spending as well. Moreover, the trend in labor market policy since the 1960s

[10] The database can be accessed at http://www.ipw.unibe.ch/content/team/klaus_armingeon/comparative_political_data_sets/index_ger.html.

[11] ALMP commitment is based on average share of total labor market policies that is devoted to ALMPs per unemployed, 1985–2007 (Armingeon data; see also Vis 2010: Table 3.1); STW commitment is based on Figure 4.3.

had been decidedly deregulatory. Previous supports for job creation and job training were progressively dismantled. In their place, a new workfare regime was put in place that mostly relies on withdrawal of benefits and forced activation.

Germany fits squarely in the Christian Democratic cluster, though if anything it comes in on the high end with respect to STW policies. Skilled workers – especially in manufacturing – enjoy multiple job protections and generous benefits. This protected core, however, exists alongside a growing low-wage sector characterized by precarious employment and low or no benefits, and in a context since 2003 featuring heightened activation. This combination of strong continued support for employment protections for insiders combined with low support for outsiders through ALMP epitomizes a trajectory of dualization. Inequality grows as precarious, low-wage jobs proliferate on the unorganized periphery.

Denmark, finally, rose over the period since the 1990s from relatively modest levels of ALMP spending to the highest level among all the rich democracies. This transformation accompanied the country's embrace of flexicurity policies that involve activation of the unemployed, including more stringent work requirements. STW policies are accordingly less well developed and also far less generous than in Germany (S. Andersen 2010: 7). Moreover, in Denmark the STW policies that do exist are specifically activating in the sense that recipients must actively seek work while on temporary layoff. Denmark's more liberal policies are also embedded in a stronger commitment to assisting workers in retraining and placement (i.e., high ALMP commitment).

LABOR MARKET POLICY IN THE UNITED STATES: FROM TARGETED ASSISTANCE TO "WORK FIRST" PROGRAMS

The United States stands out in international comparisons for its highly deregulated and flexible labor markets. The OECD employment protection index put the United States dead last among the rich democracies in the level of employment protection. The U.S. score (less than 0.5) is an order of magnitude lower than those in much of Europe, where most countries come in between 2.0 and 3.0 (see Figure 4.6). The United States has also been a laggard in terms of ALMPs throughout the postwar period. Active labor market spending as a percent of GDP (including disability category) peaked at 0.26 percent in 1985 and has declined virtually continuously to the current 0.14 percent (OECD Stat Database, accessed June 2012). Training and job creation programs in the United States have been shorter-lived and far less generous, and they reach fewer citizens than virtually any other country (Katz 1994: 272).

It is not that the American government is incapable of this type of intervention. Certainly in times of crisis, policy instruments have been devised to put people back to work in large numbers. The Works Progress Administration (WPA) during the New Deal was a high point in U.S. ALMP, employing more than three million people (out of more than nine million unemployed) and spending $1.4 billion (U.S. billion) per year from its inception until 1943 when it ended (Cook et al. 1985: 2).[12] Little remained once the crisis passed. In the postwar period, Congress enacted the weak and mostly symbolic Employment Law of 1946, which created the Council of Economic Advisors and vaguely committed the government to promoting employment and controlling inflation.

Government job creation programs were ramped up again in the late 1960s and early 1970s, first as part of President Johnson's campaign against urban poverty, and later to address unemployment in the wake of the oil crisis, but these programs were short-lived and never implemented on a very large scale (Rose 1999: 455). The CETA program in the 1970s (described in Chapter 3) in some ways marked a high point in postwar ALMP. Enrollments in CETA's direct job creation program – the Public Service Employment Program – peaked at 755,000 in April 1978 (Cook et al. 1985: 12). But the trajectory since then has moved in a deregulatory direction.

For analytic purposes, developments in the United States can be divided into three phases. In the first – roughly the 1960s through the 1970s – the government was rather heavily involved in targeted job creation and training initiatives for disadvantaged populations. The second phase, coinciding with the Reagan years, retained a minimal involvement in training programs even as all job creation measures were abandoned in favor of trickle down policies (i.e., lower taxes and labor market deregulation) aimed at spurring private-sector job growth. The period since the passage of the Clinton welfare reform of 1996 marks the beginning of the third period. Originally conceived as an attempt to convert previously failed antipoverty programs into a more forward-looking ALMP, Clinton's proposals were significantly reworked as they made their way through Congress. Direct government job creation and strong support for training were major casualties, and the resulting legislation favored "work first" policies aimed at placing the unemployed in jobs – any jobs – as quickly as possible. In short, as the government retreated first from job creation measures, then later from job training as well, what remained were often harsh workfare policies and the discipline of the market. This trend, as we will see, is quite different from that in Denmark, where activation since the 1990s was accompanied by increased government activity and spending on ALMPs.

Labor Market Policy in the Golden Era

The United States is the paradigmatic case of the kind of liberal labor regime that many observers saw as a second, equally viable path to full employment, alongside its mirror image of high unionization and high coordination

---

[12] Other New Deal programs included the Emergency Relief Administration (which preceded and was replaced by the WPA), the National Youth Administration (part of the WPA), and the Civilian Conservation Corps.

(Calmfors and Driffill 1988). Despite massive and successful job creation programs under President Franklin D. Roosevelt, after World War II Congress showed no appetite for government interventions in the labor market. However, as noted in Chapter 3, problems of structural unemployment emerging in the 1950s and 1960s sparked renewed debate on labor market policy. Democratic congressmen from declining industrial regions began to lobby for legislative action to support area redevelopment (Weir 1992: 66–67). A small minority of economists called for an expansive approach, among them Yale economist E. Wight Bakke, who in the early 1960s championed the Swedish model of broad ALMPs. But these initiatives were rejected in favor of more limited and targeted interventions.

The most significant initiatives were launched by President Johnson under the broad heading of his War on Poverty. Among these was the Job Corps, passed in 1964 and patterned after former president Roosevelt's highly successful Civilian Conservation Corps – although, unlike Roosevelt's version, the Job Corps specifically targeted disadvantaged youth. Other programs were designed to attack long-term unemployment among adult populations. The WIN program founded in 1967, for example, allowed welfare recipients to receive occupational or pre-occupational training with support from the federal government (Gold 1971: 491).

Although sometimes emphasizing skill development, these programs operated on the assumption that training alone would not suffice. As unemployment had both technological and structural components, job creation programs were part of the policy mix. "Throughout much of the 1960s and 1970s, federal policy reflected a conviction that Americans struggling to escape poverty faced both structural and deficit-demand problems. As a result, training and education policies were combined with significant public employment initiatives" (Lafer 2002: 20). For example, in 1968, President Johnson introduced a new program based on promoting partnerships between industry and government to create jobs. The Job Opportunities in the Business Sector (JOBS) program involved government subsidies for training in exchange for pledges on the part of businesses to hire workers. In introducing the JOBS initiative in his 1968 State of the Union address, President Johnson described it as "a new partnership between government and private industry to train and to hire the hard-core unemployed persons. I know of no task before us of more importance to us, to the country, or to our future."[13] But the program had already collapsed by the early 1970s, as firms turned out not to be interested in such a partnership and even less so in creating jobs for the "hard-core unemployed." Cooperation "evaporated" entirely – and funds went unclaimed – as soon as the economy grew more sluggish (Weir 1992: 93).

As with the training initiatives discussed in Chapter 3, President Johnson's labor market policies stood on fragile foundations. As Margaret Weir (1992) has argued, by steering federal funding to targeted populations – mostly the

[13] http://www.lbjlib.utexas.edu/Johnson/archives.hom/speeches.hom/680117.asp.

urban poor, and often minorities – these programs, almost by design, were vulnerable politically. By concentrating support (i.e., job placement and job training activities) on those at the low end of the labor market, these programs quickly came to be closely associated with welfare policy, "the most despised segment of social policy in America" (10, 67). Some – such as the Job Corps – survived, but many more were abandoned later or carried on in much reduced form.

When confronted with recession in 1970, Johnson's successor Richard Nixon vetoed a public employment program passed by Congress, objecting to what he called "dead-end jobs in the public sector."[14] However, as unemployment continued to rise, he agreed to the Emergency Employment Act (EEA) of 1971, which created the Public Employment Program (PEP), a two-year pilot program that came to employ 185,000 at its peak in July 1972 (Cook et al. 1985: 5–6). As part of President Nixon's New Federalism philosophy, PEP's implementation was delegated to states and local governments – "the level of government at which Republicans exercised most influence" (Weir 1992: 111). Possibly as a result, "PEP participants were better educated and less disadvantaged than participants in the more structurally oriented programs begun in the sixties, and fewer were minorities. Although the act authorized training, little money was spent for this purpose; an estimated 94 percent of the money was spent on compensation of participants" (Cook et al. 1985: 6–7).

When the PEP pilot expired in 1972, it was replaced by CETA. CETA was designed to consolidate existing programs, and it continued to reflect President Nixon's preference for state-level administration. There were three main components to CETA: training programs (administered at the state/local level); a Public Service Employment (PSE) program to operate in high-unemployment areas (greater than 6.5 percent); and federal programs for targeted groups. In the wake of the first oil shock, use of CETA funding was no longer restricted to high unemployment areas, and the number of people employed under CETA programs rose from about 100,000 in December 1974 to 350,000 in the spring of 1976. Congress reauthorized CETA's expansion in 1976 and again in 1978, and at its height in 1978 the program "provided nearly three-quarters of a million full-time jobs for adults and an additional million summer jobs for teenagers" (Lafer 2002: 21). In this period, CETA provided jobs for over 10 percent of unemployed workers (Weir 1998: 271).

However, decentralized administration had always left CETA open to misuse by local politicians as patronage, and the program came to be caught up in a series of corruption scandals in the 1970s (Weir 1992). The 1978 reauthorization was coupled with new restrictions seeking to limit the scope of the program both in terms of eligibility (so as to focus more on long-term unemployed) and duration (for all new beneficiaries, employment would be on "special projects" lasting a year or less) (Cook et al. 1985: 12–13). These restrictions sapped

---

[14] http://www.presidency.ucsb.edu/ws/?pid=2854#axzz1zro84PO3; also Weir (1992: 110).

political support for the program: with tighter eligibility requirements, the program worked less well as "pork" since the money now had to be used for the unpopular "hard core" (13). Funding was reduced under President Carter, so that by the time he left office the number of those employed in PSE was down to approximately 300,000 (10), despite an unemployment rate of 7.1 percent. His successor Ronald Reagan dismantled the program almost immediately (Weir 1992: 123–128).

The Reagan Years and Beyond

After peaking in 1981–1982 at its highest level since the Depression, unemployment began to decline through the Reagan years, bringing a certain triumphalism to the neoliberal proponents of Reagonomics. The comparisons were invariably invidious, as observers contrasted "rigid" European labor markets with buoyant employment growth in the United States and other more liberal market regimes (see, e.g., Siebert 1997). Careful observers produced a more nuanced view, noting that not all European countries were experiencing high unemployment and some that were (e.g., Denmark) also had very flexible labor markets (e.g., Nickell 1997). Generally, though, the new assumption undergirding employment policy in the United States was that there was an ample supply of jobs in the economy – "enough jobs for anyone who needed one" (Lafer 2002: 20). Unemployment came to be recast not as a matter of structural problems in the labor market or insufficient opportunity, but instead as individual-level failures based on behavioral, cultural, or motivational problems (Weir 1992: 83).

Many factors, of course, contributed to low unemployment in the United States in the 1980s and 1990s. Western and Beckett (1999) argue that high incarceration rates played a non-negligible role. They show that between 1980 and 1996, the prison population in the United States tripled to reach 1.63 million, and this despite a fall in crime rates after 1980 (1031, 1036). By removing large numbers of workers from the unemployment rolls, the penal system operated – and continues to operate – as a major labor market intervention, generating "a sizeable, non-market reallocation of labor, overshadowing state intervention through social policy" (1031).[15] In a way, incarceration operated in the United States as early retirement schemes did in many Continental European political economies, depressing unemployment rates by reducing the labor supply. The big difference is that while generous early retirement schemes redounded to the advantage of labor market insiders, labor market policy through the prison system exacerbated inequality through its highly

---

[15] They note with irony that the expenditures on courts, police, and prisons in the early 1990s "dwarfed" expenditures on unemployment benefits and employment related programs and services – with $91 billion (U.S. billion) being spent on the former and less than half that amount ($41 billion) on the latter.

unequal concentration among low SES groups – especially minorities – and its stultifying effects on their later employment prospects.[16]

In any event, strong employment growth in the United States was combined with sharply increased wage inequality and wage premiums for the more highly educated. As Katz notes, the 1980s was a period in the United States characterized by "large declines in the real earnings of less-educated and low-paid workers... associated with increased family income inequality and growing rates of poverty among working families" (Katz 1994: 239–240; Lafer 2002: 45–46). Household earnings rose, but this was only a consequence of increased working hours and especially an increase in the share of families in which both parents worked. While some observers explain these trends with reference to skill-biased technological change and the associated decline in demand for low skilled workers, institutional and political factors clearly also contributed to this outcome. The role of declining unionization and slippage in the incomes brought about by the failure of the statutory minimum wage to keep pace with median incomes (or even inflation) have already been discussed in Chapter 2.

The Reagan years were thus years of downward mobility for the working classes. Entry-level wages for male high school graduates declined nearly 20 percent between 1979 and 1989 in real terms (Mishel et al. 2012).[17] In fact, the employment growth in this period – including, notably, among women – was itself partly a consequence of the slippage in real wages. Houseman (1995) notes that "[b]ecause falling real wages among men and sharply higher divorce rates pushed many women into the labor force during the 1980's, the increase in female labor force participation [in this period was] not necessarily a sign of economic health" (17). Many of the jobs that were created in this period did not come with benefits: "Among male employees with less than a high school education, the percent not receiving any health insurance coverage through their employer rose from 42.4 percent in 1980 to 64.7 percent in 1993. Among male employees with a high school degree, the percentage not receiving any health insurance from their employer rose from 22.0 percent in 1980 to 38.0 percent in 1993. Even among male employees with some college education, the percentage receiving no health insurance on the job rose substantially from 31.0 percent to 39.5 percent between 1980 and 1993" (11). The situation was even worse for women.

Widespread downward mobility did not, however, produce a groundswell of support for increased state involvement in labor market policy. On the contrary: in this period, state policy in general and social policy in particular "came to be equated with handouts for racial minorities" (Reisch 2006: 72). The signature antipoverty program of the postwar American welfare state was Aid to Families

---

[16] "The intimate link between school failure and incarceration is clear at the bottom of the education ladder where 60 percent of black, male high school dropouts will go to prison before age thirty-five" (Western 2008).

[17] http://www.epi.org/chart/ib-327-table-1-hourly-wages-entry-level-2/.

with Dependent Children (AFDC), which provided direct cash assistance to the poor. In the 1980s, public support for helping the disadvantaged dwindled completely under President Reagan, and the AFDC came to be demonized as a program for "welfare queens." The discourse of the time was deeply antistate and opponents of welfare were successful in linking crime, welfare, and race in a toxic cocktail of antiwelfare sentiment (Soss and Schram 2007; also Quadagno 1996).

In this context, Democrats began to engage in "intense self-reflection," and ultimately came to embrace the view that they had made a grave error in the 1960s by focusing their policy initiatives on the most disadvantaged urban poor to the neglect of the white working class (Soss and Schram 2007: 112). They concluded that programs like AFDC "had fueled racial stereotypes, bred pathology among the poor, undercut public support for anti-poverty efforts, and put liberals at an ongoing political disadvantage" (112). Welfare reform under President Clinton was meant to address this problem by converting an unpopular antipoverty policy into a more forward looking ALMP. However, not all elements of what was a comprehensive package of reforms survived the legislative process. At the outset, I noted that there are different types of ALMP and the United States wound up embracing an especially coercive, punitive version.

In 1994, President Clinton sought a compromise that looks very much like what we now call flexicurity: "liberals would sign onto time limits and work requirements [for the unemployed] in exchange for conservatives signing onto substantial social investment" (Soss and Schram 2007: 112). President Clinton's original proposal coupled a two-year limit of public assistance with generous job training and health insurance benefits.[18] When the two years expired, recipients would be expected to find work but, crucially, the government would absorb the risk of continued unemployment by promising a government job "to anyone unable to find private sector employment when their two years were up" (Lafer 2002: 191–192; see also Karger 2003). Job guarantees were an integral part of the original plan; the idea of the government as employer of last resort was "critical to enabling welfare recipients to support their families through paid work" (Lafer 2002: 192).[19]

---

[18] There were certainly some punitive elements. As Beland and Waddan (2012: 49–50) point out, the 1994 reform proposal required single mothers to name the father of their child in order to enroll in welfare and allowed states to impose "family caps" (i.e., not to increase benefits for welfare recipients who had further children).

[19] The government did not expect the public employment component to be a very large part of this. According to Weaver, the administration only projected 10% of AFDC cases would be in government-provided or -subsidized employment by 2000 under its plan. Still, there were no "hard time limits" in the initial bill (i.e., time limits on provision of guaranteed jobs for those who reached the "soft time limit" on benefits) (Weaver 1998: 383).

This proposal foundered on the growing power of business and the weakness of organized labor (Weir 1998: 276–277). As we saw in Chapter 2, the political power of organized employers rose dramatically in the 1980s with the growth of the Business Roundtable and other groups. Organized labor, meanwhile, was shrinking and also becoming increasingly inward-looking. New Democrats seeking to reach out to secure new bases of support "put distance" between themselves and organized labor, pitching employment policy as aimed at the national goal of economic prosperity (276). But unions, of course, looked to Democrats to help reverse the decline in their fortunes. President Clinton's efforts to forge a compromise failed, and when the Republicans stormed Congress in 1994 with a new "Contract with America," the political sands shifted. Government supports for the unemployed and job guarantees were excised from the bill. What remained were strict time limits on receipt of welfare benefits and stringent work requirements.

The turn to workfare in the United States marked a move away from more active assistance and, for that matter, also away from any skill-based welfare-to-work strategies, embracing instead a policy organized around "immediate labor force attachment" (Peck and Theodore 2000: 124). The new era in labor market policy in the United States was heralded in 1996 when President Clinton signed the Personal Responsibility and Work Opportunities Reconciliation Act (PRWORA). Virtually gone was "all pretense of training participants in any identifiable skill whatsoever" (Lafer 2002: 14–15). What remained was assistance to the unemployed in job searching, mandatory work, short-term and minimalist training, and threat of benefit withdrawal.

PRWORA abolished AFDC and replaced it with Temporary Assistance for Needy Families (TANF). Under AFDC, states had been required by law to provide assistance to all eligible persons. TANF removed all legal entitlements to welfare. Unlike AFDC, the current program does not guarantee any amount of cash assistance for poor families, but it does institute strict time limits and work requirements for welfare recipients (Lafer 2002: 190). Moreover, TANF was implemented as a block grant program that "devolved welfare to states while demanding exacting work-participation targets" (Peck and Theodore 2000: 121). With that, a national regulatory framework was put in place that fueled competition among different states. The federal government supported local experimentation, and states were able to define their own eligibility requirements but within the context of relentless pressure to meet federally imposed job targets and spending caps (123).

Moreover, the job guarantees from the original plan had vanished. PRWORA reduced public assistance to a short-term, transitional step in the march toward full labor market participation (Karger 2003). The work-first principle underlying most of the states' welfare-to-work programs had led most states to drop all education and training. Programs "focus instead on placing participants as quickly as possible into jobs – any job, any wage" (Lafer 2002: 196). These policies are thus deeply complementary to the country's deregulated and highly fluid labor markets (Peck and Theodore 2000: 120). Their effect has been to further "individualize employment relations, intensify competitive pressure at the bottom of the labor market and enforce low-paid work" (120). The effects were magnified by the simultaneous impact of union decline, globalization (including the passage of the North Atlantic Free Trade Agreement, NAFTA), and low-skill immigration in this period. "Far from a vehicle for upward mobility, welfare-to-work programs have come to serve primarily as a disciplinary mechanism for forcing participants to embrace their fate at the bottom of the labor market" (Lafer 2002: 191).

The logic of the new activation paradigm is exemplified in regional programs that came to be held up as examples to be followed by others. Such was the case for the Greater Avenues for Independence (GAIN) program in Riverside, California. This program emphasized job search activities while downplaying the role of training, and was focused on achieving "rapid results while controlling programme costs" (Peck and Theodore 2000: 124–125). The message relentlessly conveyed to the unemployed was that "any job is a good job," and administrative structures and strategies were geared toward encouraging participants to take the first job they were offered.

Labor Market Policy and Inequality in the United States

PRWORA represents the culmination of a longer trend, one that "completed a generation-long process of devolving responsibility for public assistance to the states, eliminated the half-century old concept of entitlement for low-income children and families, and brought to fruition the longstanding preference of U.S. policymakers for work as the primary means of income support for the poor" (Reisch 2006: 74). Labor market policies organized around the work first principle individualize risk and reinforce inequality in several ways. In terms of effects on the labor market, such policies intensify competition at the low end of the labor market, driving wages down and promoting the growth of contingent labor markets. Under TANF, those whose benefits expire enter a world of irregular, low-pay, often no-benefit employment (Lafer 2002: 196–203). As Peck and Theodore (2000) put it, "these programs exacerbate inequality by promoting 'churning' at the low end of the labor market by intensifying competition for jobs" and creating a "downward pull on wages and regulatory standards" (128–129). Workfare in the United States does not so much "raise the level of employability across the labor market as a whole as increase the rate of exploitation at its lower reaches" (132).

The impact on individuals also only reinforces inequality. The relentless emphasis on rapid reentry (i.e., any job is a good job) at the expense of training means that workfare policies actually foster skill erosion by insisting that the unemployed take the first job offered regardless of its match with their skills. From the perspective of program participants, the result of churning at the low end is a pattern of "disjointed occupational progression, poor returns on education and training, and therefore lower prospects of entering the primary sector" of the non-marginally employed (Peck and Theodore 2000: 130).

Finally there is the question of how the post-reform welfare system responds to a weak labor market. Introduced at a time of very low unemployment, TANF led immediately to a sharp reduction in the number of families on welfare, from 4.4 million in August 1996 to 2.2 million four years later. Caseloads in many states continued to drop for several years after that. These developments led many observers to declare the legislation a success (Reisch 2006: 72–73). But many public policy experts were more pessimistic. Writing in 1998, Kent Weaver expressed concern: "What will happen when the nation's economy enters a downturn remains the most critical unknown about welfare reform. At present, low unemployment and a growing economy make the states' task easier in a self-reinforcing "virtuous cycle": jobs for low-skilled workers are relatively plentiful; caseload declines combined with fixed TANF federal funding makes it easier for states to spend more per recipient on transportation, child care, employment subsidies, training, and the intensive and directive case management needed to move welfare recipients into work and keep them there.... When a recession hits, however, all elements of the cycle turn vicious.... " (403–404).

In retrospect, these comments seem clairvoyant. Subsequent studies present a sobering picture of declining TANF coverage in the midst of rising poverty (Anderson et al. 2011: 35–38). Unlike the food stamp program where the federal government covers all expenses no matter how many people are enrolled, states receive fixed federal grants for TANF and must cover all overflow expenses on their own. The incentive is to cut caseloads, and indeed eleven states – many of them high unemployment regions – have cut the rolls by 10 percent or more since 2007 (DeParle 2012). In an effort to contain costs, states have shortened time limits, tightened eligibility rules and reduced benefits – to a current average of approximately $350 per month for a family of three. The result in 2012 was that "despite the worst economy in decades, the cash welfare rolls [had] barely budged"; recent studies have found "that as many as one in every four low-income single mothers is jobless and without cash aid – roughly four million women and children" (DeParle 2012).

Activation in the American context is particularly harsh when one considers the kinds of jobs into which low-skill workers are being pressed. Entry-level hourly wages for male high school graduates dropped by over 25 percent between 1979 and 2011 (mostly during the Reagan years).[20] The share of U.S. employees working in low-wage jobs now amounts to over a quarter of the workforce, topping the charts in this dubious distinction, as Figure 4.4 shows.[21]

[20] See http://www.epi.org/chart/ib-327-table-1-hourly-wages-entry-level-2/.
[21] And, of course, as Schmitt (2012) notes, in the United States, low-wage work is also associated with especially poor benefits: "Almost half of private-sector workers in the bottom fourth of the wage distribution in 2010, for example, had no paid vacations. In the same year, about

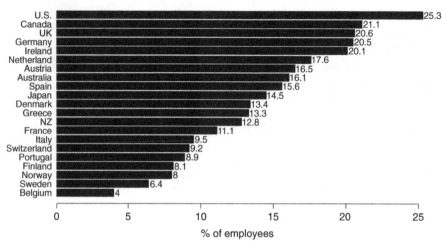

FIGURE 4.4. Share of Employees in Low-Wage Work, 2010. *Source*: OECD (2012; 2011; 2009) and Mason and Salverda (2010); data for Belgium, France, Italy, Portugal and Spain refer to 2008; data for Norway refer to 2009; data for Sweden refer to 2007; data for France and Netherlands refer to 2005; data for all other countries refer to 2010.

In some ways the pattern in labor market policy resembles that in education policy discussed in Chapter 3. There we saw that increasing college enrollment numbers are taken as an indicator of success. So it is with evaluations of TANF, in which any entry to work is viewed as progress. In both cases, political success is gauged in a very short-term perspective, with the state adopting minimalist interventions and leaving the rest to the market.

LABOR MARKET POLICY IN GERMANY

Germany has also seen the growth of a significant low-wage sector, particularly since the country implemented its own activation policies in 2003–2005 with the so-called Hartz reforms.[22] But these moves took place within the context of other policies that specifically shored up the privileges of a protected core. Previous chapters have documented strong cooperation in industrial relations and training policy to support and enhance the competitiveness of the export sectors. But achieving competitiveness through increased productivity and internal flexibility made it difficult to continue to align working standards for the less skilled with those of more productive workers in the core.

---

68 percent of private-sector workers in the bottom fourth of the wage distribution had no paid sick days ... " Health care is also a major problem: " ... in 2008, more than half (54 percent) of workers in the bottom wage quintile did not have employer-provided health insurance and more than one-third (37 percent) had no health insurance of any kind, private or public" (10).

[22] Named after Peter Hartz, the head of the commission who proposed them.

Flexibility was achieved not through across-the-board deregulation, but through selective liberalization of various forms of atypical employment – agency work, fixed-term contracts, and especially so-called mini-jobs that contribute to what is now a significant low-wage sector in Germany.

Mini-jobs refer to low-wage, part-time work that is not fully covered by social insurance contributions and in which workers do not enjoy entitlements to the usual benefits (Keller and Seifert 2006: 238; Buschoff and Protsch 2008: 61–64).[23] This form of employment had long existed on the margins as a way for students, housewives, and retirees to work a few hours to supplement family income. However, in the 1980s employers began to use mini-jobs as a cheaper alternative to regular part-time employment; in the meantime, mini-jobs account for 20 percent of low-skill service-sector jobs. The expansion of this type of employment has contributed to the growth of low-wage employment in Germany, which has increased steadily over the past decade to over 20 percent of total employment – behind only the United States, Canada, and the UK, as Figure 4.4 illustrates (Spiegel 2008; see also OECD 2012c: 247; Weinkopf n.d.: 2). The incidence of low paid employment is especially high among women in Germany.[24]

In other words, the overall trend in German labor market policy – as in industrial relations and training – is a strong bifurcation: while the vast majority (74 percent) of blue-collar workers in the manufacturing core occupy standard (permanent, full-time) jobs, among low-end service functionaries only about 37 percent hold such jobs, the rest working under atypical employment contracts of one sort or another (Eichhorst and Marx 2012b: 83). In contrast to the United States, Germany exhibits lower levels of wage dispersion among full-time employees (as we saw in Chapter 2), but compared to Denmark it is also characterized by more uneven access to the primary labor market (standard employment with benefits) (Eichhorst and Marx 2009: 3–4). The following sections trace the politics that have produced this pattern, beginning with labor market policies affecting the core and turning then to those that have contributed to the growth of the periphery.

Stabilizing the Core

In Germany, the safeguards protecting workers in standard or normal employment relationships are substantial. Germany has comparatively strong employment protection legislation for regular full-time workers, and it is actually one of very few countries in which OECD figures record an increase in employment protections for regular workers since 1985 (OECD Stat Database, accessed

---

[23] While eligible for health care through the public system, mini-jobbers do not qualify for unemployment benefits, or for pension benefits unless they themselves make voluntary contributions to pension funds – something that these low-income workers are rarely in a position to do.

[24] Over 68% of low wage earners in Germany are women.

July 2012).[25] Beyond the formal legal protections, workers who are covered
by collective bargaining often benefit from additional safeguards set down in
industry contracts; these especially protect older workers and workers with
long tenure (Ebbinghaus and Eichhorst 2007: 26). And finally, as noted in
Chapter 2, workers in the organized core – particularly in Germany's large
manufacturing companies – enjoy vigorous representation through powerful
works councils that, as we saw, have made employment security a priority and
the centerpiece of company-level pacts with their employers.

Alongside these already strong protections, the government supports measures – above all, STW (in German: *Kurzarbeit*) – that specifically benefit labor
market insiders by underwriting continued employment stability in industry.
Kurzarbeit reaches back quite far in German history,[26] and it remains a key
labor market instrument today. In 1958, government subsidies for STW – paid
to companies but passed on to workers – were initially set at a relatively generous 62.5 percent of net wages (80 percent for workers with families) for
a maximum of 14 weeks. STW policies were also a central element in major
labor market legislation in 1969 – namely, the Law for Employment Promotion
(*Arbeitsförderungsgesetz*). Under the 1969 legislation, government subsidies
were extended to cover benefits as well – 50 percent of health care contributions and 75 percent of pension fund contributions for affected workers.[27]
In 1975, under pressure from industry in the economic downturn following
the first oil shock, government subsidies for wages of short-time workers were
increased to 68 percent with a maximum duration of twenty-four months (and
in the beleaguered steel industry, to 36 months).

By the 2000s, STW benefits had been reduced somewhat but continued to
cover 60 percent of a worker's normal wage (67 percent for parents) for up to
six months. Moreover, manufacturing firms routinely top up the government
subsidies so that workers experience less dramatic declines in income despite
shorter hours. A recent collective agreement in the chemical industry, in fact,
committed firms to top up government-subsidized wages to cover 90 percent
of the worker's normal wage, in metalworking about 80 percent (see especially
Bispinck 2010b for the provisions in collective agreements on *Kurzarbeit*).

Firms must apply for *Kurzarbeit* subsidies through the local employment
agency, and such applications require the consent of works councils (Bispinck
2010b: IV). Where – as in manufacturing – firms and workers have jointly
invested in the skills required for a specific occupation, both sides share an
interest in long-term employment. Such logic does not, however, apply in

[25] Largely as a result of changes that restored employment protections that had been previously
retracted for workers in very small firms.
[26] These programs can be dated back to the 1880s, when some firms responded to downturns by reducing hours and providing the affected workers with "waiting payments" (Will
2011: 2).
[27] The law also laid out the terms of firm eligibility (companies could apply for STW subsidies on
economic grounds if one-third of workers would be affected by a decline in wages of at least
10%).

sectors that do not rely on skills (e.g., most low-end services) nor in sectors that rely on general rather than firm- or industry-specific skills where the best workers – and therefore the ones the company would most like to keep – will have more exit options.

The role and function of STW policies in Germany was vividly on display in the recent crisis.[28] In a first "rescue package" in November 2008, the government made it easier for firms to qualify for *Kurzarbeit* and expanded state subsidies by increasing the maximum period of support from previous six months to eighteen months. In a second rescue package passed just four months later, eligibility restrictions were also relaxed; companies were no longer required to demonstrate that one-third of the workforce would have to have wages cut by 10 percent in order to qualify; even a small number of workers could be affected (Bundesregierung 2009). Where *Kurzarbeit* subsidies were used for training, or where STW exceeded six months, the state agreed to cover 100 percent of social contributions rather than the usual 50 percent.[29] In July 2009, the government increased the maximum duration again, to twenty-four months, and took on even more responsibility for paying social contributions (Will 2011: 5).[30]

At the height of the crisis in 2009, fully 3.2 percent of German workers fell under STW arrangements, a higher percentage than most other countries save Italy (3.3 percent) and Belgium (5.6 percent) (Schmitt 2011). Germany's labor market performance since the Great Recession has been widely celebrated (Krugman 2010; Brenke et al. 2011; Rinne and Zimmermann 2011; Schmitt 2011).[31] Analysts attribute Germany's strong and rapid rebound largely to adjustments in working times, partly accomplished through various flextime arrangements and partly through STW, which together seem to have been sufficient to absorb the decline in labor demand. Without detracting from the many laudatory effects these policies have had, it is nonetheless important to bear in mind that these policies are not even remotely redistributive, but instead redound virtually exclusively to the benefit of those workers in the core economy who already enjoy the strongest job protections and most generous benefits.

Although manufacturing in Germany accounts for just 20 percent of total employment, almost 80 percent of those supported by STW in the 2008–2009

---

[28] See also Pancaldi (2011) for an extended comparative analysis of the use of STW in Germany and Italy.

[29] Beyond this, unions and employers in manufacturing jointly approached the government in order to secure (successfully) the coverage also of agency workers under the terms of the *Kurzarbeit* legislation. In practice, though, employers do not typically offer agency workers this option (S. Vogel 2009b) and in fact such workers appear to be used more as a buffer. For example in the immediate aftermath of the crisis many firms hired temps rather than permanent workers.

[30] The duration was later lowered again to 18 months but with the government paying 100% of contributions (Will 2011: 5–6).

[31] Against the almost universal trend toward rising unemployment, Germany's jobless rate actually fell from 8% at the beginning of 2008 to 5.6% four years later.

downturn were from manufacturing (overwhelmingly metalworking) (BA 2009: 12; see also Deeke 2005: 15). Even though unemployment is by far higher in eastern Germany than it is in the west, the heaviest concentrations in STW subsidies went to western firms, and the biggest beneficiaries were in fact the prosperous Baden-Württemberg and Bavaria regions (Schwengler and Loibl 2010: 7–8). STW policies clearly help to underwrite continued cooperation in the manufacturing core by supporting stable employment there and protecting the investments that both firms and workers have made in industry- or firm-specific skills. And while these policies did much to allow German manufacturing to bounce back quickly in the wake of the recent recession, they do not necessarily do much to reduce the inequalities that have accompanied the decline in collective bargaining coverage and the increase in atypical employment – a development to which I now turn.

Flexibilizing the Periphery

One of the consequences of the stabilization of employment in the shrinking core was to drive a general outsourcing of certain functions formerly performed within large companies to other firms that could make use of more flexible forms of employment. These trends, along with the progressive expansion of a broad range of services outside the reach of the unions, have fueled the rise of a secondary labor market, characterized by nonstandard work contracts and lower standards – for pay, working conditions, and social protection. While trade unions have successfully resisted major changes in employment protection for core workers, they experienced growing pressure to accept increased flexibility for other types of jobs. Thus, alongside the stable and still well-protected jobs, various forms of atypical employment have been on the rise in Germany.

Beginning with the Employment Promotion Act of 1985 (*Beschäftigungs-förderungsgesetz*), the government sought to enhance flexibility in the labor market by easing restrictions on various forms of atypical employment (Kittner 1985). Reforms in 1985 and 1996, for example, relaxed the rules governing fixed-term employment to allow firms to offer contracts for up to twenty-four months with no special justification. Further reforms under the red-green government of the early 2000s lowered the threshold for contract renewals for older unemployed workers. Start-up companies can also now use contract workers for up to four years with no special justification (Eichhorst and Marx 2009: 11). The 1985 law and subsequent reforms also relaxed restrictions on the use of agency workers whose maximum terms were successively extended from previously three months to twelve months in 1997 before the limit was abolished altogether in 2002 (Dekker and Kaiser 2000: 5; Mitlacher 2007: 584–585).

However, one of the most important sources of dualization is the rise of mini-jobs, which have flourished in the less unionized service sector. This type of employment dates back to the Golden Era of the 1960s and early 1970s, when these jobs were held mostly by students, housewives and others who were not interested in regular employment. Because they enjoyed benefits through their husbands or fathers, workers in these jobs were exempt from all contributions up to a threshold of earnings set at 620 DM per month (adjusted, soon after, to 630 DM, Silvia 2002: 14). Their employers paid a lump-sum tax amounting to 20 percent of the worker's earnings, but the workers were not responsible for payroll taxes. Through such arrangements, households could supplement family incomes, tax-free, while continuing to rely on benefits through male breadwinners.

The early growth of mini-jobs is a textbook example of policy drift. As non-wage labor costs grew in the 1980s and 1990s employers increasingly turned to the less expensive mini-jobs option, and as a result the number of such jobs increased well beyond the original clientele (Silvia 2002: 14; also Eichhorst and Marx 2009: 8). Service-sector firms in particular showed a distinct preference for forgoing regular forms of part-time employment in favor of mini-jobs, which were also less bureaucratic and more flexible. This form of employment has grown especially in low-skill service industries that employ a large number of women. Almost two-thirds (62 percent) of mini-jobholders are women, overwhelmingly married (Spangenberg 2005: 27; Eichhorst 2012: slide 7; Minijobzentrale 2012: 10).

The increase in this form of employment brought with it calls by unions for greater regulation, and the politics reveal a great deal about the interests and alignments behind dualization in Germany. Low-wage unions in the service sector – whose members compete most directly with mini-jobbers – pressed the government to seek to limit, if not to abolish altogether, this type of contribution-free and benefit-empty work. In the early debates of 1999, unions representing workers in the retail trade and hospitality industries called for the government to lower the threshold at which regular payroll taxes would be collected in order to limit the number of mini-jobs (HBV 1999; NGG 1999). These unions were not just concerned with the consequences for individual workers, who might be tempted to forego benefits to increase their take-home pay by avoiding contributions. They were also worried that mini-jobs would depress wages generally – particularly because these workers would have incentives to stay below the 630 DM limit, since higher earnings would push them into an employment zone (subject to full contributions) that would drastically reduce their take-home pay. Unions representing workers in low-pay sectors were joined by women's groups – including the National Council of German Women's Organizations (the Deutscher Frauenrat) – who wanted to either sharply limit these mini-jobs or see them fully covered by mandatory social insurance contributions.

Manufacturing unions were less engaged in these debates; the major industrial unions (chemical workers, metalworkers) did not submit position papers in 1999 when the issue was first mooted for legislative action by the Social

Democratic government. Their members do not typically compete for employment with mini-jobbers; in fact, many of them are married to mini-jobbers. The goal of the industrial unions in these debates was therefore not so much to secure separate benefits for this type of work as it was to thwart employer efforts to dodge their contribution obligations. They feared that the increase in mini-jobs, deliberately chosen by employers to avoid social contributions, would undermine the financial stability of the social insurance funds.[32]

Employers, for their part, vigorously opposed all proposals to curtail or limit the growth of mini-jobs. The Association of German Retailers and the Organization of Hotel and Restaurant Employers led the charge in rejecting changes to existing arrangements, arguing that this would lead to unsustainably high labor costs (DeHoGa 1999). These groups were backed up by the BDA as well as the neoliberal Free Democratic Party, which positioned itself as defender of the interests of small and medium sized firms (e.g., Bundestag 1999: 1144). Artisanal associations also criticized proposals to reduce the contribution threshold on mini-jobs, since many handicraft producers rely on their own wives – employed in this way – as an integral part of the family business.

In a first reform in 1999, the red-green government made some attempt to slow the growth of mini-jobs, prohibiting these as secondary employment and increasing the cost to employers marginally. However, it rejected the more drastic proposals of the party's left wing to limit the use of mini-jobs by lowering the threshold at which social contributions would kick in. The government also addressed the concerns of manufacturing unions that the growth of this form of contribution-free employment would undermine the social insurance funds. It did so by replacing the previous lump-sum tax with employer – but not employee – contributions to health and retirement funds (10 percent and 12 percent of wages, respectively) ("Koalitionswirren" 1998). The Federal Ministry of Labor and Social Affairs (BMAS) argued that it was not sustainable for the country's social net to be carried by fewer and fewer contribution-based jobs. In the debate over this legislation, SPD spokesman Rudolf Dressler reasoned that the shift from a tax on mini-jobs to employer contributions would bring 10 billion DM into the strapped insurance funds. These additional resources, he noted, were "urgently needed" in order to avert an otherwise "nearly unavoidable" further increase in social contributions on standard, full-time jobs ("SPD will Beitragspflicht" 1998).

The restrictions on mini-jobs in the 1999 legislation did dampen the growth of this form of employment, but other aspects of the legislation seemed to

---

[32] I thank Martin Seeleib-Kaiser for emphasizing this to me. Manufacturing unions were also – for the same reasons – skeptical of proposals aimed at reducing social contributions for low-skill workers or using funds from a newly introduced ecology tax to finance a progressive reduction of such contributions. Both of these ideas had been raised in the context of tripartite "Alliance for Work" negotiations, but were met with intense opposition in union circles (*auf das heftigste abelehnt*) (Streeck 2000: 22; see also Streeck and Heinze 1999). In these debates, manufacturing unions were criticized for cleaving to outmoded solutions aimed at rationing employment rather than stimulating the creation of new jobs (Streeck 1999; see also Gehrmann 1998).

redound more to the benefit of regular full-time workers than to mini-jobbers themselves. The switch from a lump-sum tax to employer contributions played a role in facilitating a reduction in pension contributions for regular workers – from 20.3 percent in April 1999 down to 19.1 percent by January of 2001 (Schludi 2005: 145). The law prohibited any one individual from taking a mini-job as a second job, but as before, families anchored by male breadwinners could continue to augment household income, tax-free, in this way. Meanwhile, though, not much changed for mini-jobbers outside of households with a primary breadwinner. Although such workers carry health insurance coverage through the public system, they were still not entitled to unemployment insurance, and their pension entitlements are trivial, being tied to income on what are – by definition – very low earnings.[33]

Moreover, by 2002 there was not a trace left of any effort to limit the growth of mini-jobs. On the contrary, new legislation in that year encouraged the expansion of such employment by raising the monthly pay threshold at which mandatory employer contributions kick in (from 325 to 400 euros per month), by abolishing the fifteen hour per week limit, and by again allowing mini-jobs as second jobs (Bäcker 2006). While employers had criticized the 1999 switch to contributions as bureaucratic, they welcomed the later changes that lifted the earnings threshold and eased other restrictions (Funk 2003). Firms would have to pay a higher fixed contribution than before – 25 percent of gross earnings, up from 22 percent (increased again to 30 percent in 2006) – but most employers feel this is more than compensated by the great flexibility this form of employment offers.[34] Mini-jobbers often work irregular hours (e.g., in grocery stores, they are brought in at peak hours or before store opening to stock shelves), and because the workers themselves are still exempt from social contributions, firms share in the subsidy through low wage rates (Weinkopf n.d.: 10–11).[35]

The 2002 legislation was followed by a very rapid increase in the number of mini-jobs, especially as second jobs (Eichhorst and Kaiser 2006: 33; Ebbinghaus and Eichhorst 2007: 22; see also Bäcker 2006; Mitlacher 2007: 585). This form of marginal employment climbed steeply, to nearly 7.5 million by 2010.

[33] Mini-jobbers can supplement this with individual pension contributions, but of course, given the low wages, few are actually in a position to do this.

[34] The new legislation also contained provisions for jobs paying slightly more, from 400–800 euros per month (so-called midi jobs). In this case, both employers and workers do pay contributions, though employee contributions are lower than with regular employment. Specifically, employer contributions (for health and pensions) stayed at 21% for workers earning between 400–800 euros per month. Employee contributions begin at 400 Euro, though at a reduced level, increasing in a graduated fashion and reaching the usual 21% of pay only at 800 euros per month (Bäcker 2006; Funk 2003; Neubäumer and Tretter 2008).

[35] The cost savings to employers of hiring mini-jobbers over regular part-time workers are significant (Eichhorst and Kaiser 2006; Neubäumer 2007). And, as Neubäumer points out, under regular part-time conditions, for a worker to arrive at the same net income of 400 Euro, his or her gross income – before contributions – has to be much higher (almost double) that sum. The legislation thus provides savings that the employer and employee can divide between themselves.

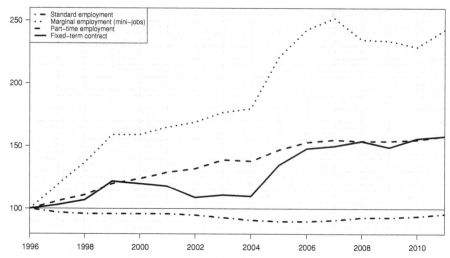

FIGURE 4.5. Trends in Different Forms of Employment in Germany, 1996–2010. *Note*: 1996 = 100. *Source*: Eichhorst (2012b: 9).

Figure 4.5 puts these developments in context by tracking the growth of mini-jobs against trends in other forms of employment since 1996. The number of standard employment contracts has been essentially flat, even declining, since the late 1990s, but the number of mini-jobs (in this figure, "marginal employment") has more than doubled, outstripping by far the growth in all other forms of atypical employment in Germany.

Service-sector employees and women make up the vast majority of those who work under such arrangements. In 2010, one in three service-sector employees worked as mini-jobbers, and retail alone accounts for about 1 million of a total of 7 million mini-jobbers (Beile and Priessner 2011: 5). While some research has shown that certain forms of atypical employment (e.g., fixed-term contracts) can serve as a bridge to permanent jobs in Germany (Gash 2008), this is not true for mini-jobs.[36]

Activation, German Style

The easing of restrictions on mini-jobs was part of a much broader package of reforms – the so-called Hartz reforms of the early 2000s – that were associated with a shift to activation and accompanied by a liberalization of other forms of

[36] Women's groups have long argued that mini-jobs do not offer women a pathway into "regular" employment so much as they put up new barriers, while at the same time further anchoring a model of female employment as a complement to the primary male breadwinner. Bäcker's (2006) work supports this, suggesting that women in mini-jobs are mostly "shunted into the traditional role of supplementing family income" (259).

atypical work as well (Konle-Seidl 2008: 6; Schnyder and Jackson 2011: 18).[37] Other measures promoted self-employment for the unemployed (so-called *ich-AG*, or Me, Inc.) and created work opportunities (at low pay) in the public sector for the long-term unemployed.[38] The share of part-time employment classified by the OECD as involuntary (i.e., for lack of being able to find a full-time job) rose steadily in Germany from about 5 percent in the late 1980s to 10 percent in the late 1990s, to 18.7 percent by 2010 (OECD Stat Database).

Unlike in Denmark, these liberalizing measures – and the accompanying activation policies – have not been strongly articulated with enhanced state support for training. On the contrary, spending on ALMP did not increase with the Hartz reforms, but instead actually declined, as Figure 4.2 shows. "Compared to 2002, spending on ALMP through 2006 has decreased of [sic] about one third. The financial volume for the most important instrument, vocational training programs, decreased from €7.2 to €2.0 billion" (Konle-Seidl 2008: 25). Whereas Demark is characterized by high ALMP spending and high income-related unemployment compensation, Germany "went in the other direction...aiming for fast placements rather than up-skilling as in the past" (Bosch and Charest 2008: 436). In short, the Hartz reforms represented a move away from "long term training and direct job creation measures to shorter programs aiming at an accelerated reintegration into the labor market" (Eichhorst and Marx 2009: 10).

In fact, labor market policy in Germany now not only allows, it also in effect subsidizes, a significant and growing low wage sector (Eichhorst and Marx 2009: 10; Astheimer 2010; Weinkopf n.d.: 10). The last of the Hartz reforms (Hartz IV) created the possibility of in-work benefits for low-income groups and, with that, the possibility to combine state financed minimum income support[39] with mini-jobs and other forms of low-pay employment. Over a quarter of recipients of Hartz IV support are working, but for wages that are so low that they also qualify for means-tested benefits (Konle-Seidl 2008: 21, 2012). Those who top up their benefits with paid work are called *Aufstocker* (loosely: "top-uppers"). For such workers, being employed in mini-jobs allows them to earn some money (tax- and contribution-free) without losing their benefits, and also has the advantage of keeping the job centers off their backs.[40] Taken together, these moves "officially sanction the raise [sic] of a low-wage sector and hence constitute a break with the German postwar

---

[37] These included the relaxation in restrictions on temporary agency work and fixed-term contracts noted previously.

[38] The latter are the so-called one euro jobs, essentially work paid at marginally more than social assistance levels (Barbier and Knuth 2010: 26).

[39] Arbeitslosengeld II, or ALG II.

[40] Regina Konle-Seidl (2012) notes that in June 2012, 681,000 *Aufstocker* were employed in mini-jobs. Self-employed (ich-AG) often apply for Hartz IV benefits as well because this entitles them to health insurance.

model that had a high-wage, high-skill, high quality production compromise at its centre" (Schnyder and Jackson 2011: 19).

Moreover, once institutionalized in this way, the low-wage sector has proved highly resistant to reform (BMAS interview, 2011). The problem is partly that the organized interests with the greatest stake in reversing these trends are weak and disorganized; as we have seen, unionization is low in services, and especially so in low-wage service sectors. Service-sector employers, for their part, resist change. They value mini-jobs for the extreme flexibility they offer, making it possible for them to pay for exactly those hours they want and no more (interview with representative of Handelsverband Deutschland, HDE, the German Retail Federation, 2011). Meanwhile, some mini-jobbers themselves prefer this type of job over full-time employment subject to high payroll taxes, especially if they can combine it with partial benefits through Hartz IV as *Aufstocker* ("Wenn sich die Arbeit nicht" 2010: 11; "Aufstocker arbeiten meist Teilzeit" 2013).

Perhaps most important politically, mini-jobs remain attractive as a source of supplementary household income. Since 1958, the German tax code provides windfalls for married couples with highly unequal incomes, and mini-job reforms have all been framed so as to continue to allow married women to get the full tax benefit (Spangenberg 2005: 27; "CDU-Spitze" 2006; Weinkopf n.d.: 11). Any attempt to reform this aspect of the tax code (*Ehegattensplitting*) has become a political third rail. The CDU is vehemently opposed under the banner of "family values" (CDU/CS-Fraktion 2011), but the Social Democrats also cannot bring themselves to embrace the idea (Zylka 2002; "SPD zweifelt am Splitting" 2011).[41] Unions, meanwhile, continue to be dominated by male breadwinners, and so they also quietly defend mini-jobs as the only tax loophole that helps their constituents.[42] While single mother mini-jobbers in Germany would benefit from a regularization of benefits, many of them work alongside other women who already enjoy benefits through their insider husbands and are simply supplementing family income. The latter are objectively identical in terms of their labor market situation, but politically they are often on the other side of the debate (Barrows 2011).

Recent developments in German labor market policy have thus helped to institutionalize and anchor a divide between well-protected standard employment relationships endowed with significant benefits on one hand, and more precarious jobs with virtually no benefits on the other. One sees again in these developments a pattern similar to that observed for industrial relations: intensified cooperation within the manufacturing core and more

---

[41] Only the Greens are unequivocally and vocally in favor of abolishing this tax benefit.

[42] Thirty-five percent of mini-jobbers live in two-income households earning more than 3,000 euros per month; the rest are split rather evenly between households earning under 2,000 euros per month and those earning between 2,000 and 2,999 euros per month (Eichhorst 2012: slide 12).

conflictual relations in low-wage service sectors, rooted in employer preferences for flexibility through the use of benefit-weak atypical employment contracts. Germany's organized labor movement has been generally quite successful in heading off deregulatory moves that would directly affect their core constituencies, while employer strategies – and increasingly, state policy – promote flexibility on the periphery. So, while the national indicators for Germany currently look rather impressive (strong economic growth, declining unemployment), behind these aggregate figures the labor market is more segmented than ever (Brönstrup 2011).

LABOR MARKET POLICY IN DENMARK

If the story of German labor market policy is broadly about stabilizing the core while flexibilizing the periphery, then the headline for Denmark is something like the opposite: liberalizing on a broader scale while stabilizing the situation of those on the periphery through measures to facilitate their (re-)integration into the core labor market. As in Germany, government policy in Denmark now leans heavily toward activating the unemployed, but activation policies are embedded in generous state support for the most vulnerable groups. Dualization is a problem in Denmark, too, but low-skill workers outside of manufacturing are better organized and represented, resulting in significantly lower levels of precarious employment and low-wage work. These outcomes explain why the Danish model of flexicurity has attracted such attention and why it figures prominently in the policy recommendations of both the EU and the OECD (C. Jørgensen 2005; Viebrock and Clasen 2009).

The rhetoric of its proponents is often rather too breathless, and I will discuss the dark side of the Danish model below. But the admiration is in many ways understandable and not unwarranted. In the 1980s, Denmark was plagued by high unemployment and growing public debt. The country managed a very impressive turnaround beginning in 1993 when the number of registered unemployed peaked at 12.4 percent before declining steadily to 5.2 percent in 2002 (J. Andersen 2010: 6). Moreover, at the same time that unemployment was being reduced, Denmark also raised overall employment levels by 6 percent, mostly through job creation in the private sector (75 percent of new jobs), which brought Denmark to an employment/population ratio of almost 78.6 percent, one of the highest in the OECD (P. Madsen 2002: 243, 2006: 323). Unemployment bottomed out in 2007 at less than 4 percent, and though it has risen again since the 2008 financial crisis, it still remains well below the OECD average (OECD 2012b: 3).

Flexicurity means different things in different contexts, but in Denmark it "combines the flexibility of the labour market often ascribed to a liberal market economy with the social safety net of the traditional Scandinavian welfare state" (P. Madsen 2006: 327). This combination of flexibility and security explains why the model has won endorsements from observers on different ends of the ideological spectrum (Viebrock and Clasen 2009). Neoliberals attribute Denmark's economic successes to low employment protections and the activating elements of labor market policy; they urge further flexibility. Defenders of social democracy stress the way the model provides support for those displaced by the market, thus reconciling "adaptability to a changing international environment [with] a solidaristic welfare system [that] protects the citizens from the more brutal consequences of structural change" (P. Madsen 2002: 243).

The Danish model is typically characterized as involving a "golden triangle" of mutually reinforcing components, namely: flexible labor markets, generous support for the unemployed, and labor market policies that actively underwrite retraining and placement. Some elements of the golden triangle – in particular, relatively low employment protection – were inherited from the past (e.g., Campbell and Hall 2006). Other elements, notably activation and training-based labor market policies are of very recent (1990s) vintage (P. Madsen 2006: 331; also Viebrock and Clasen 2009).

As is widely known, Denmark features quite fluid labor markets and high levels of mobility.[43] This country has long stood out because the level of employment protection for full-time workers is much lower than most other CMEs (Estevez-Abe et al. 2001). As Emmenegger (2010) has pointed out, in the 1970s Danish unions failed where their Swedish counterparts succeeded in winning legislation to strengthen employment protection and enhance labor's local-level codetermination rights in this area.[44] He thus argues that Danish labor's defeat in the Golden Era ironically was a crucial prerequisite for later flexicurity policies.

Figure 4.6 provides data on the level of employment protection enjoyed by permanent workers and workers on temporary contracts for the five countries covered in this book (based on OECD measures). It shows that regular full-time workers in Denmark are significantly less well protected than their counterparts in Sweden, the Netherlands, and Germany – though still better protected than those in the liberal United States.

However, what is also striking about Figure 4.6 is that protections for temporary workers in Denmark are not far behind those for regular full-time workers.[45] In addition, and very different from Germany in particular, atypical forms of employment (whether part-time or fixed-term) are much more likely to be covered by the same arrangements as standard workers – same collective

---

[43] Kristensen et al. (2011) note that 20% of the Danish labor force changes jobs each year (87).

[44] Salaried employees, however, enjoy somewhat stronger dismissal protection as a result of legislation dating back to the 1930s (Emmenegger 2009: 181–182). For a comparison of the rules for blue- and white-collar workers see CO-industri (2008: 19).

[45] As a matter of fact, when measured in terms of an alternative OECD "version 3" employment protection index – one that includes additional indicators both for permanent and temporary employment – protections for temporary workers in Denmark are actually greater than those for regular workers. Per Kongshøj Madsen (2013), for example, uses this alternative index. For a summary of the calculations involved in both indices see OECD (n.d.).

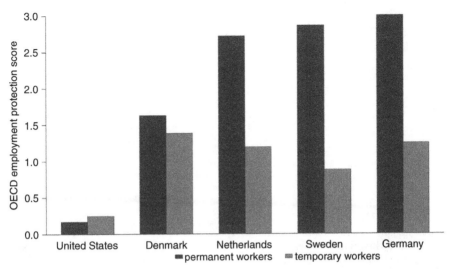

FIGURE 4.6. Strictness of Employment Protection for Permanent and Temporary Workers, Various Countries. *Source*: stats.oecd.org, accessed 5/27/2013.

bargains, same provisions for vacation, sick pay, seniority, and the like (P. Madsen 2013: 8–16).

In consequence, if Denmark's primary labor market is more fluid, its secondary labor market is overall less well developed compared to most other European countries. The share of employees on temporary contracts, for example, is low in international comparisons, as shown in Figure 4.7. The country does have a significant share of part-time work, but mostly this is a matter

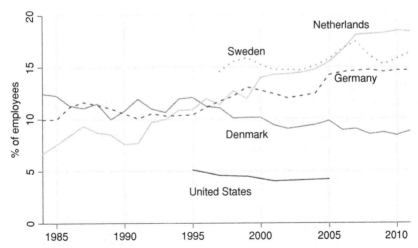

FIGURE 4.7. Temporary Employment as a Share of Total Employment, 1985–2010. *Source*: OECD Stat Database.

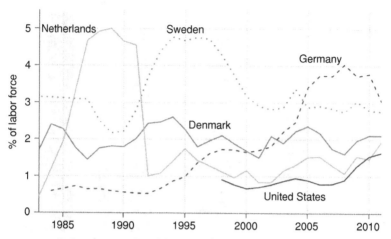

FIGURE 4.8. Involuntary Part-Time Workers as a Share of Total Labor Force, 1985–2010. *Source*: OECD Stat Database.

of choice, as indicated in Figure 4.8 by relatively low levels of involuntary part-time employment (P. Madsen 2013: 5).

The pattern we observe for Denmark is thus very different from Germany, where labor market liberalization since the 1990s has been associated with strong bifurcation between well-protected jobs in the core and a growing periphery of more precarious, atypical employment. It is not, however, that Denmark has not experienced liberalization. On the contrary, the 1990s saw a sharp turn in labor market policy toward increased activation of the unemployed. Unlike in the United States, however, these developments were followed by measures to collectivize rather than individualize the accompanying risks. The next sections explore the politics that produced these outcomes as they unfolded over time.

The Turn to Liberalization

Labor market policy in Denmark in the 1970s and 1980s bore a strong resemblance to policies in Germany. The first response of the Danish government to the increase in unemployment in the 1970s was actually classically "continental" and aimed at easing older workers out of the labor force, while supporting the unemployed with generous social transfer payments.[46] As Torfing (1999) puts it: "the main ambition in the years from 1977 to 1993 was to maintain the standard of living for the unemployed as well as possible"

---

[46] This was the aim, for example, of the Voluntary Early Retirement scheme passed in 1979, which made it possible for workers between sixty and sixty-six years old to withdraw from the labor market and draw on unemployment benefits as a bridge to receipt of pensions (P. Madsen 2007: 20).

(13; see also H. Jørgensen 2002: 173–174). The labor market programs that existed at the time were decidedly passive and served "not to support reintegration into the workforce but more to re-qualify the long-term unemployed for continued receipt of benefits" (Schulze-Cleven 2009: 190). Job training programs in many ways encouraged repeated re-qualification for benefits ("cycling") so that "the unemployed could stay within the unemployment insurance system forever" (Torfing 1999: 12–13).

The first signs of change came in 1982 with the collapse of the center-left government and the ascendance to power of Poul Schlüter, a confirmed but pragmatic neoliberal, at the head of a new center-right coalition government. Many aspects of economic policy took a strong neoliberal turn as Prime Minister Schlüter introduced a number of measures, often against intense opposition from labor and the Social Democrats. These included, among other things, the institutionalization of a hard currency regime, a massive liberalization of capital markets, and the elimination of previous cost-of-living indexation for wages and social benefits (Schulze-Cleven 2009: 190). These reforms, combined with the changes in industrial relations institutions detailed in Chapter 2 and significant decentralization in the public sector under the banner of new public management (NPM), made this a period of significant change – and conflict – in Danish politics (Schwartz 1994).

The changes in labor market policy were less dramatic than those in the area of macroeconomic policy. Sitting at the helm of a minority government in a time of soaring unemployment, Prime Minister Schlüter refrained from undertaking a major reform of unemployment insurance (Green-Pedersen 2001: 60; J. Andersen 2010: 8). Even so, the tone for labor market policy shifted considerably as "the economists took over" and argued that labor market rigidities and distortions were undermining work incentives (Torfing 1999: 14). Henning Jørgensen (2002) documents the emergence of a new discourse in Denmark in the 1980s, which "criticized the passive and expansive employment support schemes," which were being redefined as serious impediments to the proper functioning of the labor market (175–176).

The early years of the Schlüter government were turbulent, as the prime minister launched a number of initiatives that were clearly designed to reduce the influence of organized labor (Scheuer 1992: 188). Activation policies got their start in the municipalities (H. Jørgensen 2002: 175–176). In an effort to rein in spending, Schlüter's Finance Ministry introduced changes in the structure of central funding and regulation, transitioning "from a system of reimbursement for local service expenditures...to a system of shrinking block grants" (Schwartz 2001: 148). Spending cuts at the national level resulted in a decline in support for local governments, from 35.6 percent of local funding in 1982 to just 28 percent by 1985 (Schwartz 2001: 148). Faced with these developments, municipal officials began experimenting with active social policies as a way of simultaneously coping with fiscal constraints and enhancing the productivity of marginal workers (Martin and Thelen 2007: 25; Martin and Swank 2012:

chapter 9). Training programs for the unemployed figured centrally in many of these locally grown measures (Etherington 1995: 251).

The more sweeping changes came somewhat later, building on the local experiments in the 1980s but based on recommendations from a tripartite labor market commission Prime Minister Schlüter convened in 1991. The Report of the so-called Zeuthen Commission came out just before a general election that would return the Social Democrats to power. Representatives of the LO and the DA were deeply involved in the work of the commission (and together formed a majority on it), but the report also reflected the new prevailing tone in public opinion that had emerged over the years of the center-right government. Danes had become increasingly concerned "by the emergence of a dependency culture, especially among the young unemployed" and the commission recommended deep structural changes to the Danish unemployment insurance system (Torfing 1999: 21–22). The solution worked out involved a trade-off in which organized labor conceded cuts in the duration of unemployment support and stricter eligibility rules in return for a government commitment to skill formation – institutionalizing a "right and obligation" to training (Torfing 1999). As Ornston (2012) puts it, the Zeuthen Commission "replaced passive labor market measures with training, thus creating a focal point for subsequent bargaining" (103).

Danish Flexicurity

Activation in Denmark was thus put on the agenda by the center-right coalition, but it mattered a great deal that it was implemented on the basis of recommendations worked out between employers, government, and encompassing unions. So when the Social Democratic Party returned to power in 1993, the party did not use its strong majority to turn back, but instead to push forward with labor market reform along the lines recommended by the Zeuthen Commission (Green-Pedersen 2001: 60, 63). Initial measures were unambiguously liberalizing and represented a decisive "departure from a 'rights-based' to an 'obligation-based' regime in which unemployed individuals are met with increasing demands in order to receive benefits" (Ibsen and Mailand 2009: 85). A 1993 law (1) reduced the period of passive support to four years, followed by a period of three years of activation; (2) attacked the problem of cycling by specifying that, unlike previously, participation in ALMPs would not prolong eligibility for unemployment benefits; and (3) required long-term unemployed persons to work out an individual action plan with labor market representatives aimed at reintegrating them into the labor market.[47]

---

[47] Another provision also decentralized the administration of unemployment benefits in order to strengthen the link to regional labor markets. A subsequent reform in 1995 reduced the period of entitlement to passive benefits for young unskilled workers to six months, and for adults to two years. Conditionality and eligibility were the main focus, although there were also changes

However, alongside more stringent activation requirements, the supports for reintegration were also strong. The other side of flexicurity, then, is security, and through the 1990s activation policies under the Social Democrats were coupled with a vast expansion of funding for ALMPs designed to facilitate a move on the part of the unemployed back into employment (see Figure 4.2). Government funds supported measures to ease workers' reentry – through enhanced support from the public unemployment service, heightened efforts directed specifically at long-term unemployed and minorities, and stepped up efforts to provide training that was designed to meet the needs of local employers. Important initiatives in the area of continuing training discussed in Chapter 3 emerged in conjunction with these reforms, so that government policy not only supported the retraining of unemployed persons to upgrade their skills while out of work, but also promoted ongoing skill acquisition by workers who held jobs, mostly through tuition subsidies and wage supplements.

Danish efforts on this front stand out in international comparisons (Mailand 2006: 380). Between 1991 and 1996, when other countries were cutting spending in this area, Denmark doubled its expenditures on ALMP, and spending continued to rise to 1.89 percent of GDP by 2000. Outlays for training, specifically, more than tripled, from 0.25 percent of GDP in 1990 to 0.85 percent in 1996. By 1995, almost one-half of all Danes over the age of fifteen had already at some point participated in further training measures (Petersen 1997b). Based on a survey carried out in the late 1990s, Desjardins et al. (2006) report that 53 percent of unemployed Danes – the highest for any of the eighteen countries surveyed – and 43 percent of low-skilled blue-collar Danes (only surpassed by Finland) had participated in some adult education or training in the year before being interviewed (51). Figures from the Ministry of Labour record a strong increase in the number of companies providing individual plans for vocational training between 1995 and 1996, from 35 percent to almost 50 percent (Petersen 1997b).[48] In 1997, the Ministry of Labor – with support from both the DA and the LO – launched a nationwide vocational training campaign, which it carried out in collaboration with 265 local vocational training centers (Petersen 1997b). The groundwork for this effort had been laid earlier that same year by the passage of the Financial Act, which increased

to the levels of support. The 1995 law cut benefits for young persons (under twenty-five). For adults, the level of unemployment benefits remained at 90% of previous earned income for the lowest paid groups but with a ceiling. In general, benefits are indexed to wage increases, but in practice they have lagged behind so that they "gradually became a de facto flat-rate benefit . . . as the overwhelming majority [of beneficiaries] received the maximum" (J. Andersen 2010: 11). Over time, the unemployed were subjected to stricter activation requirements, not just through reduced duration but also through stricter rules on job searching (P. Madsen 2006: 334–335).

[48] Larger firms were overall much more likely to provide such plans than smaller ones: 80–90% of companies with over 100 employees did so, compared to less than 50% of companies with under 100 employees (Petersen 1997b).

expenditure by over 60 percent, from DKK 40 million to DKK 65 million, to support companies undertaking projects aimed at further training (Petersen 1997b).[49]

While many observers think of flexicurity as a strong validation of the consensus-generating powers of macro-corporatism, the truth is that the process was painful and not all groups were equally happy with the outcome. The negotiations behind the original Zeuthen Report had taken place under the center-right government's implicit but clear threat "to circumvent the authority of the business and labor organizations" if they failed to reach agreement (Martin and Thelen 2007: 26). Unskilled workers' unions, especially, opposed the initial moves toward ALMPs. These groups objected to efforts to eliminate passive benefits and to expand the labor market obligations of the unemployed. Despite the fact that it was their members who "potentially had the most to gain from upskilling [they] resented the forcible end to decommodification" (Martin and Swank 2012: 188 fn. 57).

However, the shift in collective bargaining from national-level to industry-level negotiations described in Chapter 2 had had an important effect on the position both of the LO and of low-skill unions within it. Once a powerful bloc within the LO, unskilled unions now negotiated at the sectoral level, where skilled unions dominated (Cox 2001: 482). At the same time, bargaining decentralization had robbed the LO of its role in wage setting, so that – coming up on its centennial celebrations in 1998 – the confederation was casting about for a way to reassert its leadership in the Danish political economy (EIRR 1998b: 5; Petersen 1998f). As we saw in Chapter 2, this was a year of significant turmoil in industrial relations. The government's direct legislative intervention to end the general strike in that year had prompted the LO to demand negotiations on a broader "social contract" (Mailand 2002: 85). The result was an agreement that paved the way for the confederation to assume a leading position in negotiating non-wage issues, including notably the increasingly important area of training (EIRR 1998b: 5).

Thus, the LO ultimately found in the area of training a new *raison d'être* and proceeded to define skill development as a centerpiece of its new strategy. In 1998, the DA and the LO sponsored a joint conference on vocational training and development, and rights to training began to show up in pattern-setting industrial agreements at this time. These developments were further institutionalized in 2001 with the creation of a new tripartite Board for the Labor Market's Financing of Education and Training. The board was part of an initiative "to concentrate public finances on the less skilled and on formal

---

[49] An additional DKK 105 million was made available to companies in support of projects aimed at "improving working life" (Petersen 1997b). Moreover, all of these financial measures were accompanied by an advertising campaign designed to encourage workers to demand and participate in further training measures (Petersen 1997b).

or recognized competences and to include more companies in the financing of activities," and it was expressly charged with advising the government on almost all aspects of CVET (Mailand 2006: 381).

In the end, Denmark in the 1990s settled on a course that emphasized liberalization and activation, but these initiatives were also tied to considerable support for training and retraining, not just for the most vulnerable groups but on a broad scale. As we saw in previous chapters, government subsidies for skill formation and especially adult education and training in Denmark has been very generous in comparative perspective, and unions have actively supported and promoted changes in the CVET system that have made it easier for all groups to access training at all stages in the life cycle. The result has been that liberalization in the labor market has been combined with training liberalization – but with extensive participation on the part of Denmark's encompassing unions, and especially with fulsome support from the state.

A corollary to this is that Denmark has been much less willing than Germany and other continental countries to subsidize STW, which, as we saw, protects jobs and almost always redounds to the benefit of higher-skill workers in the manufacturing core. As Søren Andersen (2010) notes, the Danish government mostly rejects the use of state subsidies to try to prevent job loss (7, italics in original; see also C. Jørgensen 2009b). Thus, Danish short time work subsidies are much less generous than those in Germany (S. Andersen 2010: 7). In Germany, as we saw, government subsidies amounting to 67 percent of a worker's previous wages are then often topped up by companies under terms laid down in industry contracts, so that workers often wind up with 80 to 90 percent of their regular pay. In Denmark, by contrast, compensation is typically around 50 percent of the base wage (i.e., *before* adding the company-level component, which, as we saw in Chapter 2, comprises a large share of the overall wage) and without any company top-ups (7). In the recent crisis, some large Danish industrial firms approached the government to extend the duration of STW benefits, but they came away empty-handed (7). So while this measure was the policy tool of choice for the Germans in the recent crisis, in Denmark "employers' associations, trade unions and the government have by and large agreed that extended coverage of the short-time work scheme should be avoided" (8).

The Danish Model under the Right

As should be clear by now, the Danish flexicurity regime was not implemented all of a piece and in a single grand bargain, let alone a consensual one. In fact, it seems like a classic case of what Zorn et al. (2006) call "retrospective sense making" – cobbled together over time but later marketed as a coherent policy package. This is why it is hard to identify a single coherent "coalition for reform" behind flexicurity. In fact, in the Danish case the liberalizing reforms came first and support for the model was not consolidated among the unskilled "beneficiaries" of these programs until after the fact. Moreover, the balance between flexibility and security continued – and continues – to be contested (Lødemel and Trickey 2001; J. Andersen 2010: 23). In the hands of less redistributively minded parties, the Danish model is always vulnerable to a tilt toward more flexibility and less security, even if it continues to rest on both elements (Larsen et al. 2001: 25; Berkel and Møller 2002; Bredgaard and Larsen 2006: 19; Larsen 2009).

The liberal-conservative coalition that governed Denmark from 2001 to 2011 – under the leadership of the liberal Venstre Party, but sometimes with the support of the anti-immigrant Danish People's Party – introduced some important changes. Among other things, conditionality and activating elements were successively tightened, particularly for the hard-core unemployed. Changes were introduced that, among other things, increased demands on the unemployed to engage in active job searching (including mandatory contact with the unemployment agencies every three months), required the unemployed to take jobs even if they would have to move, and reduced social security benefits for some groups, in particular married couples and newly arrived immigrants (P. Madsen 2006: 337).[50] The bourgeois government also reduced spending on training, which declined in absolute terms from nearly 10 billion Danish Kroner in 2000 to just over 4 billion in 2008 – or from 0.77 percent of GDP in 2000 to 0.23 percent in 2008[51] – before rebounding in response to the rise in unemployment after the financial crisis up to 7.3 billion Danish Kroner and 0.42 percent of GDP in 2010 (OECD).

Denmark is by no means free of dualist tendencies, and efforts on the part of the conservative-liberal coalition to cut costs brought these elements to the fore. The electoral successes of the xenophobic Danish People's Party channeled some such tendencies into measures that targeted immigrants specifically. In 2002, Denmark passed a new law on immigration that not only restricted access to the country, but also introduced a new, less generous social assistance scheme for immigrants from non-EU countries (Liebig 2007). The benefits under the so-called start assistance program are well below standard social assistance – between 35 and 50 percent lower, depending on the composition of the household, and benefits are least generous for households with children. Although social assistance in Denmark is still among the most generous of all the rich democracies, start assistance singles out immigrants for decidedly more miserly treatment (J. Andersen 2010: 35; Mouritsen and Olsen 2013).

---

[50] A government proposal to introduce a longer waiting period before receipt of unemployment benefits for higher-income groups encountered stiff resistance from the trade unions. Perhaps less expectedly, though, employers sided with labor on this issue, worried that benefit cutbacks would be answered by increased demands for stronger employment protection (Madsen 2006: 346–347).

[51] Although unemployment was falling as well for most of this period.

In addition, in 2005 the government instituted a program with the cheery title "New Chance for All," but which in fact increased work requirements for receipt of social assistance (as opposed to unemployment benefits). This, too, implies increased bifurcation: workers who remain close to the core workforce are supported for rather long periods on generous unemployment benefits – subject to some activation but with significant training support as well. By contrast, social assistance beneficiaries (by definition, among the least employable, and in fact also overwhelmingly of immigrant backgrounds) are subject to a harsher workfare regime – among other things expected to work at least 300 hours over two years against the threat of benefit withdrawal (J. Andersen 2010: 35–36). These developments should serve as a cautionary lesson understoring the fragility of the arrangements underlying even the most successful political economies.

TRAJECTORIES OF LIBERALIZATION IN LABOR MARKET POLICY

The shared trajectory of change in labor market policy across all three cases discussed in this chapter is clearly liberalizing; the variation mostly concerns who is activated and on what terms. The United States has long featured highly fluid labor markets with pockets of greater employment security in unionized firms, especially in industry. Here the decline of manufacturing and of unions has hastened further deregulation. Former president Clinton's signature labor market and social policies, originally conceived as an attempt to move toward a stronger commitment to training and social investment, wound up exacerbating these trends, as the "security" aspects of labor market policy were excised, leaving a harsh work first activation model that has fueled inequality by pushing low-skill workers into extremely precarious forms of low-pay employment.

In Germany, the pattern is different because here firms in the manufacturing core share with their employees an interest in stable employment relations that is rooted, among other things, in shared investments in firm- or industry-specific skills. In this case, the push for a liberalization of employment relations has been highly uneven, and manifests itself in the emergence of atypical employment, especially in the service sector. The two sides of dualization – the stabilization of the core and the flexibilization of the periphery – are not separate stories, but two sides of the same coin because extending employment guarantees to core workers is increasingly "bought" through outsourcing strategies that benefit from liberalization outside the core. The same coalition that successfully defends against liberalization within the core in this way inadvertently and indirectly fuels dualization.

Denmark, finally, has undertaken a very significant shift toward liberalization through activation since the 1990s. Low-skill workers are no less exposed to the vicissitudes of the market here than in Germany or, for that matter, in the United States. The difference lies in the system of supports on which they can rely. Generous social insurance and strong state support for training to go along with activation have so far largely "crowded out precarious jobs" and limited the growth of a secondary low-pay labor market (J. Andersen 2010: 4). What distinguishes the Danish system above all is an overall closer integration of training policy, social support, and labor market policy that – with the glaring exception of immigrants – is less organized around defending a stable core and more oriented toward facilitating the reintegration of the unemployed back into standard full-time work.

5

Coalitional Realignments and Institutional Change

The previous chapters have explored the ways in which the decline of employment in manufacturing and the transition to services have unsettled previously stable arrangements across all three of the institutional arenas under analysis here. The broad trajectory of change – in industrial relations, in vocational education and training, and in labor market policy – across all three countries is toward liberalization. This should be seen as a validation of liberalization arguments (notably Streeck 2009; also Baccaro and Howell 2011). Yet we have also seen that there are distinct varieties of liberalization, driven forward by different political dynamics and also associated with different distributional outcomes.

Writing in 1985, Gøsta Esping-Andersen argued that the political viability of the more egalitarian varieties of capitalism involves forming and maintaining alliances that shift in response to changes in class structures as capitalism itself evolves. Social democracy's traditional core constituencies – above all, blue-collar workers in industry – remain central actors in this process, not least because manufacturing itself remains a vital part of the political economies in these countries. However, as Esping-Andersen anticipated, declining employment in manufacturing also means that the survival of social democracy hinges crucially on the new coalitions these groups are able to forge with emerging new class actors – particularly lower-skill workers in the growing service sectors, but also salaried employees and white-collar workers generally. Building on the core insights that Esping-Andersen developed in his analysis of social and welfare policies, I submit that in order to explain observed distinctive trajectories of liberalization in the three arenas examined in this book, we can do no better than to ask how and to what extent such alliances are taking shape.

This chapter thus turns to two further cases – the Netherlands and Sweden – whose differences to those already analyzed provide additional insight into the politics of institutional change in the rich democracies. The Dutch case offers an opportunity to explore how a Christian Democratic country departed from the usual continental pattern to embrace a different version of flexicurity that shares some broad similarities to Scandinavia. Sweden then provides an instructive contrast to Denmark, since this is a Social Democratic bastion that nonetheless has exhibited stronger elements of dualization resembling those in Germany. To be clear, the trends that I observe in the Netherlands and Sweden do not "transport" them into a wholly different "family," in Esping-Andersen's terms. However, they do constitute significant tendencies, and understanding their causes provides additional leverage in explaining the broader cross-national patterns.

I argue that the same two factors that I have identified as important in distinguishing dualism from embedded flexibilization across families also explain more fine grained differences within families as well. Returning to the causal framework presented in Table 1.1, I show how similarities between the Netherlands and Germany can be traced to similarities in the composition of unions and employer associations and the resulting producer group dynamics, while important differences in outcomes are a result of greater state capacity in the Netherlands to broker coalitions that extend beyond the manufacturing core. In a parallel fashion, core similarities between Denmark and Sweden can be traced back to similarities in the broad inclusiveness of the labor movement, while differences between the two reflect the relative weakness of the Swedish state and associated inability to overcome the opposition of employers (especially in industry) to produce a broad national settlement.

THE NETHERLANDS

Many observers place the Netherlands alongside Denmark in the pantheon of apparently successful efforts to sustain, and by some measures even enhance, solidarity in a context marked by retrenchment and liberalization (EC 2006; Bekker and Wilthagen 2008). Understanding the political dynamics that produced the Dutch "jobs miracle" beginning in the mid-1980s is instructive because the country shares many similarities to Germany with respect to core labor market and welfare regime structures, yet reforms in the Netherlands generated outcomes that seemed to at least bend the mold of the classic Christian Democratic model.

At a time when other continental political economies were stuck in a vicious cycle of welfare without work, the Netherlands was able to reduce unemployment steadily and rather dramatically, from 12 percent in 1983 to 6 percent by 1992 and ultimately to 3.2 percent in 2007 – lower than any other country in the EU on the eve of the financial crisis (Bovenberg et al. 2008: 9). Job creation between 1985 and 1995 averaged 1.8 percent per annum, compared to a paltry 0.4 percent in the EU as a whole and 1.5 percent in the United States, which at the time was praised for its robust employment growth (Visser 1998: 270). Most strikingly perhaps, against the backdrop of a previously well entrenched male breadwinner model of employment, women entered the Dutch labor market in very large numbers. Female labor market participation rates in the Netherlands rose from 52.2 to 71.5 percent between 1993 and 2009, an increase double that of the EU average, which rose from 49.2 to 59.9 percent over that period (Visser 2011: 6).

The Dutch employment "miracle" prompts comparisons to the Danish model, but the recipe in the Netherlands was very different (Bekker and Wilthagen 2008; Keizer 2011). Whereas the Danish model is based on a high degree of labor market flexibility for full-time workers and ALMPs to boost skills and push the unemployed back into work, the Dutch jobs miracle is almost entirely a story of increasing part-time employment (Viebrock and Clasen 2009: 9–11). Ninety percent of the jobs that were created between 1985 and 1995 were part time (i.e., between twelve and thirty-six hours), and by 2009 almost half (48.3 percent) of Dutch employees worked part time (Visser 2011: 1; also Bovenberg et al. 2008: 9).[1] As in most countries, part-time work in the Netherlands is heavily female-dominated. Seventy-five percent of all employed Dutch women work part time (Bovenberg et al. 2008: 9). In the meantime, however, 31 percent of all employed men also work part time – so that the Netherlands is now the "frontrunner in male part-time work" as well (Visser 2011: 5; Bovenberg et al. 2008: 9).

Most of these workers have chosen the shorter hours. Even as the Netherlands tops all other OECD countries in the number of part-time workers as a share of total employment, it also registers the lowest levels of involuntary part-time employment (see Figure 4.8).[2] Unlike the German mini-jobs analyzed in Chapter 4, part-time jobs in the Netherlands are subject to the same rules as "standard" full-time jobs with regard to dismissal protection, health care, sick pay, and disability (Viebrock and Clasen 2009: 9–11). Part-time workers are also entitled to the usual benefits (e.g., unemployment insurance and supplementary pensions) on a pro-rated basis. By law, employers may not discriminate on the basis of working hours, so part-timers are covered by the same collective contracts regulating wages, wage supplements, bonuses, and holidays.[3] A large majority of part-time workers are covered by collective

---

[1] This is based on working hours under thirty-five per week. Using a stricter definition, with a cutoff of thirty hours per week, the figure drops to 36.1%, but this is still far ahead of all the other rich democracies. This suggests that many part-timers in the Netherlands are working four eight-hour days (Visser 2011: 1).

[2] In 2010, 4.4% of part-timers in the Netherlands were involuntary; in Germany, the equivalent statistic was 19.5%, having doubled since 2000; in Denmark, the figure in 2010 was 11.6% (stats.oecd.org).

[3] Other forms of atypical work – agency and fixed-term contract employment – are more precarious. Temporary agency workers, for example, used to be covered by the same dismissal protection as regular workers after twenty-six weeks with the agency and enjoy rights with respect to training, wage guarantees, and supplementary pensions (Viebrock and Clasen 2009). However, the length of employment required to qualify for employment protection has now been lengthened. On fixed-term contracts in the Netherlands, see Bovenberg et al. (2008: 9).

agreements – 74 percent, as compared to a coverage rate of 84 percent for full-time workers in 2006 (Visser 2011: 31–32). While part-time workers are still concentrated in the lower occupational grades, this is somewhat less true for female part-timers, more than a third of whom occupy managerial, professional or technical positions (Visser 2002: 32–33). Surveys indicate that a vast majority (around 80 percent) of part-time workers are happy with their arrangements (Keizer 2011: 158). More generally, Denmark and the Netherlands are tied for first place in overall levels of job satisfaction: nearly 90 percent of Danish and Dutch workers report themselves to be "satisfied" with their employment (Schulze-Cleven 2011: slide 18).[4]

Another major difference from Germany (and similarity to Denmark) is the increase since the 1990s in support for training, in particular CVET. In Germany, we saw that dualism in the training market has been driven in part by the dynamics of a regime in which firms control access to IVET while the state performs a "mop up" operation to provide some training for the unemployed, but where CVET is underdeveloped. By contrast, in the Netherlands, the state is more heavily involved in initial vocational training so that the economy is overall less dependent on private-sector voluntarism when it comes to the acquisition and certification of skills for youth. As importantly, CVET is much better developed in the Netherlands than in Germany. Unlike in Denmark, however, CVET in the Netherlands rests less on direct state financing (as is clear in Figure 4.2). Instead, it is premised on extensive collectively bargained branch-level training funds, which are typically financed by contributions from firms in the sector. Thanks to the use of state extension clauses – through which the government extends the terms of these agreements to cover all workers in the sector, whether or not their firm is party to the negotiations – the reach of these arrangements is almost universal (Trampusch and Eichenberger 2012: 652).[5]

Given the dismal state of the Dutch economy in the 1970s and early 1980s, there is much to praise here. Of course, the jobs success in the Netherlands has not been wholly unequivocal. Unemployment crept up again after the financial crisis (currently 5.1 percent, up from 3.1 percent in 2008) and long-term unemployment – though much reduced since the 1980s – remains a persistent problem, particularly for unskilled and non-native workers. The Netherlands also has one of the highest shares of temporary (fixed-term) employment – 18.4 percent of total employment in 2011, exceeded only by Spain and

[4] Moreover, more Dutch workers than German workers perceived their jobs to be "secure" (Schulze-Cleven 2011: slide 17, based on data from the European Foundation for the Improvement of Living and Working Conditions).

[5] Available evidence also suggests that use is made of these funds. Recent Eurobarometer data show that 41.5% of Dutch workers report that they participated in education and training during the previous year. While this is still far below Denmark's 56.2%, it is well ahead of Germany's 32.0%. In fact, the Netherlands comes in ahead of all other continental countries in this regard (Schulze-Cleven 2011: slide 16).

Portugal among the western European countries.[6] Moreover, Dutch politics, like Danish politics, have come to be inflected with a very strong strain of anti-immigrant sentiment (Rath 2009; Vasta 2007). So the Dutch model is more complex than the sometimes adoring headlines suggest. I return in Chapter 6 to the darker side of the Dutch and Danish models, but here I focus on the distinct trajectory of employment growth through the upgrading and normalization of part-time work, in addition to the role of training in the move to flexicurity in the Netherlands in the 1990s.

Explaining Dutch Flexicurity

The Dutch case poses a puzzle because there are more similarities to Germany than there are to the Nordic cases. While some observers have characterized the Netherlands as a complex blend that includes some elements from the Social Democratic model, most scholars place the country firmly in the Christian Democratic camp. All Dutch citizens are covered by universal health care, and all are entitled to a basic minimum pension. Beyond that, social protection has traditionally been based on the classic "Bismarckian" social-insurance model, financed by payroll contributions from employers and workers. Social policy is organized around status maintenance and income replacement, and traditionally strongly discouraged female employment (Hemerijck and Visser 2000: 230–233; van Wijnbergen 2002: 20).

What accounts, then, for the distinctive trajectory of development in the Netherlands? There are several candidates in the literature, but the most prominent alternatives (previewed in Chapter 1) do not seem to provide much leverage in explaining these differences. The German-Dutch comparison is paradoxical, for example, in light of power resource theory. Unionization rates in both countries are well below Nordic levels and broadly similar to one another. In fact, German unionization rates are slightly higher (see Table 2.4), and if anything Christian Democracy is even more dominant in the Netherlands.[7] Both countries feature Social Democratic parties that have held power at various points but do not remotely approach the level of power and influence exercised by Social Democratic parties in Scandinavia.

Labor market dualism theories might be invoked – although, as we saw in Chapter 1, there is some debate about the political auspices under which insider-outsider cleavages are more likely to emerge. While David Rueda (2007) has argued that Social Democrats are inclined to promote the interests of insider groups, Jonas Pontusson (2009) suggests that it is Christian Democratic governments that are more associated with dualism, while Social Democrats

---

[6] Denmark: 8.8%; Germany 14.7% (stats.oecd.org).

[7] The Christian Democratic Party has participated in every postwar government except for one relatively brief period in opposition during the Purple Coalition of Social Democrats and Liberals from 1994 to 2002.

maintain higher levels of solidarism. In the end, the Netherlands does not provide unequivocal support for either thesis. Major liberalizing reforms were undertaken under the center-right government in the 1980s, but as in Denmark these were not reversed when the Social Democrats returned to power. For example, it was a Grand Coalition government involving both Christian Democrats and Social Democrats that engaged in the most pitched battles against labor market "insiders" to reform the law on disability pay in 1991. And it was the Social Democrats who pressed on afterwards to investigate allegations of abuse of power that led to a reduction in the role of the social partners in key tripartite and bipartite forums. In light of this, it is hard to view the Dutch case as a clear confirmation of either of the two competing partisan-based arguments.

The third and by far most popular explanation for these differences is rooted in corporatism theory. The Netherlands has a relatively long tradition of tripartitism and centralized consultation between the social partners and the state at the national level. This was institutionalized in the bipartite Labor Foundation (STAR) created by organized labor and business in 1945, as well as in the tripartite Socio-Economic Council (SER) created in 1950 to facilitate consultation among unions, employers, and government on social and economic legislation.

Yet it would be hard to attribute the impressive employment outcomes in the Netherlands to the consensus-generating powers of corporatism. The Wassenaar Agreement of 1982 is typically offered as Exhibit A in support of such an argument, but this agreement was reached after more than a decade of corporatist stalemate and against a backdrop in which a freshly elected center-right government had essentially walked away from tripartitism (Hemerijck 1995: 218; also Wolinetz 1989: 87).[8] Corporatist institutions were also thoroughly discredited in the early 1990s by revelations that the social partners for years had colluded to use public resources – in particular, disability benefits – to offload onto taxpayers the costs of industrial restructuring. The scandal precipitated a major crisis, with the result that the tripartite SER lost its previous (legislatively anchored) right to be consulted on all new social and economic legislation, and the social partners were stripped of their bipartite control over the administration of social security benefits (Visser 1998: 279; Hemerijck 2003: 255). As emphasized in Chapter 1, we need to look beyond the existence (or not) of corporatist structures to the conflicts that are played out within these structures and the political dynamics that channel the policy outcomes that emerge.

---

[8] Some observers, in fact, attribute Dutch problems both before and after Wassenaar – stalemate in the 1970s and high levels of inactivity in the 1980s – to the failure of consultative institutions like STAR and SER (Therborn 1986; Delsen 2002: 9). Hemerijck (1995), for example, argued that the dismal economic performance of the Dutch in the 1970s and 1980s "bluntly refutes" Katzenstein's argument that small open economies with corporatist avenues for interest intermediation facilitate flexible adjustment to exogenous economic shocks (186–187).

In what follows, then, I propose an alternative reading of the Dutch case, one that emphasizes overlooked differences from Germany that help explain why increasing female part-time employment became the centerpiece of job creation strategies in the 1990s. A key difference goes back to the place of manufacturing. The historic center of gravity in the Dutch economy lay in services, especially banking and insurance. Industrialization came late in the Netherlands (with a major push in the 1950s and 1960s) and was based on a rather narrow range of industries and premised on a low-wage strategy that left Dutch manufacturing extremely vulnerable in the 1970s and 1980s to the entry of lower-cost producers in the developing world. While German manufacturing emerged from the economic turbulence of that period leaner but nonetheless very competitive, Dutch industry continued to decline.[9] Industrial employment was never very high (30 percent at its peak) and declined steadily and rather rapidly through the 1970s, reaching current German levels (slightly under 20 percent) in 1980 before leveling off to the approximately 10 percent seen today.

These differences have been overlooked because in the 1980s Germany and the Netherlands seemed to be on parallel tracks. Both countries were governed by Christian Democratic parties. Both countries were pursuing classic continental-conservative labor market policies that addressed unemployment by reducing the labor supply: both promoted the exit of older workers through early retirement schemes, while in the Netherlands disability benefits played a major supporting role as well. In Germany, however, the Christian Democratic government of Chancellor Helmut Kohl did not embark on a strong neoliberal course, and continued to nurture traditional institutions and practices to shore up manufacturing in this period. By contrast, Dutch Christian Democrats in the 1980s embraced a more unequivocally neoliberal approach aimed at actively promoting services as an area of traditional strength. Unlike in Germany, where the preferences and policies of all the main actors were aimed at stabilizing employment and supporting industry, the Dutch government collaborated with service-sector employers to vigorously support the growth of part-time employment, mostly outside of manufacturing.

In the Netherlands, manufacturing decline and associated higher and rising levels of inactivity among male blue-collar workers pushed women into the labor market to supplement family wages, while the legacy of the Christian Democratic welfare state – underdeveloped daycare options, among many other things – meant that part-time employment was the only "family" option (Visser 2002; Morgan 2006).[10] Both countries experienced a major corruption scandal involving bipartite oversight of social and labor market policies – the Netherlands in the early 1990s, Germany in the early 2000s. However, in

---

[9] Manufacturing employment declined everywhere, but the magnitude of the decline in the Netherlands was dramatic, and most closely matched the UK (WRR 1980: 20).

[10] In this sense, the figures on "involuntary" part-time employment may be somewhat misleading, since we do not know if parents might prefer more hours if good childcare options were more readily available.

the Netherlands the collapse of manufacturing and the effects of the neoliberal period had already largely transformed the country's economic base and employment structures – part-time work made up over a quarter of total employment and women had entered the labor market in large numbers. It was in this context that Dutch Social Democrats pivoted programmatically and turned corporatist channels of interest intermediation to new ends, taking up the interests of the new constituencies that the neoliberal interlude had created.

The Dutch Political Economy before and after Wassenaar

The Dutch had entered the postwar period with a very strong tradition in trade and finance, as well as a large agricultural sector, but a very underdeveloped industrial base (Wolinetz 1989: 82). The 1950s saw an outpouring of reports on the need for the Netherlands to industrialize, prompting the government to launch a policy "to transform the country from an agricultural into an industrial economy [concentrating] on stimulating large processing industries in energy, chemicals, food and metals" (Bouwens and Dankers 2010). Dutch industry did indeed take off, spurred by a low-wage strategy that was supported by what was called "guided" collective bargaining through the state. Annual wage guidelines were set by a Board of Government Mediators – Commissie van Rijksbemiddelaars (CvR) – under the direction and responsibility of the minster of social affairs, based on recommendations from the bipartite STAR and figures provided by the tripartite SER (van Wijnbergen 2002: 57).

All the main interest associations had reasons to accept heavy state involvement in wage formation in the early postwar years. Employers benefited because state-led bargaining consistently produced wages that ran 20 to 25 percent below those in Germany and Belgium between 1950 and 1960 (Hemerijck 1995: 200). Unions were keen to promote industrialization, convinced as they were that industrial workers would be at the heart of working-class strength and that an expansion of the country's underdeveloped welfare state could only be financed through strong export-led growth. Moreover, government involvement compensated (as well as substituted) for relatively low levels of union organization and union fragmentation because the government made liberal use of its power to extend the terms of collective agreements beyond the signatories to the contract.[11] "While before 1940, collective extension applied to less than 20% of all workers, in the 1950s collective coverage increased dramatically from 40% in 1950 to 70% in 1956," and further to 80 percent by 1995 (201).

By the end of the 1950s, Dutch industry had taken off – and as in other counties at the time, began to run up against labor shortages. Similar to other

---

[11] The Act on the Extension of Collective Agreements from 1937 was scarcely used in the first years of its existence, but it came to loom very large in postwar industrial relations.

Christian Democratic countries, the Netherlands turned to guest workers to cope with these shortages while women stayed at home. In fact, female labor market participation rates in the Netherlands were by some distance the lowest in all of Europe. In 1962, only 27 percent of Dutch women worked, a rate well below even other low-end countries such as Italy (38 percent) (Huber and Stephens 2000: 328). This would remain essentially flat in the ensuing period, rising only to 31 percent by 1975 – a figure that was still lower than the 1962 levels for all other OECD/advanced industrial countries – while other countries were increasing through this period.[12]

The late 1960s and 1970s were especially unkind to Dutch manufacturing. The biggest problem was the famous "Dutch disease" (i.e., export-smothering exchange rate appreciation due to revenues from natural resources). But the economy was weighed down by other problems as well. An elaborate set of linkages – between public- and private-sector wages, between these and the statutory minimum wage, and between the latter and the level of social benefits – created a situation in which 60 percent of the government budget came to be directly tied up in private-sector wage negotiations. Together, these developments helped to fuel a vicious cycle of inflation, rising unemployment, and fiscal crisis (Hemerijck and Visser 2000: 236–237).

Manufacturing employment dropped by 78 percent in the 1970s, as core sectors "fared far worse than in any other EC country," losing domestic share to other industrialized countries in ways that could not be compensated by export growth (WRR 1980: 20, 251–252). The Dutch textile and clothing industries were essentially wiped out between 1968 and 1973, and shipbuilding would be more or less finished by 1985. Those segments of Dutch industry that remained competitive were anchored by multinational corporations that turned outward with strategies of global expansion and diversification (Bouwens and Dankers 2010; Sluyterman 2010: 749, 753; Sluyterman and Wubs 2010). An influential report published by the widely respected Scientific Council for Government Policy – Wetenschappelijke Raad voor het Regeringsbeleid (WRR), an independent advisory council – took stock of the effects, noting that the drop in industrial share of total value added in the Netherlands in this period exceeded that in all other EC countries except the UK (WRR 1980: 251).

As in Germany, the employment effects were dealt with through liberal use of early retirement along with, in the Dutch case, disability insurance. The dependency ratio in the Netherlands (i.e., the ratio of social benefit recipients to employed persons) rose from 45.9 percent in 1970 to 68.4 percent in 1980, hit 86.4 percent in 1985, and continued at about that level through 1990, when it was 85.6 percent (van Keersbergen 1999: 364). By the beginning of the 1980s,

---

[12] For comparison, in Denmark, labor market participation among women rose by 16 percentage points (from 48% to 64%) between 1962 and 1975, in Norway by 16 percentage points (from 37% to 53%), and in Sweden by 14 percentage points (from 54% to 68%) (Huber and Stephens 2000).

the Netherlands was experiencing negative economic growth. Unemployment was well above the EU average – 11.4 percent in 1982, compared to the EU average of 8.9 and Germany at 5.9 – and 60 percent of the unemployed had been out of work for over a year (Delsen 2002: 2). Total employment dropped from 62 percent of the working-age population in 1970 to 51 percent in 1984, and by 1985, fully "one-third of the Dutch labor force was dependent on welfare benefits" (Bonoli 2012: 73). The very depth of the crisis is part of what made the subsequent turnaround so dramatic.

Most accounts of the Dutch jobs miracle begin with the Wassenaar Accord of 1982, once dubbed by Jelle Visser (1998) as "the mother of all accords" and widely seen as a turning point in the postwar evolution of the Dutch political economy. In the accord, unions exchanged wage moderation – including, most notably, abolition of automatic price compensation clauses that had been introduced in the 1960s and successfully defended only five years earlier – for decentralized negotiations over working-time reduction. That the agreement had an impact is clear: the escalator clauses disappeared almost overnight, and average real wages fell by 9 percent. Reductions in the working week, from forty to thirty-eight hours, were widely implemented between 1983 and 1986, but mainly through the addition of extra holidays. The accord immediately restored profitability in the private sector (280).

Although the Wassenaar Accord is frequently held up as a prime example of the capacity of macro-corporatism to forge consensus in the national interest, in fact state power and the "shadow of hierarchy" were crucial to forging this "consensus" (van Wijnbergen 2002). Much of what was achieved in the Wassenaar agreement had already been worked out three years earlier between the social partners in the so-called almost deal (*bijna-akkoord*) of December 1979, only to collapse in the face of opposition by low-skilled and public-sector unions (Wolinetz 1989: 92; Visser and Hemerijck 1997: 98). Elections in 1982 brought to power a new center-right government that was operating under a strict "no nonsense" motto and that firmly and credibly committed itself to intervening to impose a wage freeze and to suspend the automatic price compensation clauses by decree (van Wijnbergen 2002: 67). In this context, unions rationally gave up on defending the cost-of-living escalators, and employers – eager to avoid renewed unwanted government interventions in their affairs – agreed to what was actually rather vague language on reducing weekly working hours in decentralized negotiations and in a "cost neutral" way (Visser 1998: 279).

In terms of its accomplishments, Wassenaar did eliminate direct state intervention in wage bargaining (a lasting accomplishment, as it turns out), and it certainly brought wage moderation – partly by disentangling some of the inflationary linkages; for example, severing the link between private- and public-sector bargaining (Visser 1998: 280–281). It did not, however usher in a new era of macro-corporatist decision making. Prime Minister Ruud Lubbers was uninterested in tripartitism; he presided over an anti-concertative austerity coalition that proceeded to ram through a reform program that largely sidestepped traditional corporatist channels (Wolinetz 1989: 80, 90, 95). A core priority of the new government was to bring public-sector finances under control. Among other things, Prime Minister Lubbers reduced the statutory minimum wage, imposed sweeping cuts in spending on health and education, and reduced welfare payments by lowering the replacement rate for unemployment, sickness, and disability benefits (Salverda 2009: 14; Bonoli 2012: 74; also van Oorschot and Abrahamson 2003: 292). By 1989, long-time observers of Dutch politics were bemoaning the shift from "the politics of accommodation to adversarial politics in the Netherlands" and the "erosion" of social partnership in that country (Lijphart 1989: 139; Wolinetz 1989: 79).

Wassenaar also did not break the familiar Continental European syndrome of welfare without work, for as Anton Hemerijck (1995) shows, whatever improvements the Netherlands experienced in terms of unemployment before 1989 were mostly due to a sharp increase in hidden unemployment within the disability benefit system (187–188). In fact, the one area where corporatism survived best was in social security, where the social partners continued to jointly administer unemployment and disability benefits. As in Germany, industrial downsizing occurred partly through early retirement, but in contrast to Germany, the Dutch also famously facilitated labor market exit through the promiscuous use of disability insurance. Disability pay began in 1967 as a very modest program but grew well beyond all expectations as firms in the 1980s used it aggressively to shed redundant labor by easing less productive workers out of the labor market (Hemerijck and Visser 2000: 239; also van Wijnbergen 2002: 80).

As in Germany, such exit options provided the basis for relatively consensual downsizing. In the Netherlands, in fact, it was better to be classified as disabled than to retire early because the former came with generous benefits of virtually unlimited duration and allowed recipients to avoid the more stringent requirements of unemployment benefits (involving job searches, for example) (van Wijnbergen 2002: 80; Kuipers 2004: 155).[13] Firms, for their part, welcomed the opportunity to offload the costs of redundancies since insurance costs were not borne by the company but by the social funds and underwritten by taxpayers.[14] By the end of 1989, almost 14 percent of Dutch workers were on disability (full or partial), so that alongside the early retired and the unemployed, this meant that by the end of the 1980s about one-third of the Dutch labor force was out of work in one way or another and supported by the state (Visser 1998: 269–270; van Wijnbergen 2002: 89).

---

[13] The center-right government's move in 1985 to control social spending by tightening eligibility requirements for unemployment and lowering benefits from 80% to 70% of last wages probably enhanced the attraction of exit via disability (Visser and Hemerijck 1997: 136).

[14] Sick pay mostly came out of employer contributions, but disability benefits were primarily financed by worker contributions (Hemerijck 2003: 248).

The Rise of Part-Time Work

The rise in part-time employment in the 1980s must be understood against the backdrop of the developments discussed in the preceding section. In Germany, responses to the economic crisis in the 1970s and 1980s revolved around rationing available work while preserving standard full time employment (particularly in manufacturing). There, the Christian Democratic government sided with the more conservative chemical workers' union in promoting early retirement over the metalworkers' preferred strategy of weekly working-time reduction (see, e.g., Thelen 1991). By contrast, Dutch Christian Democrats in the 1980s were increasingly taking their cues from service employers – including especially those in traditional strongholds like finance and insurance – who were eagerly pitching part-time and fixed-term employment as an alternative source of employment growth (Visser 2002: 29). Ad Kolnaar, former chair of the social security committee of the SER, emphasizes the role of the insurance industry in these developments and also notes that the Dutch temporary agency firm Randstad grew mightily in this period to become the second largest player in the temp industry worldwide (interview, 2010). Former prime minister Lubbers similarly stresses the role of services and trade in explaining why part-time work took off during his administration. He stressed that the Dutch economy was always more centered on services and trade and "became even less like Germany in this period" (interview, 2010). Part-time employment in the Netherlands – higher than in Germany to begin with – rose steadily in the 1980s from 18.5 to 28.2 percent before leveling off temporarily in 1990 (OECD Stat Database).

Meanwhile, Dutch women – especially women whose husbands were unemployed or experiencing falling real wages (the Wassenaar effect) – faced strong incentives to supplement household income in this period (Visser 2002: 30). Real wages were declining (by 6 percent between 1970 and 1985), great swaths of manufacturing were in full collapse, and inactivity among Dutch men was rampant. Meanwhile, on the "pull" side, some of the more draconian discriminatory practices that had discouraged female employment in the Netherlands were being dismantled. For example, in 1985, married women became eligible for the first time for unemployment benefits – a change that coincided with a reduction in unemployment benefits for their possibly jobless husbands (Watson et al. 1999: 26). Unlike Germany, the Netherlands had a statutory minimum wage to which part-time workers were legally entitled so long as they worked at least one-third of normal weekly hours. Moreover, since the minimum wage had just been decoupled from private sector wages, it was still rather close to the modal wage – so by adding a part-time job for the wife, families could stay close to their previous incomes (interview with representative of WRR, 2010).

Dutch unions – heavily concentrated in manufacturing – were in deep crisis in this period. They had already suffered massive job losses in the 1970s, and continued to hemorrhage in the 1980s. The Social Democratic union confederation (FNV) lost more than 100,000 members – one-third of its total membership – between 1977 and 1987 alone (Visser 1992: 348). While union density held steady in the Netherlands at around 35 percent from 1960 to 1977, it plunged to about 20 percent by 1985 (excluding retired) (Ebbinghaus 2000: 492). The number of inactive (retired and unemployed) members rose from 8.5 percent in 1970 to 17.4 percent by 1988–1989 and continued to rise to nearly a quarter subsequently (Visser 1991: 119; Ebbinghaus 2002: 32).

The decline of manufacturing also transformed the family division of labor as the number of single breadwinner households declined steadily after 1977 from 51 percent to just 18 percent of households by 1997 (Visser 2002: 23). Driven by the preferences of rising service-sector employers and strongly supported by the center-right government, female employment in the Netherlands grew rapidly and almost exclusively through an increase in part-time employment (30). A significant transformation was accomplished in a single generation; whereas in 1973, only 10 percent of mothers with preschool age children worked outside the home, by 1998 over half did (27).

By the time the Social Democratic Party returned to government in 1989 – as junior partner in a coalition with the Christian Democrats (still under Prime Minister Lubbers) – much had transpired. Women now participated in the labor force in increasingly large numbers. Part-time employment, making up more than a quarter of total jobs, had prevailed over weekly working-time reduction as a means of redistributing work. Unions – still largely rooted in the shrinking industrial core – were coming off a bruising decade. Prime Minister Lubbers' neoliberal policies and industrial decline had taken a massive toll, especially on their core constituencies.

The return of the Left to government in a Grand Coalition might have heralded a return to encompassing concertation and tripartitism after years of dormancy. In many ways, this is what unions expected (van Wijnbergen 2002: 95–107). However, the period from 1989 to 1992 was if anything a time when social partnership reached a new low. In a dramatic and highly conflictual episode, Prime Minister Lubbers pushed through a reform of the Dutch disability regime – against widespread union protest – with the argument that the Netherlands was "sick" and in need of "strong medicine" (van Wijnbergen 2002: 82). Wim Kok, former union leader and head of the Social Democratic Party, endorsed the reform. Freshly installed as Minister of Finance in the Grand Coalition government, he was eager to demonstrate that Social Democrats, after years of languishing in opposition, were willing to take responsibility for hard choices. Union rank-and-filers who had been led to believe that the Social Democrats would not allow the reform to go through felt betrayed, and the fallout was significant. Discord within the party and unions prompted Kok to offer his resignation as head of the party, though it was declined (van Wijnbergen 2002: 100–105).

Even before the protests had subsided, corporatist institutions were thrown into a very negative limelight as a parliamentary inquiry was launched to investigate collusion by the social partners in their role as administrators of disability funds. Against theories that posit that Social Democrats are likely to defend insider interests, Dutch Social Democrats were the most zealous in their drive to investigate the scandal. Kok had to overcome resistance from the Christian Democratic Party to establish a parliamentary commission to investigate in the first place. Christian Democrats dragged their feet not only because they have their own links to the organized labor movement, but also because they worried that any move against union-employer co-administration would inevitably lead to greater state controls.[15] The Buurmeijer Commission – named after Social Democratic Chair Flip Buurmeijer – was featured in televised hearings that cast bipartite social security administration by the social partners in an extraordinarily negative light (Hemerijck and Marx 2010: 134). By the time the committee released its official report in September 1993, the findings were already "common knowledge, namely that the social partners had made 'very liberal use' of social security for purposes of industrial restructuring and social peace" (Hemerijck and Visser 2000: 242).

Similarly to the Wassenaar Accord of 1982, the crisis of corporatism was again sufficient to bring the unions and employers together to defend their roles in both collective bargaining and social policy. As the government "toyed with the idea to discontinue extension of collective agreements" the peak-level union and employer confederations responded with a spirited joint defense of the practice (Visser and Hemerijck 1997: 107). To forestall government threats to amend or possibly scrap the Extension of Collective Agreements Act of 1937, they worked out an agreement that in many ways laid the basis for new initiatives that would unfold over the next several years.

Crisis and Conversion of Dutch Corporatism: Flexicurity in the Netherlands

The "New Course" agreement of 1993 marks the beginning of the turn toward the Dutch version of flexicurity. Somewhat different from Denmark, in the Netherlands flexibility revolved around upgrading part-time work as a solution for expanding employment and reconciling work and family (Keizer 2011: 151). But similar to Denmark, changes in labor market policies were

---

[15] This concern was later vindicated when the Social Democratic Party came to power in the following election in coalition with the liberal People's Party for Freedom and Democracy (VVD). The new government proceeded to eliminate the legislation obligating the government to consult the tripartite SER, and replaced bipartite administration of social security with a new, independent public supervisory agency and new National Institute for Social Insurance (Ebbinghaus 2010: 266, 268). Ebbinghaus considers the Netherlands a case where government reforms "readjust[ed] social partnership in the social policy area to overcome reform blockages, limit[ed] social partners' externalization strategies and re-instill[ed] social responsibility" (278).

accompanied by a significant increase in support for ongoing training. Whereas in Denmark the state itself played a strong and direct role in sponsoring and financing such training, in the Netherlands, these changes ran through collective bargaining.

The shift in policy on part-time work reflects a transition that, as we have seen, had been in the works for some time. In 1989, the bipartite STAR published a joint opinion that became the basis for the New Course agreement four years later: "Noting that part-time employment had expanded rapidly, the social partners agreed that 'a halt in this development should be prevented,' something that 'might happen if part-time work remains concentrated in a limited number of sectors or jobs, or if small part-time jobs produce too limited income and career prospects'" (quoted in Visser 2002: 32). The report recommended improved standards for part-timers, as well as the right of full-time workers to reduce their working hours.

Unions and Social Democrats alike had come under increasing pressure to adapt their strategies to new conditions. The party's collaboration with the Christian Democrats on disability reform had fueled debates within the Left. Social Democratic leader Wim Kok had taken much of the heat, but so did his colleague Elske ter Veld, who was then the junior minister of social affairs and the state secretary directly responsible for the disability reform. Ter Veld, like Kok, had roots in the labor movement, but she was more attuned to the interests of female constituencies, having long served as the head of the trade union confederation's department for women (van Wijnbergen 2002: 87, 103). An internal report of the Social Democratic Party, commissioned by Party Chairwoman Marianne Sint and released in July 1991, "criticized internal party structure and decision making procedures as being dominated by 'in-groups'" (Wolinetz 1993: 107).[16] By 1992, the Social Democrats adopted major organizational changes, abolishing the party council and restructuring the party congress. Dutch feminists were ambivalent about part-time work as inherently second class, but within the FNV, women members "began to campaign for more equality between part-time and full-time workers" (Visser 2011: 15). Women remained seriously underrepresented in the unions,[17] but at the same time the traditional male breadwinner model had clearly lost its "once dominant position in the Dutch labour market," since by the early 1990s close to half (44 percent) of all adult union members were part of dual-earner households (Visser 2002: 29, 31).

---

[16] A subsequent report by a committee that included Wim Kok himself pleaded for "a more open party organization" (Wolinetz 1993: 103–104).

[17] Figures from the International Labour Organization indicate that the female share of union membership rose in the Netherlands from 20% in 1991 to 32% in 2008, although density rates lagged behind those of men. In 2001, female density in the Netherlands was 19% (29% for men). Of the 14 countries covered, only Austria and Germany had a bigger gender gap, whereas Sweden, Norway, Finland, and the UK had more female than male union members, and Canada and Ireland were virtually 50/50 (Visser 2006: 46).

Shortly after the New Course agreement was signed, the Grand Coalition of Christian Democrats and Social Democrats was replaced by the so-called Purple Coalition composed of Social Democrats and Liberals, excluding the Christian Democrats for the first time in the postwar period. The growing influence of social liberals – both within the government and in the Social Democratic Party itself – paved the way for a series of government reforms over the next seven years that regularized part-time employment by upgrading the status and benefits attached to such jobs. Major legislation in 1996 prohibited discrimination on the basis of working hours; henceforth, part-time workers were entitled to equal treatment in wages, overtime pay, holidays, bonuses, occupational pensions, and training (Bovenberg et al. 2008: 10; also van Oorschot 2004a: 20, 2004b: 216).[18] Part timers would also be covered by the same rules as full-time workers with respect to dismissal protection, probation, unemployment benefits, sick pay, and disability (Visser 2011).[19] The previous working-hour threshold for entitlement to the statutory minimum wage – which had exempted jobs involving very few hours – was eliminated (Salverda 2009: 12–13; Keizer 2011).

The New Course agreement also set the scene for improvements in the rights of temporary agency workers. In 1996, new rules were formulated in a central agreement on "Flexibility and Security," which became the basis for the law of the same name passed in 1999 (Hemerijck and Visser 2000: 242–243). These measures relaxed restrictions on fixed-term contracts while they also stabilized the employment status of agency workers by stipulating that those who were employed for over twenty-six weeks were entitled to a permanent (open-ended) contract with the agency.[20] As "regular" employees, agency workers would then be entitled to all the usual rights and benefits, including employment protection, rights to training, wage guarantees, and supplementary pensions (Bekker and Wilthagen 2008: 10; Bovenberg et al. 2008: 10; see also Viebrock and Clasen 2009: 315).

Another milestone was reached with the Working Hours Adjustment Act of 2000, which allows employees to opt for shorter– or longer–working hours. The 1993 New Course agreement had called for the adoption of a so-called

---

[18] This is the Law on Prohibition of Discrimination by Working Hours – *Wet Verbod on der scheid arbeidsduur* (WVOA).

[19] In fact, unemployment benefits operate to the slight advantage of low-income workers, which includes many part-timers. A portion of unemployment insurance is earnings related, but lower-income groups are entitled to a slightly higher replacement rate than higher-income groups (Schulze Buschoff and Protsch 2008: 65).

[20] Minister of Social Affairs Ad Melkert (2008) was privy to these negotiations, and noted that it was easier for unions to accept the growth of part-time work and the relaxation of limits on agency work as the rights and responsibilities of these groups came to be more aligned with those of "mainstream" full-time workers. In the meantime, the required length of employment to qualify for an open-ended contract, however, has been extended again, as discussed later in this chapter.

part-time clause in collective agreements, giving full-time workers a conditional right to choose fewer hours. The 2000 law strengthened and extended a worker's right to opt for fewer hours.[21] It also, crucially, facilitated reversals, giving part-time workers the option to return to full-time employment if they wished. More precisely, after the year 2000, workers in all but the smallest firms (less than 10 employees) could "adjust [their] working hours by 20 percent, from full-time to part-time or, under more restrictive conditions, from part-time to full-time, unless employers prove that compelling business reasons to the contrary exist (no replacement, impossibility of splitting the job, not enough work)" (Visser 2002: 32).[22]

Taken together, these changes upgraded the position of part-timers (and women part-timers in particular), a notable accomplishment in a country that had long lagged far behind even most other Christian Democratic countries in female employment rates.[23] Former Christian Democratic leader Lubbers argues that what he calls the "feminist dimension" to the Purple Coalition years was an effort to portray the Christian Democrats as "not friendly toward women" (interview, 2010). The idea was to position themselves at the vanguard for women's rights and in opposition to old style corporatism.

Lubbers' comments certainly capture the political debates of the time, even if the reality, as we have seen, is somewhat more complicated. As Visser (2002) has argued, part-time work grew initially out of "the market adversity of the 1980s to shore up household incomes with the decline in manufacturing jobs and wages," though it was then "discovered and promoted by politicians and, after some hesitation, adopted by trade unions and feminists" (26). In this sense, unions and the Social Democratic party were in many ways simply "opportunistically accommodat[ing] their policies" to changes in the labor market that Lubbers himself had set in motion (35). The previous Grand Coalition government of 1989 to 1993 had extended maternity leave from twelve to sixteen weeks and increased child care funding, but the Purple Coalition pushed much further, augmenting child care services through direct subsidies and mandating employer contributions (Morgan 2012: 166–167).

As in Denmark, training plays an important part in the Dutch version of flexicurity, and in this area too there have been important changes in the past two decades. When it comes to IVET (for youth), a key difference between Germany and the Netherlands is that the Dutch state plays a much larger role in financing and steering VET. In Germany, as we saw, firm-based apprenticeship

---

[21] In fact, a large number of collective agreements already had part-time clauses (70% by 1996), but unions were not satisfied with the implementation of the clauses (Visser 2002: 32; also Pruijt and Dérogée 2010; Bonoli 2012).

[22] The law prompted another increase in collective agreements with part-time clauses – from 60% in 2000 to 88% by 2009.

[23] Dutch women only got full rights to engage in independent legal contracts in 1956, and until 1957 female civil servants who married were subject to dismissal (Seeleib-Kaiser et al. 2008: 25).

dominates IVET, while state-sponsored, school-based alternatives are residual and very low status – serving mostly as a holding pattern for weaker students who have failed to land an in-firm apprenticeship. In the Netherlands, by contrast, publicly funded school-based training dominates – approximately two-thirds of trainees follow this path. It also enjoys higher status, being considered by employers as equivalent to that of firm-based training (Anderson and Hassel 2012: 185–186). Because of its stronger reliance on publicly financed vocational schools, the Dutch training system is overall much less reliant on private-sector voluntarism and therefore also less vulnerable to economic downturns, which in Germany often cause firms to reduce training precisely when it is most needed (185–186).[24]

The much larger role of the state and of vocational schools in the Netherlands also influences the content of skills, such that "*general* skills occupy an important part of the curriculum in senior secondary vocational education" (Anderson and Hassel 2012: 187, emphasis mine). Anderson and Hassel view this as important because "precisely the acquisition of general skills and competences in conjunction with specific vocational skills ... are crucial for service sector employment" (187). Moreover, when it comes to the trajectory of change in IVET, Anderson and Hassel see a growing divergence between Germany and the Netherlands. While the German system of apprentice-based IVET is mostly stable, the Dutch training system is liberalizing, both because of the increasing importance of school-based (as opposed to firm-based) training and because of the accompanying shift in content toward more general (as opposed to firm- or industry-specific) skills – and thus "moving farther away from the German regime" (190).

Equally important, as we have seen, is the issue of CVET, an area of traditional weakness in the German model. In the Netherlands, CVET is much better developed; in this case, collectively bargained sectoral training funds play an important role in supporting continuing training and lifelong learning (Tros 2009: 2). A number of industry agreements were concluded in the late 1990s under the heading of "employability," a term that reconciles employers' demand for *inzetbaarheid, mobiliteit, flexibiliteit* (availability, mobility, flexibility) with labor's concern for *weerbaarheid* (worker empowerment) (Pruijt and Dérogée 2010).

The roots of sectoral funds in the Netherlands extend back to the 1960s, but in the 1990s they were increasingly directed to supporting training. Based on contributions by firms across a given industry, they are jointly administered by the social partners to support "continuing training, apprenticeship or other

---

[24] Whereas in Germany there is little interest among unions and business for developing stronger school-based alternatives, recent reforms in the Netherlands have enhanced and improved school-based training. For example, a 1994 law significantly reorganized and streamlined publically financed vocational schools in order to give "employers (and unions) more influence on the content of VT and skill certification," in order to meet the "needs of employers as well as students, especially weak ones" (Anderson and Hassel 2012: 184–185).

forms of training" (Llorens 1998: 6).[25] In 1997, there were seventy-two such branch funds covering 1.5 million workers and providing 100 million euros for firm-based CVET. By 2002 this had grown to 99 branch funds covering over 40 percent of Dutch workers and providing 400 million euros, of which 250 million euros were going to CVET. By 2007, the vast majority of Dutch workers (86 percent) could tap these funds in order to participate in training or education (Pedersini 2009; see also Grünell 2005).

In sum, while sectoral funds to support ongoing training "play a marginal role" in Germany, they are both significant and "foundational" to CVET in the Netherlands (Berger and Moraal 2012: 382). The role of the state looms large in explaining this outcome. Although the funds are mostly based on contributions (a portion of the wage sum), the Dutch state augments the funds and encourages collective bargains that establish them by offering tax exemptions for both employees' and employers' payments toward CVET (Berger and Moraal 2012: 388; Trampusch and Eichenberger 2012: 654). More importantly still, even though training funds are founded on agreements between labor and employers, the use by the state of its right to extend the terms of these agreements to all firms in an industry (party to the agreement or not) and to all workers (union members or not) has been crucial to achieving very high coverage rates (654).

In this way, the Netherlands has achieved rather high levels of support for CVET (similar to Denmark) even though the Dutch state is less involved as a direct financier.[26] Sectoral funds "cover all kinds of employees" – white- and blue-collar, high- and low-skill – and finance various forms of training, both on-the-job training and external courses (Trampusch and Eichenberger 2012: 652). Moreover, although based on industry-level agreements, the funds can also be used for training that is designed to ease the transition to jobs in other sectors (Berger and Moraal 2012: 389).[27]

The Dutch Case in Comparative Perspective

The changes in the Netherlands over the past three decades have been significant. When compared to Germany, two differences stand out. One concerns

---

[25] The contribution rates vary by sector, from under 1% of the total wage bill in the retail industry to 3% in construction (Llorens 1998).

[26] As Figure 4.2 shows, the Dutch state is not spending much on training, though ALMP spending increased slightly in the late 1990s while passive support declined (along with unemployment).

[27] Another feature of the Dutch version of flexicurity is the institution of the "Life Course" savings account, introduced by the government in 2006 and again implemented by the social partners in collective bargaining. Such accounts allow workers to bank up to 210% of their annual pay and use the account to finance personal leave time of up to three years at 70% of their usual wage. In some cases, collective bargaining provisions call for employers to contribute to such schemes as well (Bovenberg et al. 2008: 11). Life Course savings accounts are designed to allow workers to deal flexibly with life events like parental care, education, sabbatical, or early retirement. In 2006, about 70% of collective agreements included Life Course savings account provisions (Pedersini 2009).

the extent and character of part-time work. Prompted in part by the collapse of manufacturing and fueled by active state promotion in the 1980s, the growth of part-time work in the Netherlands has outstripped that in all other countries. Subsequent reforms that "regularize" such employment have done a great deal to upgrade the conditions of part-time workers – including ensuring them access to the fruits of collective bargaining in terms of wages, training, and parental and other leaves. This contrasts with developments in Germany where, as we saw, the fastest growing segment of the part-time labor market has been mini-jobs, notorious precisely for their low pay, limited hours, and mostly absent benefits. The other difference relates to access to training, including and in some ways especially CVET, which in Germany remains underdeveloped even as trends in the Netherlands over the past twenty years have expanded opportunities for Dutch workers. Here, too, the state has played the decisive role, directly sponsoring and financing initial vocational education (through public schools) while also actively promoting continuing education and training through tax exemptions and the use of extension clauses to expand the coverage of collectively bargained sectoral training funds.

Especially in its promotion of CVET, the Netherlands shares elements with the Danish case. Yet despite the shared moniker of "flexicurity," the differences to the Danish model are also hard to overlook. Compared to Denmark, what is strikingly missing in the Netherlands is a strong public commitment to investing in skill development for the most vulnerable segments of the working class. In Denmark, state-sponsored training (especially for low-skill workers) is the single most important mechanism through which the activating elements in labor market policy are compensated and through which the attendant risks are collectivized. In the Netherlands, by contrast, continuing training runs mostly through collective bargaining. While the reach of training agreements is impressive – and a direct consequence of state extension clauses – there are still problems with respect to the training of the unemployed, who are by definition outside the ambit of collective bargaining.

The Dutch political economy therefore continues to suffer more than the Danish one from problems at the low-skill end of the labor market. Long-term unemployment, while much reduced from its historic highs in the 1980s, remains a persistent problem. Agency workers – who are concentrated in low-skill industries, particularly in services, and have spottier employment records – have been disproportionately affected by legislation that now allows derogations from equal treatment provisions through collective agreements.[28] These developments naturally tilt outcomes for these workers in the direction of increased flexibility, not security. Moreover, many of the recent gains in collective bargaining – concerning training and personal leave, for instance – remain out of reach for many of these constituencies for very pragmatic reasons. The

---

[28] For example, the social partners agreed to extend the period before a fixed-term contract becomes open-ended from twenty-six to seventy-eight weeks (Visser 2011: 11).

take-up rate for training is markedly lower for these groups – the ones arguably most in need of training – than other, better off groups.

One might summarize the difference to Denmark as follows: while the Danish flexicurity model involved a new social pact to redefine the role of the state to underwrite a broad socialization of risk, the Dutch have recalibrated policy to put more emphasis on risk sharing among the presently employed and especially within households. As we have seen, recent developments have done a great deal to incorporate a large number of Dutch women into the labor market. This development – together with the upgrading of part-time work – has created a dynamic in which the Netherlands is increasingly composed of one and a half earner families. While large numbers of Dutch men also work part-time, there is still a strong gender bias. Thus, gains for women – and for low-skill workers – in the Netherlands remain more fragile. We should therefore not be too surprised to learn that in the aftermath of the financial crisis, when cuts were made, the center-right government "turned its back on social investment by retrenching child benefits and disinvesting in education, without tinkering with passive social insurance and insider-biased labour market regulation" (Hemerijck and van Hooren 2012).

Here we see again the similarities to Germany, because in the Netherlands continued low unionization rates – especially among women and low-skill workers in the service sectors – are a crucial difference from the Scandinavian countries.[29] New benefits – such as the recent (2009) extension of parental leave – offer relief to the growing number of dual income middle-class families; however, being unpaid, such leave rights are mostly out of reach for lower income families (Hemerijck and van Hooren 2012). Measures taken by the Dutch center-right government in the 2000s have also been strikingly uneven, redounding quite explicitly to the disadvantage of low-skill precariously employed. In fact, the most recent reforms strengthen the traditional continental insurance principle "in unemployment insurance and disability benefits, with stricter coverage, increased importance of relative work history, and the linking of benefit duration to work history" (7). I take these developments as evidence of the limits to reform in a context in which the most vulnerable segments of the labor market remain mostly unorganized and therefore under-represented.

SWEDEN

If the puzzle for the Netherlands was to explain the country's embrace of a flexicurity model since the 1990s – albeit one with strong Christian Democratic overtones – the puzzle for Sweden is to explain relatively serious signs of

---

[29] In 2008, Dutch women made up less than one-third of total trade union membership (32.8%), very similar to Germany (31.8%), and far behind Scandinavia (greater than 50%) (Carley 2009).

dualism in a country long associated with strong labor and macro-corporatism. ALMPs and broad access to education and training are the centerpieces of the flexicurity model that is now seen as the most viable formula for reconciling successful economic performance with low unemployment and comparatively high levels of equality. Since these are areas of traditional Swedish strength, surely this is the country that should be the poster child today. Sweden famously pioneered ALMP in the 1950s, long before it figured at the top of EU and OECD recommendations to boost job creation and sustain growth. Moreover, when it comes to education and training, arguably no country has done more than Sweden has to break down barriers to assure that all youth have the same chances to acquire the education they need to compete for well-paid and stable jobs. In the 1960s and 1970s, Swedish Social Democrats worked to blend together vocational and academic tracks at both the lower secondary and upper secondary levels. Many of the most important reforms were undertaken by Olof Palme, who served as minister of education before becoming prime minister (serving from 1969 to 1976 and again from 1982 to 1986), and who considered the school system to be "the key to the abolition of the class society" (quoted in Rothstein 1996: 68).

In fact, Sweden does continue to do well on many fronts. The country still boasts one of the lowest levels of income inequality (especially post-tax and transfers) among the OECD countries. With a Gini coefficient of 0.259, Sweden is not as egalitarian as Denmark (0.248) but it is still at the low end when compared to the non-Nordic countries (OECD 2011a: 45).[30] Wage inequality, while significantly higher than the historically compressed wages of the 1970s, is also still extremely low by international standards – lower, in fact, in 2008 than all other countries save Norway (with which it was tied) (87).

However, more discouraging signs are also not hard to find. Unemployment since 1990 has remained stubbornly higher in Sweden than in Denmark and the Netherlands (see Figure 4.2). In fact, average unemployment in Sweden in the late 2000s was higher than in many Christian democratic countries, exceeded only by Belgium, Germany, and France (see Figure 4.1). Moreover, youth unemployment in Sweden – at 22.9 percent (2011) – is well above the Nordic average, and for that matter, the OECD average of 16.2 percent as well. The only countries with higher rates on this measure are the notoriously troubled Greece, Italy, Portugal, Spain, and Ireland (OECD 2012a). Employment protection for those in standard full-time jobs remains very strong. However, very large numbers of youth are employed on temporary contracts – 50 percent in 2009 (Lovén 2009b; Kjellberg 2011b: 78) – and the gap between their level of employment protection and that of standard workers is rather extreme, as Figure 4.6 showed. Temporary employment in Sweden is significantly higher than it is in Denmark (and exceeds even that of Germany), as Figure 4.7 showed.

---

[30] Inequality in Sweden – as in Denmark – has increased significantly since 1980, but from a particularly low base.

Finally, involuntary part-time employment in Sweden rose rapidly in the 1990s, and although it has dropped off since then, it stabilized in the 2000s at a level that is above Denmark's and close to Germany's (see Figure 4.8).

A recent OECD study examines the (diverse) sources of rising inequality across the rich democracies. In most cases in which inequality has risen over the last twenty years, this has been a function of rising wage inequality. In Sweden, inactivity, not wage dispersion, is at the root of the problem (OECD 2011a: 150). This pattern – continued strong employment protection and relative wage equality for those with full-time standard employment relationships combined with higher levels of unemployment and involuntary part-time employment – suggests dualization, and indeed this is exactly how the Swedish case is being coded by knowledgeable observers (Davidsson 2010; Lindvall 2010; Bonoli 2012; Lindvall and Rueda 2012; Obinger et al. 2012).

The contrasts to Denmark offer important insights into explaining these outcomes. Whereas Denmark addressed high unemployment in the 1990s with a major tripartite agreement around flexicurity, similar initiatives in Sweden in exactly this period collapsed in disagreement and acrimony (Anthonson et al. 2010). While Denmark ramped up active labor market spending in that period, Swedish efforts stalled. Despite continued high unemployment, spending in Sweden on ALMPs – and on training specifically – dwindled in the 2000s to levels now below Denmark and even Germany, a traditional laggard in this area (see Figure 4.2). Since the mid-1990s, Swedish inequality has increased more than Denmark, no matter what the measure: Gini coefficient, interquintile share ratio (S80/S20), or interdecile ratio (P90/P10) (OECD 2011a: 45). What has happened to the Swedish model?

Swedish Exceptionalism Revisited

The dominant theoretical frameworks seem not to offer much leverage in explaining these developments. The comparison between Denmark and Sweden is puzzling against the backdrop of power resource theory, for example. The unionization rate in Sweden has always been somewhat higher than in Denmark, and so if anything one would expect better outcomes in Sweden. The same thing holds if we observe the partisan balance of power. Sweden is legendary for the historic hegemony of the Social Democratic Party, which governed the country uninterrupted for almost four decades before 1976. The party looks a lot less invincible today,[31] but the Social Democrats still wield considerable influence (having been in power for twenty-one of the last thirty-six years) even if they no longer monopolize power.

Precisely this point might be invoked as evidence in support of dualism theories, which suggest that Social Democrats will fuel insider-outsider divisions by protecting insiders. Consistent with Rueda's arguments, active and passive

---

[31] In fact, the Center-Right has been in power since 2006.

spending on labor market policy stopped tracking unemployment in the 1990s, despite Social Democratic control of government beginning in 1994. However, as in the case of the Netherlands, the partisan complexion of government does not seem to capture the relevant trends. Austerity policies began under the center-right government of 1991 to 1993 – which, although less long-lived than its Danish counterpart in the 1980s, nonetheless involved serious retrenchment and liberalization. The Social Democrats elected to reverse some but not all of these measures upon their return to office in 1994.

Finally, corporatist theory might shed some light, since Sweden has always been seen as the paradigmatic case of macro-corporatism. As in Denmark, Swedish corporatism went through a major crisis, beginning with the breakdown of solidaristic wage policy in the 1980s. However, employers and unions still possess considerable organizational capacity, and the 1990s saw a reconsolidation and partial re-coordination of wage bargaining behind industrial leadership, accompanied (as in Denmark) by widespread decentralization in wage formation. Coordination among Swedish employers is stronger now than at any time since 1983, but the main goal of the employers' association since the 1990s has not been to restore tripartite coordination; instead, organized employers have mostly sought to keep the LO on the sidelines. Thus, unlike in Denmark, national-level concertation has itself become a source of conflict between unions and employers, and even within the union movement itself. To understand these patterns, we have to look more closely at the politics within and around Swedish macro-corporatism.

The following account explains these developments with reference to differences in the organizational landscape in Sweden and the role of the state. Similar to Denmark – and unlike in the Netherlands and Germany – women, low-skill, and service-sector workers outside the industrial core are almost as well organized as blue-collar workers in industry. The resulting strong representation has helped to establish and defend an overall more robust set of minimum conditions with respect to wages and benefits for the most vulnerable workers. However, the broad shift in employment (the rise of services, the increasing importance of salaried and professional groups) has had a more fragmenting effect in Sweden than in Denmark. Unlike in Denmark, the Swedish trade union movement has traditionally organized blue- and white-collar workers separately. So long as industry was dominant, the peak blue-collar confederation LO played the leading role in reconciling divergent interests on the labor side and negotiating with employers. Now, however, the LO is declining in membership and strength relative to white-collar confederations and has increasingly been cast in the role of defending low-skill workers (especially low-skill women workers employed by municipalities), often against and at odds with white-collar groups and more privileged segments of the working class. Industrial interests are still powerful – not so much by virtue of employment numbers but because of the importance of industry to Swedish exports. The pivotal metalworkers' union (IF Metall) straddles these divisions and has been caught between the efforts of the LO to defend elements of the previous system (above all, some measure of wage solidarism) on one hand, and the pull of white-collar groups representing different constituencies with wholly different interests on the other.

Also unlike in Denmark, the Swedish government commands precious few tools to counteract these fragmenting forces. In Denmark, the state could break through deadlocks by exercising its power to impose broad and encompassing agreements, either by linking together collective bargains across different sectors or by imposing settlements outright using its strong mediation powers. The Swedish state is not endowed with similarly strong capacities. Not quite as constrained as the German state from any intervention in collective bargaining, the Swedish state can require conflicting parties to engage in conciliation, but it can neither force agreement nor impose binding results.

If dualization in Germany involves "the bottom dropping out" for low-skill workers, in Sweden it is more a matter of the top taking off – with employers negotiating new forms of flexibility for higher-skilled workers, particularly salaried professionals and semi-professionals, while the LO defends the position of low-skill constituencies. In industrial relations, for example, the LO has continued to fight for compensation clauses for low-skill workers to keep their wages more in line with their blue-collar counterparts in manufacturing, but these elements of solidarism exist alongside widespread wage individualization benefitting salaried groups. Swedish-style dualization also manifests itself in an almost complete lack of attention to CVET alongside strong support for higher education and a flourishing of private options in primary and secondary education. In labor market policy it takes the form of a spirited (and largely successful) defense of traditional employment protections for those in standard full-time jobs, but alongside the growth of atypical employment of various sorts. Moreover, declining investment in ALMPs has translated into less support than in Denmark for measures for reintegrating the long-term unemployed.[32]

The Swedish Model in Good Times and Bad

The traditional Swedish postwar political economic model bears the names of the two labor economists who developed it – Gösta Rehn and Rudolph Meidner. Elaborated within the research department of the blue-collar confederation LO, the Rehn-Meidner model rested on two central pillars – ALMPs and centralized solidaristic wage bargaining. Sweden famously pioneered the use of ALMPs in the 1940s and 1950s, long before such an approach gained its current cachet among academics and policy makers. The goal of ALMP was to

---

[32] As Figure 4.2 shows, labor market spending on training and ALMP dropped in the 1990s and since 2000 it has not responded to unemployment. Spending on training and ALMP has trended steadily down since 1998 despite the increase in joblessness.

facilitate the smooth shift of resources out of declining industries and into growing ones through "a variety of measures designed to improve labour mobility:
information to workers about vacancies and to employers about applicants,
subsidies for relocation and, above all, vocational retraining" (Moene and
Wallerstein 1993: 387).

Centralized, solidaristic wage policy complemented ALMP. From 1956 until
1983, the broad parameters for wage settlements covering most of the economy were set at the national level in peak negotiations between the LO and
the national confederation of Swedish employers (SAF) (see, e.g., A. Martin
1991). Centralized bargaining helped maintain the competitiveness of Swedish
exports by holding back wage gains in the lower-productivity sheltered sectors. Wage compression facilitated economic adjustment by pushing low-
productivity firms out of business while rewarding high-productivity firms and
sectors with profits that could be reinvested. The economic model supported
the political compromise on which it rested. By assuming the costs of retraining workers for jobs in rising sectors rather than defending their employment
in declining ones, ALMP provided "the glue that held together the growth
coalition within the labor movement" (Pontusson 1992: 96).

Even before the oil crisis, the Rehn-Meidner model had come under strain.
In the face of painful dislocations caused by the decline of core industries such
as shipbuilding and forestry, LO head Arne Geijer could be heard remarking
that "if those concerned cannot be granted sufficient security during transitions, this will provoke political and social unrest" (quoted in Davidsson 2010:
119). The pressures for more security of employment – not in the abstract
but in the "here and now" – only picked up steam after the oil crisis and its
impact in the 1970s (Henning 1984: 214). Moreover, and as both Nycander
(2010) and Emmenegger (2010) have pointed out, the political pressures to
preserve jobs was mightily enhanced by developments that resulted in a significant increase in labor's plant-level powers in the codetermination legislation of
the 1970s. The landmark Employment Protection Act of 1974 gave local labor
representatives enormous leverage to influence the extent and terms of layoffs
by establishing the principle of "last in, first out." As Nycander emphasizes, the
legislation marked a double departure from the traditional model, both proce-
durally (going through the legislature rather than corporatist negotiations) and
substantively (protecting jobs rather than facilitating movement).[33]

These developments shifted the center of gravity in bargaining from the
national to the regional and municipal levels as "industrial policy came to be
dominated by defensive, ad hoc measures elaborated through political bargaining, with national unions playing a marginal part" (Pontusson 1992: 158).
Supported by elected municipal authorities, local unions sought to prevent
plant closings and to preserve jobs at all costs. In other words, after the

---

[33] For this reason, Nycander (2010) singles out the 1974 law as powerfully disruptive to the
traditional Swedish model.

oil crisis "Swedes seem to be no longer satisfied with a virtual guarantee of a job *somewhere* in the labour market...but instead expect a guarantee of their existing jobs" (Henning 1984: 207–208, quote from 214–215, emphasis in original). The Social Democratic government largely accommodated these demands and by 1976, subsidies to individual enterprises had grown to 90 times their 1960 levels (200).

Not much changed in 1976 with the transition to the first non-socialist government since 1932. After decades in opposition, the bourgeois parties were keen to demonstrate that they were as committed to full employment as the Social Democrats (Pontusson 1992; Steinmo 2011). Minister of Industry Nils Åsling (Center Party) conceded that since this was "the first center-right government in many, many years, we did not want to seem worse – in terms of the labor market – than the Social Democrats" (quoted in Lindvall 2010: 71).[34] The Center-Right was also deathly afraid of coming to power only to preside over industrial decline. In one major case, a leading metal producer, Gränges, was bailed out partly because bankruptcy would have confirmed "a picture of [industrial] decline" and seriously "risked the reputation and the authority of the new non-socialist government" (Garme 2001: 190–192).[35]

Moreover, not just labor representatives sought protection; manufacturing employers were also asking the government to shore up industry. Garme (2001) relates the story of when (Minister of Industry) Åsling met the "grand old man of Swedish industry, Marcus Wallenberg." The context was one in which a major Swedish steel company was failing and desperately seeking government support. Since Wallenberg held a majority share in a competing company, he might have been expected to encourage the minister to let the firm go. What he instead said was surprising and reflected the conviction that Swedish industry should be preserved at all costs. In Åsling's words, "He said to me: 'Incredible, should this old mining country with its mechanical industry not have room for its own commercial steel industry.' That made a certain impression on me" (73).[36]

Rather than change course, the conservative government continued with policies organized around "rescue operations to bail out and reconstruct corporations on the verge of bankruptcy" (Pontusson 1992: 138; also Henning 1984: 213; Garme 2001). Financial support to ailing companies was channeled through the Ministry of Industry, or what was called "Åsling's

---

[34] This goal was perhaps even more important to Minister of Labor Per Ahlmark, leader of the Liberal Party, who was keen to consolidate the image of the party as a reliable guardian of full employment (Garme 2001: 166–167).

[35] This is a company that the Social Democrats later (1989) privatized (Garme 2001: 198).

[36] This story was repeated with other companies hit by the crisis. The head of the more neoliberal Conservative Party was likewise "influenced by all the managing directors who metaphorically speaking came crawling into his room begging him to spare them bankruptcy" (Garme 2001: 184, from an interview with Lars Wohlin, economist and consultant to the government at the time).

emergency ward" (Garme 2001: 161). Rescue measures that began under the Social Democrats intensified under the bourgeois government, including takeovers in key industries such as steel and electronics; "all told, the bourgeois parties nationalized more industry during their first three years in power than the social democrats had in the previous forty-four years!" (Pontusson 1992: 140–141).[37] Christer Peterson (2011) notes that the decisions in the 1980s to devalue the currency to solve the competitiveness problems of Swedish manufacturing also "conserved old industrial structures" (188).

Even as the job mobility component of ALMP came under strain, coordinated wage bargaining also began to generate problems. As in Denmark, centralized bargaining supported wage restraint in the export industries by holding back disruptive wage increases in the sheltered sectors. What upset the deal in Sweden was a growing challenge to manufacturing leadership emanating both from within and outside the LO. Within the LO, public-sector unions took advantage of their strength and newly acquired (in 1965) right to strike to secure the inclusion of contractual provisions to compensate public-sector workers for wage drift in manufacturing. Similar clauses for other low-wage unions were concluded that allowed them to keep pace as well. Meanwhile, the LO faced a second challenge in the rising power of a separate white-collar bargaining cartel outside the ambit of the LO-SAF framework. Whereas in 1950, fourteen out of the fifteen largest Swedish unions were blue-collar LO affiliates, in the 1970s seven of the top ten unions organized service sector workers (Kjellberg 1999, 2009: 179–180).[38] Competition across these various constituencies fueled a chronic institutionalized ratcheting up of wages (A. Martin 1991: 35; Walsh 1995: 182; Pontusson and Swenson 1996: 232–233; Elvander 1997: 13).

Wage compression had created special problems for IF Metall, partly because of its effects on exports, but more immediately because of the competition it generated with its white-collar counterpart in industry. In a context in which technological change had blurred the line between skilled blue-collar and white-collar occupations, high-skill metalworkers often found themselves working in jobs very similar to those of members of the separate white-collar union Svenska Industritjänstemannaförbundet (SIF), but – because of wage compression – at a much lower rate of pay (Mahon 1991; A. Martin 1991: 36).[39] These tensions

---

[37] Moreover, these measures were accompanied by selective financial support to industry between 1976 and 1980 that was five times as high as it had been in the 1971–1976 period under Social Democratic rule (50 billion Swedish Kroner under the Center-Right versus 9 billion Swedish Kroner under the Social Democrats) (Garme 2001: 152). In fact, spending on such measures rose from an average of just 11.3% of industrial policy expenditures in the period between 1970 and 1976 (under the socialists) up to 43.8% between 1976 and 1980 under the center-right government (Pontusson 1992: 138).

[38] By 2009, nine of these top fifteen were now white-collar unions (Kjellberg 2011a: 50).

[39] Kjellberg (1992) notes that in 1984, wage differentials between the highest and lowest paid blue-collar workers in manufacturing were just 34%, far below comparable figures for Britain (210%) and the United States (490%) (108).

were sufficient to facilitate a cross-class realignment in 1983 in which manufacturing unions joined with SIF and the employers' association to precipitate
the collapse of peak-level bargaining and solidaristic wage policy.

In Search of a New Equilibrium

What followed was a period of uncertainty and disorganization in Swedish
industrial relations and politics. Over the next several years, the level of bargaining shifted several times – conducted sometimes at the industry level and
sometimes between the LO and SAF minus the metalworking industry, but just
once (after the assassination of Prime Minister Palme) at the peak level. The
stability of the traditional Swedish model had rested heavily on the capacity
of the organized representatives of labor and capital to mediate conflicts of
interest within their own ranks. By the 1980s, however, it was eminently clear
that the LO was no longer able – and SAF no longer willing – to perform
this function. Repeated attempts on the part of the LO to reconsolidate its
authority and re-establish its place at the center of wage bargaining foundered
on the opposition of skilled manufacturing unions and vehement rejection on
the part of organized employers who were now dead against any return to
peak bargaining. The 1980s saw a hardening of the lines on the union side
between proponents and opponents of recentralization, as well as a radicalization of manufacturing employers. The decisive break with the old system was
accomplished in 1990. In an initiative led by large manufacturing firms – and
with Volvo's Pehr Gyllenhammar leading the charge – SAF withdrew its representatives from all tripartite bargaining arenas and dismantled its collective
bargaining unit altogether, making a return to the status quo ante impossible.

Events of the 1980s and early 1990s drove further fragmentation and conflict, especially between manufacturing and public-sector interests. Concerned
about inflation and declining export competitiveness, the Social Democratic
government sought to reduce public sector spending, among other things,
through the privatization of some public services.[40] Since much of the LO's
core constituency was among low-skill public-sector workers, these were years
of "unprecedented conflicts" between the Social Democratic leadership and
the LO (Lindvall 2010: 110; see also Davidsson 2010: 121). By the early
1990s, it seemed that not much was left of the vaunted Swedish model. Corporatism appeared to be dead, and relations between the political and industrial
wings of the labor movement were more strained than ever before. Rather than
corporatist bargaining, wage formation in Sweden took place from 1991 to
1993 under the auspices of a government appointed commission headed by
the experienced labor mediator (and former head of the labor market board)
Bertil Rehnberg, marking an unusual "moment of extreme state regulation and
centralisation" in Swedish industrial relations (Kjellberg 2009: 183).

---

[40] Public employment fell from about 32% of total employment in 1989 to just over 25% by
2008 – and with that, from levels above to levels below the Danes (OECD 1999, 2011b).

The subsequent re-equilibration of collective bargaining in Sweden took place not with, but mostly outside and around the LO. The first post-Rehnberg collective bargaining round in 1995 was sufficiently chaotic to prompt employers who had previously resolved to decentralize bargaining to accept an overture by a consortium of blue- and white-collar unions in the industrial sectors to engage in joint negotiations over wage formation and mediation procedures for all of industry. The resulting Agreement on Industrial Development and Wage Formation (*Industriavtalet*) supports coordination in bargaining across the entire exposed sector (including blue- and white-collar unions) while also foreclosing a return to peak-level bargaining. By facilitating and institutionalizing stronger coordination between blue- and white-collar unions within industry, the *Industriavtalet* deepened the split between the metalworkers' union and the LO, as the latter increasingly found itself marginalized and representing the interests of a "rump" group of low-wage workers centering especially on municipal employees (predominantly female), who now make up the confederation's largest constituency. Subsequent efforts by the LO in the late 1990s to reinstate wage solidarism were resisted by IF Metall's leadership, who did not want low-paid municipal workers to claim "too much" (Ahlberg 1997a; see also Berg 2002).

The Social Democratic government sided with manufacturing interests in these conflicts. Crucial developments unfolded in 1998 in the context of peak negotiations over a new "Pact for Growth" that was widely seen as a possible new "Basic Agreement" along the lines of the famous Saltsjöbaden Accord of 1938. The LO was keen to reassert itself in the emerging new order and sought above all to "create tables" or forums at which confederation leaders would sit together again as in the years of the LO-SAF agreements (interview with LO leader, 2000). In one initiative, the LO proposed bargaining linkages along the lines of the Danish model, which would reinstate a measure of national-level wage coordination, and give the LO a role in the process. However, this idea was rejected not just by the government mediator Svante Öberg, but also by white-collar unions, export unions like IF Metall, and of course employers (Albåge and Öberg interviews, 1999). In the face of ongoing deadlock between the LO and the SAF, the government created a new National Mediation Authority (Medlingsinstitutet) to replace the old, weaker National Conciliator's Office (Förlikningsmannaexpeditionen) (Skiöld 2001), and tasked it with supporting (rather than replacing) the *Industriavtalet* by facilitating settlements in other sectors (Berg 1999; Skiöld 2001).

As in Denmark, the shift to industry-level contracts was accompanied by much enhanced room for company-level negotiations. However, in Denmark this was part of a negotiated trade-off that resulted in increased state support for training (especially for low-skill workers), and in which the Danish LO played the key coordinating role. In Sweden, no such deal was forthcoming, leaving the Swedish LO on the sidelines officially, though still attempting to steer wage developments through its influence within the labor movement.

Wage solidarism, however, was a harder sell under the new decentralized regime. During the years of wage compression, the returns to education had fallen by 50 percent, so white-collar unions outside the LO's ambit eagerly embraced decentralization (Edin and Holmlund 1995: 341). Wage formation generally began to be driven by the notion of "extra compensation for the (high-skilled) 'wrongly paid'" (Hibbs and Locking 2000: 764; see also Kjellberg 1998: 87–88; Fransson and Thörnquist 2004: 60). For example, the pay gap between nurses (who are organized outside the LO in the white-collar confederation TCO) and nurse's assistants (within the LO) had narrowed considerably over the 1970s and 1980s, so that by the 1990s nurses were in chronic short supply. With the market at their back, the nurses' union struck in 1995, earning their members annual wage increases of 7 percent for the entire period from 1995 to 2002 (Fransson and Thörnquist 2004: 61). Ignoring withering criticism from the LO for their "unsolidaristic" behavior, the nurses' union embraced individualized wage bargaining as a collective strategy to claim (to them, long-overdue) credit for their credentials and competencies. They urged their members to take advantage of decentralized bargaining "to raise their competitive power in the labor market through further education and/or vocational training" (Fransson and Thörnquist 2004).

Other unions of salaried employees in both the public and private sectors also often eagerly embraced decentralized wage formation in this period. For example, in 1992 an agreement between the Association for Managerial and Professional Staff (Ledarna) and the employers' association Almega contained no uniform salary increase at all, leaving wage formation entirely to the local bargaining partners. Negotiations in the state sector between the national government and high-level salaried workers – organized within the Swedish Confederation of Professional Associations (SACO) – followed suit with an agreement in 1993 that replaced fifty-two separate salary grades with fully decentralized bargaining (Ahlberg and Bruun 2005: 131). In fact bargaining decentralization in the (central) state sector had received a boost in the 1980s as widespread privatization and outsourcing resulted in workforce reductions that affected, above all, blue-collar workers. By shifting the balance of employment away from LO and its blue-collar constituents toward white-collar unions and their confederations (state-sector TCO employees and SACO), which were more amenable to wage differentiation, privatization facilitated a transition to individualized wage setting in the state sector.

Blue-collar unions were more or less forced to follow suit, but they embraced these changes more gingerly. In the Rehnberg years of state-led bargaining (1990–1993), the only way to improve on the very moderate increase set nationally was through supplementary company-level bargaining, so it was in this period that experimentation with various formulas for local bargaining took off. Almost all industry contracts now call for local bargaining. However, rather than fully individualized pay, most provide for a wage kitty – a percentage of the total plant wage bill (e.g., 2 percent of average

TABLE 5.1. *Sectoral Distribution of Wage Agreement Models in Sweden, 2010*

Agreement Model[41]	Percentage of Employees by Sector			
	Private	State	Municipal and County Council	All Sectors
1. local wage formation without nationally determined margin	6	38	5	8
2. local wage formation with a fallback regulating the size of the margin	9	62	40	25
3. local wage formation with a fallback regulating the size of the margin, plus some form of individual guarantee	1			1
4. local wage frame without an individual guarantee	12		54	7
5. local wage frame with an individual guarantee or, alternatively, a fallback regulating the individual guarantee	43			43
6. general pay increase and local wage frame	18			10
7. general pay increase	11		1	6

Source: Medlingsinstitutet Annual Report Summary (2010: 6)

wages) – to be distributed locally and according to principles laid out in the contract. Such a system allows for some differentiation of wages to reflect individual attributes (leadership, initiative, skill) but within negotiated parameters. Many contracts also specify a minimum fallback guaranteed increase to which each worker is entitled no matter what. Previous wage scales have largely disappeared, however, and only 6 percent of workers in Sweden still work under industry contracts that specify a general (percentage) pay increase with no local bargaining.

Table 5.1 displays the current sectoral distribution of various models. Those at the top of table have the most individualized wage setting and, as a general rule, the higher the skill level, the more decentralized and individualized

[41] Key:

1. Individual wage increases entirely up to local negotiations, in some cases negotiated directly between employee and employer but in all cases with unions signing off
2. Fallback is a specified kitty for the event that local bargainers cannot agree
3. Fallback is kitty plus some form of individual guarantee
4. Centrally agreed wage kitty but no individual guarantee
5. Centrally agreed wage kitty and individual guarantee
6. General pay increase for all plus kitty [quite similar to past]
7. General increase which is equal for all workers (Ahlberg and Bruun 2005)

the bargaining.[42] Salaried workers are overwhelmingly covered by contracts in which bargaining occurs exclusively at the company level. For them, "figureless" agreements are attractive because benchmarks set in other industries tend to hold them back. Blue-collar workers are more likely to be covered by contracts that feature local wage frames (kitties); many also include an individual guarantee.

In Denmark, we saw that a similar decentralization of wage formation set the scene for the Danish LO to redefine its role by shifting its emphasis from distributional (wage) issues to supply-side issues, and training in particular. In Sweden, by contrast, repeated efforts to achieve a similar macro deal have failed. In the late 1990s, the Social Democratic government had convened a tripartite commission to advise on labor market policies in general and on training specifically. Discussions centered, among other things, on the possible introduction of personal education accounts that would allow workers to access further training. Since the 1975 Act on Employees Right to Education Leave, Swedish employees have been entitled to training leave, but the financing was such that the take-up was concentrated among higher-skilled, salaried employees. Proposals for new personal education accounts were meant to redress this imbalance and bolster training among low-skilled, low-pay workers.

Negotiations foundered on the question of who would bear the costs of this initiative (Ahlberg 1997b). SAF was, in principle, in favor of such a program but insisted on voluntary rather than obligatory contributions to training funds. The largest blue-collar union (municipal workers) rejected this, arguing that without obligatory contributions by firms, the result would be "a luxury system reserved for those who can afford to study anyhow" (Ahlberg 1997b). The LO itself proposed financing through a payroll tax, and signaled that such an arrangement might compensate for the small nominal raises that many of their low-skill members had to swallow under the new decentralized wage regime despite the revived economy and renewed profits (Ahlberg 1997b). Negotiations degenerated and were broken off without a resolution.

Sustaining Solidarity in a Neoliberal Era

The comparison with Denmark helps to identify why reconsolidating macro-corporatism has been more difficult in Sweden despite its shared tradition of tripartitism and similar if not higher levels of employer and union organization. Two factors stand out. One is the extent and type of fragmentation within the labor movement, which divides unions along precisely the lines that are activated by current trends. The general shift in employment out of traditional manufacturing into services – combined with technological changes that undermine the position of low-skill workers – have played directly into pre-existing

[42] An exception is air pilots, who along with transport workers have contracts specifying general (%) increases, applied uniformly.

organizational divisions in Sweden between blue- and white-collar trade unions and associated competing union confederations. Swedish employers actually have no interest in concluding any kind of centralized agreement with the LO because they can clearly see that the LO's power is waning while that of the confederations of salaried employees – including the very decentralization-friendly SACO in particular – rises.[43]

The other difference is the role of the state, which, as we saw, was crucial to brokering a new deal in Denmark between the LO and the DA by assigning to them a role in negotiating non-wage issues and supporting this with generous funding for ALMP and training. In Sweden, the state Medlingsinstitutet has powers to delay conflicts and to attempt to encourage the bargaining parties to resolve their differences, but unlike in Denmark it can neither impose agreements nor force coordination through collective bargaining linkages. Continued strong organization among low-skill workers outside manufacturing (in services, especially retail and public municipal workers) have prevented German-style dualization (e.g., the emergence of a more or less fully unregulated zone alongside the traditional collective bargaining core). However, in contrast to Denmark, weaker state capacities have made it more difficult to achieve an overarching agreement that can reconcile the interests of the diverse constituencies on both sides of the class divide.

The dynamics in Sweden are most vividly on display in wage bargaining, an arena in which ongoing leadership struggles – both between unions and employers and between actors in different sectors – have complicated broader attempts at tripartitism. Absent a statutory minimum wage and without the possibility of state mediators to guide pay bargaining, the Swedish LO has continued to coordinate bargaining among its constituent unions. Unlike in Denmark, where the LO represents a broader range of interests (including salaried workers) and has made training the centerpiece of its program, the Swedish LO increasingly represents low-skill workers and has continued to organize its strategy primarily around wage issues. For example, the previous two bargaining rounds (2007 and 2010) were explicitly fought over securing additional increases for low-paid workers – in particular, low paid women workers – through the use of what is colloquially called the *räknesnurra*. The term comes from a nineteenth century calculating machine, a cylindrical metal device on which the user punches digits and turns a handle several times in order to produce the result.[44] These days, the term refers to a mechanism through which the LO translates the percentage increase achieved in the industrial sector into a kroner figure that is then recalculated for low-pay sectors as a percent of their lower wage levels, yielding a higher percent that is then taken as the "mark," or goal, for the low-pay sectors.

Engineering employers in Sweden fiercely reject this practice, which to them smacks of a return to LO coordination and wage solidarism. Nonetheless, the

---

[43] I thank Erik Bengtsson for emphasizing the importance of this to me.
[44] Thanks to Göran Trogen for explaining the origins of the term.

LO has achieved some modest successes with this strategy. Retail employees, for example, are relatively well organized, and the sector is dominated by a few large companies that can absorb somewhat larger settlements because their agreements do not provide for local bargaining (hence, no wage drift). So when the retail union Handels threatened a strike during the busy Easter shopping season in 2007, employers agreed to wage increases that were technically above the "mark" set by industry. This outcome fueled conflict within the peak employers' confederation – SAF's successor Svenskt Näringsliv (SN) – as manufacturing employers denounced their colleagues in retail for failing to follow the lead of industry. It also increased tensions on the labor side, particularly between low-wage, female-dominated unions and skilled male manufacturing workers who also think the exposed industry should lead bargaining (Kjellberg 2011a: 49, 68).

The subsequent 2010 wage round featured similar strategies, prompting the association for engineering employers Teknikföretagen (TF) to withdraw from the industry agreement to protest LO coordination (Kjellberg 2011b: 62). This precipitated a crisis in industrial relations because TF anchors the entire industrial-sector agreement and organizes firms accounting for about 20 percent of all workers organized by SN (Ibsen et al. 2011: 3). The condition for their return to the industry agreement was that IF Metall refrain from participating in any LO-sponsored coordination.

The metalworkers, for their part, are caught on the horns of a dilemma. Coordinating with the LO provokes intense opposition by employers and also sits badly with SIF, the union's white-collar counterpart in industry, with which (since 1997) it coordinates bargaining under the terms of the *Industriavtalet*.[45] SIF recently rejected the idea of a formal merger with the metalworkers' union, on grounds that it was too close to the LO, whose influence in their affairs would not be welcome (interview with representative of collective bargaining department for Unionen, 2010). Rather than combine forces with its blue-collar counterpart in industry, SIF merged with another white-collar union, the Salaried Employees' Union (HTF).[46]

While engineering employers vehemently reject coordination above the level of industry, as in Germany they are still supportive of coordination among firms and unions within the industrial sector. Thus, periodic outbursts directed at the LO by the metalworking employers notwithstanding, the industry agreement appears to be quite stable, and social partnership in manufacturing has weathered recent strains fairly well. For example, unlike in the more conflictual

---

[45] As noted above, SIF is the Union of Technical and Clerical Employees in Industry; it organizes white-collar employees in industrial sectors.

[46] HTF organizes a range of salaried employees in wholesale and retail industries, in the transport sector, and in travel agencies and the like. The union that emerged from its merger with SIF is called Unionen. In the 2010 bargaining round, Unionen (representing SIF members) did not wait for IF Metall to settle, causing great tensions between the two main unions in industry. Among other things, IF Metall had wanted to lengthen the duration of the contract in order to bring negotiations in that sector back in line with other LO unions.

transport and construction industries, the metalworkers' union dealt with the growing issue of migrant ("posted") labor not by organizing these workers, but instead by striking a deal with the employers' association to ensure that they would be paid the going rate (Bengtsson 2013). Another sign of resilient social partnership within Swedish industry is the behavior of the metalworkers' union and the employers' association in the context of the recent crisis, as they together approached the government to request STW policies similar to those in Germany that could preserve employment in manufacturing (interview with representative of collective bargaining department, Teknikföretagen, 2012). When their appeals for state support were rejected, they settled for collectively bargained funds instead (see also Kullander and Norlin 2010).

The groups that that have been critical of the industry agreement represent rather diverse interests. On the union side, for example, the more militant transport and construction unions have been critical of the new regime because they see it as a constraint, especially on industrial action. Beyond this, gender-based criticisms emanate especially from female-dominated unions such as Handels and the municipal workers' union (Kommunal), who, as noted, have constantly probed the boundaries of the new system even if not seeking to dismantle it.[47] On the employers side, Almega – a sprawling association of service-sector firms – has openly challenged the role of industry in wage setting and demanded much more radical (liberalizing) changes to the entire bargaining system (Kjellberg 2011b: 69). However, partly no doubt because of this diversity of interests, the industry agreement appears quite stable at present.

Dualization through Drift in Sweden

Policy stalemate and inaction define the conditions under which drift thrives, and drift is in turn associated with dualization. Despite periodic efforts to reinvigorate Swedish corporatism through a new national-level bargain, unions and employers are far apart on the content of any such deal (Lovén 2009a). Continued efforts on the part of the LO to bolster the wages of low-skill workers help to explain why fewer full-time workers in Sweden have fallen into the low-wage zone (see Figure 4.4). At the same time, an important gap has opened up between well-protected, full-time jobs and a growing number of more precarious forms of employment.

As noted in the previous sections, employment protection for full-time workers is much stronger in Sweden than in Denmark, and this has emerged as a flashpoint in the face of liberalization efforts. In the early 1990s, the center-right government sought far-reaching changes to the 1974 Employment Protection Legislation (the "last in, first out" rule described earlier). But the resulting legislation was reversed immediately when the Social Democrats returned to power in 1994 (Davidsson 2009: 11). However, even as Swedish unions "used

---

[47] I thank Erik Bengtsson for these points.

every possible means at their disposal" to defend employment protection for permanent workers, flexibility was increased for atypical workers through a relaxation of restrictions on fixed-term and temporary employment (12; see also Davidsson 2010: 128–129). The difference from Denmark is clear in Figure 4.6. While in Denmark temporary workers enjoy protections that are nearly on par with those in standard employment, the gap between the two in Sweden (as in Germany) is vast.

Thus, while employer efforts to dismantle existing employment protections for regular workers have so far been thwarted, as in Germany it is not hard for Swedish employers to find ways around these constraints. Temporary employment increased steadily after 1990, but particularly after a 1996 law was passed that eased restrictions on such jobs (see Obinger et al. 2012: 192). Involuntary part-time employment also soared in Sweden in that period before dropping back somewhat, as Figure 4.8 shows. Engblom (2009) notes that Sweden is above the average of the fifteen core members of the EU on both fixed-term and part-time work (5).

Sweden has followed other countries in instituting new activation provisions to push the unemployed back into work,[48] but unlike in Denmark this has not been accompanied by the same well-elaborated system for retraining. Major skill formation initiatives were launched in the late 1990s under the Social Democrats, but these were targeted interventions of limited duration. For example, an ambitious "Adult Education Initiative" (AEI, a.k.a. the "Knowledge Lift") program inaugurated in 1997 focused on unemployed workers with low education. Participants were enrolled in regular adult education courses offered through existing municipal adult education centers (KOMVUX). This was a huge program, "unprecedented in its size and scope" (Albrecht et al. 2005; see also Forslund and Krueger 2008: 22; Schnyder 2012: 12). Stenberg and Westerlund report that "between the autumn semester of 1997 and the spring semester 1999, individuals in the AEI represented 1.2 to 1.5% of the total labour force" (2008: 55–56). But when it expired, it was folded back into the regular adult education system and supported at a much lower level – 10,000 training slots per year, versus 100,000 at its peak (55–56). Another short-term program, the Swedish Information Technology (SWIT) program also targeted the unemployed while addressing nationwide shortages in IT skills, but this initiative lasted only two years – from 1998 to 2000. When the SWIT and "Knowledge Lift" programs ran out, spending on ALMP, and training in particular, trended sharply down in Sweden, as Figure 4.2 showed (Lindvall 2010: 165ff).

Another big contrast to Denmark (and similarity to Germany) is the relative underdevelopment of CVET. In Denmark, activation was closely connected

---

[48] One of the most important reforms since the 1990s was the new "Activity Guarantee" program of 2000 that eliminated the possibility to re-qualify for unemployment benefits by participation in labor market programs (Forslund and Krueger 2008: 15, 19, 32).

to training initiatives within the existing system of (firm- and school-based) vocational training. In Sweden, by contrast, the separate vocational track for youth was eliminated decades ago. Firms are also not obligated to provide CVET for adults, this being a matter negotiated at the sectoral or enterprise level (CEDEFOP 2009: 33). A pilot program launched in the late 1990s and fully institutionalized in 2002 introduced more CVET and sought to increase employer involvement in its provision. But Swedish unions are skeptical of giving firms more control over the content of training, and employers face fewer incentives than in Denmark to provide such training on a broad scale (Lindell 2004, 2006: 235). CVET thus remains relatively underdeveloped, and the volume of state-sponsored training in Sweden pales in comparison to that in Denmark and even the Netherlands.[49]

Meanwhile, the policies of the center-right government since 2006 have intensified activation without many of the compensatory policies we saw in Denmark, thus exacerbating dualism. The previous "Activity Guarantee" passed by the Social Democrats in 2000 was replaced with a new "Jobs and Employment Guarantee" that involved more stringent activation requirements (Schnyder and Jackson 2011). The center-right government has also continued to encourage the emergence of a secondary labor market by flexibilizing agency work further, loosening restrictions on fixed-term employment, reducing unemployment benefits for part-time workers, and most recently and controversially by introducing tax breaks for hiring household help (23–24; Bowman and Cole 2009; Engblom 2009: 6–7; Obinger et al. 2012: 194).

New training opportunities were introduced in 2009, but they are targeted at "problem" populations, while voluntary CVET for the already employed runs through the social partners. This separation of state-sponsored training (for targeted groups) shares similarities with Germany, and it contrasts starkly with the more integrated system of training in Denmark, in which employers participate, with state support, in providing training for all kinds of workers. By contrast, Swedish ALMP now includes a dizzying array of different programs in the context of a general shift away from more general active labor market supports toward programs targeted more at specific problem groups, such as the long-term unemployed, youth, and immigrants (Obinger et al. 2012: 194).

The Swedish Case in Comparative Perspective

Overall, the comparison between Sweden and Denmark underscores the difficulties of constructing and sustaining political support for solidarity in a neoliberal era. The two countries share several structural prerequisites, including a high level of organization and strong coordinating capacity on both sides of

---

[49] A 2009 reform transferred responsibility for adult VET to the new Agency for Higher Vocational Education, charged with developing and implementing a unified structure for higher vocational education and training (CEDEFOP 2009).

the class divide. Unlike in Germany, and similar to Denmark, organized labor in Sweden has a strong footing not just among traditional blue-collar groups, but also among workers within the emerging service sectors, from salaried professionals to low-skill workers. Strong organization among the latter has been crucial to preventing the emergence of an essentially unregulated zone of employment as in Germany, even if it has not suppressed dualist tendencies entirely.

Here, the differences to Denmark come to the fore. In Sweden, the historic separation of white- and blue-collar workers into distinct trade union confederations has meant that the growth in unionization in much of the service sector and among salaried employees has come at the direct expense of the LO. IF Metall – the pivotal blue-collar union for engineering – now sits uneasily at the intersection of ongoing strains between the LO and white-collar unions. The dominant political dynamic involves a see-sawing in which the LO has been able to enlist manufacturing unions in partial defense of traditional institutions and practices – sometimes even including elements of wage solidarism across industries – while unions of salaried workers pursue an increasingly independent course.[50] Continued coordination among blue-collar unions behind LO leadership has prevented extreme downward dualization by securing compensatory gains for its low-skilled constituents. However, precisely this has also radicalized Swedish employers, especially in manufacturing. Engineering employers so far have had enough veto power to prevent a return to peak-level coordination, but without commanding sufficient strength to dictate outcomes in other sectors.

To the extent that Swedish engineering employers are united around an agenda that seeks to marginalize the LO, the prospects for a peak-level deal involving trade-offs between the interests of the more privileged segments of the working class and low-skill workers (LO's main constituencies) seem rather dim. Indeed, repeated attempts to conclude a comprehensive "Pact for Growth" covering a broad range of issues have so far foundered. SN demands a renegotiation of the employment protection legislation from the 1970s and of the rules governing secondary strikes – two issues the LO considers non-negotiable. Consistent with the logic of drift, stalemate may, in fact, be employers' preferred outcome for the time being, because meanwhile the strength of white-collar confederations like SACO – which are not attached to traditional arrangements – grows apace. In fact, somewhat ominously for the low-skill constituencies that the LO represents, SN has initiated negotiations with the white-collar cartel on a possible Grand Bargain – without the LO.[51]

---

[50] These groups have also been significant beneficiaries of Sweden's recent "choice revolution," which since the 2000s has increased the number of private options across a broad range of social services – from education to day care and eldercare to health care (Blomqvist 2004: 140). As Blomqvist shows, private providers (health care, schools, etc.) tend to be over-represented in higher income areas.

[51] I thank Johan Davidsson for bringing this to my attention.

Unlike in Denmark, the Swedish state has mostly been unable to break the deadlock. The state can cajole and implore, but it lacks strong powers to force a negotiated solution that could bridge the interests within the union movement and among firms with divergent interests – let alone across the class divide. In short, while strong organization, especially on the labor side, seems important to preventing a free-fall into German-style dualization, tendencies in that direction are still present in Sweden. As in Denmark, manufacturing interests led the break with tripartitism, but in Sweden the weakness of the state has so far complicated re-coordination around an alternative, more encompassing coalition.

Summing up the lessons from this chapter as a whole, then, we can say that the Dutch-German comparison showed that a narrowly based union movement puts sharp limits on achieving high levels of equality, even if a stronger state makes at least certain forms of solidarism possible. The Denmark-Sweden comparison demonstrates the continuing importance of strong organization, especially among low-skilled workers, while highlighting the role of the state in brokering coalitions that can reconcile their interests with those of traditional manufacturing and emerging salaried employees.

6

The Future of Egalitarian Capitalism, in Light of Its Past

A central goal of this study has been to attempt to reframe the debate on varieties of capitalism, and in so doing, to shed some light on observed divergent trajectories of institutional change in the political economies of the rich democracies. For the past two decades, scholarship in this area has equated the political-economic institutions associated with liberal capitalism with inequality and those associated with coordinated capitalism with higher levels of social solidarity. Debates have focused on the sources of stability in traditional institutions and the extent of change, particularly within the CMEs. VofC scholars see existing arrangements in these countries as fundamentally robust and resilient due to their efficiency effects – and in consequence of these, to employers' continuing support for them. VofC critics, by contrast, see these institutions as under siege in the face of a broad neoliberal offensive, and argue that their survival depends on labor's capacity to resist. Against this backdrop, the clear implication seemed to be that the best way to preserve egalitarian capitalism is through a vigorous defense of the institutions that have traditionally defined coordinated capitalism.

The preceding chapters analyzed the political dynamics at work across five countries – the United States, Germany, Denmark, the Netherlands, and Sweden – and in three important institutional arenas – industrial relations, vocational education and training, and labor market policy. Rather than rely on assumptions about the relevant interests, I investigated empirically what employers and unions in different sectors and countries have sought to achieve in these realms. While confirming a broad, shared trajectory of liberalization, I found that there are in fact different varieties of liberalization associated with different distributive outcomes. My analysis links distinct constellations of interests and political-coalitional dynamics to three broad trajectories of change – deregulatory liberalization, dualization, and embedded flexibilization.

Against the conventional wisdom, I found that not every defense of traditional institutions is solidarity promoting, and not every move toward liberalization undermines social solidarity. In Germany, the successful defense of institutions associated with coordinated capitalism across all three realms has come bundled with declining coverage and increasing inequality through dualization. Meanwhile, Denmark has witnessed significant departures from the practices associated with strategic coordination across each of these institutional arenas. Pay bargaining is more decentralized than in the organized sectors in Germany, with wages being largely set at the firm or even individual level. Training is increasingly individualized and organized around promoting general rather than specific skills. Labor market policy is not based on guaranteeing workers stable careers within a firm or industry, but on facilitating movement of workers across firms and even sectors. These developments do not square with the logic behind the classic CME model, but they do seem to be compatible with continued relatively high levels of equality.

The three trajectories of change I have identified conform broadly to Esping-Andersen's famous trilogy – deregulation (associated with LMEs), dualization (associated with continental Christian democratic countries), and embedded flexibilization (associated with Scandinavian social democratic countries). Clearly, generous social policy remains the sine qua non of high levels of social solidarity, and the "embedded" part of the embedded flexibilization trajectory that I have identified depends heavily on what Christer Peterson (2011) has called the "enabling welfare state" to prevent liberalization in these three institutional arenas from degenerating into "sheer deregulation" as in the liberal economies (209). Throughout my analysis, the United States has thus served as an important bounding case, throwing into sharp relief the conditions – above all, strong representation of labor interests both in politics and in the market – that are necessary to protect the most vulnerable groups in society.

In this study, I have focused on collective bargaining, vocational education and training, and labor market institutions – leaving changes in welfare regimes mostly to the side. Further research on the connections between changes in the political-economic institutions at the center of the present study and those that define distinctive welfare regimes is clearly needed (but see, for example, Huber and Stephens 2012). Some authors have suggested that the dynamics that shape political-economic institutions such as industrial relations or training operate on a somewhat different logic from those that govern welfare state institutions, with the former being driven more by an organized-interest (or producer-group) logic, while social and welfare policy is more dominated by electoral politics. Like my own analysis, this raises the possibility that the two realms do not move in tandem. Where my analysis departs somewhat from the usual understandings is in a different view of what is stable and what is changing. Most VofC scholars suggest that the political-economic institutions – collective bargaining, training, employment protection – in CMEs are largely stable, while welfares regimes are changing rather fundamentally. My argument is something like the opposite: I see political-economic institutions (driven by organized interest group politics) as undergoing significant changes even as the core logic of the three well-known welfare state families has proved remarkably robust.[1]

As an analysis of change, my study sheds light on why the institutions of egalitarian and coordinated capitalism coincided and complemented one another in the Golden Era of postwar capitalist development, and why they do not do so now. An important body of historical work taught us that the institutions of coordinated capitalism rested on a strong cross-class coalition between manufacturing firms and their employers (e.g., Swenson 2002). My study shows that the decline of employment in manufacturing and the transition to services has meant that the strong and in some ways still resilient cross-class coalition that was so central to the politics of coordination in the CMEs is no longer able (labor) or willing (employers) to exercise political leadership for the economy as a whole. Moreover, across all of the rich democracies, new constituencies have emerged in the context of the service transition as a growing number of women entered the labor market, and as various forms of atypical employment have increased in size and significance at both the high and low ends of the income spectrum. For many of these constituencies, the traditional institutions of strategic coordination are either no longer desirable (white-collar salaried employees), no longer obtainable (many low-skill atypical workers), or no longer cover the very different risks these groups face in the market (professionals, working parents). In such a context, the defense of traditional arrangements may be a recipe for institutional erosion and drift.

THE COALITIONAL FOUNDATIONS OF EGALITARIAN CAPITALISM

Classic literature on the political economy of the advanced industrial countries tells us that egalitarian capitalism depended on the alliances that social democracy's core constituencies were able to forge with other groups (e.g., Przeworski and Sprague 1986). The successes of the Nordic countries in this regard depended not just on the strength and organization of labor, but also on the coalitions that working-class parties were able to forge with representatives of other economic interests, notably farmers (Esping-Andersen 1985; Gourevitch 1986). Similarly today, the survival of the more egalitarian varieties of capitalism appears to hinge crucially on the alliances that the representatives of traditional manufacturing are able to forge with emerging new interests that are increasingly central to the new post-industrial economy. Such coalitions do not emerge from thin air, but instead, as I have argued, reflect differences in the organizational and political resources that the relevant groups – organized labor, business, and the state – inherit from the past and can bring to bear in the present.

---

[1] I thank an anonymous reviewer for emphasizing this to me.

Similar to Esping-Andersen's classic analysis of social policy, contemporary changes in the political-economic institutions at the center of my own analysis also seem to be inextricably related to the legacy of political choices that go back to the Golden Era of postwar capitalist development. In the LMEs, no stable settlement between labor and capital was reached, not even in the manufacturing core. Although unions achieved some organizational strength in industry, employers themselves never developed the kind of coordinating capacities necessary to support high-skill production (Hall and Soskice 2001). Individual firms thus experienced union influence as a competitive drag, and employers sought to preserve competitiveness through an aggressive attack on organized labor (Thelen 2004). The decline of manufacturing only amplified these dynamics, as the transition to services took place under the auspices of a coalition between traditional industrial interests and rising service-sector firms under a broad neoliberal banner. The result has been a dismantling of those coordinating capacities that once existed and a collapse of unions – and with that, rising inequality at both ends of the income spectrum, as the wages and salaries of top earners have taken off and low-income groups have seen their position decline relative to the median.

The Christian democratic countries, by contrast, saw the institutionalization of stronger cross-class coalitions in industry in the immediate postwar period (Iversen and Soskice 2010). In many of these cases, traditional blue-collar interests have continued to dominate the producer-group landscape. Unions are still more heavily concentrated in manufacturing, with low organization among women and in the service sectors. In such countries, the transition to services has often taken place under the auspices of a solid cross-class coalition in manufacturing that has been successful in defending many of the traditional arrangements of coordinated capitalism. However, the same coalition that has been so successful in heading off across-the-board deregulatory liberalization often presides over growing dualization, which proceeds quietly – through drift – as employment shifts out of areas in which unions are well anchored and into sectors where they simply never established a foothold (e.g., Palier and Thelen 2010).

Finally, contemporary political dynamics in the social democratic countries have also been profoundly shaped by past developments – above all, the relatively early entry of women into the labor market and the associated growth of services, both public and private (Huber and Stephens 2000: 327; see also Pontusson 2009). In these countries, public-sector unions represent a strong and well-organized counterweight to manufacturing. Women now make up a majority of the union movement in most of these countries, and low-skill occupations are also well organized. Encompassing organization has not eliminated conflicts of interest; on the contrary, as we have seen, the Scandinavian countries have featured massive clashes, not just between unions and employers but also within the labor movement itself. In fact, some of the most significant changes documented in my analysis emerged out of these conflicts, and they

FIGURE 6.1. Export Dependence on Manufacturing in 2009 and Spending on Active Labor Market Policy as Percentage of GDP per Unemployed in 2008. *Sources*: OECD (ALMP); UN Comtrade SITC Rev 4. (Exports)

reflect negotiated trade-offs between constituencies – skilled manufacturing workers, public-sector workers, and unskilled service-sector employees – with very different interests.

Eric Patashnik's (2008) work has shown that institutional change often involves elements of both decomposition and re-composition, and he argues that the durability of reform depends heavily on the extent to which new policies "upset inherited coalitional patterns and stimulate the emergence of new vested interests and political alliances" (4). In this context, it is perhaps no coincidence that the relatively more "solidaristic" outcomes in each of the two "within-family" comparisons underwent a much more intense turn to neoliberalism in the 1980s. In that period, policy in the Netherlands under the Christian democratic Prime Minister Lubbers pivoted sharply toward liberalizing labor markets and promoting the service sector, even as Lubbers' German counterpart Helmut Kohl was pursuing a more moderate course and doubling down on support for manufacturing. Similarly, in the Danish-Swedish comparison, it was Denmark that underwent the more dramatic neoliberal turn, as Conservative Prime Minister Poul Schlüter forged ahead with liberalizing moves across all three of the institutional arenas analyzed in this book. Sweden's embrace of neoliberalism in this period was much more halting and tentative in comparison. Applying Patashnik's insights, we might argue that the strong neoliberal turn promoted coalitional reconfiguration by unsettling previous coalitions and opening the way for the formation of new alliances, both within classes and across the class divide.

It is also perhaps no coincidence that among the CMEs, the Netherlands and Denmark rely much less heavily on manufacturing than the other rich democracies. Figure 6.1 provides comparative data on the value of manufacturing exports as a percentage of total exports. In the Netherlands, by

2009 manufacturing exports made up just 57 percent of total exports, and in Denmark 65 percent. Reliance on manufacturing in these countries is thus well below that in other CMEs (e.g., Sweden's 77 percent and Germany's 83 percent) and even below notable LMEs like the United States and the UK.[2]

However, Figure 6.1 also makes clear that Denmark and the Netherlands stood out before the financial crisis in another dimension as well, namely in spending on ALMPs (measured as a percent of GDP per unemployed person). Thus, my analysis also emphasized the crucial constructive role played by the state in promoting and underwriting broadly solidaristic outcomes. In Denmark, the re-equilibration of tripartitism and a strong national settlement depended heavily on an explicit deal – brokered and sponsored by the state – to reconcile the interests of low-skill workers (especially, but not exclusively, in the service sectors) with those of more privileged blue- and white-collar groups. This deal involved a significant conversion of centralized bargaining institutions away from wage solidarism and toward an emphasis on human capital formation above all. In this sense, the flexicurity trade-off for which Denmark is now so famous was not so much the product of a coherent social coalition as it was a mechanism for forging one.

In short, state social policy remains central to the new politics of social solidarity, but it is a different kind of state and a different kind of policy than in the past. As Esping-Andersen emphasized long ago, salaried white-collar employees are increasingly central to the social democratic alliance. Salaried groups, especially professionals and semi-professionals, are not necessarily against the welfare state and they often favor universalism. However, they tend to embrace a different version of universalism, one that emphasizes individual development, internationalization, gender equality, and meritocracy (Häusermann and Kriesi 2012; Morel et al. 2011). In the three realms under analysis here, reconciling the interests of these groups with those of more vulnerable segments of the working class seems to imply different kinds of interventions based above all on a social investment logic (see, e.g., Hemerijck 2013; Huber and Stephens 2012; Morel et al. 2011). Where wage differentials are increasingly based on merit, state policy plays a key role in guaranteeing and subsidizing educational opportunities for all. Where greater employment security requires more general skills, the state has an important role to play in financing investments that the private sector will not. Where labor markets are more flexible, state policy is crucial for underwriting re-training opportunities throughout the life course.

[2] The story is similar if one looks at manufacturing as a percentage of GDP. Here, too, Denmark and the Netherlands are at the low end among CMEs (manufacturing accounted for 13% of GDP in each in 2009). Only France (11%) and Norway (10%) record lower figures, while most other CMEs are much higher (e.g., Germany at 19%). The figure for Sweden is between the extremes at 16%. Turning to employment in manufacturing as a percentage of total employment, the Netherlands again records the lowest level (10.8% in 2009). Denmark is somewhat higher at 13.7%, but again significantly below Germany at 19% and even Sweden at 16%. All figures from the OECD.

Education and training thus occupy a very central role in the new politics of social solidarity, and as we have seen, this is precisely an area in which it seems possible to find common ground across groups that are otherwise very differently situated in the labor market.

POSSIBILITIES AND PITFALLS OF EMBEDDED FLEXIBILIZATION

I have argued that the kinds of interventions associated with embedded flexibilization involve forging and maintaining encompassing coalitions and, with that, a strong "community of fate," to use Ahlquist and Levi's felicitous term (2013: 22 and passim). There is sometimes a kind of breathlessness in scholarly accounts of cases such as Denmark – and, to a lesser extent, the Netherlands – which have been held up by the OECD and others as exemplars of a new flexicurity model. So before we leave these cases it is important to note once again that there is also a dark side to these models.

Both the Netherlands and Denmark feature a particularly virulent strain of anti-immigrant sentiment, expressed especially strongly in the electoral arena. The Dutch Party for Freedom – Partij voor de Vriheid (PVV) – rose rapidly in the 2000s on a strongly anti-immigrant (especially anti-Muslim) message. Under the leadership of the outspoken Geert Wilders, it became the third largest party in parliament, and until recently played a key role in supporting a minority government led by Prime Minister Mark Rutte. Although the PVV's share of the popular vote declined in the last (2012) election, with 10 percent of the electorate behind it, the party is still a force in Dutch politics ("Dutch surprise" 2012).

The xenophobic Danish People's Party – Dansk Folkeparti (DF) – was founded somewhat earlier in 1995, and its rapid rise in popularity played an important role in promoting a major reform of Danish immigration law in 1999 – producing one of the most restrictive immigration regimes in Europe today (Liebig 2007; Rydgren 2010).[3] The DF continues to enjoy success at the polls, garnering around 15 percent of votes, making it the third largest party in Denmark. Between 2001 and 2011, the DF provided crucial support allowing the center-right minority government to remain in power. The party's influence in that period is clear among other things in the policies described in Chapter 4 that imposed restrictions on immigrants specifically in receipt of social benefits (Liebig 2007; Mouritsen and Olsen 2013). Similar to radical right parties in the Netherlands and elsewhere in Europe, the DF invokes ethno-nationalist rhetoric about preserving Denmark's distinctive national character (Rydgren 2010: 57, 63).

---

[3] Subsequent reforms in the 2000s further increased restrictions on immigration, despite the fact that Denmark has one of Europe's smallest immigrant populations, just 7% according to Liebig (2007: 9; on the reforms, see also Rydgren 2010). Recent legislation, for example, tightened rules for family reunification and made it more difficult for immigrants to claim social benefits (see, for example, "On the March" 2011 and "Ins and Outs" 2013).

The Danish radical right is significantly more prominent and influential than its Swedish counterpart. In Sweden, the mainstream parties "have erected a cordon sanitaire" against the radical right, while in Denmark the behavior of the mainstream parties has contributed to legitimizing the DF and its agenda (Rydgren 2010: 58 and passim). Some of Denmark's notable political-economic successes, therefore, must be read against the backdrop of an immigration policy that has become more restrictive and in fact openly hostile to immigrants. For example, the otherwise laudable decline in the difference in employment rates for native Danes and non-Western immigrants – from a forty-two point difference in the mid-1990s to a twenty-four point difference today – compares favorably to Sweden, which continues to suffer from a wider employment gap, but which also features a far less restrictive immigration policy ("Ins and Outs" 2013).[4]

The point here is that a strong defense of social solidarity – a strong internal "community of fate" – in the Netherlands and Denmark seems to have come bundled with strict boundaries to the outside.[5] To the extent that this is true, the Netherlands and Denmark do not so much reflect the absence of an insider-outsider divide as a different line of cleavage.

NEW CHALLENGES, NEW FORMULAS

The pattern that emerges from the empirical analysis in this book is consistent neither with traditional VofC theory (which emphasizes institutional stability) nor with alternative perspectives that equate all liberalizing moves with a decline in social solidarity. Figures 6.2 and 6.3 provide a picture (admittedly crude) of how we might think about how the broad policy choices facing the rich democracies have shifted since the 1980s. They situate these countries in a two-dimensional space that maps variation in coordination in labor markets (in the VofC sense) on one dimension and levels of equality on the other. Thus, the x-axis captures what we can think of as reflecting whether countries have adopted labor market policies that are overall "market-countenancing" (toward the left: lower employment protection, high flexibility through ALMP) or more "protective" (toward the right: stronger employment protections, less spending on ALMP). It is based on a simple two-variable index that taps differences in levels of employment protection for regular workers and spending on ALMPs. The y-axis records countries' positions relative to one another in terms of two measures of overall inequality (again based on a simple two-variable index composed of poverty rate and post-tax Gini coefficient). Countries more to the top are more egalitarian by these measures than those toward the bottom.

Figure 6.2 captures the "state of affairs" across the rich democracies on these two dimensions for the 1980s. What we can see here is that in the Golden

---

[4] 84% of native Swedes have a job, compared to 51% of non-Europeans, and fully 46% of the unemployed in Sweden are non-Europeans ("Ins and Outs" 2013).
[5] I thank David Soskice for emphasizing this to me.

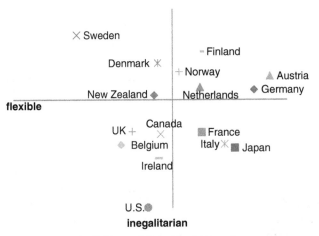

FIGURE 6.2. Flexibility and Equality Mid-1980s

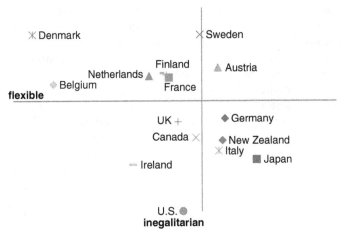

FIGURE 6.3. Flexibility and Equality, Mid-/Late 2000s

Era of postwar capitalism, countries tended (with a few exceptions) to form a broad "swath" that runs from the southwest to the northeast quadrant – countries with more flexible labor markets were associated with higher levels of inequality, while those with more protected labor markets were associated with higher levels of equality at the national level.[6]

By the late 2000s, however, the picture had changed rather dramatically, as Figure 6.3 shows. By this time, the countries characterized by more protected (less flexible) labor markets were increasingly plagued by higher inequality.

[6] Sweden is an exception because of the importance of ALMP to the original Rehn-Meidner model of the 1950s and 1960s (see Chapter 5).

For example, labor markets in Germany, Japan, and Italy all remained more protected, but these economies had also become decidedly less egalitarian. By contrast, in a number of other cases, labor markets became more flexible, but without the country succumbing to higher levels of inequality. For instance, Denmark, Austria, and the Netherlands all become relatively more flexible by these measures while also inhibiting the growth of poverty and inequality. Overall, the population of countries occupying the northeast quadrant (high protection, high equality) has thinned out considerably and the swath now runs from northwest to southeast.

Without wishing to over-interpret this admittedly very simple picture, I want to suggest that while LMEs continue to combine flexible labor markets with high inequality, CMEs increasingly find themselves pulled in one of two directions. Some countries have clearly gone down the route of dualization, preserving traditional protections but for a shrinking core (from the northeast to the southeast quadrant). By contrast, the countries that maintained higher levels of equality are not those that are defending traditional labor market policies and practices (northeast quadrant), but those that precisely embrace elements of market as opposed to strategic coordination, alongside compensatory social policies that prevent a slide into the inegalitarian Anglo-Saxon model – thus migrating toward the northwest rather than the southwest quadrant.

The overall pattern that emerges from my analysis shares some similarities with recent work by Schneider and Paunescu (2011), who track policy and institutional reforms in the rich democracies between 1990 and 2005, and link these to shifts in sector-specific comparative advantage. Based on a set of measures that capture the core features that are widely seen as distinguishing LMEs from CMEs, Schneider and Paunescu show that many of the continental political economies continue to exhibit an institutional and policy clustering that is broadly consistent with the original (coordinated) model. However, they observe very significant changes in a subset of CMEs – namely Denmark, Sweden, the Netherlands, and Finland – all of which moved in this period toward more flexible LME-like institutions and practices.[7] Schneider and Paunescu are less interested in the distributional consequences of this, focusing instead on changes in the composition of exports. Thus they show that the "non-mover" CMEs continue to enjoy comparative advantage in medium-technology exports, but that the "mover country" CMEs (i.e., those that have experienced significant liberalization) have shifted increasingly toward the kind of high-tech (research and development intensive) exports traditionally associated with LMEs.[8]

---

[7] In a similar vein, an index developed by the right-libertarian Fraser Institute shows Sweden, Denmark, and Finland all "catching up" to the United States on their measures of "economic freedom" (see "Ins and Outs" 2013).

[8] Their distinction between high- and medium-tech sectors is based on the OECD classification of industries (for details, see Schneider and Paunescu 2011: 5). Darius Ornston (2012) argues in the same direction, documenting how some of Europe's most corporatist political economies

For my purposes here, what is important is that the liberalizing policy and institutional changes that Schneider and Paunescu document for mover political economies (Denmark, Sweden, the Netherlands, and Finland) have not come bundled with the same high levels of inequality that are characteristic of the classic LME model. So while they are struck by the embrace of liberalization by such political economies in important areas, my analysis emphasizes the re-embedding of liberalization in these countries in arrangements and policies that have headed off Anglo-Saxon-style inequality.

The analysis presented here contains both good news and bad news for LMEs. The VofC literature tends to emphasize structural constraints and strong path dependency, in which countries are "born" coordinated or liberal in the late nineteenth century. If we then follow the conventional wisdom, the liberal economies are more or less doomed to higher levels of inequality. The message of my book is more hopeful, or so I think, because it opens possibilities for policy innovations that do not rely on a country having inherited from the past particular institutional features associated with coordinated capitalism. The good news, then, is that once we unbundle coordinated and egalitarian capitalism, we can see new possibilities to achieve more egalitarian outcomes even in liberal political economies.

The bad news, though, is that it appears that other features that are still lacking in LMEs – encompassing interest associations (especially unions) and state strength – are more important than ever. Organization on the employer side is helpful because, as usual, from labor's perspective the only thing worse than a strong and organized business class is a weak and disorganized one (Martin and Swank 2012). However, we have also seen that well-organized employers are by no means sufficient. What has channeled employer strength and organization in directions consistent with economic efficiency *and* equality is encompassing unions and a strong and active state. And these are, of course, elements that are still in short supply in most LMEs.

SUMMING UP

By exploring empirically the expressed interests of key actors in the political economy and analyzing the conflicts among them in three arenas of central relevance to the literature on VofC, we gain insight into distinctive trajectories of change in the rich democracies. Four broad conclusions follow from my analysis.

(1) *Employer coordination may be necessary but is by no means sufficient to secure the survival of egalitarian capitalism.*

have shifted since the 1980s toward increased emphasis on exports based on the type of high-tech "big" innovation that we have traditionally associated with LMEs rather than the usual CME-style incremental technological change.

In the 1980s and 1990s, the conventional wisdom in the political economy literature was upended by a powerful wave of revisionist research that emphasized the constitutive role of employers and business associations in forging and sustaining many of the institutional arrangements we now associate with egalitarian capitalism. Whereas the corporatism literature explained cross-national differences with reference to the structure and strength of the labor movement, a new wave of theorizing emphasized instead employer organization and associated capacity for strategic coordination as the core underlying distinction between different varieties of capitalism. Most recently, Martin and Swank (2012) developed a powerful case that strong peak business associations support broadly egalitarian outcomes through their impact on employers' conceptions of their long-term interests and their capacity to resist short-termism and a competitive race to the bottom.

My analysis confirms the importance of employer organization, but it adds a strong caveat. While high coordinating capacity among firms may be necessary for high levels of social solidarity, it is by no means sufficient. The case studies in the preceding chapters feature ample evidence of Hilferding's enduring insight that the political management of capitalism is more difficult where capitalists do not have the capacity to act collectively. At the same time, though, we have also seen many cases in which coordinated employers brought their considerable organizational powers to bear in pursuit of goals that are distinctly corrosive with respect to social solidarity – to eliminate unions (as in the U.S. case), to prevent reforms that would shore up eroding collective bargaining coverage (Germany), and to block a return to forms of coordination that could restore the influence of the LO as the primary representative of low-skill workers (Sweden). As the foregoing analysis shows, the question is not simply: Are employers capable of coordination? But rather: Who is coordinating with whom and to do what?

(2) *High levels of organization and unity of the labor side are indispensable for continued high levels of social solidarity.*

By contrast, the analysis in the preceding chapters reaffirms one of the core arguments of power resource theory, demonstrating that weakness and fragmentation on the labor side are devastating to egalitarian capitalism. The United States is paradigmatic, for in this case union weakness is a key factor in explaining the rise of inequality over the past decades. Other cases, however, serve as a powerful reminder that unions that are strong but whose power is concentrated in specific sectors are ill-placed to sustain social solidarity on a broad scale. Where – as in Germany – organized labor has failed to extend its reach beyond the traditional manufacturing core, the institutional arrangements characteristic of egalitarian capitalism are susceptible to institutional erosion and dualization through drift. Indeed, one of the key features distinguishing the continental from the Nordic cases is the extent to which labor constituencies outside the industrial core – including salaried employees, women, and low-skill workers in the private-service sector – are organized and fully represented within the labor movement. Where this is the case, traditional arrangements have not been dismantled, but rather (often) converted to new goals that reflect the interests of emerging constituencies on the labor side and reconcile these with those of traditional manufacturing interests.[9]

(3) *State support is crucial to sustaining solidarity in the current neoliberal period.*

The role of the state in supporting social solidarity – through its impact on labor unity, on employers' cooperation, and especially on mediating the impact of liberalization, particularly for the most vulnerable groups in society – cannot be overemphasized. In the United States, the policies of the government, especially during the Reagan years, actively hastened the collapse of organized labor and the decline in collective bargaining. In Denmark, by contrast, state interventions in the 1990s were crucial to maintaining labor unity and to brokering a coalition between skilled and unskilled workers based on a trade-off between wage decentralization on one hand and strong support (and subsidies) for retraining on the other. And in the Netherlands and Sweden, reductions in support for training under center-right governments in the context of continuing activation policies have contributed to growing inequality.

Moreover, as we have seen, it is not just what governments do, it is also what they do not do. The erosion of collective bargaining in Germany is in large measure a function of state inaction and incapacity in the face of clear signs of dualization. The principle of collective bargaining autonomy in Germany goes back to a time when unions sought to put up defenses against encroachments by a hostile state. However, as recent trends show, the equality-enhancing effects of this depend heavily on continuing encompassing coverage. The distributional impact of collective bargaining autonomy shifts considerably when, as in the current period, union coverage shrinks and the state is unable or unwilling to address the resulting gap through traditional measures (e.g., extension clauses) or new initiatives (e.g., a statutory minimum wage). The failure of the state to respond, as much as active state policy, has contributed to the growth of a new low-pay sector in that country. The same general point holds in a different way in Sweden, where (compared to Denmark) the more limited powers of the state (e.g., the relative weakness of state mediation) has contributed to ongoing conflict and instability in industrial relations, even if coverage rates remain higher than in Germany.

(4) *Institutional reproduction requires the ongoing mobilization of new support coalitions.*

---

[9] My findings are also parallel to that of an emerging body of work on electoral behavior that tells us that the kinds of alliances that are likely to form are deeply influenced by the networks that link these groups together as voters (see, e.g., Iversen and Soskice 2010 and Lupu and Pontusson 2011).

In previous work, I have argued that the reproduction of political-economic institutions is not a matter of inertia or stasis, or even of simple feedback effects. More than this, in fact, I have argued that because the economic and political environment in which institutions are embedded changes over time, the survival of these arrangements is often heavily laced with elements of institutional change. Thus, finally and perhaps most provocatively, I have argued that changes in the coalitional base on which traditional institutions rest will inevitably bring with them important changes in the form these institutions take and the functions they perform in the market and in society.

The political economy literature traditionally has associated egalitarian capitalism with institutions that support and sustain high levels of strategic coordination among employers. For the institutions at the center of my analysis, that has meant coordinated wage bargaining and associated wage compression, vocational training systems that encourage the acquisition of industry- or firm-specific skills, and labor market policies that support strong employment protection and long job tenures. These are, of course, exactly the institutions that at least some segments of capital are most keen to liberalize today. But what complicates the politics is that many of these traditional institutions also do not necessarily reflect the rather different interests of (nor address the different risks faced by) emerging constituencies on the labor side. To underscore just a few of the observations from the case studies above: Salaried workers (Esping-Andersen's crucial white collar strata) chafe at collective bargaining arrangements aimed at wage solidarism and that therefore hold their salaries back. Women are often disadvantaged by employment and training arrangements that served male blue-collar workers well in the era of manufacturing dominance. Low-skill workers who are especially exposed to the vagaries of the market may benefit less from training systems that are premised on the assumption of stable employment in a particular firm or industry than from more flexible arrangements that open avenues to accumulate more general (portable) skills across the life course.

For all these reasons, negotiating the terms of change – the trajectory of liberalization – is more than a matter of successful defense of traditional arrangements. In fact, as I have argued, where institutions continue to reflect the interests of a shrinking manufacturing core, liberalization is likely to proceed anyway, albeit quietly through erosion and drift. Maintaining high levels of social solidarity thus requires forging new alliances, reconfiguring institutions to accommodate the interests of new groups, and reconciling them with those of traditional interests. Along with a growing number of other scholars, I emphasize social investment policies that have the potential to reconcile otherwise conflicting interests of firms and workers in a neoliberal era (e.g., Hemerijck 2013; Huber and Stephens 2012; Morel et al. 2011). Such policies are aimed at "changing the role of the state from a passive guarantor of well-being to an active creator of future growth" while at the same time providing protections for vulnerable constituencies who may not be well covered by traditional arrangements (Gingrich and Ansell 2012: 1, 4).

However, while my analysis suggests that some paths may be more fruitful than others, I have not identified any unequivocally positive model that can be held up as embodying all the possibilities and none of the pitfalls. Rather, I have shown how difficult it is to forge these new coalitions and how their stability depends upon ongoing social mobilization and the active support of the state.[10] Moreover, if the preceding chapters are any indication, this is a process that is still very much underway.

In the end, the argument in this book draws upon the strengths of all three of the schools of thought reviewed in Chapter 1. From the power-resource theorists, I take the key insight that employer interests are conceived and articulated in a context in which the power and organization of labor is a key (perhaps *the* key) fact around which they must organize their strategies and goals – even if I do not see coalitional politics and possibilities as reducible to a question of labor strength against capital. From the dualism theorists, I take the insight that contemporary market trends complicate unity on the labor side through their differential impact on workers in different sectors who occupy different kinds of positions in the market – though I combine this with an analysis of how these same trends also manifest themselves in divisions among employers, producing different kinds of coalitional alignments with different results. And with the corporatism theorists, I argue that a high level of employer organization is a crucial precondition for continued high levels of social solidarity – though I do not assume that employers' capacity to coordinate among themselves assures their willingness to cooperate with labor, and instead emphasize the role of the state in facilitating ongoing renegotiation of the form and especially many of the functions of corporatist bargaining over time (Iversen 1999; Thelen and Kume 2006).

Returning to the debate between VofC and its critics, I submit that we do not have to choose between the alternatives as typically presented in the literature – between the reproduction in perpetuity of varieties of capitalism that emerged in the nineteenth century on one hand, and egalitarian capitalism as a fleeting model doomed to inexorable exhaustion on the other. An examination of the political-coalitional underpinnings of the institutions of egalitarian capitalism reveals ongoing contestation and significant shifts in the political coalitions on which they rest. It turns out that these institutions may survive least well when they continue to rely solely on the coalitions of the past, and remain most robust where they have been carried forward by new social coalitions and turned to significantly new ends.

---

[10] As Wolfgang Streeck emphasizes, and as we have also seen in the case studies presented in this book, social investment policies (being based, typically, on discretionary spending) are always especially vulnerable to rollback in a period of ongoing fiscal strain.

APPENDIX A

Components of Index and Descriptions of Variables for Figure 1.1

The x- and y-coordinates reflect the weighted average of several variables (see next section). Before averaging, each variable is standardized using the following OECD formula:

$$I_{qc}^t = \frac{x_{qc}^t - \min_c(x_q^{to})}{\max_c(x_q^{to}) - \min_c(x_q^{to})}.$$

After standardization, values range from 0 to 1, with 1 indicating the maximum observed value.

Coordination Dimension (x-axis)

Weight	Name
1	Wage Coordination (Swank: WAGEBC)

Lane Kenworthy's wage-setting coordination scores as an index with 5 categories:

- 1 = fragmented wage bargaining, confined largely to individual firms or plants;
- 2 = mixed industry- and firm-level bargaining, with little or no pattern-setting and relatively weak elements of government coordination such as setting of basic pay rate or wage indexation;
- 3 = industry-level bargaining with somewhat irregular and uncertain pattern-setting and only moderate union concentration;
- 4 = centralized bargaining by peak confederation(s) or government imposition of a wage schedule/freeze, without a peace obligation;
- 5 = centralized bargaining by peak confederation(s) or government imposition of a wage schedule/freeze, with a peace obligation.[1]

---

[1] See http://www.u.arizona.edu/~lkenwor/data.html for documentation.

1   Labor-Management Coordination (Swank: LABMANC)

Labor-management cooperation as extent of long-term, voice-based purchaser-supplier relationships.

Source: Lane Kenworthy and Alex Hicks, Departments of Sociology, University of Arizona and Emory University, "Economic Cooperation in 18 Industrialized Democracies."

1   Power of Peak Employer Organization (Swank: EMPPOW)

Powers of national peak employers' confederation as a 0 to 4 score for basic employers' association powers – control over lockouts, collective bargaining strategy, collective funds.

Source: Miriam Golden, Michael Wallerstein, and Peter Lange, "Unions, Employers, Collective Bargaining and Industrial Relations for 16 OECD Countries, 1950–2000," Department of Political Science, UCLA; Franz Traxler et al, 2001, National Labour Relations in International Markets (Oxford U. Press, 2001); late 1990s–2005: country-specific sources and labor and industrial relations periodicals.

Solidarity Dimension (y-axis)

−1   Youth Unemployment (OECD Stat Database)
−1   Involuntary Part-Time Employment (OECD Stat Database)
 1   Collective Bargaining Coverage (OECD: 2004)

APPENDIX B

Components of Index for Figures 6.2 and 6.3

The index uses the same methodology as in Figure 1.1

Flexibility Dimension (x-axis):

Weight	Name
1	employment protection index (OECD Stat Database)
−1	active labor market spending as percentage of GDP (OECD Stat Database)

Equality Dimension (y-axis):

−1	poverty rate (OECD Stat Database)
−1	post-tax Gini coefficient (OECD Stat Database)

Bibliography

ABC News. 2009. "Daimler Reaches Labor Deal at Sindelfingen Plant." December 9.

Acemoglu, Daron. 1998. "Why Do New Technologies Complement Skills? Directed Technical Change and Wage Inequality." *Quarterly Journal of Economics* 113 (4):1055–89.

Acemoglu, Daron, James A. Robinson, and Thierry Verdier. 2012. "Can't We All Be More Like Scandinavians? Asymmetric Growth and Institutions in an Interdependent World." *NBER Working Paper Series.* Cambridge, MA: National Bureau of Economic Research.

Addison, John T., Claus Schnabel, and Joachim Wagner. 2007. "The (Parlous) State of German Unions." *Journal of Labor Research* 28 (1):3–18.

Ahlberg, Kerstin. 1997a. "Blue-Collar Unions Concentrate on Low-Paid Workers." In *EIROnline*: Eurofound. http://www.eurofound.europa.eu/eiro/1997/10/feature/se9710145f.htm.

Ahlberg, Kerstin. 1997b. "Personal Educational Accounts May Complement Collectively Agreed Measures." In *EIROnline*: Eurofound. http://www.eurofound.europa.eu/eiro/1997/08/feature/se9708132f.htm.

Ahlberg, Kerstin, and Niklas Bruun. 2005. "Sweden: Transition through Collective Bargaining." In *Collective Bargaining and Wages in Comparative Perspective*, ed. T. Blanke and E. Rose. The Hague: Kluwer Law International.

Ahlquist, John, and Margaret Levi. 2013. *In the Interest of Others: Leaders, Governance, and Political Activism in Membership Organizations.* Princeton, NJ: Princeton University Press.

Aktürk, Sener. 2011. "Regimes of Ethnicity: Comparative Analysis of Germany, the Soviet Union/Post-Soviet Russia, and Turkey." *World Politics* 63 (1):115–64.

Albrecht, James, Gerard J. van den Berg, and Susan Vroman. 2005. The Knowledge Lift: The Swedish Adult Education Program That Aimed to Eliminate Low Worker Skill Levels. Bonn: IZA.

Andersen, Jørgen Goul. 1984. "Decline of Class Voting or Change in Class Voting? Social Classes and Party Choice in Denmark in the 1970s." *European Journal of Political Research* 12:243–59.

Andersen, Jørgen Goul. 1992. "The Decline of Class Voting Revisited." In *From Voters to Participants: Essays in Honour of Ole Borre*, ed. P. Gundelach and K. Siune. Aarhus: Forlaget Politica.

Andersen, Jørgen Goul. 2010. "Activation as Element of Two Decades of Labour Market Policy Reforms in Denmark." Background paper for presentation at International Symposium, "Activation or Basic Income? Towards a Sustainable Social Framework," Tokyo, February 26.

Andersen, Søren Kaj. 2010. *Tackling Job-Losses: Varieties of European Responses.* Copenhagen: FAOS.

Andersen, Søren Kaj, and Mikkel Mailand. 2005. "The Danish Flexicurity Model: The Role of the Collective Bargaining System." Copenhagen: FAOS.

Anderson, Karen M, and Anke Hassel. 2012. "Pathways of Change in CMEs: Training Regimes in Germany and the Netherlands." In *The Political Economy of the Service Transition*, ed. A. Wren. Oxford: Oxford University Press.

Anderson, Theresa, Katharine Kairys, Michael Wiseman. 2011. "Activation and Reform in the United States: What Time has Told." Working Paper, George Washington Institute of Public Policy, Washington, DC, July 1.

Anthonson, Mette, Johannes Lindvall, and Ulrich Schmidt-Hansen. 2010. "Social Democrats, Unions, and Corporatism: Denmark and Sweden Compared." *Party Politics* 46 (September): 1030–57.

Arpaia, A., N. Curci, E. Meyermans, J Peschner, and F. Pierini. 2010. "Short Time Working Arrangements as Responses to Cyclical Fluctuations." Occasional Paper 64 of the European Commission Directorate-General for Employment, Social Affairs and Equal Opportunities. Brussels: European Commission.

Astheimer, Sven. 2010. "Wenn sich die Arbeit nicht mehr lohnt." *Tageszeitung*, January 19.

"Aufstocker arbeiten meist Teilzeit," 2013. *Die Zeit*, July 18. http://www.faz.net/aktuell/wirtschaft/wirtschaftspolitik/armut-und-reichtum/studie-aufstocker-arbeiten-meistens-teilzeit-12286335.html.

Autor, David H., Lawrence F. Katz, and Melissa S. Kearney. 2008. "Trends in U.S. Wage Inequality: Revising the Revisionists." *The Review of Economics and Statistics* 90 (2):300–23.

BA (Bundesagentur für Arbeit). 2009. Der Arbeitsmarkt in Deutschland: Kurzarbeit, Aktuelle Entwicklungen. Berlin: Bundesagentur für Arbeit.

Baccaro, Lucio, and Chris Howell. 2011. "A Common Neoliberal Trajectory: The Transformation of Industrial Relations in Advanced Capitalism." *Politics & Society* 39 (4):521–63.

Baccaro, Lucio, and Richard M. Locke. 1998. "The End of Solidarity? The Decline of Egalitarian Wage Policies in Italy and Sweden." *European Journal of Industrial Relations* 4 (3):283–308.

Bäcker, Gerhard. 2006. "Was heisst hier geringfügig? Minijobs als wachsendes Segment prekärer Beschäftigung." *WSI-Mitteilungen* 56 (5):255–261.

Baethge, Martin. 1999. "Glanz und Elend des deutschen Korporatismus in der Berufsbildung." *Die Mitbestimmung online* 4:15.

Baethge, Martin, Heike Solga, and Markus Wieck. 2007. *Berufsbildung im Umbruch.* Berlin: Friedrich-Ebert-Stiftung.

Barbier, Jean-Claude, and Matthias Knuth. 2010. "Of Similarities and Divergences: Why There is No Continental Ideal-Type of 'Activation Reforms'." *CNRS Working Paper Series*. Paris: CNRS.

Barrows, Samuel. 2011. "Inside-Outsiders: The Role of Partner Job Status in the Formation of Welfare Preferences." Paper presented at the Midwest Political Science Association Meetings, Chicago, March 31–April 1.

BDA (Bundesvereinigung der deutschen Arbeitgeberverbände). 2007. "Beschluss, Sitzung des Präsidiums: Bilanz in der Tarifautonomie wahren: Position der Arbeitgeber zur Mindestlohndebatte," Position Paper. Berlin: BDA.

BDA (Bundesvereinigung der deutschen Arbeitgeberverbände). 2010. "Kompakt: Mindestlohn," Position Paper. Berlin: BDA.

Becker, Gary S. 1993. *Human Capital*. 3rd ed. Chicago: University of Chicago Press.

Beile, Judith and Christine Priessner. 2011. "Industrial Relations Developments in the Commerce Sector in Europe: Country Report Germany." Brussels: European Foundation for the Improvement of Living and Working Conditions.

Bekker, Sonja, and Ton Wilthagen. 2008. Europe's Pathways to Flexicurity: Lessons Presented from and to the Netherlands. Tilburg: Tilburg University.

Beland, Daniel and Alex Waddan. 2012. *The Politics of Policy Change: Welfare, Medicare, and Social Security Reform in the United States*. Washington, DC: Georgetown University Press.

Bengtsson, Erik. 2013. "Swedish Trade Unions and European Union Migrant Workers." *Journal of Industrial Relations* 55 (2):174–89.

Berg, Annika. 2002. "Blue-Collar Workers' Pay Falls Behind." In *EIROnline*: Eurofound. http://www.eurofound.europa.eu/eiro/2002/12/feature/se0212104f.htm.

Berger, Klaus, and Dick Moraal. 2012. "Tarifliche Weiterbildungspolitik in den Niederlanden und in Deutschland." *WSI Mitteilungen* 5:382–90.

Bernhardt, Annette, Ruth Milkman, Nikolas Theodore, Douglas Heckathorn, and Mirabai Auer. 2009. *Broken Laws, Unprotected Workers: Violations of Employment and Labor Laws in America's Cities*. Los Angeles: UCLA Institute for Research on Labor and Employment.

BIBB (Bundesinstitut für Berufsbildung). 2005. "Schaubilder zur Berufsbildung: Strukturen und Entwicklungen." Bonn: BIBB.

BIBB (Bundesinstitut für Berufsbildung). 2010. AusbildungPlus 2004–2010. www.ausbildungplus.de.

BIBB (Bundesinstitut für Berufsbildung). 2011a. "Berufsbildungsbericht 2011." Berlin: BIBB.

BIBB (Bundesinstitut für Berufsbildung). 2011b. "Duale Studiengänge immer beliebter." *Press release*. Berlin: BIBB.

Bishop, John H. 1995. "Vocational Education and At-Risk Youth in the United States." *CAHRS Working Paper Series*. Ithaca, NY: Cornell University ILR School.

Bispinck, Reinhard. 2010a. "Niedriglöhne und der Flickenteppich von (unzureichend) Mindestlöhnen in Deutschland." *WSI Report*. Düsseldorf: WSI.

Bispinck, Reinhard. 2010b. Tarifliche Regelung zur Kurzarbeit. Düsseldorf: WSI.

Blagg, Deborah. 2012. "Exploring the Outcomes of Economic Loss." *Radcliffe Magazine*. http://www.radcliffe.harvard.edu/news/radcliffe-magazine/exploring-outcomes-economic-loss.

Blomqvist, Paula. 2004. "The Choice Revolution: Privatization of Swedish Welfare Services in the 1990s." *Social Policy and Administration* 38 (2):139–55.

BMBF (Bundesministerium für Bildung und Forschung). 2000. Berufsbildungsbericht. Berlin: BMBF.

BMBF (Bundesministerium für Bildung und Forschung). 2001. Berufsbildungsbericht. Berlin: BMBF.

BMBF (Bundesministerium für Bildung und Forschung). 2005. Reform der Berufsbildung. Berlin: BMBF.

BMAS (Bundesministerium für Arbeit und Soziales). 2011. Verzeichnis der für allgemeinverbindlich erklärten Tarifverträge. Bonn: BMAS.

Bohle, Dorothee, and Bela Greskovits. 2009. "Varieties of Capitalism and Capitalism 'tout court'." *European Journal of Sociology* 3:355–86.

Bonoli, Giuliano. 2005. "The Politics of the New Social Policies: Providing Coverage Against New Social Risks in Mature Welfare States." *Policy & Politics* 33 (3):431–49.

Bonoli, Giuliano. 2012. *The Origins of Active Social Policy*. Oxford: Oxford University Press.

Bosch, Gerhard. 2008. "Auflösung des deutschen Tarifsystems." *Wirtschaftsdienst* 88 (1):16–20.

Bosch, Gerhard, and Jean Charest. 2008. "Vocational Training and the Labour Market in Liberal and Coordinated Economies." *Industrial Relations Journal* 39 (5):428–47.

Bosch, Gerhard, Claudia Weinkopf, and Thorsten Kalina. 2009. "Mindestlöhne in Deutschland." Düsseldorf: Friedrich Ebert Stiftung.

Bouwens, Bram, and Joost Dankers. 2010. "The Invisible Handshake: Cartelization in the Netherlands, 1930–2000." *Business History Review* 84 (4):751–72.

Bovenberg, Lans, Ton Wilthagen, and Sonja Bekker. 2008. "Flexicurity: Lessons and Proposals from the Netherlands." *CESifo DICE Report* 6 (4):9–14.

Bowman, John R., and Alyson M. Cole. 2009. "Do Working Mothers Oppress Other Women? The Swedish 'Maid Debate' and the Welfare State Politics of Gender Equality." *Journal of Women in Culture and Society* 35 (1):157–84.

Bredgaard, Thomas, and Flemming Larsen. 2010. "External and Internal Flexicurity." Paper presented at the 2010 Meeting of the IIRA European Congress, Copenhagen, June 28–July 1.

Brenke, Karl, Ulf Rinne, and Klaus F. Zimmermann. 2011. "Short-Time Work: The German Answer to the Great Recession." *IZA Discussion Paper 5780*. Bonn: IZA.

Broadberry, Stephen N. 1993. "Manufacturing and the Convergence Hypothesis: What the Long-Run Data Show." *Journal of Economic History* 53 (4):772–95.

Bronfenbrenner, Kate. 2009. "No Holds Barred: The Intensification of Employer Opposition to Organizing." *EPI Briefing Paper*. Washington, DC: Economic Policy Institute.

Brönstrup, Carsten. 2011. "Arbeitsmarkt ist gespalten wie lange nicht." *Tageszeitung*, May 30.

Brown, Bettina Landard. 2002. "School to Work after the School to Work Opportunities Act." Columbus, OH: Center on Education and Training for Employment.

Büchtemann, Christoph F., Jürgen Schupp, and Dana Soloff. 1993. "Roads to Work: School-to-Work Transition Patterns in Germany and the United States." *Industrial Relations Journal* 24 (2):97–111.

Buhse, Malte. 2012. "Auf Azubisuche in Bulgarien." In *Zeit Online*. http://www.zeit.de/wirtschaft/2012-08/lehrstellen-deutschland.

"Bundesarbeitsgericht lässt mehrere Tarifverträge zu." 2010. In *Spiegel Online*, June 23. http://www.spiegel.de/wirtschaft/unternehmen/0,1518,702404,00.html.

Bundesregierung, Deutsche. 2009. "Konjunkturpaket II: Die Krise Meistern," February 25. http://www.bundesregierung.de/Content/DE/Artikel/2009/01/2009-01-27-zweites-konjunkturpaket.html.

Bundestag, Deutscher. 1999. "Minutes of the Deutscher Bundestag 14. Wahlperiode, 17. Sitzung, 22. Januar 1999." Bonn: Deutscher Bundestag.

Buschoff, Karin Schulze and Paula Protsch. 2008. "(A-)Typical and (In-)Secure? Social Protection and Non-Standard Forms of Employment in Europe." *International Social Security Review* 61 (4):51–73.

Busemeyer, Marius. 2009. *Wandel trotz Reformstau: Die Politik der beruflichen Bildung seit 1970*. Frankfurt: Campus.

Busemeyer, Marius R., and Torben Iversen. 2012. "Collective Skill Systems, Wage Bargaining, and Labor Market Stratification." In *The Political Economy of Collective Skill Formation*, ed. M. Busemeyer and C. Trampusch. Oxford: Oxford University Press.

Busemeyer, Marius, and Christine Trampusch. 2012. "The Comparative Political Economy of Collective Skill Formation." In *The Political Economy of Collective Skill Formation*, ed. M. Busemeyer and C. Trampusch. Oxford: Oxford University Press.

Calmfors, Lars, and John Driffill. 1988. "Centralization of Wage Bargaining." *Economic Policy* 3 (6):13–61.

Campbell, John L., and John A. Hall. 2006. "Introduction: The State of Denmark." In *National Identity and the Varieties of Capitalism: The Danish Experience*, ed. J. L. Campbell, J. A. Hall, and O. K. Pedersen. Montreal: McGill-Queen's University Press.

Card, David. 2001. "The Effect of Unions on Wage Inequality in the U.S. Labor Market." *Industrial and Labor Relations Review* 54 (2):296–315.

Carley, Mark. 2009. "Trade Union Membership 2003-2008." In *EIROnline*: Eurofound. http://www.eurofound.europa.eu/eiro/studies/tn0904019s/tn0904019s.htm.

CDU/CSU-Fraktion. 2011. "Hände weg vom Ehegattensplitting." *Press release*. Berlin: CDU/CSU-Fraktion, November 1, http://www.cducsu.de/Title_haende-weg_vom _ehegattensplitting.htm.

"CDU-Spitze erwägt Ehegattensplitting-Reform," 2006. *Handelsblatt* June 16. http://www.handelsblatt.com/politik/deutschland/cdu-spitze-erwaegt-ehegattensplitting-reform.htm.

CEDEFOP. 2009. *Vocational Education and Training in Sweden*. Luxembourg: European Centre for the Development of Vocational Training.

CEDEFOP. 2012. *Vocational Education and Training in Denmark*. Luxembourg: European Centre for the Development of Vocational Training.

CO-industri. 2008. *Flexicurity: A Danish Trade Union View*. Copenhagen: CO-industri.

Cook, Robert F., Charles F. Adams, and V. Lane Rawlins. 1985. "The Public Service Employment Program." In *Public Service Employment: The Experience of a Decade*, ed. R. F. Cook, C. F. Adams, and V. L. Rawlins. Kalamazoo, MI: W.E. Upjohn Institute for Employment Research.

Cort, Pia. 2002. "Vocational Education and Training in Denmark." In CEDEFOP Panorama Series. Luxembourg: European Centre for the Development of Vocational Training.

Cowie, Jefferson. 2010. *Stayin' Alive*. New York: The New Press.

Cox, Robert Henry. 2001. "The Social Construction of an Imperative." *World Politics* 53:463–98.

Crouch, Colin. 1993. *Industrial Relations and European State Traditions*. Oxford: Clarendon Press.

Crouch, Colin, David Finegold, and Mari Sako. 1999. *Are Skills the Answer?* Oxford: Oxford University Press.

Culpepper, Pepper D., and Kathleen Thelen. 2007. "Institutions and Collective Actors in the Provision of Training: Historical and Cross-National Comparisons." In *Skill Formation: Interdisciplinary and Cross-National Perspectives*, ed. K.-U. Mayer and H. Solga. New York: Cambridge University Press.

Daimler AG. 2010. "Daimler AG zieht Tariferhöhung auf Februar vor." Stuttgart, November 29, 2010. http://www.daimler.com/dccom/0-5-7153-49-1351662-1.html.

Daley, Suzanne, and Nicholas Kulish. 2012. "Brain Drain Feared as German Jobs Lure Southern Europeans." *New York Times*, April 28.

Dansk Arbejdsgiverforening. 2013. *Arbejdsmarkedsrapport 2012*. København: Dansk Arbejdsgiverforening.

Dansk Arbejdsgiverforening. 2005. *Arbejdsmarkedsrapport 2004*. København: Dansk Arbejdsgiverforening.

Dansk Arbejdsgiverforening. n.d. *Flexicurity in Denmark*. Copenhagen: DA.

Darren, Mara and David Levitz. 2010. "Referendum Quashes Hamburg School Reform, Cripples Coalition," Deutsche Welle, July 19, 2010, www.dw.de/referendum-quashes-hamburg-school-reform-cripples-coalition/a-5814250.

Davidsson, Johan Bo. 2009. "The Politics of Employment Policy in Europe: Two Patterns of Reform." Presented at ECPR Conference. Lisbon. April 14–19.

Davidsson, Johann. 2010. *Unions in Hard Times: Labor Market Politics in Western Europe*. Ph.D. Thesis, Department of Political and Social Sciences, European University Institute, Florence.

Deckstein, Dinah, Sebastian Ramspeck, and Janko Tietz. 2006. "Schnell Rein, Schnell Raus." *Der Spiegel* 5/2008. December 30. http://www.spiegel.de/spiegel/spiegelspecial/d-59462272.html.

Deeke, Alex. 2005. Kurzarbeit als Instrument betrieblicher Flexibilität: Ergebnisse aus dem IAB-Betriebspanel 2003. Berlin: Bundesagentur für Arbeit.

DeHoGa (Deutscher Hotel- und Gaststättenverband). 1999. "Stellungnahme des Deutschen Hotel- und Gaststättenverbandes DEHOGA zum Entwurf eines Gesetzes zur Neuregelung der geringfügigen Beschäftigungsverhältnisse." Position paper submitted to Parliamentary Committee (Ausschuss für Arbeit und Sozialordnung), Drucksache 14/280. Bonn: Deutscher Bundestag.

DeHoGa (Deutscher Hotel- und Gaststättenverband). 2010. *Tarifsynopse für das Hotel- und Gaststättengewerbe*. Berlin: Deutscher Hotel- und Gaststättenverband.

Dekker, Ronald, and Lutz C. Kaiser. 2000. "Atypical or Flexible: How to Define Non-Standard Employment Patterns: The Cases of Germany, the Netherlands, and the United Kingdom." Tilburg Institute for Social Security Research and German Institute for Economic Research.

Delsen, Lei. 2002. *Exit Polder Model? Socioeconomic Changes in the Netherlands*. Westport, CT: Praeger.

DeParle, Jason. 2012. "Welfare Limits Left Poor Adrift as Recession Hit." *New York Times*, April 7, www.nytimes.com/2012/04/08/us/welfare-limits-left-poor-adrift-as-recession-hit-html.

"Der beste Mann der IG Metall war der Arbeitgeberchef," *Der Tagesspiegel*, June 29, 2003: 24.

Desjardins, Richard, Kjell Rubenson, and Marcella Milana. 2006. *Unequal Chances to Participate in Adult Learning: International Perspectives*. Paris: UNESCO.

Dettmer, Markus, Peter Müller, and Janko Tietz. 2011. "Kehrtwende der Kanzlerin," *Der Spiegel* 45/2011. November 7.

Dølvik, Jon-Erik. 2007. "The Nordic Regimes of Labour Market Governance: From Crisis to Success-Story?" Fafo-paper 2007: 07. In *Fafos Rådsprogram 2006–2008*. Copenhagen: Fafo.

Dribbusch, Heiner. 2004. "Debate on Introduction of Statutory Minimum Wage." In EIROnline: Eurofound. http://www.eurofound.europa.eu/eiro/2004/09/feature/DE0409205F.htm.

Dribbusch, Heiner. 2009. "Germany: Wage Formation." In *EIROnline*: Eurofound. http://www.eurofound.europa.eu/eiro/studies/tn0808019s/de0808019q.htm.

Due, Jesper, and Jørgen Steen Madsen. 2008. "The Danish Model of Industrial Relations: Erosion or Renewal?" *Journal of Industrial Relations* 50:513–29.

Due, Jesper, Jørgen Steen Madsen, and Christian Lyhne Ibsen. 2012. LO's andel af de fagligt organiserede er for først gang under 50 pct. Copenhagen: FAOS.

Due, Jesper, Jorgen Steen Madsen, C. Strøby Jensen, and L. K. Petersen. 1994. *The Survival of the Danish Model*. Copenhagen: DJØF Forlag.

"Dutch Surprise." 2012. *The Economist*, September 15.

Ebbinghaus, Bernhard. 2000. "Denmark." In *Trade Unions in Europe since 1945*, ed. B. Ebbinghaus and J. Visser. Oxford: MacMillan.

Ebbinghaus, Bernhard. 2002. "Trade Unions' Changing Role: Membership Erosion, Organisational Reform, and Social Partnership in Europe." *EU Paper Series*. Madison: European Union Center, University of Wisconsin.

Ebbinghaus, Bernhard. 2010. "Reforming Bismarckian Corporatism: The Changing Role of Social Partnership in Continental Europe." In *A Long Goodbye to Bismarck? The Politics of Welfare Reform in Continental Europe*, ed. B. Palier. Amsterdam: Amsterdam University Press.

Ebbinghaus, Bernhard, and Werner Eichhorst. 2007. "Distribution of Responsibility for Social Security and Labour Market Policy, Country Report: Germany." *Amsterdam Institute for Advanced Labour Studies Working Paper*. University of Amsterdam.

Ebner, Christian, and Rita Nikolai. 2010. "Duale oder schulische Berufsausbildung? Entwicklungen und Weichenstellungen in Deutschland, Österreich, und der Schweiz." *Swiss Political Science Review* 16 (4):617–48.

EC. 2006. *Employment for Europe*. Luxembourg: Office for Official Publications of the European Community.

Economist, The. 2013. "The Next Supermodel: Why the World Should Look at the Nordic Countries." Special Report. February 2.

Edelstein, Benjamin. n.d. "Continuity and Change in the German School System: Structural School Reform in Historial Perspective," Dissertation Prospectus, Wissenschaftszentrum Berlin für Sozialforschung.

Edin, Per-Anders, and Bertil Holmlund. 1995. "The Swedish Wage Structure: The Rise and Fall of Solidarity Wage Policy?" In *Differences and Changes in Wage Structures*, ed. R. B. Freeman and L. F. Katz. Chicago: University of Chicago Press.

Edwards, Richard C., Michael Reich, and David M. Gordon. 1973. *Labor Market Segmentation*. Lexington, MA: D.C. Heath and Company.

Eichhorst, Werner. 2012. "Reformen der geringfügiger Beschäftigung und deren arbeitsmarktpolitischen und fiskalischen Effekte." Paper presented at the 2012 Meeting of SASE. Boston, June 28–30.

Eichhorst, Werner. 2012. "The Unexpected Appearance of a New German Model," IZA Discussion Paper No. 6625, Bonn: Forschungsinstitut zur Zukunft der Arbeit.

Eichhorst, Werner and Lutz C. Kaiser. 2006. "The German Labor Market: Still Adjusting Badly?" IZA Discussion Paper No. 2215, Bonn: Forschungsinstitut zur Zukunft der Arbeit.

Eichhorst, Werner, and Paul Marx. 2009. "Reforming German Labor Market Institutions: A Dual Path to Flexibility." *IZA Discussion Papers*. Bonn: IZA.

Eichhorst, Werner, and Paul Marx. 2012a. "Non-Standard Employment across Occupations in Germany: The Role of Replaceability and Labor Market Flexibility." IZA Discussion Paper 7662. Bonn: Forschungsinstitut zur Zukunft der Arbeit.

Eichhorst, Werner, and Paul Marx. 2012b. "Whatever Works: Dualisation and the Service Economy in Bismarckian Welfare States." In *The Age of Dualization*, ed. P. Emmenegger, S. Häusermann, B. Palier, and M. Seeleib-Kaiser. Oxford: Oxford University Press.

EIRR. 1998a. "Denmark: New Trade Union Structure Proposed." *European Industrial Relations Review* 297 (October):4–5.

EIRR. 1998b. "Denmark: Tripartism under Pressure." *European Industrial Relations Review* 298 (November):5.

Elvander, Nils. 1997. "The Swedish Bargaining System in the Melting Pot." In *The Swedish Bargaining System in the Melting Pot: Institutions, Norms, and Outcomes in the 1990s*, ed. N. Elvander and B. Holmlund. Solna: Arbetslivsinstitutet.

Emmenegger, Patrick. 2009. *Regulatory Social Policy: The Politics of Job Security Regulations*. Bern: Haupt.

Emmenegger, Patrick. 2010. "The Long Road to Flexicurity: The Development of Job Security Regulations in Denmark and Sweden." *Scandinavian Political Studies* 33 (3):271–94.

Emmenegger, Patrick, Silja Häusermann, Bruno Palier, and Martin Seeleib-Kaiser, eds. 2011. *The Age of Dualization: Structure, Policies, Politics*. Oxford: Oxford University Press.

Engblom, Samuel. 2009. "Regulatory Frameworks and Law Enforcement in New Forms of Employment National Report: Sweden." In *World Congress of Labour and Social Security Law*. Sydney.

Esping-Andersen, Gøsta. 1985. *Politics Against Markets: The Social Democratic Road to Power*. Princeton, NJ: Princeton University Press.

Esping-Andersen, Gøsta. 1990. *Three Worlds of Welfare Capitalism*. Princeton, NJ: Princeton University Press.

Estevez-Abe, Margarita. 2006. "Gendering the Varieties of Capitalism: A Study of Occupational Segregation by Sex in Advanced Industrial Societies." *World Politics* 59 (1):142–75.

Estevez-Abe, Margarita, Torben Iversen, and David Soskice. 2001. "Social Protection and the Formation of Skills: A Reinterpretation of the Welfare State." In *Varieties of Capitalism: The Institutional Foundations of Comparative Advantage*, ed. P. A. Hall and D. Soskice. New York: Oxford University Press.

Etherington, David. 1995. "Decentralisation and Local Economic Initiatives: The Danish Free Local Government Initiative." *Local Economy* 10 (3):246–58.

"Falscher Ort, falsche Zeit," *Süddeutsche Zeitung*, June 30, 2003: 2.

Ferguson, Thomas, and Joel Rogers. 1979. "Labor Law Reform and Its Enemies." *The Nation*, January 6–14: 19–20.

Finegold, David, and David Soskice. 1988. "The Failure of Training in Britain: Analysis and Prescription." *Oxford Review of Economic Policy* 4 (3):21–53.

"'Flächentarif als Modell für die Zukunft': Präsident von Gesamtmetall sieht Fortschritte bei Sicherung von Arbeitsplätzen in Deutschland," *Süddeutsche Zeitung*, November 20, 2006.

Fleming, Daniel, and Henrik Søborg. n.d. "Skill Formation, Employment Relations and Institutional Support." Roskilde University: Roskilde University Denmark.

Forslund, Anders, and Alan Krueger. 2008. "Did Active Labour Market Policies Help Sweden Rebound from the Depression of the Early 1990s?" *Center for Economic Policy Studies Working Paper 1035*. Princeton, NJ: Princeton University.

Fransson, Susanne, and Christer Thörnquist. 2004. "Gender, Bargaining Strategies and Strikes in Sweden." In *Nordic Equality at a Crossroads: Feminist Legal Studies Coping with Difference*, ed. E.-M. Svensson, A. Pylkkänen, and J. Niemi-Kiesilinen. Hants: Ashgate.

Freeman, Richard B. 2007. "Do Workers Still Want Unions? More than Ever." *EPI Briefing Paper*. Washington, DC: Economic Policy Institute.

Führin, Katharina, and Rene Pfister. 2011. "Grünes Lob, Schwarzer Frust." *Der Spiegel* 27 (July 4). http://www.spiegel.de/spiegel/print/d-79303792.html.

Funk, Lothar. 2003. "New Legislation Promotes 'Minor Jobs'," *EIROnline*: Eurofound. http://www.eurofound.europa.eu/eiro/2003/02/feature/DE0302105F.htm.

Garme, Cecilia. 2001. *Newcomers to Power*. Uppsala: Uppsala University Library.

Gash, Vanessa. 2008. "Bridge or Trap? Temporary Workers' Transitions to Unemployment and to the Standard Employment Contract." *European Sociological Review* 24 (5):651–668.

Gehrmann, Wolfgang. 1998. "Bündnis in Arbeit." *Die Zeit*, December 10. http://www.zeit.de/1998/51/199851.buendnis_.xml.

Gingrich, Jane and Ben Ansell. 2012. "The Dynamics of Social Investment: Human Capital, Activation, and Care," Paper presented at the conference "The Future of Democratic Capitalism," Duke University, October 11–13.

Glyn, Andrew. 2006. *Capitalism Unleashed: Finance Globalization and Welfare*. Oxford: Oxford University Press.

Godard, John. 2009. "The Exceptional Decline of the American Labor Movement." *Industrial and Labor Relations Review* 63 (1):82–108.

Gold, Stephen F. 1971. "The Failure of the Work Incentive (WIN) Program." *University of Pennsylvania Law Review* 119 (3):485–501.

Goldfield, Michael. 1987. *The Decline of Organized Labor in the United States*. Chicago: University of Chicago Press.

Gordon, David M., Richard Edwards, and Michael Reich. 1982. *Segmented Work, Divided Workers: The Historical Transformation of Labor in the United States*. New York: Cambridge University Press.

Gourevitch, Peter. 1986. *Politics in Hard Times*. Ithaca, NY: Cornell University Press.

Graf, Lukas. 2011. "Locating Hybridity at the Nexus of VET and HE: The Case of Dual Study Programs in Germany." Berlin: WZB.

Green-Pedersen, Christoffer. 2001. "Minority Governments and Party Politics: The Political and Institutional Background to the 'Danish Miracle.'" *Journal of Public Policy* 21 (1):53–70.

Groll, Tina, and Marcus Gatzke. 2012. "'Ein Mindestlohn in Deutschland hilft auch Europa.'" In *Zeit Online*. http://www.zeit.de/wirtschaft/2012-02/interview-ursula-von-der-leyen.

Grollmann, Philipp, Susanne Gottlieb, and Sabine Kurz. 2003. *Co-operation between Enterprises and Vocational Schools: Danish Prospects*. Bremen: Institut Technik und Bildung.

Grünell, Marianne. 2005. "2004 Annual Review for the Netherlands." In *EIROnline*: Eurofound. http://www.eurofound.europa.eu/eiro/2005/01/feature/nl0501104f.htm.

Güßgen, Florian. 2006. "Mindestlohn-Debatte: Wieviel soll es sein?" *Stern.de*. March 14. http://www.stern.de/politik/deutschland/mindestlohn-debatte-wieviel-soll-es-sein-557672.html.

Hacker, Jacob. 2002. *The Divided Welfare State: The Battle over Public and Private Social Benefits in the United States*. New York: Cambridge University Press.

Hacker, Jacob. 2006. *The Great Risk Shift*. New York: Oxford University Press.

Hacker, Jacob, and Paul Pierson. 2010a. "Drift and Democracy: The Neglected Politics of Policy Inaction." Paper presented at the 2010 Meeting of the American Political Science Association, Washington, DC (August).

Hacker, Jacob, and Paul Pierson. 2010b. *Winner-Take-All Politics: How Washington Made the Rich Richer – and Turned its Back on the Middle Class*. New York: Simon and Schuster.

Hacker, Jacob, and Paul Pierson. 2010c. "Winner-Take-All Politics: Public Policy, Political Organization, and the Precipitous Rise of Top Incomes in the United States." *Politics & Society* 38 (2):152–4.

Hacker, Jacob, Philipp Rehm, and Mark Schlesinger. 2013. "The Insecure American: Economic Experiences, Financial Worries, and Policy Attitudes." *Perspectives on Politics* 11 (1):23–50.

Halepli, Leo. n.d. The Political Economy of Immigrant Incorporation: The Cases of Germany and the Netherlands. London: London School of Economics.

Hall, Peter A., and Daniel Gingerich. 2009. "Varieties of Capitalism and Institutional Complementarities in the Political Economy." *British Journal of Political Science* 39:449–82.

Hall, Peter A., and David Soskice, eds. 2001. *Varieties of Capitalism: The Institutional Foundations of Comparative Advantage*. New York: Oxford University Press.

Hall, Peter A., and Kathleen Thelen. 2009. "Institutional Change in Varieties of Capitalism." *Socio-Economic Review* 7:7–34.

Halperin, Samuel. 1994. "School-to-Work: A Larger Vision." Paper presented at Statewide School-to-Work Conference, Newport, RI, November 4.

Handelsblatt. 2006. "CDU-Spitze erwägt Ehegattensplitting-Reform." *Handelsblatt*, June 16.

Hansen, Hal. 1999. "Caps and Gowns: Historical Reflections on the Institutions that Shaped Learning for and at Work in Germany and the United States, 1800–1945." *Business and Economic History* 28 (1):19–24.

Hassel, Anke. 1999. "The Erosion of the German System of Industrial Relations." *British Journal of Industrial Relations* 37 (3):484–505.

Hassel, Anke. 2011. "The Paradox of Liberalization: Understanding Dualism and the Recovery of the German Political Economy." Paper presented at the Conference of the Council for European Studies, Barcelona, June 20–22.

Hassel, Anke. 2012. "The Paradox of Liberalization: Understanding Dualism and the Recovery of the German Political Economy." *British Journal of Industrial Relations*: 1–18.

Hassel, Anke and Britta Rehder. 2001. "Institutional Change in the German Wage Bargaining System: The Role of Big Companies." *MPIfG Working Paper 01/9*. Cologne: MPIfG.

Häusermann, Silja and Hanspeter Kriesi. 2012. What Do Voters Want? Dimensions and Configurations in Individual-Level Preferences and Party Choice. Paper presented at the conference "The Future of Democratic Capitalism," Duke University, October 11–13.

HBV. 1999. "Schriftliche Stellungnahme zur öffentlichen Anhörung am 10. Februar 1999." Position paper submitted to the Parliamentary Committee (Ausschuss für Arbeit und Sozialordnung, Drucksache 14/280). Bonn: Deutscher Bundestag.

Hemerijck, Anton. 1995. "Corporatist Immobility in the Netherlands." In *Organized Industrial Relations in Europe: What Future?* ed. C. Crouch and F. Traxler. Aldershot: Avebury.

Hemerijck, Anton. 2003. "A Paradoxical Miracle: The Politics of Coalition Government and Social Concertation in Dutch Welfare Reform." In *Konzertierung, Verhandlungsdemokratie und Reformpolitik im Wohlfahrtstaat: Das Modell Deutschland im Vergleich*, ed. S. Jochem and N. A. Siegel. Opladen: Leske + Budrich.

Hemerijck, Anton. 2013. *Changing Welfare States*. Oxford: Oxford University Press.

Hemerijck, Anton, and Ive Marx. 2010. "Continental Welfare at a Crossroads: The Choice between Activation and Minimum Income Protection in Belgium and the Netherlands." In *A Long Goodbye to Bismarck? The Politics of Welfare Reform in Continental Europe*, ed. B. Palier. Amsterdam: Amsterdam University Press.

Hemerijck, Anton, and Franca van Hooren. 2012. *Stress-Testing the Dutch Welfare State, Once Again*. Amsterdam: VU University.

Hemerijck, Anton, and Jelle Visser. 2000. "Change and Immobility: Three Decades of Policy Adjustment in the Netherlands and Belgium." *West European Politics* 23 (2):229–56.

Henning, Roger. 1984. "Industrial Policy or Employment Policy? Sweden's Response to Unemployment." In *Unemployment: Policy Responses of Western Democracies*, ed. J. Richardson and R. Henning. London: Sage.

Herrigel, Gary. 1996. *Industrial Constructions: The Sources of German Industrial Power*. New York: Cambridge University Press.

Hibbs, Douglas A., and Håkan Locking. 2000. "Wage Dispersion and Productive Efficiency: Evidence for Sweden." *Journal of Labor Economics* 18 (4):755–82.

Hicks, Josh. 2013. "Obama nominates new NLRB Members as House threatens to halt board actions," *Washington Post*, www.washingtonpost.com (published April 9, 2013).

Hijzen, Alexander, and Danielle Venn. 2011. "The Role of Short-Time Work Schemes during the 2008–09 Recession." *OECD Social, Employment and Migration Working Papers*. Paris: OECD.

Hilferding, Rudolf. 1910. *Das Finanzkapital*. Vienna: Wiener Volksbuchhandlung.

Höpner, Martin. 2000. "Unternehmensverflechtung im Zwielicht." *WSI-Mitteilungen* 53:655–63.

Höpner, Martin. 2007. "Coordination and Organization: The Two Dimensions of Nonliberal Capitalism." *MPIfG Discussion Paper 07/2012*. Cologne: MPIfG.

Höpner, Martin, and Lothar Krempel. 2003. "The Politics of the German Company Network." *Competition and Change* 8 (4):339–56.

Höpner, Martin, and Maximilian Waclawczyk. 2012. "Opportunismus oder Ungewissheit? Mitbestimmte Unternehmen zwischen Klassenkampf und Produktionsregime." *MPIfG Discussion Paper 12/1*. Cologne: MPIfG.

Houseman, Susan N. 1995. "Job Growth and the Quality of Jobs in the U.S. Economy." *Upjohn Institute Working Papers*. Kalamazoo, MI: W.E. Upjohn Institute for Employment Research.

Howell, Chris. 2003. "Varieties of Capitalism: And Then There Was One?" *Comparative Politics* 36 (1):103–24.

Huber, Evelyne, and John D. Stephens. 2000. "Partisan Governance, Women's Employment, and the Social Democratic Service State." *American Sociological Review* 65 (3):323–42.

Huber, Evelyne, and John D. Stephens. 2012. "Post-Industrial Social Policy," Paper presented at the conference "The Future of Democratic Capitalism," Duke University, October 11–13.

"Hungerlohn trotz Vollzeitjob." 2010. *Spiegel online*. November 19. http://www.spiegel.de/wirtschaft/soziales/billiglohnsektor-hungerlohn-trotz-vollzeitjob-a-729972.html.

Ibsen, Christian Lyhne. 2012. *The "Real" End of Solidarity?* Presented at a workshop at the Institute for Work and Employment Research, MIT, Cambridge, MA.

Ibsen, Christian Lyhne. 2013. *Consensus or Coercion: Collective Bargaining Coordination and Third Party Intervention*. Ph.D. Thesis, Department of Sociology, University of Copenhagen.

Ibsen, Christian Lyhne, Søren Kaj Andersen, Jesper Due, and Jørgen Steen Madsen. 2011. "Bargaining in the Crisis: A Comparison of the 2010 Collective Bargaining Round in the Danish and Swedish Manufacturing Sectors." *Transfers: European Review of Labour and Research* 17 (3):323–39.

Ibsen, Christian Lyhne, Trine Pernille Larsen, Jørgen Steen Madsen, and Jesper Due. 2011. "Challenging Scandinavian Employment Relations: The Effects of New Public Management Reforms." *The International Journal of Human Resource Management* 22 (11):2295–2310.

Ibsen, Christian Lyhne, and Mikkel Mailand. 2009. "Flexicurity and Collective Bargaining: Balancing Acts Across Sectors and Countries." *FAOS Forskningsnotat*. Copenhagen: FAOS.

Imel, Susan. 1999. "School-to-Work Myths and Realities No. 4." Columbus, OH: Center on Education and Training for Employment.

"The Ins and the Outs: Immigration and Growing Inequality are Making the Nordics less Homogenous." 2013. *The Economist*, February 2. http://www.economist.com/news/special-report/21570836-immigration-and-growing-inequality.htm.

Iversen, Torben. 1996. "Power, Flexibility and the Breakdown of Centralized Wage Bargaining: The Cases of Denmark and Sweden in Comparative Perspective." *Comparative Politics* 28 (4):399–436.

Iversen, Torben. 1999. *Contested Economic Institutions: The Politics of Macroeconomics and Wage Bargaining in Advanced Democracies*. New York: Cambridge University Press.

Iversen, Torben, and Frances Rosenbluth. 2010. *Women, Work and Power: The Political Economy of Gender Inequality.* New Haven, CT: Yale University Press.

Iversen, Torben, and Frances Rosenbluth. 2012. "The Political Economy of Gender in Service Sector Economies." In *The Political Economy of the Service Transition,* ed. A. Wren. Oxford: Oxford University Press.

Iversen, Torben, and David Soskice. 2009. "Distribution and Redistribution: The Shadow from the Nineteenth Century." *World Politics* 61 (3):438–86.

Iversen, Torben, and David Soskice. 2010. "Dualism and Social Coalitions: Inclusionary versus Exclusionary Reforms in an Age of Rising Inequality." Paper presented at the 2009 Annual Meeting of the American Political Science Association, Toronto, September 3–6.

Iversen, Torben, and John D. Stephens. 2008. "Partisan Politics, the Welfare State, and the Three Worlds of Human Capital Formation." *Comparative Political Studies* 41 (4/5):600–37.

Iversen, Torben, and Anne Wren. 1998. "Equality, Employment, and Budgetary Restraint: The Trilemma of the Service Economy." *World Politics* 50 (4):507–46.

Jørgensen, Carsten. 2004. "New Collective Agreements Concluded in Industry." In *EIROnline*: Eurofound. http://www.eurofound.europa.eu/eiro/2012/06/articles/de1206019i.htm.

Jørgensen, Carsten. 2005. "Seminar Highlights Flexicurity in the Labour Market." In *EIROnline*: Eurofound. http://www.eurofound.europa.eu/eiro/2005/06/feature/dk0506103f.htm.

Jørgensen, Carsten. 2009a. "Denmark: Collective Bargaining and Continuous Vocational Training." In *EIROnline*: Eurofound. http://www.eurofound.europa.eu/eiro/studies/tno804048s/dko804049q.htm.

Jørgensen, Carsten. 2009b. "Les conséquences de la récession économique [Consequences of the Economic Recession in Denmark]." *Chronique Internationale de l'IRES* 121 (November).

Jørgensen, Henning. 2002. *Consensus, Cooperation and Conflict: The Policy Making Process in Denmark.* Cheltenham: Edward Elgar.

Kapstein, Ethan. 1996. "Workers and the World Economy." *Foreign Affairs* 75 (3):16–37.

Karger, Howard Jacob. 2003. "Ending Public Assistance: The Transformation of US Public Assistance Policy into Labour Policy." *Journal of Social Policy* 32 (3):383–401.

Karlson, Nils. 2010. *Four Cases of Decentralized Bargaining.* Stockholm: Ratio Institute.

Katz, Harry, and Owen Darbishire. 1999. *Converging Divergences.* Ithaca, NY: Cornell University Press.

Katz, Lawrence F. 1994. "Active Labor Market Policies to Expand Employment and Opportunity." In *Reducing Unemployment: Current Issues and Policy Options.* Kansas City, MO: Federal Reserve Bank of Kansas City.

Keizer, Arjan. 2011. Non-Regular Employment in the Netherlands. Tokyo: JILPT.

Keller, Berndt and Hartmut Seifert. 2006. "Atypische Beschäftigungsverhältnisse: Flexibilität, soziale Sicherheit und Prekarität." *WSI Mitteilungen* 5:235–240.

Kitschelt, Herbert, Peter Lange, Gary Marks, and John D. Stephens. 1999a. "Convergence and Divergence in Advanced Capitalist Democracies." In *Continuity and Change in Contemporary Capitalism,* ed. H. Kitschelt, P. Lange, G. Marks, and J. D. Stephens. New York: Cambridge University Press.

Kitschelt, Herbert, Peter Lange, Gary Marks, and John D. Stephens, eds. 1999b. *Continuity and Change in Contemporary Capitalism*. New York: Cambridge University Press.

Kittner, Michael. 1985. *Beschäftigungsförderungsgesetz*. Cologne: Bund Verlag.

Kjellberg, Anders. 1992. "Sweden: Can the Model Survive?" In *Industrial Relations in the New Europe*, ed. A. Ferner and R. Hyman. Oxford: Blackwell.

Kjellberg, Anders. 1998. "Sweden: Restoring the Model?" In *Changing Industrial Relations in Europe*, ed. A. Ferner and R. Hyman. Oxford: Blackwell.

Kjellberg, Anders. 2009. "The Swedish Model of Industrial Relations: Self-Regulation and Combined Centralisation-Decentralisation." In *Trade Unionism since 1945: Towards a Global History*, ed. C. Phelan. Bern: Peter Lang Publishing Group.

Kjellberg, Anders. 2011. "Trade Unions and Collective Agreements in a Changing World." In *Precarious Employment in Perspective: Old and New Challenges to Working Conditions in Sweden*, ed. A. Thörnquist and A.-K. Engstrand. Brussels: Peter Lange.

Klausen, Jytte. 1999. "The Declining Significance of Male Workers: Trade-Union Responses to Changing Labor Markets." In *Continuity and Change in Contemporary Capitalism*, ed. H. Kitschelt, P. Lange, G. Marks, and J. D. Stephens. New York: Cambridge University Press.

"Koalitionswirren um geringfügige Beschäftigung." 1998. *Frankfurter Allgemeine Zeitung*, November 19.

Kochan, Thomas A., Harry C. Katz, and Robert B. McKersie. 1994. *The Transformation of American Industrial Relations*, 2nd ed. Ithaca, NY: ILR Press.

Konle-Seidl, Regina. 2008. "Changes in the Governance of Employment Services in Germany since 2003." *IAB Discussion Papers*. Nuremberg: IAB.

Konle-Seidl, Regina. 2012. "Wirkung von Hartz IV auf die Rückkehr in die Arbeit." Paper presented at conference on Soziale Herausforderungen. Paris: CIRAC, February 13.

Krämer, Birgit. 2010. "Agreement to safeguard Jobs signed in Metalworking Industry." In *EIROnline*: Eurofound. http://www.eurofound.europa.eu/eiro/2010/04/articles/de1004029i.htm.

Krämer, Birgit. 2011. "Germany: EIRO Annual Review 2009." In *EIROnline*: Eurofound. http://www.eurofound.europa.eu/eiro/studies/tn1004019s/de1004019q.htm.

Kremen, Gladys Roth. 1974. MDTA: The Origins of the Manpower Development and Training Act of 1962. Washington, DC: U.S. Department of Labor.

Kreysing, Matthias. 2001. "Vocational Education in the United States: Reforms and Results." *European Journal: Vocational Training* 23:27–35.

Kristensen, Peer Hull. 2006. "Business Systems in the Age of the 'New Economy': Denmark Facing the Challenge." In *National Identity and the Varieties of Capitalism: The Danish Experience*, ed. J. L. Campbell, J. A. Hall, and O. K. Pedersen. Montreal: McGill-Queen's University Press.

Kristensen, Peer Hull, Maja Lotz, and Raimo Rocha. 2011. "Denmark: Tailoring Flexicurity for Changing Roles in Global Games." In *Nordic Capitalisms and Globalization: New Forms of Economic Organization and Welfare Institutions*, ed. P. H. Kristensen and K. Lilja. Oxford: Oxford University Press.

Krugman, Paul. 2010. "The Conscience of a Liberal." *New York Times*, September 2.

Kuipers, Susanne. 2004. *Cast in Concrete? The Institutional Dynamics of Belgian and Dutch Social Policy Reform*. Amsterdam: Eburon.

Kullander, Mats and Jenny Norlin. 2010. "Social Partners Review Temporary Layoff Agreements," *EIROnline*: Eurofound. http://www.eurofound.europa.eu/eiro/2009/12/articles/se0912019i.htm.

Kuo, Alexander. 2009. *The Political Origins of Employer Coordination, Political Science.* Ph.D. Thesis, Stanford University, Palo Alto, CA.

Kupfer, Antonia. 2010. "The Socio-Political Significance of Changes to the Vocational Education System in Germany." *British Journal of Sociology of Education* 31 (1):85–97.

Kupfer, Franziska, and Andrea Startz. 2011. *Dual Courses of Study: The Supply and Demand Situation.* Berlin: BIBB.

Lacey, Nicola. 2008. *The Prisoners' Dilemma: Political Economy and Punishment in Contemporary Democracies.* Cambridge: Cambridge University Press.

Lafer, Gordon. 2002. *The Job Training Charade.* Ithaca, NY: Cornell University Press.

Lamparter, Dietmar. 2012. "Liegt hier unsere Zukunft?" *Die Zeit*, January 12.

Lassen, Morten, John Houman Sørensen, Anja Lindkvist Jørgensen, and Rasmus Juul Møberg. 2006. *A Study of the Impact of Skills Needs and Institutional and Financial Factors on Enterprise-Sponsored CVT in Denmark.* Aalborg: Aalborg University Center for Labour Market Research.

Lesch, Hagen. 2010. "Tarifeinheit: BDA und DGB mit einer Stimme." In *Gewerkschaftsspiegel.* Cologne: Institut der deutschen Wirtschaft.

Levy, Jonah. 1999. "Vice into Virtue? Progressive Politics and Welfare Reform in Continental Europe." *Politics & Society* 27 (2):239–73.

Liebig, Thomas. 2007. "The Labour Market Integration of Immigrants in Denmark." *OECD Social, Employment and Migration Working Papers No. 50.* Paris: OECD.

Lijphart, Arend. 1989. "From the Politics of Accommodation to Adversarial Politics in the Netherlands." *West European Politics* 12:139–54.

Lindbeck, Assar, and Dennis J. Snower. 1988. *The Insider-Outsider Theory of Employment and Unemployment.* Cambridge, MA: MIT Press.

Lindell, Mats. 2004. "From Conflicting Interests to Collective Consent in Advanced Vocational Education: Policymaking and the Role of Stakeholders in Sweden." *Journal of Education and Work* 17 (2):257–77.

Lindell, Mats. 2006. "From Formulation to Realisation: The Process of Swedish Reform in Advanced Vocational Education." *Education + Training* 48 (4):222–40.

Lindvall, Johannes. 2010. *Mass Unemployment and the State.* Oxford: Oxford University Press.

Lindvall, Johannes, and David Rueda. 2012. "Insider-Outsider Politics: Party Strategies and Political Behavior in Sweden." In *The Age of Dualization: The Changing Face of Inequality in Deindustrializing Societies*, ed. P. Emmenegger, S. Häusermann, B. Palier, and M. Seeleib-Kaiser. Oxford: Oxford University Press.

Llorens, Maria Caprile-Clara. 1998. "Collective Bargaining and Continuing Vocational Training in Europe." In *EIROnline*: Eurofound. http://www.eurofound.europa.eu/eiro/1998/04/study/tn9804201s.htm.

Locke, Richard M., and Kathleen Thelen. 1995. "Apples and Oranges Revisited: Contextualized Comparisons and the Study of Comparative Labor Politics." *Politics & Society* 23 (3):337–67.

Lødemel, Ivar and Heather Trickey (eds.). 2001. *'An Offer You Can't Refuse:' Workfare in International Perspective.* Bristol: The Policy Press.

Lovén, Karolin. 2009a. "Deadlock in Negotiations on New Central Agreement." In *EIROnline*: Eurofound. http://www.eurofound.europa.eu/eiro/2009/03/articles/se0903029i.htm.

Lovén, Karolin. 2009b. "Social Partners Disagree on Solutions for Youth Unemployment." In *EIROnline*: Eurofound. http://www.eurofound.europa.eu/eiro/2009/08/articles/se0908019i.htm.

Lundberg, Urban, and Klaus Petersen. 2012. "Wanted: A Good Cleavage! Body Snatchers, Desperadoes and the Real McCoy." Presented at a workshop on "Political Cleavages: Revolutions and Conflicts in the 21st Century," Paris (March).

Lupu, Noam, and Jonas Pontusson. 2011. "The Structure of Inequality and the Politics of Redistribution." *American Political Science Review* 105 (2):316–36.

Lynch, Lisa M. 1994. *Training and the Private Sector: International Comparisons.* Chicago: University of Chicago Press.

Madsen, Jørgen Steen. 1998. "1998 Annual Review for Denmark." In *EIROnline*: Eurofound. http://www.eurofound.europa.eu/eiro/1998/12/feature/dk9812107f.htm.

Madsen, Per Kongshøj. 2002. "The Danish Model of Flexicurity: A Paradise–with Some Snakes." In *Labour Market and Social Protections Reforms in International Perspective*, ed. H. Sarfati and G. Bonoli. Aldershot: Ashgate.

Madsen, Per Kongshøj. 2006. "How Can it Possibly Fly? The Paradox of a Dynamic Labour Marekt in a Scandinavian Welfare State." In *National Identity and the Varieties of Capitalism: The Danish Experience*, ed. J. L. Campbell, J. A. Hall, and O. K. Pedersen. Montreal: McGill-Queen's University Press.

Madsen, Per Kongshøj. 2007. "Distribution of Responsibility for Social Security and Labour Market Policy. Country Report: Denmark." Working Paper 07/51, Amsterdam Institute for Advanced Labour Studies. Amsterdam: University of Amsterdam.

Madsen, Per Kongshøj. 2013. "Labour Market Flexibility in the Danish Service Sector: Same, Same, but Still Different." Paper presented at Conference on Non-Standard Employment in Comparative Perspective, Bonn, May 25–26.

Madsen, Per Kongshøj, and Henrik Larsen. 1998. "Training and Development in the Danish Context: Challenging Education?" *Journal of European Industrial Training* 22 (4/5):158.

Mahon, Rianne. 1991. "Lonetagare and Medarbetare? The Swedish Unions Confront the 'Double Shift'." Paper presented at workshop on The Changing Place of Labor in European Society: The End of Labor's Century? Center for European Studies, Harvard University, November 23–24.

Mahoney, James, and Kathleen Thelen. 2009. "A Theory of Gradual Institutional Change." In *Explaining Institutional Change: Ambiguity, Agency, and Power*, ed. J. Mahoney and K. Thelen. New York: Cambridge University Press.

Mailand, Mikkel. 1999. *Denmark as a Further Training Utopia?* Copenhagen: FAOS.

Mailand, Mikkel. 2002. "Denmark in the 1990s: Status Quo or a More Self-Confident State?" In *Policy Concertation and Social Partnership in Western Europe: Lessons for the 21st Century*, ed. S. Berger and H. Compston. New York: Berghahn.

Mailand, Mikkel. 2006. "Dynamic Neo-Corporatism: Regulating Work and Welfare in Denmark." *Transfer* 3/06 12 (3):371–87.

Mailand, Mikkel. 2009. "Corporatism in Denmark and Norway: Yet Another Century of Scandinavian Corporatism?" *WSI Mitteilungen* 1.

Mares, Isabela. 2000. "Strategic Alliances and Social Policy Reform: Unemployment Insurance in Comparative Perspective." *Politics & Society* 28 (2):223–44.

Martin, Andrew. 1991. "Wage Bargaining and Swedish Politics: The Political Implications of the End of Central Negotiations." *Center for European Studies Working Paper Series #6*. Harvard University.

Martin, Andrew, and George Ross, eds. 1999. *The Brave New World of European Labour: Comparing Trade Unions Responses to the New European Economy.* Oxford: Berghahn.

Martin, Cathie Jo. 2000. *Stuck in Neutral: Business and the Politics of Human Capital Investment Policy.* Princeton, NJ: Princeton University Press.

Martin, Cathie Jo. 2012. "Political Institutions and the Origins of Collective Skill Formation Systems." In *The Political Economy of Collective Skill Formation*, ed. M. Busemeyer and C. Trampusch. Oxford: Oxford University Press.

Martin, Cathie Jo, and Jette Steen Knudsen. 2010. "Scenes from a Mall: Retail Training and the Social Exclusion of Low-Skilled Workers." *Regulation & Governance* 4:345–64.

Martin, Cathie Jo, and Duane Swank. 2004. "Does the Organization of Capital Matter?" *American Political Science Review* 98 (4):593–611.

Martin, Cathie Jo, and Duane Swank. 2012. *The Political Construction of Business Interests: Coordination, Growth and Equality.* New York: Cambridge University Press.

Martin, Cathie Jo, and Kathleen Thelen. 2007. "The State and Coordinated Capitalism: Contributions of the Public Sector to Social Solidarity in Post-Industrial Societies." *World Politics* 60 (October):1–36.

Martin, John P. 1998. "What Works Among Active Labor Market Policies: Evidence from OECD Countries' Experiences." Paris: OECD.

Mayer, Karl Ulrich, and Heike Solga. 2008. "Skill Formation: Interdisciplinary and Cross-National Perspectives." In *Skill Formation: Interdisciplinary and Cross-National Perspectives*, ed. K. U. Mayer and H. Solga. New York: Cambridge University Press.

Medlingsinstitutet. 2010. "Summary of the Annual Report: Wage Bargaining and Wage Formation in 2010," in National Mediation Office Sweden, *Annual Report 2010.* http://www.mi.se/files/PDF-er/ar_foreign/eng_smftn_feb2011.pdf.

Meiritz, Annett and Philipp Wittrock. 2008. "Entsendegesetz: Sieben Branchen für den Mindestlohn." *Spiegel online.* March 31. http://www.spiegel.de/wirtschaft/entsendegesetz-sieben-branchen-fuer-den-mindestlohn-a-544363.html.

Melkert, Ad. 2008. "The Dutch Job and Welfare Experience." Paper presented at International Workshop on "Jobs and Equity in a Global World," Santiago, Chile, January 8.

Minijobzentrale. 2012. *Aktuelle Entwicklungen im Bereich der geringfügigen Beschäftigung.* Essen: Die Minijob Zentrale.

Ministeriet, Undervisnings. 2008. *Adult Vocational Training in Denmark.* Copenhagen: Ministry of Education.

Ministry of Children and Education in Denmark. 2012. *Education and Training in Denmark: Facts and Key Figures.* Copenhagen: Ministry of Children and Education.

Mishel, Lawrence, Josh Bivens, Elise Gould, and Heidi Shierholz. 2012. *The State of Working America.* Washington, DC: Economic Policy Institute.

Mitlacher, Lars W. 2007. "The Role of Temporary Agency Work in Different Industrial Relations Systems." *British Journal of Industrial Relations* 45 (3):581–606.

Moene, Karl Ove, and Michael Wallerstein. 1993. "The Decline of Social Democracy." In *The Economic Development of Denmark and Norway since 1870*, ed. K. G. Persson. Aldershot: Edward Elgar.

Moody, Kim. 2007. *US Labor in Trouble and Transition: The Failure of Reform from Above, the Promise of Revival from Below*. New York: Verso.

Morel, Nathalie, Bruno Palier, and Joakim Palme. 2011. "Beyond the Welfare State as We Knew it?" In *Towards a Social Investment Welfare State?* ed. N. Morel, B. Palier, and J. Palme. Bristol: Policy Press.

Morgan, Kimberly J. 2006. *Working Mothers and the Welfare State*. Stanford: Stanford University Press.

Morgan, Kimberly J. 2012. "Promoting Social Investment through Work-Family Policies: Which Nations Do It and Why?" In *Towards a Social Investment Welfare State?* ed. N. Morel, B. Palier, and J. Palme. Bristol: Policy Press.

Mouritsen, Per and Tore Vincents Olsen. 2013. "Denmark between Liberalism and Nationalism." *Ethnic and Racial Studies* 36 (4):691–710.

NCES. 2012. "The Condition of Education." National Center for Education Statistics, U.S. Department of Education. http://nces.ed.gov/programs/coe/.

NEA (National Education Authority). 2008. *The Danish Vocational Education and Training System*. Copenhagen: Danish Ministry of Education.

Nelson, Moira. 2010. "The Adjustment of National Education Systems to a Knowledge-Based Economy: A New Approach." *Comparative Education* 46 (4):463–86.

Nelson, Moira. 2012. "Continued Collectivism: The Role of Trade Self-Management and the Social Democratic Party in Danish Vocational Education and Training." In *The Political Economy of Collective Skill Formation*, ed. M. Busemeyer and C. Trampusch. Oxford: Oxford University Press.

Nelson, Moira, and John D. Stephens. 2012. "The Service Transition and Women's Employment." In *The Political Economy of the Service Transition*, ed. A. Wren. Oxford: Oxford University Press.

Neubäumer, Renate. 2007. "Mehr Beschäftigung durch weniger Kündigungsschutz?" *Wirtschaftsdienst* 3:1–8.

Neubäumer, Renate, Harald Pfeifer, Günter Walden, and Felix Wenzelmann. 2011. "The Costs of Apprenticeship Training in Germany: The Influence of Production Processes, Tasks, and Skill Requirements." University of Koblenz and BIBB.

Neubäumer, Renate and Dominik Tretter. 2008. "Mehr atypische Beschäftigung aus theoretischer Sicht." *Industrielle Bezhiehungen* 15 (3):256–278.

NGG. 1999. "Stellungnahme der Gewerkschaft Nahrung-Genuss-Gaststätten zur Anhörung des Bundestagsausschusses für Arbeit und Sozialordung zum Thema 'geringfügige Beschäftigung' am 10. Februar 1999." Position paper submitted to Parliamentary Committee (Ausschuss für Arbeit und Sozialordnung, Drucksache 14/280). Bonn: Deutscher Bundestag.

Nickell, Stephen. 1997. "Unemployment and Labor Market Rigidities: Europe versus North America." *Journal of Economic Perspectives* 11 (3):55–74.

"Niedriglöhne machen Betriebsräten zunehmend zu schaffen." 2010. *Böckler impuls* 17:4–5.

Nielsen, Søren. 1995. *Vocational Education and Training in Denmark*. Brussels: CEDE-FOP.

Nycander, Svante. 2010. "Misunderstanding the Swedish Model," unpublished manuscript, Stockholm.

Obinger, Herbert, Peter Starke, and Alexandra Kaasch. 2012. "Responses to Labor Market Divides in Small States since the 1990s." In *The Age of Dualization: The Changing Face of Inequality in Deindustrializing Societies*, ed. P. Emmenegger, S. Häusermann, B. Palier, and M. Seeleib-Kaiser. Oxford: Oxford University Press.

OECD. 1999. *OECD Historical Statistics 1960–1997*. Paris: OECD.

OECD. 2002. Thematic Review of Adult Learning: Denmark. Paris: OECD.

OECD. 2004. Employment Outlook. Paris: OECD. http://www.oecd.org/els/emp/34846881.pdf.

OECD. 2006. "Boosting Jobs and Incomes." In *Employment Outlook*. Paris: OECD.

OECD. 2008. *Growing Unequal? Income Distribution and Poverty in OECD Countries*. Paris: OECD.

OECD. 2010. "Moving Beyond the Jobs Crisis: Further Material," Annex 1.A1. The Institutional Features of Short-Time Work Schemes in OECD Countries. Paris: OECD.

OECD. 2011a. *Divided We Stand: Why Inequality Keeps Rising*. Paris: OECD.

OECD. 2011b. "Employment in General Government and Public Corporations." In *Government at a Glance 2011*. Paris: OECD.

OECD. 2011c. "Education at a Glance 2011." Paris: OECD.

OECD. 2012a. "Employment and Labour Markets: Key Tables from OECD." Paris: OECD. http://www.oecd-ilibrary.org/employment/employment-and-labour-markets-key-tables-from-oecd_20752342.

OECD. 2012b. *OECD Economic Surveys: Denmark*. Paris: OECD.

OECD. 2012c. *OECD Outlook 2012*. Paris: OECD.

OECD. 2012. OECD.Stat Database. Paris: OECD.

OECD. n.d. Calculating Summary Indicators of Employment Protection Strictness. Paris: OECD.

OECD. n.d. OECD Stat Database. stats.oecd.org.

"On the March: Populist Anti-Immigration Parties are Performing Strongly Across Northern Europe." 2011. *The Economist*, March 17, http://www.economist.com/node/18398641/print.

Orloff, Ann. 1993. "Gender and the Social Rights of Citizenship: The Comparative Analysis of Gender Relations and Welfare States." *American Sociological Review* 58:303–28.

Ornston, Darius. 2012. *When Small States Make Big Leaps: Institutional Innovation and High-Tech Competition in Western Europe*. Ithaca, NY: Cornell University Press.

Osterman, Paul. 2011. "The Promise, Performance, and Policies of Community Colleges." In *Reinventing Higher Education*, ed. B. Wildavsky, A. P. Kelly, and K. Carey. Cambridge, MA: Harvard Education Press.

Palier, Bruno. 2005. "Ambiguous Agreement, Cumulative Change: French Social Policy in the 1990s." In *Continuity and Discontinuity in Institutional Analysis*, ed. W. Streeck and K. Thelen. Oxford: Oxford University Press.

Palier, Bruno, and Kathleen Thelen. 2010. "Institutionalizing Dualism: Complementarities and Change in France and Germany." *Politics & Society* 38 (1):119–48.

Pancaldi, Federico. 2011. "Capitalists against Crisis: Employers and Short Time Work in Germany and Italy, 2008–2010." Paper presented at ESPAnet Annual Conference, Valencia, September 8–10.

Paster, Thomas. 2009. *Choosing Lesser Evils: The Role of Business in the Development of the German Welfare State from the 1880s to the 1990s.* Ph.D. Thesis, Department of Political and Social Sciences, Florence, European University Institute.

Patashnik, Eric M. 2008. *Reforms at Risk: What Happens After Major Policy Changes Are Enacted.* Princeton, NJ: Princeton University Press.

Peck, Jamie, and Nikolas Theodore. 2000. "'Work First': Workfare and the Regulation of Contingent Labour Markets." *Cambridge Journal of Economics* 24:119–38.

Pedersini, Roberto. 2009. "Flexicurity and Industrial Relations." In *EIROnline*: Eurofound. http://www.eurofound.europa.eu/eiro/studies/tn0803038s/tn0803038s-3.htm.

Petersen, Kåre F. V. 1997a. "The Danish Model Under Threat?" In *EIROnline*: Eurofound. http://www.eurofound.europa.eu/eiro/1997/08/feature/dk9708122f.htm.

Petersen, Kåre F. V. 1997b. "Ministry of Labour Launches Vocational Training Campaign." *EIROnline*: Eurofound. http://www.eurofound.europa.eu/eiro/1997/03/feature/dk9703104f.htm.

Petersen, Kåre F. V. 1997c. "Women's Trade Union Fights for its Independent Status." In *EIROnline*: Eurofound. http://www.eurofound.europa.eu/eiro/1997/10/feature/dk9710134f.htm.

Petersen, Kåre F. V. 1998a. "1998 Bargaining Round Ends in Major Conflict." In *EIROnline*: Eurofound. http://www.eurofound.europa.eu/eiro/1998/04/inbrief/dk9804166n.htm.

Petersen, Kåre F. V. 1998b. "1998 Collective Bargaining Commences in Industry." In *EIROnline*: Eurofound. http://www.eurofound.europa.eu/eiro/1998/01/feature/dk9801147f.htm.

Petersen, Kåre F. V. 1998c. "Breakthrough in Industry on Brink of Conflict." In *EIROnline*: Eurofound. http://www.eurofound.europa.eu/eiro/1998/03/feature/dk9803158f.htm.

Petersen, Kåre F. V. 1998d. "Parliament Intervenes to End Major Conflict." In *EIROnline*: Eurofound. http://www.eurofound.europa.eu/eiro/1998/05/feature/dk9805168f.htm.

Petersen, Kåre F. V. 1998e. "Social Partners Accept Joint Mediation Proposal for 1998 Bargaining Round." In *EIROnline*: Eurofound. http://www.eurofound.europa.eu/eiro/1998/04/feature/dk9804163f.htm.

Petersen, Kåre F. V. 1998f. "Third Reform of Labour Market Policy is Underway." In *EIROnline*: Eurofound. http://www.eurofound.europa.eu/eiro/1998/09/feature/dk9809177f.htm.

Peterson, Christer. 2011. "Sweden: From Large Corporations towards a Knowledge-Intensive Economy." In *Nordic Capitalisms and Globalization: New Forms of Economic Organization and Welfare Institutions*, ed. P. H. Kristensen and K. Lilja. Oxford: Oxford University Press.

Pierce, Brooks. 2001. "Compensation Inequality." *Quarterly Journal of Economics* 116 (4):1493–1505.

Piketty, Thomas, and Emmanuel Saez. 2003. "Income Inequality in the United States, 1913–1998." *Quarterly Journal of Economics* 118 (1):1–39.

Pontusson, Jonas. 1992. *The Limits of Social Democracy: Investment Politics in Sweden.* Ithaca, NY: Cornell University Press.

Pontusson, Jonas. 1997. "Between Neo-Liberalism and the German Model: Swedish Capitalism in Transition." In *Political Economy of Modern Capitalism*, ed. C. Crouch and W. Streeck. Thousand Oaks, CA: Sage.

Pontusson, Jonas. 2005a. *Inequality and Prosperity: Social Europe vs. Liberal America.* New York: Century Foundation.

Pontusson, Jonas. 2005b. "Varieties and Commonalities of Capitalism." In *Varieties of Capitalism, Varieties of Approaches*, ed. D. Coates. London: Palgrave.

Pontusson, Jonas. 2009. "Once Again a Model: Nordic Social Democracy in a Globalized World." In *Futures of the Left*, ed. James Cronin, George Ross, and James Shoch. Durham, NC: Duke University Press.

Pontusson, Jonas. 2013. "Trade Unions and Redistributive Politics." Geneva: University of Geneva.

Pontusson, Jonas, and Peter Swenson. 1996. "Labor Markets, Production Strategies, and Wage Bargaining Institutions." *Comparative Political Studies* 29 (2):223–50.

Powell, Justin J.W., and Heike Solga. 2011. "Why Are Higher Education Participation Rates in Germany So Low? Institutional Barriers to Higher Education Expansion." *Journal of Education and Work* 24 (1):49–68.

Pruijt, Hans, and Pascal Dérogée. 2010. "Employability and Job Security, Friends or Foes? The Paradoxical Reception of Employacurity in the Netherlands." *Socio-Economic Review* 8:437–60.

Przeworski, Adam, and John Sprague. 1986. *Paper Stones: A History of Electoral Socialism.* Chicago: University of Chicago Press.

Quack, Sigrid, and Swen Hildebrandt. 1996. "Rekrutierung, Berufsausbildung und Personaleinsatz: Deutsche und französische Kreditinstitute im Anpassungsprozess an veränderte Markbedingungen." *Zeitschrift für Berufs- und Wirtschaftspädagogik* 92:467–89.

Quack, Sigrid, Jacqueline O'Reilly, and Swen Hildebrandt. 1995. "Structuring Change: Training and Recruitment in Retail Banking in Germany, Britain, and France." *International Journal of Human Resource Management* 6 (4):759–94.

Quadagno, Jill. 1996. *The Color of Welfare: How Racism Undermined the War on Poverty.* New York: Oxford University Press.

Rath, Jan. 2009. "The Netherlands: A Reluctant Country of Immigration." *Tijdschrift Voor Economische En Sociale Geografie* 100 (5):674–81.

Ravitch, Dana. 2012. "How, and How Not, to Improve the Schools." *New York Review of Books*, March 22.

Rehder, Britta. 2003. *Betriebliche Bündnisse für Arbeit in Deutschland: Mitbestimmung und Flächentarif im Wandel.* Frankfurt: Campus.

Rehm, Philipp, Jacob Hacker, and Mark Schlesinger. 2012. "Insecure Alliances: Risk, Inequality, and Support for the Welfare State." *American Political Science Review* 106 (2):386–406.

Reich, Helmut. 2010. "IG Metall: Die kompromissbereite Gewerkschaft." *Zeit Online.* January 25. http://www.zeit.de/wirtschaft/2010-01/ig-metall-huber.

Reich, Robert. 1996. "Investing in People 'Good for Us as a Nation,' Says Secretary of Labor." In *National Center for Research in Vocational Education*, University of California, Berkeley. http://ncrve.berkeley.edu/CW73/Reich.html.

Reisch, Michael. 2006. "Welfare Reform and the Transformation of the U.S. Welfare State." In *The Promise of Welfare Reform: Political Rhetoric and the Reality of Poverty in the Twenty First Century*, ed. K. M. Kilty and E. Segal. Binghamton, NY: Haworth Press.

Rinne, Ulf, and Klaus F. Zimmermann. 2011. "Another Economic Miracle? The German Labor Market and the Great Recession." *IZA Discussion Paper 6250*. Bonn: IZA.

Rose, Nancy E. 1999. "Jobs for Whom? Employment Policy in the United States and Western Europe." *Journal of Economic Issues* 33 (2):453–60.

Rosenbaum, James E. 2001. *Beyond College For All*. New York: Russell Sage Foundation.

Rosenbaum, James E. 2011. "The Complexities of College for All: Beyond Fairy-Tale Dreams." *Sociology of Education* 84 (2):113–7.

Rothstein, Bo. 1996. *The Social Democratic State: The Swedish Model and the Bureaucratic Problems of Social Reforms*. Pittsburgh, PA: University of Pittsburgh Press.

Rueda, David. 2007. *Social Democracy Inside Out: Government Partisanship, Insiders, and Outsiders in Industrialized Democracies*. Oxford: Oxford University Press.

Ruggie, John Gerard. 1982. "International Regimes, Transactions, and Change: Embedded Liberalism in the Postwar Economic Order." *International Organization* 36 (2):379–415.

Rydgren, Jens. 2010. "Radical Right-wing Populism in Denmark and Sweden: Explaining Party System Change and Stability." *SAIS Review of International Affairs* 30 (1): 57–71.

Sacchi, Stefano, Federico Pancaldi, and Claudia Arisi. 2011. "The Economic Crisis as a Trigger of Convergence? Short-Time Work in Italy, Germany and Austria." *Carlo Alberto Working Papers*. Milan: University of Milan.

Sako, Mari. 2012. "Professionals Between Market and Hierarchy in Comparative Political Economy." Paper presented at the Conference of the Society for the Study of Socio-Economics, Boston. June 28–30.

Salverda, Wiemer. 2009. "The Dutch Minimum Wage: A Radical Reduction Shifts the Main Focus to Part Time Jobs." *AIAS Working Paper 09-71*. Amsterdam: AIAS University of Amsterdam.

Scharpf, Fritz. 1997. *Games Real Actors Play*. Boulder, CO: Westview.

Scheele, Alexandra. 2001. "Unified Service Sector Union (ver.di) Created." In *EIROnline*: Eurofound. http://www.eurofound.europa.eu/eiro/2001/04/feature/de0104220f.htm.

Scheuer, Steen. 1992. "Denmark: Return to Decentralization." In *Industrial Relations in the New Europe*, ed. A. Ferner and R. Hyman. Oxford: Basil Blackwell.

Scheuer, Steen. 1998. "Denmark: A Less Regulated Model." In *Changing Industrial Relations in Europe*, ed. A. Ferner and R. Hyman. Oxford: Blackwell.

Scheuer, Steen. 2007. "Dilemmas of Collectivism: Danish Trade Unions in the Twenty-First Century." *Journal of Labor Research* 28 (2):233–54.

Schludi, Martin. 2005. *The Reform of Bismarckian Pension Systems*. Amsterdam: Amsterdam University Press.

Schmitt, John. 2011. "Labor Market Policy in the Great Recession: Some Lessons from Germany and Denmark." Washington, DC: Center for Economic and Policy Research.

Schmitt, John. 2012. "Low-Wage Lessons." Washington, DC: Center for Economic and Policy Research.

Schmitt, John, and Alexandra Mitukiewicz. 2011. "Politics Matter: Changes in Union-ization Rates in Rich Countries, 1960–2010." Washington DC: Center for Economic and Policy Research.

Schmitt, John, and Ben Zipperer. 2009. "Dropping the Ax: Illegal Firings During Union Election Campaigns, 1951–2007." Washington, DC: Center for Economic and Policy Research.

Schneibel, Gerhard. 2010. "Siemens Agrees to Open-Ended Employment Guarantee." *Deutsche Welle*, September 23. http://www.dw.de/siemens-agrees-to-open-ended-employment-guarantee/a-6039620.

Schneider, Martin R., and Mihai Paunescu. 2011. "Changing Varieties of Capitalism and Revealed Comparative Advantages from 1990 to 2005: A Test of the Hall and Soskice Claims." *Socio-Economic Review* 10:731–53.

Schnyder, Gerhard. 2012. "Like a Phoenix from the Ashes? Reassessing the Transfor-mation of the Swedish Political Economy Since the 1970s." *Journal of European Public Policy* 19 (8):1126–45.

Schnyder, Gerhard, and Gregory Jackson. 2011. "Diverging Paths of Post-Fordism: The German and Swedish Models from the Oil Shocks to the Global Financial Crisis." Paper presented at Council for European Studies, Barcelona, June 20–22.

Schochet, Peter Z., John Burghardt, and Sheena McConnell. 2008. "Does Job Corps Work? Impact Findings from the National Job Corps Study." *American Economic Review* 98 (5):1864–86.

Schulten, Thorsten. 1999a. "Verdi Overture: Five Unions Agree to form Unified Ser-vice Sector Union." In *EIROnline*: Eurofound. http://www.eurofound.europa.eu/eiro/1999/11/feature/de9911225f.htm.

Schulten, Thorsten. 1999b. "Union Demands Statutory Minimum Wage." In *EIROnline*: Eurofound. http://www.eurofound.europa.eu/eiro/1999/11/inbrief/de9911221n.htm.

Schulten, Thorsten. 2002. "Pilot Agreements Signed in Metalworking After Strike." In *EIROnline*: Eurofound. http://www.eurofound.europa.eu/eiro/2002/05/feature/de0205206f.htm.

Schulze-Cleven, Tobias. 2009. *Flexible Markets, Protected Workers: Adjustment Path-ways in Europe's New Economy*. Ph.D. Thesis, Political Science, University of Cali-fornia, Berkeley.

Schulze-Cleven, Tobias. 2011. "Diverging Pathways to Flexibility: Labor Market Adjustment in Germany and Denmark during Neoliberal Times." Paper presented at Center for European Studies Visiting Scholars Seminar, Cambridge, MA, March 30.

Schulze-Cleven, Tobias. n.d. "Toward Lifelong Learning in Europe? Policy Feedback, Union Strategy and the Politics of Continuing Education." Manuscript, Center for European Studies, Harvard University.

Schulze Buschoff, Karin, and Paula Protsch. 2008. "(A-)typical and (In-)secure? Social Protection and 'Non-Standard' Forms of Employment in Europe." *International Social Security Review* 61 (4):51–73.

Schwartz, Herman. 1994. "Small States in Big Trouble." *World Politics* 46 (4):527–55.

Schwartz, Herman. 2001. "The Danish 'Miracle': Luck, Pluck, or Stuck?" *Comparative Political Studies* 34 (2):131–55.

Schwengler, Barbara, and Veronika Loibl. 2010. "Beschäftigung, Arbeitslosigkeit und Kurzarbeit: Aufschwung und Krise wirken regional unterschiedlich." *IAB Kurzbericht* 1. Nürnberg: Institut für Arbeitsmarkt- und Berufsforschung.

Seeleib-Kaiser, Martin, Silke van Dyk, and Martin Roggenkamp. 2008. *Party Politics and Social Welfare*. Cheltenham: Edward Elgar.

Shierholz, Heidi. 2009. "Fix It and Forget It: Index the Minimum Wage to Growth in Average Wages." *EPI Briefing Paper*. Washington, DC: Economic Policy Institute.

Siebert, Horst. 1997. "Labour Market Rigidities: At the Root of Unemployment in Europe." *Journal of Economic Perspectives* 11 (3):37–54.

Silvia, Stephen. 2002. "The Rise and Fall of Unemployment in Germany." *German Politics* 11 (1):14.

Simonsen, Marianne, and Lars Skipper. 2006. "The Incidence and Intensity of Formal Lifelong Learning." Department of Economics, University of Aarhus.

Skocpol, Theda. 1985. "Bringing the State Back In: Strategies of Analysis in Current Research." In *Bringing the State Back In*, ed. P. B. Evans, D. Rueschemeyer, and T. Skocpol. New York: Cambridge University Press.

Sluyterman, Keetie. 2010. "Introduction: Changing Business Systems in the Netherlands in the Twentieth Century." *Business History Review* 84 (4):737–50.

Sluyterman, Keetie, and Ben Wubs. 2010. "Multinationals and the Dutch Business System: The Cases of Royal Dutch Shell and Sara Lee." *Business History Review* 84 (4):799–822.

Smith, Michael. 2000. "Warning over IT Skills Gap." *Financial Times*, March 7, 3.

Solga, Heike. 2009. "Der Blick nach vorn: Herausforderungen an das deutsche Ausbildungssystem." *WZB Discussion Papers*. Berlin: WZB.

Solga, Heike. 2010. "Vier Thesen zur Reform des deutschen Ausbildungssystems." *Pädagogik* 62 (6):46–9.

Sørensen, John Houman, and Grethe Jensen. 1988. *The Role of the Social Partners in Youth and Adult Vocational Education and Training in Denmark*. Berlin: CEDEFOP.

Soss, Joe, and Sanford F. Schram. 2007. "A Public Transformed? Welfare Reform as Policy Feedback." *American Political Science Review* 101 (1):111–27.

Spangenberg, Ulrike. 2005. "Neuorientierung der Ehebesteuerung: Ehegattensplitting und Lohnsteuerverfahren." *Hans Böckler Stiftung Working Paper*. Düsseldorf: Hans Böckler Stiftung.

"SPD will Beitragspflicht für Billig-Jobs einführen." 1998. *Handelsblatt*, August 11.

"SPD zweifelt am Splitting für Ehegatten." 2011. *Zeit Online*, January 11. http://www .zeit.de/politik/deutschland/2011-01/SPD-Splitting-Ehegatten.htm.

Spiegel. 2008. "Ländervergleich: Niedriglohnsektor wächst in Deutschland rasant." *Spiegel online*, April 18. http://www.spiegel.de/wirtschaft/laendervergleich-niedrig lohnsektor-waechst-in-deutschland-rasant-a-548185.html.

Spiegel. 2010a. "Unternehmen fordern Mindestlohn für Leiharbeiter." *Spiegel online*, October 5. http://www.spiegel.de/wirtschaft/soziales/druck-auf-regierung-unternehmen-fordern-mindestlohn-fuer-leiharbeiter-a-721442.html.

Spiegel. 2010b. "Hungerlohn trotz Vollzeitjob." *Spiegel online*. November 19.

Spiegel. 2011a. "Gewerkschaften kritisieren CDU-Mindestlohnpläne als nicht verfassungskonform." *Der Spiegel* 45/2011. November 6.

Spiegel. 2011b. "Gewerkschaften loben Merkels Mindestlohnwende." *Spiegel online,* October 31. http://www.spiegel.de/politik/deutschland/cdu-initiative-gewerkschaften-loben-merkels-mindestlohn-wende-a-794987.html.

Steedman, Hilary, and Karin Wagner. 2005. "Changing Skill Needs in Europe and Responsiveness of Apprenticeship/Work-Based Learning." Paper presented at the Jacobs Foundation Conference on Interdisciplinary Perspectives on Skill Formation and the Reform of Vocational and Professional Training. Schloss Marbach, April 14–16.

Steinmo, Sven. 2011. "Why is Sweden so Successful?" Manuscript, European University Institute, Florence, Italy.

Stenberg, Anders, and Olle Westerlund. 2008. "Does Comprehensive Education Work for the Long-Term Unemployed?" *Labour Economics* 15:54–7.

Stephan, Jennifer L, James E. Rosenbaum, and Ann E. Person. 2009. "Stratification in College Entry and Completion." *Social Science Research* 38:572–93.

Stephens, Geralyn E. 1995. "A Comparative Analysis of Findings: Smith-Hughes Act of 1917 and the School-to-Work Opportunities Act of 1994." Institute of Education Sciences. http://www.iab.de/194/section.aspx/Publikation/k100202n02.

Stettes, Oliver. 2005. "Modernisation of Metalworking Pay Framework starts in four Regions." In *EIROnline*: Eurofound. http://www.eurofound.europa.eu/eiro/2005/04/feature/deo504106f.htm.

Stratmann, Karlwilhelm. 1994. "Das duale System der Berufsbildung: Eine historisch-systematische Analyse." In *Lernorte im dualen System der Berufsbilder*, ed. G. Pätzold and G. Walden. Berlin und Bonn: Bundesinstitut für Berufsbildung.

Streeck, Wolfgang. 1989. "Skills and the Limits of Neo-Liberalism." *Work, Employment & Society* 3:90–104.

Streeck, Wolfgang. 1991. "On the Institutional Conditions of Diversified Quality Production." In *Beyond Keynesianism*, ed. E. Matzner and W. Streeck. Aldershot: Edward Elgar.

Streeck, Wolfgang. 1999. "Die Gewerkschaften im Bündnis für Arbeit." *MPIfG Working Papers* 99/11 (October). Cologne: MPIfG.

Streeck, Wolfgang. 2000. "Ist die Einrichtung eines "Niedriglohnsektors" die letzte Beschäftigungschance für gering qualifizierte Arbeitnehmer?" In *Niedriglohnsektor und Lohnsubventionen im Spiegel des Arbeits- und Sozialrechts*, ed. Otto Brenner Stiftung. Frankfurt: Bund.

Streeck, Wolfgang. 2005. "From State Weakness as Strength to State Weakness as Weakness." In *Governance in Contemporary Germany: The Semisovereign State Revisited*, ed. S. Green and W. E. Paterson. Cambridge, MA: Cambridge University Press.

Streeck, Wolfgang. 2009. *Re-Forming Capitalism*. Oxford: Oxford University Press.

Streeck, Wolfgang. 2010. "Noch so ein Sieg, und wir sind verloren: der Nationalstaat nach der Finanzkrise." *Leviathan* 38 (2):159–73.

Streeck, Wolfgang, and Rolf Heinze. 1999. "An Arbeit fehlt es nicht." *Der Spiegel* 19/1999, May 5.

Streeck, Wolfgang, and Daniel Mertens. 2010. "Politik im Defizit: Austerität als fiskalpolitisches Regime." *Der moderne Staat* 3 (1):7–29.

Streeck, Wolfgang, and Kathleen Thelen. 2005. "Introduction: Institutional Change in Advanced Political Economies." In *Beyond Continuity: Institutional Change in Advanced Political Economies*, ed. W. Streeck and K. Thelen. Oxford: Oxford University Press.

Streeck, Wolfgang, and Kozo Yamamura, eds. 2001. *The Origins of Nonliberal Capitalism: Germany and Japan*. Ithaca, NY: Cornell University Press.

Swenson, Peter. 1989. *Fair Shares: Unions, Pay and Politics in Sweden and Germany*. Ithaca, NY: Cornell University Press.

Swenson, Peter. 2002. *Capitalists Against Markets*. New York: Oxford University Press.

"Tarifeinheit: IG Metall widerspricht dem DGB." 2010. *Der Spiegel* 26:68.

Thelen, Kathleen. 1991. *Union of Parts: Labor Politics in Postwar Germany*. Ithaca, NY: Cornell University Press.

Thelen, Kathleen. 2001. "Varieties of Labor Politics in the Developed Democracies." In *Varieties of Capitalism*, ed. P. A. Hall and D. Soskice. New York: Oxford University Press.

Thelen, Kathleen. 2004. *How Institutions Evolve: The Political Economy of Skills in Comparative-Historical Perspective*. New York: Cambridge University Press.

Thelen, Kathleen. 2007a. "Contemporary Challenges to the German Vocational Training System." *Regulation and Governance* 1 (3):247–60.

Thelen, Kathleen. 2007b. "Skill Formation and Training." In *The Oxford Handbook of Business History*, ed. G. Jones and J. Zeitlin. Oxford: Oxford University Press.

Thelen, Kathleen. 2009. "Institutional Change in Advanced Political Economies." *British Journal of Industrial Relations* 47 (3):471–98.

Thelen, Kathleen. 2010. "Economic Regulation and Social Solidarity: Conceptual and Analytic Innovations in the Study of Advanced Capitalism." *Socio-Economic Review* 8:187–207.

Thelen, Kathleen. 2012. "Varieties of Capitalism: Trajectories of Liberalization and the New Politics of Social Solidarity." *Annual Review of Political Science* 15:137–59

Thelen, Kathleen, and Marius Busemeyer. 2012. "Institutional Change in German Vocational Training: From Collectivism toward Segmentalism." In *The Political Economy of Collective Skill Formation*, ed. M. Busemeyer and C. Trampusch. Oxford: Oxford University Press.

Thelen, Kathleen, and Ikuo Kume. 2006. "Coordination as a Political Problem in Coordinated Market Economies." *Governance* 19 (1):11–42.

Thelen, Kathleen, and Christa van Wijnbergen. 2003. "The Paradox of Globalization: Labor Relations in Germany and Beyond." *Comparative Political Studies* 36 (8):859–80.

Therborn, Göran. 1986. *Why Some People are More Unemployed than Others*. London: Verso.

Torfing, Jacob. 1999. "Workfare with Welfare: Recent Reforms of the Danish Welfare State." *Journal of European Social Policy* 9 (1):5–28.

Trampusch, Christine. 2007. "Industrial Relations as a Source of Solidarity in Times of Welfare State Retrenchment." *Journal of Social Policy* 36 (2):197–215.

Trampusch, Christine. 2009. *Der erschöpfte Sozialstaat: Transformation eines Politikfeldes*. Frankfurt: Campus.

Trampusch, Christine, and Pierre Eichenberger. 2012. "Skills and Industrial Relations in Coordinated Market Economies: Continuing Vocational Training in Denmark, the Netherlands, Austria, and Switzerland." *British Journal of Industrial Relations* 50 (4):644–66.

Troltsch, Klaus. 2005. "Berufsbildung und Strukturwandel: Zum Einfluss wirtschaftsstruktureller Veränderungen auf das betriebliche Ausbildungsstellenangebot seit 1980." In *Der Ausbildungsmarkt und seine Einflussfaktoren*, ed. BIBB. Bonn: BIBB.

Tros, Frank. 2009. "The Netherlands: Flexicurity and Industrial Relations." In *EIROnline*: Eurofound. http://www.eurofound.europa.eu/eiro/studies/tn0803038s/nl0803039q.htm.

Ulrich, Joachim Gerd. 2005. "Probleme bei der Bestimmung von Ausbildungsplatznachfrage und Ausbildungsplatzangebot." In *Der Ausbildungsmarkt und seine Einflussfaktoren*, ed. BIBB. Bonn: BIBB.

Ulrich, Joachim Gerd. 2008. "Jugendliche im Übergangssystem: eine Bestandsaufnahme." In *bwp@ Spezial* 4. http://www.bwpat.de/ht2008/ws12/ulrich_ws12-ht2008_spezial4.shtml.

"Unternehmen fordern Mindestlohn für Leiharbeiter." 2010. *Spiegel online*. October 5. http://www.spiegel.de/wirtschaft/soziales/druck-auf-regierung-unternehmen-fordern-mindestlohn-fuer-leiharbeiter-a-721442.html.

van Keersbergen, Kees. 1999. "Contemporary Christian Democracy and the Demise of the Politics of Mediation." In *Continuity and Change in Contemporary Capitalism*, ed. H. Kitschelt, P. Lange, G. Marks, and J. D. Stephens. New York: Cambridge University Press.

van Oorschot, Wim. 2004a. "Balancing Work and Welfare: Activation and Flexicurity Policies in the Netherlands, 1980–2000." *International Journal of Social Welfare* 13:15–27.

van Oorschot, Wim. 2004b. "Flexible Work and Flexicurity Policies in the Netherlands: Trends and Experiences." *Transfer* 2:208ff.

van Oorschot, Wim, and Peter Abrahamson. 2003. "The Dutch and Danish Miracles Revisited: A Critical Discussion of Activation Policies in Two Small Welfare States." *Social Policy & Administration* 37 (3):288–304.

van Wijnbergen, Christa. 2002. *Imposing Consensus: State Steering of Welfare and Labor Market Reforms in Continental Europe*. Ph.D. Thesis, Political Science, Northwestern University, Evanston, IL.

Vanselow, Achim. 2009. "Entfesseln oder Einhegen? Zeitarbeit in der Krise." *IAQ Report*. Universität Duisberg/Essen: Institut Arbeit und Qualifikation

Vartiainen, Juhana. 2011. "Nordic Collective Agreements: A Continuous Institution in a Changing Economic Environment." In *The Nordic Varieties of Capitalism. Comparative Social Research* (28), ed. Lars Mjøset. Emerald Group Publishing Limited: 331–63. http://www.emeraldinsight.com/books.htm?chapterid=17004237.

Vasta, Ellie. 2007. "From Ethnic Minorities to Ethnic Majority Policy: Multiculturalism and the Shift to Assimilationism in the Netherlands." *Ethnic and Racial Studies* 30 (5): 713–40.

Viebrock, Elke, and Jochen Clasen. 2009. "Flexicurity and Welfare Reform: A Review." *Socio-Economic Review* 7:305–31.

Vis, Barbara. 2010. *Politics of Risk-Taking: Welfare State Reform in Advanced Democracies*. Amsterdam: Amsterdam University Press.

Visser, Jelle. 1991. "Key Issues for Labour Market and Social Policy." Report prepared for the Organisation for Economic Cooperation and Development. Paris: OECD.

Visser, Jelle. 1992. "The Netherlands: The End of an Era and the End of a System." In *Industrial Relations in the New Europe*, ed. A. Ferner and R. Hyman. Cambridge, MA: Blackwell.

Visser, Jelle. 1998. "Two Cheers for Corporatism, One for the Market: Industrial Relations, Wage Moderation and Job Growth in the Netherlands." *British Journal of Industrial Relations* 36 (2):269–92.

Visser, Jelle. 2002. "The First Part-time Economy in the World: A Model to be Followed?" *Journal of European Social Policy* 12 (1):23–42.

Visser, Jelle. 2006. "Union Membership Statistics in 24 Countries." *Monthly Labor Review* (January):38–49. http://www.bls.gov/opub/mlr/2006/01/art3full.pdf.

Visser, Jelle. 2011. "Flexibility and Security in Post-Standard Employment Relations: The Case of the Netherlands." *Working Paper*. Amsterdam Institute of Advanced Labour Studies: University of Amsterdam.

Visser, Jelle, and Anton Hemerijck. 1997. *A Dutch Miracle: Job Growth, Welfare Reform, and Corporatism in the Netherlands*. Amsterdam: Amsterdam University Press.

Vogel, David. 1978. "Why Businessmen Distrust Their State: The Political Consciousness of American Corporate Executives." *British Journal of Political Science* 8 (1):45–78.

Vogel, David. 1983. "The Power of Business in America: A Re-Appraisal." *British Journal of Political Science* 13 (1):19–43.

Vogel, Sandra. 2009a. "Minimum Wages in Postal Services Suspended." In *EIROnline*: Eurofound. http://www.eurofound.europa.eu/eiro/2009/01/articles/de0901029i.htm.

Vogel, Sandra. 2009b. "New Allowances for Short-Time Work in Bid to Offset Economic Crisis." In *EIROnline*: Eurofound. http://www.eurofound.europa.eu/eiro/2009/04/articles/de0904039i.htm.

Vogel, Sandra. 2009c. "New Collective Agreement in Metalworking Sector." In *EIROnline*: Eurofound. http://www.eurofound.europa.eu/eiro/2009/05/articles/de0905049i.htm.

Vogel, Sandra. 2010. "Assessing Employee Representation and Collective Bargaining Coverage." In *EIROnline*: Eurofound. http://www.eurofound.europa.eu/eiro/2010/05/articles/de1005029i.htm.

Vogel, Sandra. 2011. "Social Partners Debate Pay Rises." In *EIROnline*: Eurofound. http://www.eurofound.europa.eu/eiro/2010/12/articles/de1012019i.htm.

Völk, Daniel. 2011. "Strukturen des dualen Studienangebots in Deutschland," Institut für Hochschulforschung. Presentation in Duisburg, October 14.

Wallerstein, Michael. 1999. "Wage-Setting Institutions and Pay Inequality in Advanced Industrial Societies." *American Journal of Political Science* 43:649–80.

Walsh, Janet. 1995. "Convergence or Divergence? Corporatism and the Dynamics of European Wage Bargaining." *International Review of Applied Economics* 9 (2):169–91.

Watson, C. Maxwell, Bas B. Bakker, Jan Kees Martijn, and Ioannis Halikias. 1999. *The Netherlands: Transforming a Market Economy*. Washington, DC: International Monetary Fund.

Weaver, R. Kent. 1998. "Ending Welfare As We Know It." In *The Social Divide: Political Parties and the Future of Activist Government*, ed. M. Weir. Washington, DC: Brookings Institution Press.

Weinkopf, Claudia. n.d. "Germany: Precarious Employment and the Rise of Mini-Jobs." *Comparative Perspectives Database Working Paper Series*. http://www.genderwork.ca/cpdworkingpapers/weinkopf.pdf.

Weinkopf, Claudia, and Gerhard Bosch. 2010. "The Minimum Wage System and Changing Industrial Relations in Germany (Executive Summary)." Report prepared for the research project "Minimum wage systems and changing industrial relations in Europe" for the European Commission, DG Employment, Social Affairs and Equal Opportunities, September.

Weir, Margaret. 1992. *Politics and Jobs: The Boundaries of Employment Policy in the United States*. Princeton, NJ: Princeton University Press.

Weir, Margaret. 1998. "Wages and Jobs: What is the Public Role?" In *The Social Divide: Political Parties and the Future of Activist Government*, ed. M. Weir. Washington, DC: Brookings Institution Press.

Weir, Margaret. 2010. "Beyond the Plant Gates: Postwar Labor and the Organizational Substructure of Liberalism." *Institute for Research on Labor and Employment Working Paper Series*. Berkeley: University of California, Berkeley.

"Wenn sich die Arbeit nicht mehr lohnt." 2010. *Frankfurter Allgemeine Zeitung*, January 20: 11.

Werner, Dirk. 2004. "Ausbildung zwischen Strukturwandel und Investitionskalkül." Paper presented at Expert Workshop. Bonn, July 1–2.

Western, Bruce. 1997. *Between Class and Market: Postwar Unionization in the Capitalist Democracies*. Princeton, NJ: Princeton University Press.

Western, Bruce. 2008. "Reentry: Reversing Mass Imprisonment." *Boston Review*, July/August.

Western, Bruce, and Katherine Beckett. 1999. "How Unregulated is the U.S. Labor Market? The Penal System as a Labor Market Institution." *American Journal of Sociology* 104 (4):1030–60.

Western, Bruce, and Jake Rosenfeld. 2011. "Unions, Norms, and the Rise of U.S. Wage Inequality." *American Sociological Review* 76 (4):513–37.

Wiarda, Jan-Martin. 2011. "Dual an der Spitze: An den einstigen Berufsakademien (heute DHBW) studieren Baden-Württembergs beste Abiturienten." *Die Zeit*, July 21. http://www.zeit.de/2011/30/C-Dual.

Wiesmann, Gerrit. 2012. "Germany Sets Gold Standard for Training." *Financial Times Online*, July 9. http://www.ft.com/intl/cms/s/0/98d8d6c6-c67e-11e1-963a-00144feabdc0.html.

Wilkinson, Frank, ed. 1981. *The Dynamics of Labour Market Segmentation*. London: Academic Press.

Will, Henner. 2011. *Germany's Short Time Compensation Program: Macroeconom(etr)ic Insight*. Düsseldorf: Institut für Makroökonomie und Konjunkturforschung.

Wilson, Hugh A. 2004. "The Development of America's Postwar Active Labor Market Policy: The Demise of the Big Bang Theory." Paper presented at the 2004 Meeting of the Midwest Political Science Association. Chicago, April 15–18.

"Wir müssen mehr leisten." 2003. *Die Zeit*, June 26: 18.

"Wirtschaft warnt vor endlosen Grabenkämpfen." 2010. *Spiegel Online*, June 23. http://www.spiegel.de/wirtschaft/soziales/0,1518,702495,00.html.

Wolinetz, Steven B. 1989. "Socio-Economic Bargaining in the Netherlands: Redefining the Post-War Policy Coalition." *West European Politics* 12 (1):79–98.

Wolinetz, Steven B. 1993. "Reconstructing Dutch Social Democracy." *West European Politics* 16 (1):97–111.

Wren, Anne, Máté Fodor, and Sotiria Theodoropoulou. 2012. "The Trilemma Revisited: Institutions, Inequality and Employment Creation in an Era of ICT-Intensive Service Expansion." In *The Political Economy of the Service Transition*, ed. A. Wren. Oxford: Oxford University Press.

WRR. 1980. *Industry in the Netherlands: Its Place and Future*. The Hague: Netherlands Scientific Council.

Zorn, D., Frank Dobbin, Julien Dierkes, and M. Kwok. 2006. "The New New Firm: Power and Sense-Making in the Construction of Shareholder Value." *Nordiske Organisationsstudier* 3.

Zylka, Regine. 2002. "SPD und Grüne uneins über Ehegattensplitting." *Berliner Zeitung*, October 4.

Index

Jeremy M. Weinstein, *Inside Rebellion: The Politics of Insurgent Violence*

Stephen I. Wilkinson, *Votes and Violence: Electoral Competition and Ethnic Riots in India*

Jason Wittenberg, *Crucibles of Political Loyalty: Church Institutions and Electoral Continuity in Hungary*

Elisabeth J. Wood, *Forging Democracy from Below: Insurgent Transitions in South Africa and El Salvador*

Elisabeth J. Wood, *Insurgent Collective Action and Civil War in El Salvador*

Printed in the USA
CPSIA information can be obtained
at www.ICGtesting.com
LVHW041551221223
767232LV00001B/83